FROM INSURRECTION TO REVOLUTION IN MEXICO

JOHN TUTINO

# From Insurrection to Revolution in Mexico

*Social Bases of Agrarian Violence*
*1750-1940*

PRINCETON UNIVERSITY PRESS

LIBRARY OF CONGRESS CATALOGING IN PUBLICATION DATA
WILL BE FOUND ON THE LAST PRINTED PAGE OF THIS BOOK

ISBN 0-691-07721-5

PUBLICATION OF THIS BOOK HAS BEEN MADE POSSIBLE BY A GRANT
FROM THE PUBLICATION PROGRAM OF THE NATIONAL ENDOWMENT
FOR THE HUMANITIES, AN INDEPENDENT FEDERAL AGENCY

THIS BOOK HAS BEEN COMPOSED IN LINOTRON BASKERVILLE

CLOTHBOUND EDITIONS OF PRINCETON UNIVERSITY PRESS BOOKS
ARE PRINTED ON ACID-FREE PAPER, AND BINDING MATERIALS ARE
CHOSEN FOR STRENGTH AND DURABILITY. PAPERBACKS, ALTHOUGH
SATISFACTORY FOR PERSONAL COLLECTIONS, ARE NOT USUALLY
SUITABLE FOR LIBRARY REBINDING

PRINTED IN THE UNITED STATES OF AMERICA
BY PRINCETON UNIVERSITY PRESS
PRINCETON, NEW JERSEY

*For
Jane,
María,
and
Gabriela*

# CONTENTS

## LIST OF TABLES

Why do people rebel? What leads poor people, usually struggling to stay alive, to risk death by taking up arms against those who rule? And when do insurrections lead to changes in the way poor people live? These questions are especially important in Mexican history. A country characterized by extremes of inequality and exploitation since the Spanish conquest, Mexico experienced mass insurrections during only one era of its modern history. The three centuries of Spanish colonial rule, though rife with social tensions, were remarkable for the few major insurrections that developed. It was during the years between 1810 and 1930, from the independence era to the early twentieth-century revolution, that Mexico generated repeated agrarian insurrections. This study seeks to understand why the Mexican poor chose that century to challenge their rulers, and why it was not until after 1910 that their insurrections began to change the structures of state and society in Mexico.

My primary goal is to explain the actions of the majority of insurgents who were rebel followers. Not always sharing interests with rebel leaders, it was they who risked life to make insurrections mass movements. Few of the tens of thousands of Mexican rural insurgents left records of their goals. But their actions can be studied through comparative social history. By comparing agrarian social changes across numerous Mexican regions during two centuries, and relating them to the presence or absence of insurrections, we may begin to understand why rural poor people became insurgents.

This work, then, offers an explanation of why agrarian insurrections became so common in Mexico from 1810 to

1930, and of how these uprisings helped shape modern Mexico. In addition, the analytical approach and conclusions may contribute to the internationally comparative discussions of the origins of insurrections and the roles such violent mass mobilizations play in the making of the modern world.

Such a book cannot be a research monograph. During recent years, I have completed much research on Mexican society during the period from 1750 to 1870. That work is the basis of this analysis. But research into the letters and labor accounts of landowners and estate administrators; into governmental records of land disputes and rebellions; and into varied other materials must deal with particular questions in limited regions. I have presented these studies in a dissertation and in several essays aimed primarily at others who study Mexican history. (The appendices here also present some research materials.) My goal in this book is to bring together the results of my specialized studies and those of many others in an interpretive synthesis.

The book divides into two parts. One probes the origins of the first mass insurrections of modern Mexican history—those of the independence era. The second examines developments from 1810 to 1910, seeking the roots of the violent conflicts of the early twentieth century. A period of intensive study of eighteenth-century Mexico, in which I have been but one of many participants, has led to a new and more detailed understanding of social developments before independence. In contrast, analysis of agrarian life during the nineteenth century has begun to intensify only recently. The first part of the book, then, can synthesize my investigations with many others' and with some confidence link the social changes of the eighteenth century to the emergence or absence of insurrections in 1810. The second part of the book remains more exploratory. It seeks to relate the explanations proposed for the uprisings of the independence era to the complex developments of the following century, and to the origins of the revolution that began in 1910.

Throughout, my goal is to refine questions and propose explanations that should be debated, perhaps discarded, perhaps refined, as research and analysis continues.

I have been working on these problems for nearly two decades, though I began to write this book more recently. During that time, I have incurred countless debts—intellectual, financial, institutional, and personal. I can only acknowledge directly the help of a few.

As I began to study history as an undergraduate, William Green introduced me to a critical approach to the discipline. Holy Cross College allowed me an entire academic year to study the Mexican revolution under the guidance of Warren Schiff. As a graduate student, I worked with several scholars who have influenced this work: James Lockhart initiated me to colonial social history. Nettie Lee Benson led me through the labyrinths of nineteenth-century Mexican politics and convinced me that they did matter. And Richard N. Adams introduced me to social theory and persuaded me that history is more analytical when it is theoretically informed.

Kim Rodner, my colleague at Carleton College, has helped me to bring my studies into a comparative, international context. My students at St. Olaf and Carleton have pressed me in the same direction, often asking how my studies of Mexican peasants in past centuries relate to current issues. This book is an attempt to respond to their concerns.

Many friends read parts of this work as it evolved, and offered suggestions along with encouragement. For such assistance I thank Richard N. Adams, David Brading, Jonathan Brown, Patrick Carroll, Guillermo de la Peña, Enrique Florescano, Tulio Halperin Donghi, Hugh Hamill, John Super, and Eric Van Young. León Narvaez, Kim Rodner, William Taylor, and two readers for Princeton University Press, Walter Goldfrank and Mark Wasserman, read and commented upon versions of the complete manuscript. None of these scholars agrees with all my approaches and conclusions. Their assistance and support is thus doubly appreciated.

I owe a less personal, but no less important, debt to many others who have preceded me in studying Mexico. Their contributions are but minimally acknowledged in the footnotes and bibliography. While writing this book, I was fortunate to participate in the working group on Rural Uprisings in Mexico led by Friedrich Katz and sponsored by the Joint Committee on Latin American Studies of the American Council of Learned Societies and the Social Science Research Council during 1981 and 1982. That group twice brought together scholars from Mexico, Europe, and the United States to present and discuss essays on many of the questions treated here. Many of my ideas were formed and refined in that unique environment. And my colleagues in the Carleton-St. Olaf study group on States in Capitalist Economies, funded by a Northwest Area Foundation grant in 1982 and 1983, helped me explore the issues of state and society that inform this analysis.

The help of innumerable librarians and archivists has been crucial. I must thank those at the Benson Latin American Collection of the University of Texas at Austin Library, at Washington State University, and at the Bancroft Library, Berkeley; in Mexico City at the Archivo General de la Nación, the Instituto Nacional de Antropología e Historia, the Hemeroteca Nacional, and the Biblioteca Nacional; and in Minnesota at St. Olaf, Carleton, and the University of Minnesota.

As the book neared completion, Sandy Thatcher of Princeton University Press offered needed encouragement, copyeditor Eve Pearson brought me nearer to clarity, and Andrew Mytelka guided the work through press with skill and good humor. Gregory Chu and the Cartography Lab of the University of Minnesota drew the maps.

Financial and institutional support has come from many

sources. My parents paid for, and Holy Cross College sanctioned, a year of intellectual freedom as a Fenwick Scholar in 1968-1969. The History Department of the University of Texas at Austin awarded me an NDEA-Title IV fellowship during 1971 and 1972 that supported research in the Benson Collection and at Washington State. That department also allowed me a home as a Visiting Scholar in 1983-1984. A Fulbright-Hays dissertation research fellowship financed my work in Mexico City during all of 1973. The National Endowment for the Humanities has three times supported my work—with a Summer Stipend in 1977, a Summer Seminar led by the late Stanley Ross in 1979, and a yearlong fellowship in 1983-1984. For six months of 1981, the History Department and the Latin American Center of the University of California, Berkeley, provided time and an environment to facilitate research and writing. And since 1977, St. Olaf and Carleton Colleges have repeatedly provided summer support, research and travel allowances, and funds for manuscript preparation.

The most persistent support has come from my wife Jane. She encouraged me to study Mexican history and provided much of our income as I pursued seemingly endless graduate studies. Together we have survived the difficult, seminomadic life of international scholarship—while working to establish family life. When the book became too absorbing, she kept me connected to family and friends.

I dedicate this study to Jane and our daughters María and Gabriela. Our girls' lives span the few years I have been working directly on the book. They are my constant reminder that historical inquiry has no business becoming separated from living concerns. They may read this some day and perhaps understand why daddy keeps going to school even though he is a grownup.

Footnote references to published works include only the author's last name and a short title. Full citations are in the bibliography.

The following abbreviations are used in references to archival sources and collections of published documents:

Archival Collections:

AGN   Archivo General de la Nación, Mexico City.

CPP   Conde de Peñasco Papers, Benson Latin American Collection, the University of Texas at Austin.

FEN   Fernando Espinosa y Navarijo Papers, Benson Latin American Collection.

INAH  Instituto Nacional de Antropología e Historia, Microfilm, Mexico City.

JSE   José Sánchez Espinosa Papers, Benson Latin American Collection.

PCR   Papeles de los Condes de Regla, Washington State University Library.

WBS   W. B. Stevens Manuscripts, Benson Latin American Collection.

Collections of Published Documents:

FCA   *Fuentes para la historia de la crisis agrícola de 1785-1786*, ed. by Enrique Florescano (Mexico: Archivo General de la Nación, 1981), 2 Vols.

FHEM  *Fuentes para la historia económica de Mexico*, ed. by Enrique Florescano and Isabel Gil (Mexico: Instituto National de Antropología e Historia, 1973-1976), 3 Vols; Vol. 1: *Descripciones económicas*

*generales de Nueva España*; Vol. 2: *Descripciones económicas regionales de Nueva España: Provincias del
Norte, 1790-1814*; Vol. 3: *Descripciones económicas regionales de Nueva España: Provincias del Centro, Sud-
este, y Sur, 1766-1827.*

# INTRODUCTION

# CHAPTER ONE

# Agrarian Life and Rural Rebellion

## AGRARIAN VIOLENCE IN MODERN MEXICO

In 1910, Emiliano Zapata led the villagers of Anenecuilco, in the state of Morelos south of Mexico City, in a fight over lands claimed by a nearby sugar estate. He quickly gained fame as a defender of village rights against the haciendas that dominated the economic life of the region. At the same time, Francisco Madero, son of one of the richest ranching, mining, and banking families of northern Mexico, led a rebellion against Porfirio Díaz, the aging patriarch who had ruled Mexican politics since 1876. Zapata's program was simple and radical: he demanded the return of community lands to peasant villagers. Madero's program was moderate and complicated: he demanded electoral democracy and effective justice. He did mention agrarian justice, a vague goal that became the basis for a tenuous alliance with Zapata early in 1911. That link between the political dissident and the agrarian insurgent helped strengthen a revolt that soon forced Díaz to flee Mexico and allowed Madero to take over the national government.

Before the end of 1911, Madero had claimed the presidency in elections he deemed fair. Zapata kept demanding the immediate return of lands to the Morelos villagers. Madero answered with talk of caution and delay, leading Zapata to rise again—this time against the reformist president he had helped install. Madero and the federal army could not defeat Zapata. Often citing that failure, conservative forces led by General Victoriano Huerta ousted and killed Madero early in 1913. Zapata remained in rebellion. During the years of revolutionary civil wars that followed,

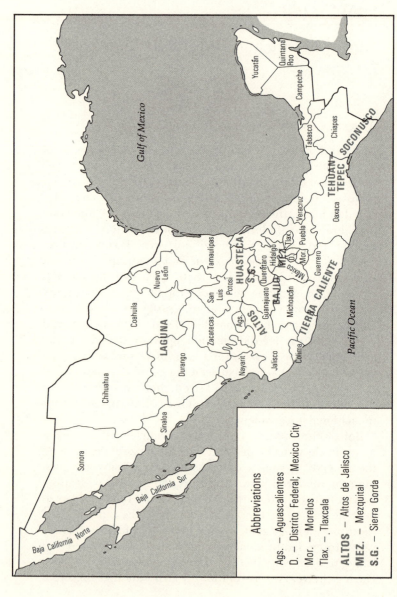

Mexico: States and Regions

Abbreviations

Ags. – Aguascalientes
D. – Distrito Federal; Mexico City
Mor. – Morelos
Tlax. – Tlaxcala
**ALTOS** – Altos de Jalisco
**MEZ.** – Mezquital
**S.G.** – Sierra Gorda

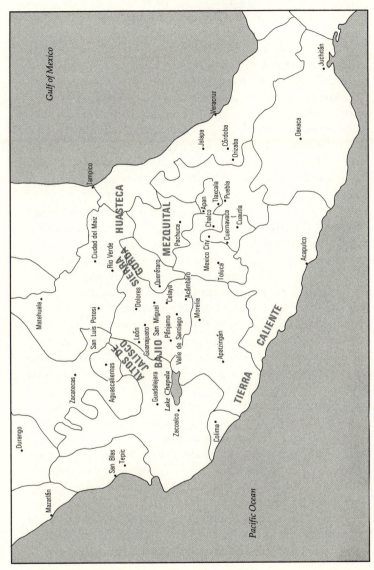

Central Mexico: Cities and Regions

the agrarian insurgents of Morelos fought tenaciously against any faction that claimed national power but would not distribute lands among the villagers of central Mexico. In time, those competing for national power learned that they had to adopt agrarian reform proposals—however reluctantly—in order to recruit troops and supporters in rural Mexico. By 1917, a faction led by Venustiano Carranza, another wealthy estate owner from northern Mexico, controlled the government and wrote a new constitution. That charter allowed, but did not mandate, radical agrarian reform. Land distribution remained minimal—and Zapata remained in rebellion. He was murdered treacherously in 1919.

A year later, Alvaro Obregón toppled Carranza and claimed the presidency with the help of surviving Zapatistas. To pay his debt to the long-rebellious villagers of Morelos, as well as to pacify them, Obregón began to expropriate and redistribute lands formerly owned by sugar estates. After a decade of insurrection, destruction, and bloodshed, the 1920s finally brought an unprecedented victory to the villagers of Morelos. They obtained lands to grow maize. They could continue to live as peasants a while longer.[1]

Morelos quickly became an example for other rural Mexicans. The politicians working to build a postrevolutionary state in the 1920s kept proclaiming their devotion to agrarian reform. But only the most persistent and often violent rebels, like the Zapatistas, received land from the new leaders of Mexico. The lesson was clear: only those who threatened the regime got land; thus those seeking land must threaten the regime. The early 1920s therefore brought numerous rural revolts, as villagers fought to claim the government's attention.[2]

Then, late in 1926, another massive regional agrarian revolt exploded in the west central states of Jalisco and Michoacán. Its wrath fell upon those who claimed to rule in

[1] On the Zapatistas, see Womack, *Zapata* and Warman, *Y venimos.*
[2] For example, see Friedrich, *Agrarian Revolt.*

the name of "the revolution." The rebels of the late 1920s were not villagers with deep roots in the communalism of Mexico's indigenous and colonial past, as were those who fought with Zapata. Rather, this second wave of agrarian insurrection developed among the *rancheros* of west central Mexico. Rancheros formed a rural middle sector. They held their lands as private property. They were more Hispanized in culture and were tied closely to the institutional Catholic Church. Yet they remained poor peasant farmers. Few lived even comfortably. They raised most of their own food, while also selling small surpluses of crops or livestock at local or regional markets.

During the 1920s, many rancheros began to fear that they would become the victims of the much talked about agrarian reform. The government was obviously friendly with surviving landed elites, yet it owed a clear political debt to many peasant rebels. In that dilemma of the postrevolutionary state, the lands of the rancheros—often extensive, but of poor quality—could appear an easy target for redistribution. Reluctant reformers in the government might thus be able to give lands to the agrarian poor without expropriating landed elites.

While these tensions escalated, Plutarco Elías Calles became president in 1924. A revolutionary most hesitant to begin radical reforms, he pressed his most vehement attacks against the Catholic Church. The rancheros of Jalisco, Michoacán, and surrounding regions watched as a spat between the president and the bishops led to the closing of their churches and the suspension of all services. The massive insurrection called the Cristero revolt followed. For three years, beginning in 1926, rancheros of west central Mexico (with little Church support) pressed an agrarian revolt in defense of their lands and their religion against postrevolutionary leaders whose policies seemed to threaten ranchero life.[3]

[3] On the Cristero revolt, see Meyer, *La cristiada*, and Díaz and Rodríguez, *El movimiento cristero*.

The Cristero rebellion ended in 1929, more due to a compromise between the state and bishops—and to rebel exhaustion—than to clear military victories by the government. The strength of the Cristero revolt made it plain that rural Mexico would not be pacified, that no regime would remain secure, until "the agrarian question" was addressed in a comprehensive reform. At that juncture, the great depression struck Mexico in 1930. The wealth and power of many elites—especially of landholders producing for export markets—were suddenly undermined. Persistent agrarian insurgents, from the Zapatistas through the Cristeros, forced political leaders to face the need for agrarian reform. The depression so weakened the Mexican economy, and the elites that profited from it, that a major reform became possible.

Lázaro Cárdenas assumed the presidency in 1934. Born in Michoacán, in the heartland of the Cristero revolt, Cárdenas had fought his way to the rank of general and the position of Governor of Michoacán during the decades of revolutionary conflicts. Once president, he implemented the vast agrarian reforms allowed by the 1917 Constitution. The landed base of Mexico's traditional elite was destroyed by Cárdenas' expropriation of over 20,000,000 hectares (nearly 50,000,000 acres) of rural lands. And nearly 800,000 rural families obtained plots as members of newly organized *ejido* communities during Cárdenas' term from 1934 to 1940.[4]

The agrarian insurgents who fought and often died during the years of revolutionary conflict had finally won a major, but partial, victory. They had fought for *tierra y libertad*—land and liberty. They got *tierra y el estado*—land and the state. Arguing that the recipients of ejido lands had to be protected, Cárdenas' state retained unprecedented powers over them. Many peasants received lands, only to face

---

[4] On Cárdenas, see Hamilton, *Limits of State Autonomy*. The land reform figures are from p. 237.

persistent pressures to support the government politically and to participate in the commercial economy. For most, support for Cárdenas came easily. He had given them land. But many were less ready to move into the commercial economy. That was not the peasant utopia of land and autonomy. But Cárdenas' massive land redistribution did satisfy enough rural Mexicans to bring a rapid reduction of agrarian violence. After 1940, Mexico moved into a new era in which a stable postrevolutionary regime grappled with the problems of rapid capitalist development in a society with a large, recently mobilized, and now entrenched peasant population.

The agrarian insurrections, political wars, and radical reforms that began in 1910 and culminated with Cárdenas brought an agrarian social revolution to Mexico.[5] That revolution laid the foundations of modern Mexico—a nation of political stability, with spectacular yet uneven economic growth and persistent mass poverty.

The revolution was not, of course, exclusively an agrarian movement. It revolved around alliances and conflicts among numerous factions with varying programs. From 1910 to 1914, uneasy alliances among upper-class reformers and agrarian radicals focused on eliminating first the Díaz regime and then its remnants under General Huerta. Once Huerta was forced out in 1914, and the old regime clearly defeated, revolutionary factions squared off against each other. Two visions of Mexico remained primary within revolutionary conflicts: nationalist, capitalist reformers led

[5] For a general interpretation of the Mexican revolution focused on agrarian concerns, see Gilly, *La revolución interrumpida*. In *The Great Rebellion*, Ramón Eduardo Ruíz argues that the conflicts of the early twentieth century were neither agrarian nor revolutionary. He reaches that conclusion by emphasizing the goals of elite leaders and the failures of industrial workers. He downplays agrarian reform policies forced on reluctant elites by adamant agrarian rebels. And by closing his analysis in 1924, Ruíz does not have to account for the Cristero revolt and Cárdenas' reforms.

by Madero and later Carranza faced agrarian, anticapitalist revolutionaries epitomized by Zapata.

(Pancho Villa, who led the largest armies of the revolutionary era, attempted to incorporate multiple factions into his Division of the North. He represented the ranchero peasants of the Chihuahua highlands as well as the irate rural laborers and sharecroppers of the Laguna cotton region. He tried to lead discontented segments of the upper and middle classes at the same time. And he hoped to be a Mexican nationalist without confronting the powerful United States' interests in the northern borderlands that were his home base. That diversity of vision and of political base helped Villa amass huge armies. The irreconcilable conflicts thus incorporated within his movement no doubt contributed to Villa's eventual defeat.)

From 1910 to 1940, the nationalist-capitalists—Madero, Carranza, Obregón, Calles, and yes, Cárdenas—won all the major military and political battles. They controlled the state from 1915 on. Left to themselves, they would have attempted only moderate, nationalist reforms. But they had to deal with adamant agrarian revolutionaries who were often beaten, but rarely accepted defeat. The persistence of the rural radicals, often in guerrilla bands, repeatedly forced political leaders intent on building a more capitalist Mexico to include agrarian reforms in their programs. It was the vehement agrarian insurgents who inserted the revolutionary elements into the civil wars that tore Mexico apart early in the twentieth century.[6]

The result was a revolutionary conflict that ended in stalemate. Agrarian revolutionaries forced the massive redistribution of lands by often reluctant nationalist-capitalists who controlled the state and the national economy. The Cárdenas reforms institutionalized that stalemate in a remarkable state that has endured for half a century. Postrev-

---

[6] The best analysis of the complex forces in the Mexico revolution is in Katz, *The Secret War in Mexico*.

olutionary Mexico is a society in which millionaire industrialists must coexist with millions of landed peasants. The partial victory of the agrarian revolutionaries meant an equally partial victory for elites who envisioned a more nationalist but thoroughly capitalist Mexico. Agrarian insurgents left an indelible mark on modern Mexico.

Every student of the Mexican revolution recognizes its agrarian roots. Few have examined the historical origins of the rural violence that helped transform modern Mexico. Most explanations of the agrarian violence that began in 1910 point first to the legacies of inequity left by the Spanish conquest of the sixteenth century, and then emphasize the more recent disruptions of rural life set off by the rapid economic development of the late nineteenth century. Such emphases suggest that long-festering agrarian grievances left by Spanish colonialism were made unbearable by the rapid changes of the Díaz era—resulting in revolution.

The timing of agrarian insurrections in Mexican history, however, raises questions about such explanations. The long colonial era, after all, is notable for its enduring agrarian stability, despite obvious inequities. Spanish elites built large landed estates while Mexican peasants retained but minimal village fields. Yet the Spanish colonial state and elites dominated Mexico for nearly three centuries after 1521 without a standing army. There were many local rural protests, generally riots of brief duration, but most aimed to restore an accepted colonial agrarian structure, not to challenge it.[7]

It was thus a radical departure from colonial tradition when in 1810 Father Miguel Hidalgo raised tens of thousands of rural rebels in an insurrection that lasted for four months. There followed a number of smaller regional up-

[7] On the late rise of the colonial military, see Archer, *The Army in Bourbon Mexico*. On colonial revolts, see Taylor, *Drinking, Homicide, and Rebellion*.

risings that often used guerrilla tactics to hold out for years. It was between 1810 and 1816, then, that the colonial agrarian peace collapsed and Mexico experienced its first round of large, enduring, and multiregional rural uprisings. All were defeated before Mexican elites claimed their own, conservative national independence in 1821. There would be no social revolution in Mexican independence. But it was the Hidalgo revolt and the other uprisings of the independence era that marked the transition from colonial centuries of agrarian stability to over a century of escalating conflict.

The agrarian institutions left by Spanish colonialism, the expansive haciendas and the constricted peasant villages, were in place during the centuries of stability from 1600 to 1800, as well as during the era of conflict that began in 1810. Those institutional structures alone will not account for the development of mass rural violence in Mexico. And the dislocations of the late-nineteenth-century Díaz era, often most damaging to the rural poor, developed too late to explain the emergence of mass agrarian violence. Díaz policies and economic programs can only account for the continuation and intensification of rural violence already widespread in Mexico by 1876.

From 1810 to 1930, Mexico experienced a prolonged era of agrarian violence. It began with the Hidalgo revolt and the other uprisings of the independence era. The end of Spanish rule in 1821, however, did not bring peace to rural Mexico. By the late 1840s, amidst international war, political instability, and economic disruptions, a new round of agrarian insurrections engulfed widespread areas of Mexico. Multiple regional uprisings recurred in waves in the late 1860s and again in the late 1870s.[8] By the mid-1880s, Díaz had put down the last round of insurrections, restored political stability, and pressed on with his program of rapid economic development. The later years of the Díaz era brought apparent peace and prosperity to rural Mexico.

[8] See Reina, *Las rebeliones campesinas.*

Beneath the surface, however, the difficulties of the rural poor deepened. The Díaz years produced an agrarian compression that exploded into revolutionary conflicts when the state collapsed in 1911.

This study offers an explanation of the emergence of massive agrarian violence in Mexico early in the nineteenth century, and then traces the persistence and escalation of rural conflicts until the outbreak of the revolutionary period early in the twentieth century. I am looking to find the agrarian origins of the Mexican revolution in the social history of the years from 1750 to 1910. The remainder of this introduction explores an approach to understanding changing ways of rural life and the origins of agrarian rebellions. The first section of historical analysis studies the regional agrarian changes and the imperial economic and political developments that converged to generate the Hidalgo revolt in the Bajío region of Mexico in 1810. It goes on to look comparatively at other Mexican regions where the rural poor variously joined, ignored, or opposed the Hidalgo revolt and other uprisings between 1810 and 1816. And having thus examined the social bases of insurrection and loyalty—or at least inactivity—in the independence era of the early nineteenth century, in the second section I trace agrarian social changes and the proliferation of rural violence from 1821 to 1940, and offer an explanation for the revolutionary conflicts of the early twentieth century. The conclusion attempts to place my understanding of agrarian violence in Mexico in an internationally comparative context.

## AGRARIAN LIFE AND REBELLION: AN ANALYTICAL APPROACH

Why rural people rebel and periodically become protagonists in violent revolutionary struggles has become a major focus of debate. From the French revolutionary outbursts of 1789, through the early twentieth-century conflicts in

Mexico and Russia, to the recent upheavals in China, Vietnam, and Central America, rural violence has fueled revolutionary confrontations. Not all revolutions rely primarily on peasant violence—Cuba and Iran seem important exceptions. Nor has all large-scale and sustained agrarian violence resulted in social revolution—the Hidalgo revolt in Mexico is but one of many crushed insurrections. But during recent centuries, agrarian violence has been central to social transformations in many and diverse nations.

The rising tide of agrarian conflict has recently claimed the attention of many social analysts. In his groundbreaking *Social Origins of Dictatorship and Democracy*, Barrington Moore, Jr., emphasizes the importance of peasants—and particularly the presence or absence of violence by or against peasants—in explaining the varied political outcomes of the transformations to urbanized and industrialized ways of life in England, France, the United States, China, Japan, and India. In *Peasant Wars of the Twentieth Century*, Eric Wolf focuses on the importance of agrarian violence in the revolutionary struggles of Mexico, Russia, China, Vietnam, Algeria, and Cuba. These two comparative studies brought peasants to the center of scholarly attention in the late 1960s and set an agenda for continuing analysis and debate.

Moore and Wolf converge in emphasizing that peasants have become more rebellious as the expansion of commercial capitalism undermined long-established ways of agrarian life. Moore concludes that "the most important causes of peasant revolutions have been the absence of a commercial revolution in agriculture led by the landed upper classes and the concomitant survival of peasant social institutions into the modern era when they are subject to new stresses and strains." Crises emerge when "new and capitalist methods of pumping the economic surplus out of the peasantry have been added, while the traditional ones lingered or were intensified." Wolf concurs, and adds that the impact of capitalism on peasants goes beyond increased exploitation.

He argues that "What is significant is that capitalism cut through the integument of custom, severing the people from the accustomed social matrix in order to transform them into economic actors, independent of prior social commitments to kin and neighbors."⁹

Moore and Wolf thus agree that peasant rebellion responds in large part to grievances stimulated by the rapid, exploitative, and socially disruptive incursions of capitalism into agrarian societies. They also emphasize that for such rebellions to persist and eventually bring about social change, the insurgents must be tightly organized, free of elite or state domination of daily affairs, and favored by the weakness, division, or breakdown of the coercive powers of the state.¹⁰ Only under such favorable conditions can the grievances generated by the incursions of capitalism lead to sustained insurrections with potentially revolutionary results.

Many others have carried on the discussions begun by Moore and Wolf. In *Peasants, Politics, and Revolution,* Joel Migdal looks closely at the results of capitalist penetration into peasant communities. He argues that when agrarian people are incorporated into world capitalist markets, their once inward-looking local economies and cultures are turned outward. Peasants then face the opportunities as well as the inconsistencies of capitalism while becoming more involved with national, even international, social and political relations. Migdal emphasizes that these developments have often brought more difficulties than opportunities to peasants, creating mounting discontent. He then gives extensive consideration to the relations between frustrated villagers and rebel leaders and concludes that effective leadership and organization are essential for turning

---

⁹ Moore, *Social Origins,* pp. 477, 473; Wolf, *Peasant Wars,* p. 379.
¹⁰ Moore, *Social Origins,* pp. 457, 459, 469, 476; Wolf, *Peasant Wars,* pp. 284, 290, 291.

peasant grievances into the basis of effective revolutionary movements.

Jeffrey Paige's study, *Agrarian Revolution*, is an ambitious attempt to generalize about the origins and outcomes of agrarian conflicts in the export economies of the Third World. He outlines comparatively the economic structures and social relations of numerous export enclaves, with detailed case studies focused on Peru, Vietnam, and Angola. Paige argues that agrarian conflicts are best understood by focusing analysis on the interaction of the powers held by agrarian elites with the means of survival available to the working poor. Paige's conclusions have been challenged, often because his assumptions do not seem to apply to cases other than those he studied.[11] Certainly his assumption that elites with power based on capital rather than land are economically strong enough to forego the use of coercion against their workers seems inapplicable to much of Latin America. And Paige's assertion that landed peasants do not have the cohesion necessary for mass, sustained insurrection is contradicted by much of Mexican history.[12] But he makes the essential contribution of insisting that any understanding of agrarian conflict requires careful analyses of the evolving relations between agrarian elites and the working masses.

In *The Moral Economy of the Peasant*, James Scott seeks out the perceptions of peasants who have risked their lives in insurrections. He argues persuasively that poor cultivators in Southeast Asia see their world through a moral lens that takes subsistence as a basic human right. He concludes that the denial of that right is at the root of peasant uprisings. Scott emphasizes more precisely that peasants are most sensitive to the security of their subsistence—their ability to expect a minimally acceptable means of survival year after year. It is when peasant subsistence becomes insecure, when

---

[11] See Skocpol, "What Makes Peasants Revolutionary," pp. 354-359.
[12] Paige, *Agrarian Revolution*, pp. 18-40.

the available sustenance falls below a minimum threshold of survival in recurrent years of crisis, that peasants become ready to take the risks of insurrection. Scott argues that the commercialization of the economy of Southeast Asia under British and French colonial rule, along with the increasingly rigid exactions of the colonial states, led to such widespread insecurities of subsistence. The result was a series of uprisings that began in the depression era of the 1930s and persisted into the era of conflict after World War II.

Scott sees threats to subsistence security as the fundamental causes of agrarian insurrections. He is aware, however, that such developments do not alone provoke and sustain mass uprisings. He states that the outbreak of insurrection also "depends on a host of intervening factors—such as alliances with other classes, the repressive capacity of dominant elites, and the social organization of the peasantry itself."[13] But Scott's analysis makes it plain that such considerations are of secondary importance. Only after peasants have reached the peak of rage essential to taking the risks of rebellion can such larger relations come into play.

Barrington Moore has also turned his attention to the roots of insurrections as perceived by the rebels. His *Injustice: The Social Bases of Obedience and Revolt* focuses primarily on urban workers' revolts in modern Germany. But again Moore provides seminal insights into basic questions—insights that often help illuminate rural as well as urban protests. He begins by acknowledging that the poor of all modern societies have complaints against their rulers. But Moore emphasizes that the emergence of acute grievances is essential to the outbreak of rebellion. What must develop is "politically effective moral outrage." And he argues that "For this to happen, people must perceive their situation as the consequence of human injustice: a situation that they

[13] Scott, *Moral Economy*, p. 4.

need not, cannot, and ought not endure."[14] To some extent, perceptions of injustice vary. Established expectations help define what people perceive as acceptable or unendurable. But Moore argues against ultimate relativism. He emphasizes that "suffering in the forms of hunger, physical abuse, or deprivation of the fruits of hard work is indeed objectively painful for human beings."[15]

For acute suffering to create the sense of outrageous injustice fundamental to rebellion, Moore believes that the sufferers must conquer the "illusion of inevitability."[16] He sees that conquest as most likely to occur during times of rapid social changes, especially when massive increases in production are accompanied by worsening deprivations and disruptions in the lives of the poor. Moore thus returns to his argument from *Social Origins* that sudden incursions of capitalism generate rebellions. But he has moved toward viewing capitalism from the vantage of the poor. He thus stresses that rebellion is most likely when the sudden worsening of conditions is manifest, and "where the causes of misery appear to the sufferers as due to the acts of identifiable superiors."[17]

Moore also examines the political opportunities for insurrection from the perspective of the poor. He notes that the same rapid social changes that often create an acute sense of injustice among the poor may also provoke divisions among powerholders. When no elite faction predominates, some may seek mass support. Thus emerge the classic "outside agitators," disgruntled elites adopting popular issues and seeking mass support against competing elite factions. Moore joins Scott in arguing that while such agitators cannot create rebellions, they can begin uprisings based on grievances already deeply felt. For Moore, such agitators are often the "indispensible if insufficient cause" of rebel-

[14] Moore, *Injustice*, p. 459.
[15] Ibid., p. 460.
[16] Ibid., p. 462.
[17] Ibid., pp. 468-471, quote from p. 471.

lions.[18] Agitators repeatedly bring to the outraged poor the critical news that elites are divided and the state weakened. The same agitators often help organize rebel forces and may profess a unifying ideology. They may be essential to the endurance of an insurrection. But agitators do not cause rebellions.

Recent studies of agrarian insurrections began by emphasizing the exploitative and disruptive effects of capitalism on peasants suddenly incorporated into volatile markets. Further refinements emphasize the ways that the rural poor perceive and respond to such developments. All note the importance of rebel leadership in organizing insurrections, helping them endure, and allowing them a role in larger social transformations. Each author brings a personal emphasis to his work, but those discussed here converge in viewing mass peasant uprisings as reactions against injustices perceived as imposed by capitalist elites and allied states.

Criticism of such explanations is now emerging. Samuel Popkin argues in *The Rational Peasant* that most of the studies discussed above take the perspective of moral economists. He believes that they romanticize precapitalist peasant ways of life by proposing views of traditional communities as exceptionally egalitarian and cohesive. Popkin counters that peasants are individualists who seek personal and family benefits before community welfare. They are long accustomed to living subject to exploitative elites. Popkin's analysis is a useful warning against a careless reading of Wolf, Migdal, and Scott. But close attention to their works reveals that all explicitly state most of what Popkin accuses them of ignoring. The "moral economists" are not blind to peasants' self- and family interests, or to traditional village inequalities. They do see those interests and inequalities, however, as locally based, mediated by personal relationships, and subject to local pressures demanding

[18] Ibid., p. 472; Scott, *Moral Economy*, p. 173.

basic rights to subsistence. If the old village ways have often seemed attractive once lost, it is not because old villages were utopian communities. Rather, it is because peasant villagers, once incorporated into economies and polities dominated by capitalist markets, often find their lives changed for the worse by elites and market forces they can barely perceive and cannot affect—at least without the violent statements of insurrection.

Theda Skocpol also questions the analyses of peasant insurrections that emphasize the negative consequences of capitalism. Her book, *States and Social Revolutions*, compares the origins and outcomes of the French, Russian, and Chinese revolutions. She emphasizes once again that massive peasant insurrections were fundamental to the triumph of revolutionary leaders in all three conflicts. Yet Skocpol argues that peasant grievances, whether or not generated by capitalist incursions, do not explain such revolutionary insurrections. She states that "Peasants always have grounds for rebellion against landlords, state agents, and merchants who exploit them." She thus argues that "the degree to which grievances that are always at least implicitly present can be collectively perceived and acted upon"[19] is the crucial factor in the origins of peasant uprisings. The assumption that all peasants live with latent grievances, thus that all are potential insurgents, seems unfounded. Yet in a more recent discussion, Skocpol modifes her position only slightly: "For impoverished and exploited peasants in many places may *potentially* be amenable to revolutionary mobilization—*if* a revolutionary organization can establish itself with some minimal security, and *if* its cadres can address peasant needs successfully."[20]

Skocpol argues that modern peasant revolutions cannot be attributed directly to the consequences of commercial capitalism. She maintains that commercialization was mini-

[19] Skocpol, *States and Social Revolutions*, p. 115.
[20] Skocpol, "What Makes Peasants Revolutionary," p. 365.

mal in China in the decades before peasants there sustained one of the most thorough revolutions of the twentieth century.[21] She thus concludes that peasant grievances are considerations secondary to the organizational solidarity of communities, the relative power of political and economic elites within those communities, and the general strength or weakness of the state. Above all, Skocpol argues that it has been breakdowns of the state's coercive powers, usually caused by failures in international conflicts, that unleash peasants into revolutionary insurrections. Her fine analysis of the relations among international conflicts, state powers, and agrarian insurrections is a major contribution to our understanding of modern revolutions.[22]

But Skocpol's attempt to shift attention away from peasant grievances appears misplaced. She may be correct that commercial capitalism had little to do with why Chinese peasants joined the revolution there. Yet that conclusion only leaves the incursion of capitalism thesis as a generalization not applicable to every case. There is too much evidence that capitalist penetration has provoked extreme grievances and led to mass insurrections among peasants elsewhere to allow a Chinese exception to end consideration of the question.

Perhaps it is more important to emphasize that in one of the most comprehensive examinations of peasant grievances, James Scott makes it clear that peasants in Southeast Asia did not rebel against an abstraction called capitalism. They rebelled against persistent threats to their security of subsistence—which Scott sees as caused by the penetration of export capitalism and colonial state demands.[23] Capitalism is too general a concept representing too many diverse realities to directly explain the origins of peasant insurrec-

---

[21] Ibid., pp. 370-371.

[22] Skocpol, *States and Social Revolutions*, 115-117.

[23] It is unfortunate that in her critique of the incursion of capitalism thesis, Skocpol cites Scott's essay on "Hegemony and the Peasantry" but not his more detailed analysis of peasant insurrections in *Moral Economy*.

tions. But the analysis of peasant grievances should not be abandoned. It should be pursued more precisely, following Scott's lead of seeking the causes of uprisings as the rural poor perceive them.

From these studies of insurrections in widely scattered areas of the world, a few general propositions about the origins of mass rural uprisings seem warranted: rapid and severe deteriorations of rural social conditions, often but not always associated with the sudden imposition of commercial capitalism, create essential bases of discontent. For discontent to become acute, peasant difficulties must be clearly perceived as caused by human actors—landed elites, the state, or both. Yet when such acute grievances produce a pervasive sense of outrage and injustice among peasants, they do not automatically turn to insurrection. However outraged, the rural poor generally wait for evidence that powerholders are weak and/or divided before they will take the risks of an uprising. The news of such opportunities for insurrection is often brought to peasants by outside agitators—elite renegades calling for revolt against those in power. Although such rebel leaders do not cause insurrections, they often do precipitate rural revolts. And they repeatedly take pivotal roles in organizing agrarian rebels and forging their links with other groups. Elite agitators are of secondary importance to the origins of peasant insurrections; they are often essential to the success or failure of such movements.

From the perspective of the rural poor, then, mass insurrections result from critical meetings of grievances and opportunities. Both are essential to the outbreak of mass uprisings. Yet historically as well as analytically, grievances precede opportunities. Divisions among elites, breakdowns of state power, and the persuasions of rebel leaders only become important after agrarian grievances have peaked. Yet we know much more about the opportunities for insurrections than about the grievances that bring peasants to take advantage of them. Studies of state powers and of rebel leaders are numerous. Analyses of dominant elites, their cohesion, and their relations with states seem less plentiful. But materials on states, elites, and rebel leaders are sufficient to allow Skocpol to provide a perceptive, integrated analysis of opportunities for insurrection in *States and Social Revolutions*.

Our more thorough understanding of opportunities than of grievances is evident in Walter Goldfrank's recent analysis of the origins of the Mexican revolution of 1910. He concludes that four conditions were essential. One of those is "widespread rural rebellion." The other three are a "tolerant or permissive world context" (that is, a weakness or preoccupation of the world powers most committed to preventing revolution), "a severe political crisis paralyzing the administrative and coercive capacities of the state," and "dissident elite political movements."[24] Goldfrank analyzes the opportunities that allowed agrarian violence to begin and endure in Mexico in terms of three interacting developments. Mass agrarian discontent is postulated as singularly important, but the available studies of rural rebellions allowed him to explain those insurrections only minimally.

Among the major interpretive works considered here, only Scott's study of the origins of peasant rebellions in Southeast Asia and Moore's analysis of industrial protests in Germany devote substantial attention to the perceptions of the poor. We still know too little about why and how the rural masses come to feel the outrage of injustice and begin to ponder taking the deadly risks of insurrection. The analysis of Mexican uprisings attempted here focuses primarily on the origins of agrarian grievances, addressing opportunities for rebellion when appropriate.

It is not easy to study the grievances that stimulate rural uprisings. It is ultimately impossible to know with any certainty the views and values of long-dead, often illiterate, agrarian people. But we may approximate such an under-

[24] Goldfrank, "Theories of Revolution," p. 148.

standing by looking carefully at their complex and often varied ways of life. If we can see in detail both the possibilities and limitations faced by agrarian people, and then relate those conditions to the presence or absence, timing, and endurance of rebellions, we may approach an understanding of how decisions about insurrection were made. Such understanding is necessarily limited, open to reinterpretation, and perhaps subject to sharp debate. But if debate serves to focus more research and analysis on the lives and perceptions of the rural poor then the effort is justified.

Analysis must begin with concepts capable of revealing differences in the ways rural people live as they change over the years. I share with Eric Wolf and James Scott the assumption that the agrarian poor are concerned first with family subsistence. The endless work of survival must take precedence over all other activities. Wolf has provided a helpful categorization of agrarian ways of life based on how people attain subsistence. The three basic types are peasants, rural laborers, and farmers. All live as rural cultivators subject to states and economic elites, and all provide a surplus to benefit those powerholders. But as Wolf emphasizes, peasants, rural laborers, and farmers live, face rulers, and produce surpluses in very different ways.

*Peasants* are families and communities who have access to the lands and tools needed for subsistence production, and who produce for consumption most (but rarely all) of their basic necessities. In contrast; *laborers* work in the service of others in exchange for the necessities of subsistence, or the means to purchase them. And *farmers* are cultivators who sustain themselves by producing a limited number of goods to sell or otherwise exchange for subsistence goods.[25] Few families, of course, have been pure peasants, producing all of their subsistence without recourse to wage labor or mar-

[25] Wolf, *Peasants*, pp. 1-17. The emphasis on subsistence production reflects the ecological approach developed earlier by Julian Steward in *Theory of Culture Change*.

kets. Similarly, few have lived as pure farmers, wholly dependent on the market and growing nothing for family consumption. Pure laborers, fully dependent on wage income, are more common, yet in rural areas many engage in supplementary production or trade activities. Classification should focus on the *primary* means of subsistence, always noting the presence and relative importance of other activities. Thus, peasants live primarily by consuming family produce; laborers subsist primarily by working for others; and farmers live primarily by market exchange.

The distinctions among peasants, laborers, and farmers are basic to agrarian social analyses. Yet a brief study of any agrarian society reveals important variations in the lives of people who are peasants, laborers, or farmers. And such variations are often crucial to the origins of rural uprisings. To examine such distinctions, basic questions of subsistence remain critical. And the variations of the social relations linking elites and the rural poor are especially important considerations, as Jeffrey Paige insists.[26] The ways that such power relations facilitate or inhibit the production or attainment of subsistence is crucial to rural peoples' perceptions of their larger societies—and to their attitudes toward insurrection.

A focus on the interplay of four variable characteristics helps to highlight important differences in agrarian ways of life and to explain often complex social changes. One characteristic is material and at least potentially measurable: the *material conditions*, that is, the standard of living, of the population in question. The other three are more qualitative and describe the impact of power relations on the lives of the rural poor. They are the relative *autonomy*, *security*, and *mobility* of agrarian families. Each of these characteristics tells a great deal about how the poor attain their subsist-

[26] See Paige, *Agrarian Revolution*, p. 9. A more basic theoretical statement of the importance of social relations of power, or inequality, is in Richard N. Adams, *Energy and Structure*.

ence, while also describing varying social and cultural avenues left open to them. And each may be valued differently by different rural people.

*Material conditions* are obviously important. Any understanding of rural ways of life demands knowing whether people have enough food, clothing, shelter, fuel, and other basic goods; whether they enjoy some margin of comfort above subsistence; or whether they lack basic necessities and thus face persistent deficiencies of nutrition and health. It is equally essential to know whether material conditions are generally stable, improving, or declining. Such considerations of standards of living are common in studies of rural life and insurrections.

But analysis of the material lives of the poor is not sufficient for understanding agrarian ways of life, their changes, and the origins of rebellions. Extreme poverty does not necessarily lead to insurrection. As Wolf emphasizes, disruptions of established social relations are as important as worsening exploitation in provoking outrage and rebellion. A focus on peoples' relative autonomy, security, and mobility helps delineate the nature of disruptive social changes.

*Autonomy* reflects peoples' abilities to produce the necessities of subsistence independently. In general, peasants are the most autonomous of agrarian people, for by definition they directly produce the majority of their subsistence goods.[27] Farmers' autonomy is reduced; although they control their production, they depend on markets to sell their produce and to obtain many essential goods. And laborers are the least autonomous of agrarian people. By definition they do not control production and they generally live by

[27] The importance of peasant autonomy has long been noted. See, for example, John Stuart Mill, *Principles of Political Economy*, p. 252. Yet others have ignored or downplayed that independence. For a discussion that emphasizes peasant autonomy and speculates about why it is so often ignored, see Davydd Greenwood, "Political Economy and Adaptive Processes," pp. 6-8.

buying in markets they cannot control. Such variations in autonomy are basic to the differences among peasants, laborers, and farmers.

But differences in autonomy are equally important among those generally classed as peasants, farmers, and even laborers. For example, peasants owning ample, fertile, and well-watered lands perhaps enjoy the most autonomy possible among socially subordinate people. Others who must rent lands are less autonomous. And tenants with long-term rights are surely more autonomous than those facing annual rental agreements. Thus, while autonomy is a fundamental characteristic of all peasant life, it varies among peasants in different situations, and those variations deserve close attention in studies of social change and rebellion.

Peasants not only sustain themselves with great autonomy, they also tend to value that independence highly. Historians have emphasized that European peasants prized above all their ability to control the lands and tools essential to subsistence autonomy, while adapting cultural values that reinforced the desirability of maximum independence.[28] Students of contemporary peasants have noted the importance of autonomy less emphatically. Joel Migdal suggests that peasants have a "fear of dependency on outsiders";[29] James Scott's analysis indicates why modern peasants appear more fearful of dependence than positively attached to autonomy. While they cherish the ability to subsist independently, for many, by the early twentieth century, such autonomy was but a distant memory of a long lost way of life.[30] Yet Arturo Warman's fine analysis of the social history of the peasants of Morelos, Mexico, makes plain their staunch attachment to the goal of subsistence auton-

[28] See Bloch, *Feudal Society*, 1, 7; Duby, *The Early Growth*, p. 56; Goubert, *The Ancien Régime*, p. 69.
[29] Migdal, *Peasants, Politics, and Revolutions*, p. 16.
[30] Scott, *Moral Economy*, pp. 7, 36.

omy long after population growth and commercialization had reduced any real independence to a minimum.[31]

*Security* is the ability to attain subsistence consistently—to expect a minimally acceptable standard of living through the foreseeable future. Security is not directly linked to the ways of life of peasants, laborers, or farmers. Among peasants, security varies with the area and quality of lands, the conditions of access to lands, the regularity of rainfall, and many other considerations. Among laborers, security differs depending on the availability of workers, their skills, their organization, and much more. Among farmers, security varies with their lands, debts, tenancy relations, the crops raised, and market conditions.

For James Scott, as noted earlier, "subsistence security" is the key moral right demanded by peasants.[32] An examination of his analysis of Southeast Asia in conjunction with Shepard Forman's study of *The Brazilian Peasantry* suggests that it is especially when the rural poor lack autonomy and are locked into social relations of dependence that security becomes their paramount concern. Peasants dependent on landlords for access to lands, laborers dependent on estate operators for employment, and farmers dependent on elites to obtain lands, or on merchants for access to credit and markets, all tend to devote great effort to claiming secure access to those essential factors of survival. And they tend to adapt values that also prize that security. All people surely value security to a degree, but it becomes most important, at times an apparent obsession, among rural poor people held in lives of dependence.

*Mobility* is the ability to choose among multiple means of attaining subsistence. Can rural families choose whether to live as peasants, laborers, or farmers? More often, however, mobility concerns whether people have options within one prevailing way of life. Can peasants move to new lands, or

---

[31] Warman, *Y venimos.*
[32] Scott, *Moral Economy,* p. 6.

are they rooted by law, custom, or scarcity to a given plot? Are laborers restricted to one employer by lack of alternatives or by some coercion? Or can they choose among multiple positions? Can farmers choose the lands they cultivate, the crops they raise, the merchant with the lowest rate of interest, and the buyer offering the highest price? Given such diverse questions, levels of mobility vary widely among the agrarian poor. Yet mobility can become a central concern in rural welfare. Scott notes that "varieties of employment opportunities" have become "safety valves" compensating for losses of autonomy or security.[33]

Analysis of the interaction of material conditions, autonomy, security, and mobility helps describe complex agrarian changes and the origins of insurrections. Ultimately, explanation must be historical—focused on the developments of a given society. But before turning to Mexican history, a few general comments about the relations among material conditions, autonomy, security, and mobility may be helpful.

First, material standards of living are not simple or directly linked to levels of autonomy, security, or mobility. A very autonomous peasant may enjoy material comfort or face starvation. An exceptionally mobile laborer may earn high wages or a pittance. Autonomy, security, and mobility are tied to the ways people attain their subsistence. But their standards of living also depend on available resources, tools, skills, organizations, and many other factors. Only an examination of historical conditions can explain the material situation of particular people.

Second, the more qualitative considerations of autonomy, security, and mobility are linked together in more predictable ways. Most predictable is the near impossibility of the poor attaining high levels of all three at the same time. For example, peasant subsistence cultivators typically enjoy great autonomy, yet have limited security in the face of climatic uncertainties and minimal mobility because of scarce land resources. Laborers have little autonomy, widely varying levels of security, and often substantial mobility—unless bondage or other coercion eliminates that mobility, yet perhaps increases their security. Most of the rural poor attain high levels of but one among autonomy, security, and mobility. They may simultaneously have limited levels of another, while finding the third precluded. Autonomy, security, and mobility tend to vary in complex relations of inversion—gains in one usually bring losses of another.

Finally, while autonomy, security, and mobility are all generally seen as desirable, they are rarely viewed as equally important. As long as autonomy is possible, at times when it seems but remotely possible, such independence of subsistence appears the primary goal of the rural poor. Peasants have long endured extreme poverty, painful insecurities, and obvious immobility while clinging to cherished autonomy. During recent centuries, population growth, commercialization, and the concentration of resource controls have combined to undermine agrarian autonomy. At different times and by varying routes, rural families across the globe have faced the collapse of their ability to subsist with even limited independence. For most, survival has become tied to social relations of dependence. They live as direct subordinates of landed elites, employers of rural labor, and merchants who provide credit and market goods. When such dependence predominates, security become the primary concern of the rural poor. Only certain access to tenancies or jobs can cushion social relations of dependence. Yet such security has also tended to diminish in recent times. Continued population growth, accelerating monopolization of resources, and the development of "labor-saving" techniques of production have resulted in the creation of "surplus workers." Such conditions allow landlords and employers to ignore the security of their dependents, using threats—and realities—of evictions and lost jobs to raise rents and lower wages. Only mobility, access to multiple opportunities to gain income or sustenance, can protect the rural poor from such insecurities. In Scott's phrase: "Ownership was prized over tenancy and tenancy over casual labor . . . even though they might overlap in terms of income."[34] In the terms used here: autonomy is prized over dependence; with dependence, security becomes essential; and with insecurity, mobility is the only compensation.

What social changes, then, are likely to generate the extreme grievances basic to agrarian insurrections? That is the primary question of the historical analysis that follows. An outline of the conclusions may be previewed here: declining standards of living—scarce food, falling wages, rising rents, etc.—are conducive to rebellions, but rarely provoke them alone. It is when particular social changes that are especially painful to the poor accompany declining standards of living that the grievances of insurrection become acute. Peasants accustomed to subsistence autonomy become outraged when that independence is threatened or undermined by visible elite or state actors—and when that loss of autonomy is not compensated by access to ways of life that are dependent yet secure. Those accustomed to lives of dependence become outraged and move toward insurrection when their security is undermined by the evident acts of powerholders—and when their loss of security is not compensated by a new mobility. Simply stated, long-autonomous peasants suddenly forced into dependence without security, and long-secure dependents rapidly made to face insecurity without mobility, tend to become outraged at the injustices imposed upon them by the powerful. Should an opportunity for insurrection develop, such irate agrarian people often become violent insurgents.

Whether such insurgents become revolutionaries depends in part on their numbers, but also upon their leaders and their organization. The endurance and success of agrarian rebels also depend on relations with other political

[34] Ibid., p. 38.

actors and the larger context of the conflict—and even upon prevailing economic and strategic conditions in the world at the time. But from the perspective of the rural poor, all these considerations are questions of opportunity. They choose to become rebels because they are outraged by grievances that their families suffer.[35]

These generalizations are but guides to help explain historical developments. To illustrate the utility of the approach proposed here, as well as to introduce Mexican agrarian conditions, this chapter concludes with an outline of the varying agrarian structures of different Mexican regions in the eighteenth century, toward the end of the colonial era.

Colonial Mexico generated two primary agrarian patterns, with important variations within each. Across the central and southern regions, most rural people lived as relatively autonomous peasants in landed communities. Across the more northerly regions, most agrarian families were dependent laborers or tenants at large landed estates. The complex regional evolution of Mexican agrarian social relations can be analyzed by examining each of the two dominant patterns, the variations within them, and their relative importance in different regions.

In the highlands of central and southern Mexico, landed peasant communities were the principal rural social units. Peasants had cultivated maize and other food crops there for centuries before the Spanish conquest. The Spanish colonial state reserved to the peasants who survived the postconquest depopulation catastrophe at least a remnant of community subsistence lands. Interspersed among these

[35] Scott notes that insurrection demands that peasant difficulties have "tangible" causes in elite or state actions. See *Moral Economy*, p. 58. He sees the collapse of security when peasants are dependent as "a second threshold." See ibid., p. 40. In "Hegemony and the Peasantry," p. 291, he also concludes that the causes of peasant uprisings are little different in crushed insurrections and more successful revolutions. Different outcomes depend more on peasants' relations with other groups.

peasant communities were numerous large estates owned and operated by colonial elite families. But in the central and southern regions, these estates were primarily economic institutions. The rural population overwhelmingly lived in peasant villages to the end of the colonial era. That peasant population faced difficult conditions, eking out subsistence on limited community lands. Yet as landholding residents of peasant communities, they enjoyed great autonomy in producing that meager subsistence. Their security, however, was minimal. They lived by raising crops subject to the vagaries of Mexican rainfall. And they had little mobility. They were legally free to move, but their access to lands depended on continuing residence in their home communities.

The subsistence autonomy of central and southern Mexican peasants was complemented by local political independence. The colonial state allowed community governments, led by local notables, to oversee the use of community lands, collect local taxes, organize local fiestas, and generally mediate relations with outsiders. As William Taylor has shown, the preservation of local autonomy of subsistence and independence of government was critical to community peasants. They protested, rioted, and sporadically rebelled in the late colonial era when that village autonomy was threatened.[36]

Of course, this peasant community autonomy was limited. Local political leaders were subject to higher Spanish authorities. And peasant subsistence autonomy was never complete. Although most villagers raised most of their staple maize, as well as other foods, built their own homes, and made much of their own clothing, they always needed some goods they did not produce. To obtain these, families with ample lands marketed surplus produce. But most community peasants had no surplus. To sustain their families, they had no choice but to labor periodically at estates near their

[36] See Taylor, *Drinking, Homicide, and Rebellion*, pp. 113-151.

villages. The estates thus obtained seasonal workers needed for planting, cultivating, and harvesting their large crops, and the peasants received earnings that were essential to supplement their subsistence production. Such villagers were clearly incorporated into the colonial commercial economy. But they were incorporated through an agrarian structure that preserved substantial subsistence autonomy—an autonomy they prized.

Across central and southern Mexico, there were important variations within this pattern of agrarian social relations organized around landed peasant communities. Where village lands were ample and fertile, peasant autonomy was greatest. Where lands were scarce or of poor quality, autonomy diminished. Similarly important to variations of peasant life were links with urban markets. Where urban consumers were numerous and nearby, the development of commercial estates was generally greater, allowing less land for peasant communities. Thus, autonomy would decline and dependence on estate labor would increase. Conversely, where peasants lived in communities far from substantial markets, estate development was usually restricted and peasant autonomy more easily preserved. And finally, the relations between peasant numbers and community land resources always conditioned the relatively autonomy of peasant families. When population declined during the century after the conquest, peasant autonomy increased—unless community lands were lost at the same rate that the population fell. And when peasant numbers increased during the decades after 1650, autonomy inevitably diminished—peasant communities could rarely expand their land holdings. The autonomy of peasants living in landed communities varied greatly in colonial Mexico. But that autonomy remained the defining characteristic of peasant life in the central and southern highlands.[37] And it was severe

[37] This view of peasant Mexico is based on Gibson, *Aztecs*; Taylor, *Landlord and Peasant*; and Tutino, "Creole Mexico."

threats to that autonomy that most commonly produced protests and revolts among villagers.

In striking contrast, across northern Mexico, agrarian social relations developed a radically different pattern. These more arid regions were inhabited mostly by nomads before the conquest. By 1600, war and disease had pressed these natives toward extermination—or regions far from Spanish interests. Spaniards could thus settle northern Mexico with little attention to indigenous patterns of settlement. Colonial elites dominated the building of the Mexican north, organizing rural production around great landed estates. The majority of the agrarian poor who migrated north during the colonial era had no choice but to live as estate dependents. Given the sparse northern population, estate residents often enjoyed standards of living better than those prevailing in more densely populated regions to the south. They also enjoyed substantial security and good mobility throughout most of the colonial era. Nothern elites facing labor shortages often lamented that mobility. But their attempts to restrict the movement of workers met with little success. Dependence on agrarian elites was the defining characteristic of agrarian life in northern Mexico. Given that dependence, agrarian families made security a primary goal. Where eighteenth-century changes undermined that security, insurrection was substantial in 1810. Where that security endured, however, revolt was stifled.

Again, there were important variations within this northern Mexican pattern of rural life. Where large estates predominated on good arable lands, a tenantry might develop that enjoyed a limited autonomy of production, yet faced increased insecurities due to market and climatic inconsistencies, within social relations still defined by their dependence on elite landowners. Where lands were more arid and grazing predominated, dependent employment of cowboys and shepherds remained the characteristic social relation. Where such workers were scarce, their acceptance of dependence was often rewarded by security. But when population exceeded labor demands, that security could vanish rapidly. And estate residents close to northern towns and mining centers might enjoy substantial mobility, while those in more isolated regions often had little choice but to remain at estates that ruled their lives.[38]

Agrarian social relations varied as much among northern estate dependents as among the village peasants of central and southern Mexico. The result was a complex, regionally varied agrarian structure. In most regions, rural families lived primarily as villagers or as estate residents. But regions of peasants always included some estate dependents. And regions dominated by great estates inevitably included a few peasant communities struggling to survive in a hostile environment. In addition, colonial Mexican rural societies usually included rancheros—relatively independent farmers who were neither powerful elites nor impoverished peasants. Rancheros survived in small numbers interspersed among the peasant villages and commercial estates of the central and southern highlands. They lived in larger numbers in northerly regions dominated by great estates. And rancheros might even predominate numerically in a few areas where peasants were few and large estates had not developed.[39] Given these complexities, agrarian social relations in colonial Mexico can only be studied in regional perspective.

The analysis that follows begins with a lengthy and detailed examination of agrarian changes in the Bajío, and seeks to explain why a secure, but dependent, rural population was forced in the late eighteenth century to endure worsening poverty and a new, intense insecurity—engendering the sense of outrage and injustice that set off the Hidalgo revolt of 1810. That explanation is then tested and refined by examining agrarian social relations in other

[38] This analysis of estate-dominated regions reflects Tutino, "Life and Labor."

[39] On rancheros, see Brading, *Haciendas and Ranchos*.

provinces, comparing regions of rebellion with regions of loyalty and passivity. My goal is to explain the social origins of the agrarian insurrections that began early in the nineteenth century, and then to trace the expansion of rural conflicts until the agrarian revolution that began in 1910.

# PART ONE

# THE ORIGINS OF INSURRECTIONS, 1750–1816

# CHAPTER TWO

# Social Origins of Insurrection:
# The Bajío, 1740–1810

ON SEPTEMBER 16, 1810, Father Miguel Hidalgo y Costilla called on his parishioners in the small Mexican town of Dolores to join him in revolt against the Spanish colonial regime. Numerous townsfolk as well as many residents of nearby estates quickly followed their pastor into rebellion. Several hundred became insurgents on that first day of revolt.[1] Turning south across the fertile Bajío region, first to the town of San Miguel and then to Celaya, the rebellion grew to an estimated 25,000 insurgents within two weeks. And by the middle of October, after capturing the mining center of Guanajuato, the insurrection included nearly 80,000 rebels.[2]

This massive revolt was very much an agrarian uprising. Hidalgo did recruit town dwellers in Dolores, San Miguel, and Celaya, along with mine workers from Guanajuato. But a large portion of the rebels of 1810—probably a solid majority—were tenants and employees of rural estates in the Bajío. The memoirs of Pedro García, a participant in the revolt, emphasize the recruitment of rebels as the insurgents passed through the countryside. Every rural settlement seemed to provide new insurgents.[3] The conservative politician and historian Lucas Alamán, who lived through the revolt as a youth in Guanajuato and later studied it in detail, described Hidalgo's rebellion as the rising of a whole rural people. He emphasized that many rebel officers were estate

---

[1] Alamán, *Historia de Méjico*, I, 242.
[2] Hamill, *Hidalgo Revolt*, p. 124.
[3] García, *Con el cura Hidalgo*, pp. 36, 43-46, 58, 64.

managers and foremen, while most cavalry were estate cowboys, and the majority of foot soldiers were estate laborers.[4] That view is corroborated by the letters written by the manager of a large estate near San Miguel. He reported that at least 75 of his employees, tenants, and subtenants joined the revolt and then participated in several attacks on the property.[5] Hidalgo focused his proclamations on political grievances against the Spanish regime in Mexico. His followers, however, repeatedly aimed their violence against the landed estates of the Bajío and nearby areas.[6] The Hidalgo revolt was an agrarian insurrection, despite the more political goals of its leader.

The massive revolt that erupted in the Bajío in the autumn of 1810 broke nearly three centuries of agrarian stability and peace in central Mexico. It began a long era of rural violence. During the colonial centuries, there had been many rural protests, but most of these conflicts involved only single peasant communities. Few protests before 1810 lasted more than a day. And most colonial revolts attempted not to force social change, but to redress particular, local grievances. In striking contrast, the Hidalgo revolt of 1810 was larger, longer, and more violent. It recruited tens of thousands of rebels from a wide area of north central Mexico who fought vehemently against the colonial regime for four months. The mass rising led by Hidalgo was crushed militarily in January of 1811, but several offshoot rebellions carried on for years. What Hidalgo began, many continued. During the years that followed, while Mexico grappled with the dilemmas of new nationhood, agrarian conflicts proliferated. And rural rebels began to adopt programs calling for structural changes in Mexican life.[7]

---

[4] Alamán, *Historia de Méjico*, I, 244-246.

[5] JSE, vol. 214, no. 122, 18 Nov. 1810; no. 127, 3 Feb. 1811; no. 130, 4 May 1811; no. 131, 3 Dec. 1811.

[6] JSE, vol. 214, no. 121, 10 Oct. 1810; no. 122, 18 Nov. 1810.

[7] See Taylor, *Drinking, Homicide, and Rebellion*, and Tutino, "Agrarian Social Change."

Analysis of the agrarian origins of the Hidalgo revolt contributes directly to understanding the era of Mexican independence. It also helps explain the transformation of Mexican agrarian history from a long era of peace and stability to over a century of endemic, violent conflict. And such an inquiry may contribute to the wider, comparative discussions of the social origins of agrarian violence—violence that continues to play a major role in societies in Latin America and elsewhere.

Most studies of the Hidalgo revolt have focused on the lives and actions of elites. We know much about Hidalgo and other rebel leaders, and about the ideologies they proclaimed in challenging Spanish rule.[8] We know little, however, about why tens of thousands of estate tenants and laborers joined the insurrection. Yet without that mass support, Hidalgo would be known as but one among many Mexican conspirators who protested Spanish rule with little success. It was the emergence of mass, sustained, agrarian rebellion for the first time in the modern history of Mexico that made Hidalgo and the revolt he led significant. The origins of that mass insurrection deserve close attention.

Lucas Alamán, the nineteenth-century heir to a colonial fortune, presumed in his classic *Historia de Méjico* that the Mexican masses harbored old, enduring hatreds against their rulers—hatreds sparked into violent rebellion by the proclamations of Hidalgo and his fellow conspirators.[9] Alamán's presumption that the Mexican poor held long-festering grievances is most revealing of the anxieties that plagued Mexican elites in the nineteenth century. The same presumption also relieved the aristocratic historian of the need to study the lives and interests of the rebel masses. But it is clear that old grievances of Spanish colonialism cannot explain the Hidalgo revolt. Those long-standing complaints

---

[8] See, for examples, Alamán, *Historia de Méjico*, I, 154-258; Hamill, *Hidalgo Revolt*, pp. 1-116; Timmons, *Morelos*, and Villoro, *Proceso ideológico*.

[9] Alamán, *Historia de Méjico*, I, 244.

were certainly shared by the rural poor across Mexico. But only the agrarian people of the Bajío and a few nearby areas rebelled massively in 1810.

Eric Wolf began the modern study of the origins of the Hidalgo revolt by focusing on its regional uniqueness. He emphasized that the insurrection emerged in the Bajío, the most fertile region of central Mexico. Colonial society there was more commercial, perhaps more capitalist, than in other Mexican regions. The Bajío's integrated complex of commercial agriculture, textile manufacturing, and silver mining set it apart. Wolf argued that the leading families of the Bajío were emerging capitalists, increasingly resentful of colonial restrictions on their entrepreneurship. Yet when he briefly addressed the origins of the mass rebellion, Wolf followed Alamán in emphasizing long-standing colonial tribute obligations and labor regulations.[10]

For both the nineteenth-century politician-historian and the twentieth-century anthropologist-historian, a rural people with very old complaints rebelled suddenly in 1810 because a small clique of discontented elites called them to arms. Given the prevalence of such views, explanations of the Hidalgo revolt have continually focused on rebel leadership.

More recently, Jorge Domínguez has emphasized the importance of the crisis of the Spanish imperial state that preceded the insurrection. A division or weakening of state power has been pivotal to the unleashing of mass, sustained agrarian violence in many societies.[11] And a crisis of the colonial state did set the stage for the Hidalgo revolt. When in 1808 Napoleon captured Madrid and the Spanish king, Mexico and other colonial regions faced unprecedented questions. Heated debates among colonial elites probed the colony's place in an empire without a king. Conspiracies

[10] Wolf, "Mexican Bajío," pp. 182, 191.
[11] Domínguez, *Insurrection or Loyalty*, pp. 137-151, 170-171.

seeking independence developed. And it was the failure of one such conspiracy that touched off the Hidalgo revolt.

By linking the emergence of rebel leadership with the crisis of the colonial state, explanations of the Hidalgo revolt become more complex, but they remain focused on elites. Yet, can the sudden uprising of tens of thousands of rural poor people be explained primarily by the breakdown of colonial legitimacy and the emergence of a clique of leaders ready to call the masses—presumably harboring old grievances—to arms? Again, the regional uniqueness of the mass insurrection calls such political explanations into question. The crisis of imperial legitimacy and the old grievances of Spanish colonialism affected all Mexican regions. But the Hidalgo revolt began in the Bajío and found substantial support only in a few nearby regions. The state crisis, disaffected provincial elites, and old grievances surely contributed to the insurrection of 1810, but they cannot explain its regional origins in the Bajío.

Although the actions of powerholders are obviously important to the origins of most rebellions, it is ultimately the decisions of numerous subordinates to risk life in challenging those who rule that make rebellions. Therefore, the evolving lives and values of the rebel populace demand primary attention in any analysis of the origins of mass insurrection.

Fortunately, the social history of agrarian Mexico has been a flourishing field of analysis in recent years. Few agrarian societies are so well studied, and analyses of the century before 1810 are especially plentiful and detailed.[12] They reveal that rural Mexicans faced difficult changes during the late eighteenth century. This analysis asks: were

---

[12] The modern agrarian history of Mexico was begun by François Chevalier in his pioneering *La formación*. Subsequent studies basic to this analysis are Gibson, *Aztecs*: Florescano, *Precios del maíz*, and *Estructuras y problemas*; Taylor, *Landlord and Peasant*, and *Drinking, Homicide, and Rebellion*; Brading, *Miners and Merchants*, and *Haciendas and Ranchos*; Morin, *Michoacán* and Van Young, *Hacienda and Market*.

social changes in the Bajío different and perhaps more damaging than those in other regions? Can different patterns of agrarian change explain the intensity of insurrection in the Bajío as well as the weakness of uprisings elsewhere? I believe they can. Detailed study of the Bajío suggests that acute, new grievances developed there after 1750, fueling the insurrection. And comparative analysis of other regions indicates that those grievances were all but unique to the Bajío in late eighteenth-century Mexico. A specific, regional, social crisis, not old complaints against Spanish rule, generated the mass outrage mobilized by Hidalgo in 1810.

Agrarian poor people do not decide to rebel easily. Life for most is an ongoing struggle to survive, to produce or otherwise obtain the necessities of survival. Such people are understandably reluctant to take the deadly risks of insurrection. But when their lives are threatened by uncertainties of subsistence, and when those threats have clear social origins, many consider taking the chances of rebellion. Once a social structure has placed life at risk, risking life in search of social change seems a less drastic step—especially if the crisis of subsistence has visible causes that may be altered by the insurrection.

The agrarian history of the Mexican Bajío illustrates one social process that transformed a stable agrarian society into a breeding ground of insurgents. During the colonial era, the vast majority of the rural residents of the region lived as estate dependents. From the sixteenth century, the Spanish regime had allowed a provincial gentry to all but monopolize the best lands in the Bajío. The majority of the region's inhabitants thus had no choice but to live as dependents— either as tenant cultivators, employees, or both. While the gentry lived in nearby towns, enjoying leisure and luxury, the rural majority worked the land to gain a modest subsistence. These were social relations of evident and extreme inequality. Yet before the later decades of the eighteenth century, the dependents who cultivated Bajío estates enjoyed substantial security and standards of living that compared favorably with those in other Mexican regions. Subsistence was not generally a problem, for tenancies and permanent jobs were regularly available at Bajío estates. Agrarian relations of dependence were compensated with ample security and material benefits, and rural unrest remained minimal in the Bajío during most of the colonial era.

After 1750, however, the security and minimal comfort that cushioned these lives of dependence gave way to worsening insecurities accompanied by declining material conditions. Dependence that was earlier accepted—at times even sought—because it brought security and an acceptable subsistence became a grievance because it forced hunger and insecurity onto growing numbers of rural families. As the agrarian crisis deepened, problems also struck the Bajío textile and mining industries. After 1785, employment became increasingly insecure for both urban weavers and the many rural women who spun yarn. By 1810, mining employment at Guanajuato was rapidly collapsing. Converging agrarian and industrial crises left many in the Bajío ready to strike violently against provincial elites and the colonial regime. When Father Hidalgo called them to arms in 1810, tens of thousands of the Bajío poor responded by assaulting the landed estates and other institutions of elite power that dominated their lives.

## AN HISPANIC AGRICULTURAL FRONTIER, 1550–1740

To the Spanish conquerors of Mexico, the Bajío must have presented a strange sight. There lay a fine agricultural basin left vacant by Mexicans they had come to know as skilled cultivators. A few Tarascan and Otomí peasants lived on the southern flanks of the fertile depression, but most of the Bajío lacked a settled population in the early sixteenth century. Archaeological studies reveal that centuries earlier the region had supported an agricultural population. But long before the Spanish conquest, the attacks of warring nomads from the arid plateau to the north had turned the Bajío into an empty buffer between bellicose northerners and settled cultivators.[13]

This region without people did not attract the first Spanish conquerors. They came to rule people, not to work the land. In 1530, Querétaro was founded as a grazing outpost at the southeastern edge of the Bajío. Few people migrated there, however. Until the late sixteenth century, the Bajío lay at the northern limit of Spanish Mexico—more home to sheep than to Spaniards or to Indians.[14]

Two intersecting developments led to the agricultural colonization of the region late in the sixteenth century. Beginning in 1545, valuable silver mines were discovered at Zacatecas, Guanajuato, and elsewhere in the mountains of the arid country just north of the Bajío. Profitable mines gave Spaniards the incentive to take on the fierce nomads of northern Mexico. And growing mining towns created a demand for food and livestock that could not be met by production in the dry country around the mines. In response, beginning in the 1560s, a process of conquest and settlement began to shelter the Bajío from the nomads' wrath while building an economy based on supplying produce to the expanding mining towns.

The emergence of the mining economy coincided with a new interest among Spaniards in claiming lands and building estates in Mexico. The first conquerors had profited amply by collecting tributes and periodic labor services from Mexican peasants through encomienda rights.[15] Early Spanish wealth in Mexico was thus based on the survival of the native peasant economy. The conquerors congregated

[13] Diehl, "Pre-Hispanic Relationships," pp. 270-272.

[14] Chevalier, *Formación*, p. 79; Super, "Agricultural Near North," pp. 231-239.

[15] Simpson, *The Encomienda*.

where Mexican peasants were most numerous and their agriculture most intensive—especially in the central highlands around Mexico City. But Old World diseases and the social dislocations of conquest rapidly destroyed the Mexican population—a depopulation that would reach 95 percent by the early seventeenth century. That destruction of the peasant population also undermined the conquerors' ability to profit from peasant tributes and labor services.

With peasants ever more scarce and lands increasingly vacant after 1550, the conquerors' heirs began to claim land. They organized commercial estates to raise the food and livestock for growing colonial cities and mining towns—and to generate the profits essential to the aristocratic lives they expected to live. Strategically placed just south of the mines and just north of the central highlands, the vacant Bajío plains attracted Spanish estate builders in the later years of the sixteenth century.

For Spaniards to occupy the Bajío, however, they had to overcome the resistance of nomadic Indians who fought long and hard to prevent European occupation of their homelands. The first Spanish attempts at settlement failed. San Miguel was founded in 1546 by friars who planned to congregate nomadic natives in the uplands just northeast of the Bajío basin, along the road to the mines recently found at Zacatecas. The project was abandoned in 1551. Then, in 1555, Viceroy Luis de Velasco ordered the establishment of a Spanish town at San Miguel. Settlers were to be attracted by grants of 40 hectares (one hectare is 2.47 acres) of arable land, as well as house lots and access to pasturage. They were expected to defend themsleves and the region against attacks by the nomads. Settlement at the second San Miguel began early in the 1560s, followed quickly by a similar colonization to the northwest at San Felipe. And once these towns began to provide a buffer against the increasingly angry Indians, Celaya was settled in the 1570s on the Bajío plain, followed shortly by the founding of León and other towns. In each new settlement, Spaniards received from 40 to 80 hectares of cropland, plus house lots in town, and access to pasturage nearby.[16]

Spanish colonists, however, were not the only immigrants into the Bajío in the late sixteenth century. Otomí and Tarascan Indians, who lived just south of the fertile basin, had coveted its fertile soils, but for years their nomadic enemies had blocked their access to those lands. With the Spanish conquest, many Indian cultivators joined the Spaniards as subordinate allies in the conquest and settlement of the Bajío. The Otomí were especially prominent. Long subject to the Mexicans (Aztecs) of Tenochtitlan (now Mexico City), while facing the direct pressures of the northern nomads, Otomí leaders led many of their people into the warfare and colonization that created the Spanish Bajío.[17]

The nomads, of course, did not welcome this new incursion into their territory. Beginning in the 1550s, the Guamaraes began to attack settlements of Indian cultivators. They probably focused their assaults on Indian newcomers because they were old enemies, and because they did not have the more deadly weapons of the Spaniards. The Pames generally limited their attacks to Spaniards' livestock until the 1570s, when they began to strike Spanish settlements more directly. And in 1585, the Jonaces attacked the Spanish town of Zimapán, just southeast of the Bajío. Through the 1570s and 1580s, then, the eastern Bajío saw persistent conflict between Spanish, Otomí, and Tarascan immigrants and the nomads fighting to keep the newcomers out.[18]

By the 1590s, the Spaniards and their allies had the upper hand. Old World diseases continued to kill Indians, including the nomads, while Spanish immigration increased. In addition, communities of conquered and Christianized

---

[16] Chevalier, *Formación*, pp. 47-49; Powell, *Soldiers, Indians, and Silver*, pp. 67-68, 152-154.

[17] Ibid., pp. 70-71, 139, 163-164; Super, *Vida en Querétaro*, pp. 181-182.

[18] Powell, *Soldiers, Indians, and Silver*, pp. 28, 37, 60, 144, 183.

Indians were brought in from the more densely settled regions around Mexico City and Tlaxcala. They built communities not only in the Bajío, but also further north around San Luis Potosí where silver had recently been discovered. The nomads, especially the Pames and the Jonaces, retreated into the rugged highlands called the Sierra Gorda, just northeast of the Bajío. By 1595, a town—optimistically named San Luis de la Paz—was settled by Spaniards, along with Mexican, Tarascan, and Otomí Indians, at the point where the Bajío uplands meet the all but impenetrable Sierra Gorda. From then on, the fertile Bajío belonged to the Spaniards—and less directly to those Indians willing to live there under Spanish rule.[19] (The nomads, though much reduced in numbers and territory, did not disappear. They found a refuge in the Sierra, a bastion that remained uncolonized by Spaniards until the middle of the eighteenth century. And as we shall see, the Indians of the Sierra Gorda remained ready to fight Spanish encroachment when it finally came toward the end of the colonial era.)

By 1600, then, half a century of warfare and colonization had built the foundations of the modern Bajío. Querétaro, the gateway to the region from central Mexico, was already a growing commercial city with an expanding textile industry, surrounded by estates raising grain as well as livestock. Meanwhile, the smaller Bajío towns such as Celaya, Salamanca, and León were being surrounded by new estates, often with irrigated croplands, built by a dynamic regional gentry.[20] By the early sixteenth century, the Bajío had already developed the regional mix of commercial agriculture, mining, and textile manufacturing that Eric Wolf found unique when he studied eighteenth-century developments there.

[19] Ibid., pp. 195-197.
[20] See Super, "Agricultural Near North," pp. 232-239; Chevalier, *Formación*, pp. 47-48; Brading, *Haciendas and Ranchos*, pp. 17-18, 39-41; Bakewell, "Zacatecas," p. 227; Basalenque, *Historia de la Provincia*, pp. 214, 296.

Settled by Spaniards who expelled the few nomadic natives, the Bajío developed along European, commercial patterns. The region was built by a profit-seeking gentry eager to respond to market opportunities. By the 1630s, over 300 estates in the Bajío produced large harvests of wheat and maize, as well as livestock, supplying not only local markets but also the mining centers to the north. Most heavily cultivated were the plains of the eastern basin around Celaya and nearby towns. There, 137 estates raised large harvests of maize and only slightly less wheat, supplemented by small herds of livestock. The more westerly reaches of the basin around Irapuato, León, and Silao remained less developed, emphasizing maize production and limited cattle grazing. The northeast uplands around San Miguel and San Felipe by 1630 included many small growers of maize, who were crowded by a small number of large-scale stock grazers. The southwest uplands were as yet barely settled.[21]

A region of commercial cultivation, dominated by a town-dwelling gentry, the Bajío lacked the numerous landed peasant communities that defined the structure of agrarian society in central and southern Mexico. Such communities provided Indian peasants with at least limited local rule and independent access to subsistence lands. The Bajío, in contrast, was built around Spanish towns and Spaniards' commercial estates, and peasants who came to cultivate the soil of the newly settled region had no choice but to live within that European, commercial structure.

The early Bajío gentry held fertile lands and faced expanding markets. Their problem was to attract and retain a work force to cultivate their estates—for they had no intention of tilling the soil with their own hands. A small Indian population lived in communities near Querétaro and Celaya, with rights to plots of community lands. But most who migrated into the Bajío had to live as dependents of the gentry. Indian migration followed estate development—

___

[21] See Appendix A, Table A.1.

very slowly. The eastern Bajío that raised the largest crops of labor-intensive maize and wheat also had the most dense Indian population in the region by the 1630s. Yet even there, settlements of Indians on Spanairds' estates rarely reached even 50 households. In the uplands where stock grazing demanded fewer workers, and in the western basin where cultivation was just beginning, Indian settlements rarely approached 20 households.[22]

The Indian immigrants who settled the early Bajío were of diverse regional and cultural origins. It is essential to remember that the idea of "Indians" was a Spanish-imposed notion that lumped together all natives of the New World for purposes of taxation and general subordination. Thus, the general classification of estate workers in the early Bajío as Indians reveals little—and may be misleading. Many Otomí families had migrated from the dry areas between the Bajío and the highlands around Mexico City. Tarascans came from regions to the southwest where they had lived in a society long resistant to Mexican (Aztec) domination. Otomí and Tarascans preserved their own languages, as did the Nahuatl speakers who came into the Bajío from the highlands around Mexico City. The region's Indians also included a small number of former nomads. Thus, from its earliest colonial settlement, the Bajío had an "Indian" population of diverse cultural and linguistic origins.[23]

When they arrived in the Bajío, most of those Indians had no choice but to live as dependents in a regional society ruled by Spaniards. The migrants had left peasant communities that allowed the survival of indigenous languages and culture, partially sheltered from contacts with Spaniards, their language, and their commercializing culture. Such life was not possible for Indians in the Bajío. The majority of the early migrants lived as *laboríos*, resident employees of Spaniards' estates. Most settlements of laboríos

[22] See Appendix A, Table A.2.
[23] López Lara, ed., *Obispado de Michoacán*, pp. 77, 156, 165, 175.

were small, generally fewer than ten households, and included Indians of diverse language and culture.[24] Others lived on Spaniards' lands as *terrazgueros* who paid annual rents for the use of a small plot. Such tenants lived more independently than the laboríos, but all remained dependent on the Spaniards who controlled Bajío estates and dominated regional life.[25] Living in small settlements that mixed several indigenous cultures under the rule of Spaniards, Mexican migrants into the Bajío found it difficult to preserve their native languages and ways of life.

They had to adapt quickly to European ways. They worked the land with plow teams, and other Old World tools of cultivation.[26] Their constant dealings with estate owners and managers required the use of Spanish. And Christianity came to the Bajío Indians in Spanish. Among the long-established peasant peoples of central and southern Mexico, the missionary church preached in native tongues. But the mixing of peoples of many cultures and languages in the Bajío foiled even the best linguists among the missionaries. An ecclesiastical survey of the 1630s laments that priests trained in but one Mexican language were struggling to reach their converts in the Bajío. The conclusion: "In truth, they understand little."[27] Both the economic and ecclesiastical structures of the Bajío worked to favor Spanish as a lingua franca among the Indian population. The result was a relatively rapid Hispanization of the Indian migrants.[28] The colonial state persisted in calling them "Indians" in order to collect their tributes—the colonial head tax on Indians. But Spanish dominance and native diversity worked rapidly to leave the Indians of the Bajío far less Indian—both linguistically and culturally—than the peasant villagers of central and southern Mexico.

[24] Ibid., pp. 69, 70, 75, 143, 165, 176-178.
[25] Ibid., pp. 75, 80.
[26] Ibid., 80; Lavrin, "Convento de Santa Clara," p. 86.
[27] López Lara, ed., *Obispado de Michoacán*, pp. 69-70.
[28] Super, "Agricultural Near North," p. 233.

The rapid Hispanization of the region was accelerated by the early arrival of growing minorities of mestizos and mulattoes—people of mixed Spanish-Indian and Spanish-African-Indian ancestry. Many became artisans in Bajío towns. Others owned or leased modest farms. A few employed Indian dependents. Most mestizos and mulattoes, however, worked only with family labor. And some joined the Indian majority living as estate dependents. In general, the mestizos and mulattoes of the early Bajío settled into the economic and cultural space separating, yet linking, the Spanish gentry and the Indian majority.[29]

What brought mestizos, mulattoes, and especially Indians into the Bajío during the formative period before 1640? These were years of declining population in the peasant communities of central and southern Mexico. Pressures of landlessness were not generally important in pushing migrants toward the Bajío. And except for a few enslaved Africans, no organized coercion forced migrants into the region.[30] In general, the immigrants were neither coerced nor economically pressed to leave their homes to settle at the new estates being built to serve the expanding mining economy of north central Mexico. One result of the absence of such pressures was the small number of migrants arriving before 1630. The Bajío gentry repeatedly lamented the lack of laborers.[31]

Because there was neither organized coercion nor population pressures on the resources of peasant villagers living to the south, the early Bajío gentry had to provide incentives to attract migrants to become agrarian dependents. The early part of the seventeenth century saw mining entrepreneurs offering both high wages and shares of the silver ore to attract and retain workers.[32] Among the Bajío gentry, it became necessary to offer wages well above those

[29] López Lara, ed., *Obispado de Michoacán*, pp. 70, 75, 177, 178.

[30] Chevalier, *Formación*, p. 56.

[31] Morin, *Michoacán*, p. 31.

[32] Del Río, "Sobre la aparición," pp. 92-111.

prevailing in more southerly regions, guaranteed subsistence rations of maize, plus the free use of small plots of estate lands in order to recruit even small numbers of estate dependents.[33] The early labor accounts of the several estates operated by the Convent of Santa Clara at Querétaro include numerous examples of the use of such incentives.[34] To attract even a few Mexican peasants away from the relative autonomy of life in the landed villages to the south, Bajío estate operators had to offer both increased material rewards and guaranteed security of subsistence.

The formative period of Bajío settlement, from about 1560 to 1635, was characterized by an expanding market for estate produce, largely the result of the growth of silver mining at Guanajuato, Zacatecas, and elsewhere. Responding to that incentive, a provincial gentry organized wars against nomadic Indians, settled towns, and developed estates—consolidating their control of the region's best croplands. To attract a small working population into the region, commercial cultivators had to offer favorable working and living conditions to Mexican migrants from the south. High wages, subsistence rations, and access to land brought the few early migrants willing to leave their communities into the Bajío—where they lived as agrarian dependents in an Hispanic world.

By 1640, however, the first boom of Bajío estate agriculture had passed. Tithe receipts, which generally reflect the level of commercial cultivation, had increased from 25,000 pesos in 1590, to 57,000 pesos in 1625, to 85,000 pesos in 1635. But by 1640 receipts had fallen back to 50,000 pesos, and they would remain near that reduced level into the 1660s.[35] The period of estate building and expanding commercial cultivation was over. The agricultural economy of the Bajío stabilized at a level well below the peak attained in

[33] Morin, *Michoacán*, p. 32.

[34] Lavrin, "Convento de Santa Clara," pp. 85-87.

[35] Morin, *Michoacán*, p. 30.

the 1630s. From the early 1640s, the Bajío gentry began to complain about declining profits as overproduction drove prices down. They discussed the decades of prosperity in the past tense.[36]

Yet the end of estate expansion and the decline of gentry profits did not curtail the migration of peasants from central and southern Mexico into the Bajío. The number of adult men who paid tributes as Indians in the Bajío tripled during the last two thirds of the seventeenth century—a time when the population grew little in the more densely settled regions of central Mexico.[37] Migration into the Bajío continued because the decline of commercial expansion did not alter the basic regional conditions that favored families of estate dependents.

In his detailed study of agrarian society at León, D. A. Brading called the years before 1740 the "golden age" of Bajío rancheros. Located in the western reaches of the Bajío, León had been sparsely settled during the period of the first mining boom. Because of this, many who migrated there after 1640 were able to obtain land and live as modest commercial farmers who owned plow teams, other livestock, and generally sustained themselves in modest comfort, though not wealth.[38]

Only a minority of migrants into the Bajío during the seventeenth century could become landowning rancheros. The majority came to live as tenants or employees of the gentry's estates. Yet those dependents also obtained favorable living and working conditions during the decades after 1640. The accounts of the six estates operated by the Convent of Santa Clara in the countryside around Querétaro in 1668 list 129 Indian workers, an average of 22 per estate. Of those employees, 99 were heads of households receiving maize rations. Thus, each of the six estates had about 17 de-

---

[36] Chevalier, *Formación*, p. 56; Basalenque, *Historia de la Provincia*, pp. 296, 314.

[37] Miranda, "Población indígena," pp. 188-189.

[38] Brading, *Haciendas and Ranchos*, pp. 149-162; quote from p. 171.

pendent Indian families. Individual earnings averaged over six pesos monthly, and several families included more than one wage earner. Subsistence rations were provided in addition to wages at no charge. Such earnings were substantially higher than those prevailing at the time in the densely settled regions around Mexico City.[39]

Perhaps more important, while most workers at estates near the capital were recruited seasonally from peasant communities, those at the Santa Clara estates in the Bajío were employed year round. The willingness of Bajío estate operators to provide employees with high earnings, guaranteed maize rations, and secure annual employment reflected the persisting scarcity of workers in the region. Labor shortages repeatedly forced estate managers to loan employees to neighboring properties in order to complete planting and harvesting on time. One manager reported that he was working to attract newcomers to his estate through "good treatment." And a most revealing entry in the Santa Clara accounts notes the payment of 500 pesos in one year to hire plow teams owned by neighboring small holders—whether tenants or ranchero landowners is not known.[40] Apparently, Bajío estates faced labor shortages while surrounded by small cultivators who owned plow teams. The availability of lands for more independent cultivation, whether through ownership or tenancies, helped to maintain the high wages and exceptional security offered to those who would become estate employees. Together, such conditions kept a slow but steady stream of migrants coming into the Bajío through the middle century of the colonial era.

The residents of Bajío estates often owed substantial debts to the properties they served. At the Santa Clara estates, 110 of the 129 employees owed an average of six

[39] Lavrin, "Convento de Santa Clara," Table vi, pp. 112-113; for rural wages in the Valley of Mexico, see Gibson, *Aztecs*, p. 251.

[40] Lavrin, "Convento de Santa Clara," p. 87.

months' wages. Traditionally, it has been argued that these debts forced employees to remain at the estates, suggesting that the material benefits indebted estate residents gained were offset by a loss of personal freedom, because they lost mobility. Such an interpretation is not sustained by the evidence from the Bajío. Workers owed debts because estates allowed them income in goods and money in excess of their allotted wages. Thus, debts indicate an even higher level of material income. And if such debts were intended by estate operators as means to force workers to remain at estates, they repeatedly failed. At the Santa Clara estates, 10 percent of the indebted workers left without paying their debts in the single year of 1668.[41] In his study of León in the more westerly reaches of the Bajío, Brading also concludes that workers' debts primarily revealed payments in excess of wages, payments needed to attract and retain workers in times of sparse population and labor shortages. They had little coercive effect.[42] Thus, the high level of debts among workers in the Bajío during the seventeenth century is but one more indicator of the favorable material conditions of the agrarian majority. Estate operators had to offer high wages, maize rations, full annual employment, and the substantial overpayments that created debts in order to recruit and maintain a dependent rural population in the Bajío during the century after 1640.

The evidence detailing the lives of agrarian families in the Bajío during the period from 1570 to 1740 remains sparse. But all that is available points to one conclusion: before the middle of the eighteenth century, the Bajío remained a region that offered favorable opportunities to a still sparse working population. A fortunate few could purchase lands and become independent rancheros. Many more cultivated lands they leased from estates. And those

[41] Ibid., Table vi, pp. 112-113.

[42] Brading, *Haciendas and Ranchos*, 76-77; for a parallel argument based on study of central highland Mexico, see Tutino, "Provincial Spaniards," pp. 187-192.

without even the minimal resources to be tenants obtained secure and well-compensated employment at estates always short of workers. Few among the agrarian poor could aspire to join the regional gentry. The rural majority found living conditions characterized by dependence, but compensated by good material conditions and substantial security—conditions that compared favorably with life to the south in the central highlands. As a result, enough Mexicans were willing to leave the relative autonomy of life in the peasant communities for the secure dependence of the Bajío to keep the population of that once empty basin growing throughout the seventeenth century.

Woodrow Borah called that period *New Spain's Century of Depression*. The evidence from the Bajío suggests that Borah's characterization applies best to the provincial gentry. The collapse of the mining boom after 1635 did bring reduced profits to Bajío estate operators. The accounts of the Santa Clara convent indicate that its several properties generated only basic sustenance for the religious community and few profits from the 1640s to 1700. Because of this the convent sold off its rural estates early in the eighteenth century when more profitable investments became available in mortgage banking and urban real estate.[43] But while the Bajío gentry suffered a modest economic decline, times were not so depressed for the rural majority. The sparse population, for Borah the root cause of the depression, allowed important benefits to those who lived in the minimally settled Bajío. The evidence of ranchero landholding, prosperous tenant cultivation, and secure and well-remunerated employment among estate dependents—along with the continuing current of immigration—all suggest that among those who came to Bajío with modest expectations, the seventeenth century brought modestly good times.

[43] Lavrin, "Convento de Santa Clara," pp. 104-105.

## Agrarian Transformation and Crisis, 1740–1810

The formative years of colonial society in the Bajío were characterized by a mining boom, the rapid growth of commercial estates, and a declining Mexican population that provided but a few migrants for the newly settled region. The century from 1640 to 1740 brought a less dynamic mining economy, little growth and few profits in commercial agriculture, and a small but slowly growing Mexican population that sent a steady stream of migrants into the Bajío. Both sets of conditions allowed the rural poor there to obtain material benefits and security while living as estate dependents. In contrast, the second half of the eighteenth century brought new developments that imposed deteriorating conditions on the lives of the agrarian majority. Mining boomed once again. Commercial estate cultivation expanded rapidly and became increasingly profitable. And the population of Mexico sustained high rates of growth—growth especially rapid in the Bajío. Elites gained strength while the structure of labor scarcity that had long favored the rural population rapidly disappeared.

Crisis resulted from the intersection of commercial expansion and population growth—developments that separately appear favorable, but in combination forced worsening poverty and painful insecurities onto the families living at Bajío estates. Economic growth was led by the export-oriented mining sector and favored the urban minority of Mexicans. Bajío estates began to concentrate increasingly on producing more of the wheat, fruits, and vegetables that brought high prices when sold to more affluent urban Mexicans. They were less and less concerned with raising maize—the staple of the working poor. The combination of the shift away from maize production and population growth forced a deepening crisis of subsistence onto the rural poor of the Bajío—a crisis that became deadly in 1785 and 1786, years of starvation in the Bajío.

The population of the bishopric of Michoacán, of which the Bajío was the largest part, nearly tripled from 1700 to 1760, and almost doubled again between 1760 and 1810. Several local parish censuses indicate that the population of the Bajío in 1810 was five times larger than in 1700.[44] Mining production grew at a similar pace. Before 1725, the average annual silver output in the bishopric—meaning the average production at Guanajuato—remained about one million pesos. By the late 1740s it had risen to about three million pesos yearly. A modest recession followed in the 1750s and early 1760s, but boom growth soon resumed. By the 1790s, annual silver production at Guanajuato averaged over five million pesos.[45]

Agriculture in the Bajío also expanded, but it lagged far behind the growth of the population. Tithe receipts that averaged around 100,000 pesos yearly before 1725 had risen to only 300,000 pesos by the early 1780s. Receipts then shot up to nearly 500,000 pesos annually by the early nineteenth century, but that jump reflected the sharp rise in prices caused by food scarcities, not an expansion of production.[46] Because economic activity was led by an export enclave while the rural population lost bargaining power, the growth of population and of mining did not bring a similar expansion of food production. Mass poverty resulted, along with new and deepening insecurities, together afflicting the agrarian majority during an era of economic growth.

The most visible social consequence was widening class polarization. As wealth was accumulated in mining and related commercial activities, the Bajío gentry became more powerful. Brading's study of León reveals that beginning around 1740 a group of families that had profited handsomely from mining at Guanajuato were buying rural es-

44 Morin, *Michoacán*, pp. 48, 59.
45 Ibid., pp. 94-95.
46 Ibid., pp. 103, 108.

tates. They continued the classic tradition of elite families taking wealth accumulated in very profitable but exceptionally risky mining ventures and investing for security with modest profits in landed estates. And as families with mining wealth sought lands around León in the 1740s, they generally bought out local rancheros whose holdings had been fragmented by expanding families and partible inheritances. The financial reinforcement of the landed elites at León thus came at the expense of the rancheros, many of whom had no choice but to become estate tenants or employees.[47]

The new wealth brought into the Bajío landed elite by the beneficiaries of the mining boom at Guanajuato extended beyond León. The Septién family profited enormously from both mining and commerce at Guanajuato and then invested in extensive estates in the eastern Bajío. The clan quickly claimed leadership in the landed oligarchy of Querétaro.[48] Don Juan Antonio de Santa Ana took the profits from his shares of the great Valenciana mine and purchased properties worth 450,000 pesos around the Bajío town of Salamanca. During the second half of the eighteenth century, he lived there as patriarch, still investing in mining and trade at Guanajuato, operating a silver refinery there, while overseeing his expanding commercial estate operations.[49] Such diverse and profitable economic activities became more common among Bajío elite families after 1750. A modest provincial gentry was being transformed into a wealthy regional elite that profited from silver mining and trade while still ruling the Bajío's increasingly lucrative commercial cultivation.[50]

[47] Brading, *Haciendas and Ranchos*, pp. 159, 171.
[48] Brading, *Miners and Merchants*, pp. 312-319; JSE, vol. 213, no. 171, 27 Sept. 1789; AGN, Padrones, vol. 39, fols. 1-2, 1791; *Gazeta de México*, 17 Feb. 1789; 30 Jan. 1808.
[49] PCR, uncatalogued materials, folder dated 1792; WBS, vol. 134, fol. 82, 1788; *Gazeta de México*, 17 Apr. 1795.
[50] Moreno Toscano, "Economía regional," pp. 124-125.

Financially strengthened elite families facing expanding markets for estate produce found workers readily available, thanks to rapid population growth. Estate owners and managers responded by rapidly transforming production patterns, which also imposed worsening conditions on estate dependents. At first glance, the change appears primarily economic and only the continuation and completion of developments long underway. During the sixteenth century, most Bajío estates primarily grazed livestock, only secondarily harvesting grains. The first mining boom from 1570 to 1635, however, brought increasing production of grains on the fertile bottom lands of the basin, with livestock displaced toward the nearby uplands. That structure remained generally stable through the years of economic stagnation of the later seventeenth century. Then, during the second quarter of the eighteenth century, Bajío estates once again began to rapidly increase grain production while livestock grazing moved out of the region.

The eighteenth-century transformation was more complex, however. The foods of the elite and the more comfortable urban population—wheat, fruits, and vegetables—increasingly took over the best irrigated lands in the Bajío basin. Maize, the staple of the rural poor, was relegated to less fertile, nonirrigated fields. And livestock all but left the Bajío, leaving former pastures, marginal croplands at best, for the expansion of maize cultivation. The production of maize on such unproductive soils was left to poor tenant families. They took the risks of that marginal cultivation.[51]

The transformation came first to the easterly sections of the basin, where by 1785 estates planted three times as much wheat as maize. The indigenous staple then remained the primary crop in the western basin and the adjacent uplands. In the Salamanca area of the eastern Bajío, maize plantings still exceeded wheat in 1785. But at the eleven es-

[51] Brading, *Haciendas and Ranchos*, pp. 21-22, 27, 33, 79-80; Morin, *Michoacán*, p. 255; Tutino, "Life and Labor," p. 344.

tates of the seven largest growers there, wheat plantings substantially exceeded maize, and the majority of the maize was in the care of tenants—probably on the least fertile estate lands. It was the fifteen small growers at Salamanca who kept maize the primary crop there—and they too had turned much of that crop over to tenants. Even where maize apparently still predominated, it is clear that by 1785 the staple of the poor was being left to poorer soils and poorer cultivators.[52]

This transformation of estate production came later to the northeast uplands of the Bajío—the home of the Hidalgo revolt. At San Miguel, tithe receipts show that wool and other livestock products dominated estate production until 1720, with maize and other crops only 20 percent of the total. By 1740, crops had risen to 30 percent. After 1750, grains never fell below 60 percent of tithe income from San Miguel, and by late in the century they approached 80 percent.[53] In half a century, San Miguel changed from a region of grazing estates producing minimal crops to a region of cropland. The large herds of livestock had moved elsewhere.

Dolores lies just north of San Miguel, farther from the fertile soils of the Bajío basin. A region of dry, marginal lands, Dolores was first a recipient of the livestock moving out of the core areas of the Bajío. Before 1750, tithe receipts from Dolores indicate a rapid expansion of herds there, but after 1760, even the most marginal of lands around Dolores were rapidly turned over to maize production. In the 1780s, crops accounted for over 50 percent of tithe income there. By the end of the eighteenth century, then, the structural transformation of Bajío estate production was nearly complete. The most fertile, irrigated bottom lands specialized in wheat, fruits, and vegetables for the wealthier, more Hispanic minority of the population. Maize—basic to the sur-

[52] See Appendix A, Tables A.3 and A.4.
[53] Galicia, *Precios y producción*, Gráfica no. 7, p. 51.

vival of the rural and poor majority—was left to more marginal lands, often uplands long used only for grazing. And livestock had moved out of the Bajío to more arid pastures farther north.[54]

That transformation was engineered by powerful elites responding to opportunities brought by the Guanajuato silver bonanza. The change was allowed by the rapid expansion of the dependent agrarian population of the Bajío. Increased crop production required much more labor that did the grazing activities that left the region. Without the rapid growth of the agrarian population, the shift to more intensive cultivation would have been impossible.

The labor demands of grain cultivation were not only large, but seasonal. In central and southern Mexico, estates met those fluctuating labor needs by recruiting workers seasonally from nearby peasant communities. Peasants earned supplemental cash income while estates paid their field workers only during the few months they were needed. The paucity of such communities in the Bajío precluded such a solution there. During the seventeenth century, while workers remained scarce, Bajío estate operators had to employ year round many workers that they needed only part of each year. But the population growth of the eighteenth century allowed Bajío elites a more profitable solution to their labor needs—just as markets expanded.

Growing numbers of poor families could be offered small tenancies on estate lands formerly used for grazing. The tenants would raise maize for their own consumption, and perhaps a small surplus for sale in good years. Many undertook the hard work of opening former pastures for cultivation. And as long as the plots let to the tenants were small and subject to the vagaries of annual rainfall, family members would have to work seasonally for wages in the irrigated fields reserved for more profitable estate crops. Thus, the agrarian transformation of the Bajío in the eighteenth

[54] Ibid.; Hurtado López, *Dolores Hidalgo*, pp. 9, 23-25, 79, 81, 83.

century brought about the simultaneous expansion of direct estate production and tenant cultivation. The two were linked. Marginal tenant production maintained a poor and dependent population that was employed seasonally in estate fields. Elite estate owners, along with a few major tenants, thus claimed the profits of producing the foods of the wealthy. Simultaneously, ever more numerous tenants, subtenants, and sharecroppers struggled to raise maize on marginal lands, while laboring periodically in estate fields— to gain no more than a minimal subsistence for their expanding families.[55]

The agrarian transformation of the Bajío struck the rural majority hard. Most families remained dependents, living on estates owned by elites. The agrarian population remained of heterogenous origins, including families designated as Indians, mestizos, mulattoes, and even a few poor Spaniards. Those classed as Indians remained the largest group among the rural poor, but most Bajío Indians lived on estates and spoke Spanish in an increasingly Hispanic world.[56] And rural families of diverse origins continued their long tradition of living, working, and marrying together, generally moving toward becoming a homogeneous mestizo agrarian population, more Hispanic than indigenous in culture.[57]

The persistence of estate dependence, miscegenation, and Hispanization indicates important continuities in the cultural lives of the Bajío poor. But the structural transformation of estate production during the late eighteenth century imposed new difficulties on the agrarian majority. Although they continued to live as estate dependents, rural families in the Bajío began to face deepening poverty and new insecurities. With the end of labor scarcities, they had

[55] Brading, *Haciendas and Ranchos*, p. 155; Tutino, "Life and Labor," pp. 351-353; Morin, *Michoacán*, pp. 253, 255, 272, 290.
[56] See Appendix C, Tables c.1 and c.2.
[57] Tutino, "Life and Labor," pp. 339-350.

little choice but to adapt to the declining conditions that estates offered.

As late as the middle of the eighteenth century, Bajío employers were offering incentives to attract migrants to the region. The wealthy Sauto family operated a major textile workshop at San Miguel. In 1768, it provided houses, irrigated garden plots, dry lands for raising chickens and nopal cactus, as well as access to pastures for the 108 families that worked for them. Many had recently arrived from central Mexico, still clinging to indigenous ways, enticed into the Bajío by promises of homes, gardens, and pasturage—and enough land for each family to raise as many as 100 maguey cactus and to keep small numbers of swine.[58] Around 1750, then, Bajío elites still held out material incentives to migrants who would come and serve them.

After the 1760s, however, migration into the Bajío slowed dramatically. The 1792 militia census indicates that the vast majority of Spaniards, mestizos, and mulattoes had been born there—among the rural populace, most often at the estates where they lived as adults. Yet migration had not ceased in Mexico. Instead, those who left the densely populated regions of the central highlands increasingly began to move to the coastal lowlands or past the Bajío into the arid northern plateau country. Neither the tropical coasts nor the dry north were as attractive to settlement as the Bajío if climate and soil quality were the primary issues. It was the drastic deterioration of agrarian social conditions in the Bajío that sent migrants elsewhere in the later eighteenth century.[59]

The population of the region did continue to expand, but that growth was more due to local reproduction than to

[58] AGN, Tierras, vol. 932, exp. 1, fols. 229-233, 2 Mar. 1768. Sam Kagan kindly brought this survey to my attention.

[59] Galicia, *Precios y producción*, p. 17; Moreno Toscano, "Economía regional," p. 122; Brading, *Miners and Merchants*, pp. 228-229; Morin, *Michoacán*, pp. 66-70, 282.

continuing immigration.[60] The rate of population growth slowed after 1760. Apparently, rural families struggling to scrape together the bare necessities of life from insecure tenancies and seasonal labor began to have more children who might help in the endless work of survival. Such expanded families could help cushion the difficulties facing individual families; but the resulting population growth continued to assist elites who saw profit in undermining the standards of living and the security of the Bajío majority.

Another sign of the deteriorating rural conditions in the region after 1750 was the collapse of slavery. African slaves had long formed part of the working population of colonial Mexico. In Mexico, in contrast to many other colonies, slaves were never a mass labor force. Instead, they were a small but strategic minority of workers used for more permanent, specialized, and often supervisory, work. With a large, conquered population of Indian peasants, Spaniards in Mexico paid for expensive African slaves only when permanent workers were scarce and thus expensive to employ.[61] In the Bajío, important slave minorities had labored in towns and at rural estates since the sixteenth century. But after 1750, Bajío elites abandoned their slave work forces.

In 1768, the Sautos of San Miguel still owned fifteen slaves. Most, however, were men married to free women—who would thus leave only free children. Such marriages were a common means of liberating offspring among Mexican slaves who were always a small minority in a large population of free Indians and mestizos. Another thirteen slaves owned by the Sautos had died recently, while seven had fled successfully. A leading family of San Miguel had clearly decided that slavery was no longer important to their enterprises. Deceased slaves were not replaced, runaways

---

[60] Brading, *Haciendas and Ranchos*, p. 52, reports an average of 6.6 baptized children per marriage at León between 1750 and 1810.

[61] This role of slave labor is emphasized in Morin, *Michoacán*, pp. 257-258.

were not retrieved, and those remaining were leaving a new generation of free mulattoes.[62]

Others also abandoned slavery late in the eighteenth century. In the 1770s, the Puerto de Nieto estate, just east of San Miguel, included only the remnants of a once larger slave population. There, too, the combination of slave deaths without replacements, successful flights, and marriages to free women had left a much reduced slave community. For the manager, the remaining slaves—including only a few adult men, but many elderly, women, and children—were a costly burden. Free employees were seen as more available—and less expensive.

The few young slave men who might still provide years of work were sent north to San Luis Potosí, where continuing labor shortages made them valuable at other estates owned by the same family. Most of the slaves at Puerto de Nieto, however, were sold off rapidly, for whatever anyone would pay. Most brought only 30 to 50 pesos, a tenth of what a slave had cost in Mexico a century earlier. Some were bought by urban families who wanted household servants. But the most common buyers were the slaves themselves. For sums equivalent to little more than a year's wages, many purchased their own freedom.[63] For Bajío elites, the end of labor scarcities made slavery irrelevant—or too expensive.

The declining earnings of estate employees that eased the end of slavery are evident in surviving labor accounts. The hacienda named La Barranca lay about 20 kilometers south of Querétaro. Typical of Bajío estates, it raised wheat on its best irrigated lands, maize on fields relying on irregular rains, and livestock only in wooded uplands. Accounts from 1768, 1770, and 1776 detail the earnings of over 50 permanent employees—the favored group of estate dependents. Earnings had declined since the seventeenth century.

---

[62] AGN, Tierras, vol. 932, exp. 1, fols. 229-233, 2 Mar. 1768.

[63] FEN, no. 33, 8 Nov. 1774; no. 44, 9 Jan. 1779; JSE, vol. 213, no. 37, 26 Feb. 1782; no. 51, 28 Sept. 1782; no. 50, 9 Oct. 1782; no. 59, 26 Mar. 1783.

Most employees at La Barranca obtained only 4 pesos monthly, compared to the 6 pesos common a century earlier at the Santa Clara estates in the same region. And in the late eighteenth century, employees at Barranca had to work a full 30 days to earn a month's pay. The majority who labored an average of 270 days each year were paid for only 9 months and earned only 36 pesos. Such annual earnings were much less than those that had prevailed in the region a century earlier. Only a small group of more skilled and supervisory employees at La Barranca received 4 pesos each calendar month, thus 48 pesos for the year—still less than the average earnings at the Santa Clara estates in 1668.

Yet the regular employees of La Barranca retained important security. They still received weekly rations of maize in addition to their wages. And they continued to receive payments beyond their allotted wages, leaving many indebted to the estate. Debts averaged half a worker's annual income. Overpayments had apparently shrunk at the same rate as the workers' wage levels. Unfortunately, the distribution of debts among the employees at La Barranca is not known. Thus, we do not know if larger overpayments were used to attract field workers, or more to reward favored supervisors and skilled craftsmen.[64] It is clear that both the wage earnings and the debts (overpayments) of the employees of this eastern Bajío estate in the 1760s and 1770s were substantially less than those of the workers at the Santa Clara estates in the 1660s. The eighteenth-century employees remained relatively secure, enjoying regular work and receiving maize rations. But their earnings were falling.

Parallel developments are evident in the accounts of the Ybarra estate, located to the northwest between León and San Felipe. In 1783, the majority of Ybarra's 79 employees earned 4 pesos monthly and were accounted as working 9 to 10 months of the year, producing annual earnings of 36 to 40 pesos, plus the still-customary maize rations. Such

[64] Morin, *Michoacán*, pp. 215-221.

earnings were comparable to those prevailing at La Barranca a decade earlier. But the employees at Ybarra in the 1780s received much smaller overpayments. Only 68 percent of the workers owed debts, and most owed less than 12 pesos—only a third of a year's income. Meanwhile, nearly a third of Ybarra's employees were owed back earnings by the estate—the management had not paid them in full for work already done. A minority of the Ybarra employees did owe large amounts to the estate, often in excess of 20 pesos. But it was primarily supervisors and skilled personnel who had received large overpayments as rewards for valued services.[65]

The permanent employees of La Barranca and Ybarra did not face extreme poverty during the second half of the eighteenth century. Although their earnings were much less than those prevailing in the Bajío a century earlier, they remained a favored group in eighteenth-century Mexico. In the densely settled countryside around Mexico City, the few permanent estate employees often received only 3 pesos monthly, plus maize rations—with no overpayments.[66] The regular employees of Bajío estates in the later eighteenth century thus obtained relatively high, if declining wages, guaranteed maize rations, and overpayments (also declining) beyond their wages. They faced deteriorating material conditions, but retained the security that compensated for lives of dependence.

As the agrarian transformation of the Bajío accelerated, however, permanent employees became an ever smaller part of the rural population. Tenant families facing mounting difficulties were becoming more numerous. By the late 1760s, La Barranca had settled 53 tenants in its highlands, away from the estate's main operations. They cleared former pastures and woodlands for cultivation, paying rents while enhancing the value of the property. The neighbor-

[65] Tutino, "Life and Labor," pp. 357-363.
[66] Tutino, "Creole Mexico," Chapter 6.

ing San Lucas hacienda settled 60 tenants in similar conditions at the same time. And by 1783, Ybarra had 42 tenants tilling estate lands.[67] The majority paid small rents, for they planted but small plots of marginal lands. When the climate cooperated and summer rains were good, they produced enough maize for their families and a small surplus for sale. But in the recurrent years of irregular rains, to say nothing of years of drought, tenant families struggled at the margin of subsistence. The insecurities of such tenancies are plain. They became especially painful when crops failed and rents had to be paid.

These insecure tenants formed a pool of workers available for low-paying day labor at the estates. Even less secure were growing numbers of *arrimados*—the poorest of estate residents. These squatters, who lived on estate lands so poor that they were not charged rents, were expected to labor seasonally in estate fields for wages even lower than those paid to tenants. Squatters were the poorest and most insecure residents of Bajío estates in the late eighteenth century.[68]

The growing number of families living as poor tenants and squatters had profound social consequences. The estates' access to a growing population of poorly paid, seasonal laborers no doubt explains the declining earnings allowed the remaining permanant employees. The problems faced by tenant and squatter families were more severe. They struggled to sustain themselves by combining insecure cultivation and seasonal wage labor. And as estates turned their best, irrigated fields over to wheat and vegetable cultivation, maize was left to be raised by poor tenants on the most marginal lands. The Bajío's maize harvests became increasingly irregular, resulting in recurrent years of

---

[67] Morin, *Michoacán*, pp. 215-221; Tutino, "Life and Labor," pp. 365-368.

[68] Morin, *Michoacán*, pp. 215-221.

scarcity, famine, and death among the poorest inhabitants of the region.

Before 1760, the price of maize in the Bajío had varied annually and seasonally, depending on the size of the harvest. But there was no long-term trend toward an increase in the cost of the basic staple. Production increased enough to keep pace with the growing population, and whenever harvests were plentiful, the price of maize returned to the low level of 2 to 4 reales (1 peso equaled 8 reales) per fanega (1 fanega is about 1.5 bushels). But after 1770, as the shift toward production of maize by tenants on marginal lands accelerated, maize prices began a steady climb. Even following the best harvests, a fanega of maize cost no less than 4 to 6 reales. And by the late 1780s, 10 reales per fanega was the lowest price of maize in the Bajío.[69]

The developing crisis of maize production, a crisis of subsistence for the poor in the Bajío, became deadly apparent during the famine years of 1785 and 1786. Two years of drought, combined with severe frosts in the summer of 1785, produced two years of starvation that killed tens of thousands of Bajío residents—Table 2.1 calculates over 85,000 casualties in 1786 alone.[70] These years of catastrophic famine are generally portrayed as the worst natural disaster of eighteenth-century Mexico—after all, drought and frost triggered the famine. But in actuality the structural agrarian crisis caused by the transformation of Bajío estate agriculture lay at the root of the catastrophe. The origins of the famine that killed nearly 15 percent of the Bajío's population in one year were not entirely "natural." Periodic drought is part of the Mexican environment. Throughout much of the colonial era, one role of Bajío estate production was to raise surpluses of maize when times were good, and then store the grain until years of scarcity.

[69] Galicia, *Precios y producción*, pp. 72, 77; Brading, *Haciendas and Ranchos*, pp. 180-183; Morin, *Michoacán*, pp. 116, 190-191, 193.

[70] See, for comparison, the calculations in Brading, *Miners and Merchants*, p. 232, and Morin, *Michoacán*, pp. 56-57.

TABLE 2.1
Death Rates in the Intendancy of Guanajuato, 1786

| Zones and Jurisdictions | Population c. 1792 | Deaths[a] 1786 | Deaths per 1,000 Pop.[b] |
|---|---|---|---|
| AGRARIAN ZONES | | | |
| Eastern Bajío | | | |
| Celaya | 67,801 | 5,238 | 72 |
| Salvatierra | 24,995 | 2,460 | 90 |
| Acámbaro | 10,074 | 3,775 | 275 |
| Total | 102,870 | 11,517 | 101 |
| Northeast Uplands | | | |
| San Miguel | 22,587 | 4,356 | 162 |
| Dolores | 15,661 | 3,062 | 163 |
| San Felipe | 17,721 | 1,397 | 73 |
| Total | 55,969 | 8,815 | 136 |
| Western Bajío and Uplands | | | |
| Silao | 28,631 | 6,292 | 180 |
| Irapuato | 30,701 | 4,755 | 134 |
| León | 23,736 | 4,910 | 171 |
| Piedragorda | 10,952 | 955 | 85 |
| Pénjamo | 20,952 | 1,480 | 66 |
| Total | 114,309 | 18,398 | 139 |
| Known Agrarian Zones | 273,148 | 38,730 | 124 |
| Other Agrarian Zones (estimated) | 183,056 | 25,994[c] | 124 |
| Total Agrarian Zones | 456,204 | 64,724 | 124 |
| MINING ZONE | | | |
| Guanajuato | 55,412 | 20,771 | 273 |
| INTENDANCY TOTAL | 516,616 | 85,495 | 143 |

SOURCES: Population figures from Cook and Borah, *Essays*, II, Table 2.4 pp. 217-219; and from FHEM, III, 34-35; death figures from FCA, Doc. 311, pp. 892-895; and from Morin, *Michoacán*, Table II.3, p. 56.

[a] Total funerals reported by clergy; surely underreports deaths.

[b] Calculated by adding 1792 population to 1786 deaths to approximate 1786 population, and then dividing that figure into the deaths reported.

[c] Estimated by applying death rate of 124 per thousand to known population.

Bajío elites profited from sales during times of dearth—and supplies of that essential staple were available to the poor, if at extortionate prices. But during the late eighteenth century, estate operators saw greater, or at least more regular, profits in selling wheat, fruits, and vegetables to a growing and increasingly affluent urban minority. Their estates served less and less as a reserve granary for the Bajío, the mining regions, and the central highlands to the south. As maize was relegated to marginal lands cultivated by poor tenants, production failed to keep pace with population growth. The margin between subsistence and scarcity narrowed in the best of years. By the 1780s, the Bajío lacked the stores of maize that might sustain the poor through times of dearth. Many would pay with their lives.

Although the combination of drought and frost that set off the famine of 1785 and 1786 reached as far south as the highlands around Mexico City, starvation and mass mortality were concentrated in the Bajío.[71] In that afflicted region, death was most common in the urbanized mining center of Guanajuato. But mortality was also extremely high in the rural areas of the Bajío basin and the northeast uplands. The variation of death rates across the Bajío resulted in part from the movement of desperate people in search of food. The priest at Silao reported that 3,563 unidentified people from outside his parish had died in the fields and along the roads near the town.[72] And the exceptionally high death rates at Guanajuato was surely inflated by the death there of people who had straggled into the rich city hoping to take advantage of relief services. Obviously, many failed.

The organization of relief during these years of catastrophe reveals much about Bajío society at the end of the colonial era. Beginning in the fall of 1785, as soon as the frosts of late summer had destroyed the maize in the fields, the city councils of Querétaro, Guanajuato, Celaya, and smaller

[71] FCA, Table 311, pp. 892-895.
[72] FCA, Table 311, p. 892.

towns like León, began to work to assure that maize would be supplied to town residents. In most cases, city elites (who were generally rural estate owners) provided money as loans at no interest so town authorities could buy maize to sell later to urban consumers.[73] The viceregal authorities, led by the Regent of the High Court of Mexico City, Vicente de Herrera y Rivero, took special interest in finding maize for Guanajuato, the colony's leading silver producer, and secondarily for Querétaro, a major commercial hub. Herrera sought maize in the lower and warmer Huasteca region of eastern San Luis Potosí, to the northeast of the Bajío beyond the Sierra Gorda, to supply the cities he considered essential to colonial prosperity.[74]

There is no evidence of organized relief for the rural poor of the Bajío. They were left to suffer without assistance. As estate residents, the agrarian families of the Bajío had neither leaders nor institutions to organize relief. They had no village councils to voice their desperate concerns, nor in most instances even a rural priest to speak for them. They lived as dependents of an elite that ran estates for profit. In the view prevailing among estate operators, permanent estate employees were awarded maize rations—an important protection against the famine. But the expanding population of tenants and squatters who lived on their estates and provided essential seasonal labor received no such support. They were poor, numerous, and apparently considered expendable. A report from the priest at Chamacuero, one of the few small villages in the Bajío, reveals the fears of the rural poor at the beginning of the famine. The maize then held in the town and at nearby estates would provide for only a third of local needs until the harvest of 1786. Yet even those small supplies were being bought by relief organizations in the city of Celaya. The residents of one estate began to threaten to claim by force the

[73] FCA, pp. 177-209, 221-222, 270-277, 328-341.
[74] FCA, pp. 145-151.

maize they had produced but could not consume. They threatened violence to prevent starvation.[75] Relief efforts clearly followed the structure of the agrarian economy in the Bajío in 1786. The upper classes and other urban dwellers received preference, while the rural poor suffered.

The Bishop of Michoacán, Fray Antonio de San Miguel, apparently understood that the famine was the result of the changing structure of estate production in the Bajío. He saw that expanded maize cultivation on the most fertile, irrigated fields could help solve the crisis of 1785 and prevent a recurrence. Therefore, he offered 40,000 pesos in loans to Bajío estate cultivators, if they would plant maize on their irrigated lands during the winter of 1785 and 1786. The crops would be harvested by early summer in 1786, six months sooner than the next nonirrigated maize. Specifically, the bishop offered, at no interest, loans of 72 pesos for each fanega of maize planted on irrigated lands. He stated that since such planting generally cost only 40 pesos per fanega, the recipients would have 32 pesos to invest in other endeavors.[76]

The results of the bishop's efforts were limited. In the Salvatierra jurisdiction, plantings of maize nearly doubled from 340 fanegas in 1785 to 628 fanegas in 1786, accompanied by an equal reduction in wheat—indicating a real shift of irrigated lands to maize. But Salvatierra was an exception. It had the greatest concentration of religious landlords in the Bajío, estate operators who clearly responded to their bishop and led the local shift to producing irrigated maize.[77] In contrast, at Acámbaro, Valle de Santiago, and Salamanca there were but limited increases in maize production, ranging from only 5 to 13 percent. And in León and adjacent uplands to the west, maize planting declined slightly in 1786 while wheat production expanded.[78] In

[75] FCA, pp. 387-388.
[76] FCA, pp. 262-268.
[77] FCA, Doc. no. 256.
[78] FCA, Doc. nos. 257, 258, 259, 260.

general, Bajío estates did not shift production substantially in response to the famine. They continued to emphasize wheat and other foods for wealthier townspeople—thereby prolonging the scarcity.

The aftermath of the famine years of 1785 and 1786 confirmed that the subsistence crisis in the Bajío was not merely an unfortunate natural calamity, but the result of the new regional agrarian structure. The thousands of deaths caused by the famine reduced the demand for maize and might have lowered prices once good harvests returned. But maize prices never fell to prefamine levels—suggesting that truly good harvests of maize never returned to the region. Years of scarcity became recurrent in the Bajío. Barely recovering from the crisis of 1786, the areas around Celaya, San Miguel, and Dolores experienced another period of dearth in 1789 and 1790. Maize prices quickly shot up from a low of 10 reales to 40 reales per fanega. The staple remained scarce and expensive for over a year. At Dolores, over 1,600 residents survived only because of local relief efforts.[79] Similar scarcities recurred through the 1790s and the early 1800s, culminating in the second great famine of the Bajío—the scarcity of 1809 and 1810 that helped touch off the Hidalgo revolt.

The catastrophe of 1785 and 1786 did nothing to slow the tragic transformation of Bajío agriculture. The 1790s and early 1800s brought a new dimension to the mounting insecurities of the rural poor. Increasing numbers of tenants were evicted from Bajío estates. As crop prices rose rapidly, estate owners looked to raise the rents of those tenants still holding more fertile lands, thereby insuring that elites rather than tenants would reap the profits of rising prices. Tenant families of modest means often could not pay and were evicted—generally with little notice and with-

[79] Brading, *Haciendas and Ranchos*, p. 194; Galicia, *Precios y producción*, p. 72; Hurtado López, *Dolores Hidalgo*, p. 94; *Gazeta de México*, 28 July 1789; 27 Apr. 1790; 22 June 1790.

out compensation for improvements they had made during their years as renters. Evicted families were obviously hurt. They were suddenly forced to seek new means of life, and generally that meant taking on the rental of the most marginal lands on the fringes of the Bajío.

The spate of evictions in the late eighteenth century had painful repercussions on those remaining at Bajío estates. Hacienda residents never had the right of independent community organization enjoyed by villagers in central and southern Mexico. Yet while living, working, and marrying together for generations, Bajío estate residents cemented informal—but no less important—community relationships. They maintained extended families, organized local religious celebrations, resolved periodic conflicts, and generally sustained a community environment. As evictions tore long-established families out of estate communities, their solidarity was weakened, though not fully undermined. Families that remained never knew who would be the next to go. Insecurity of subsistence was thus compounded by insecurities in community social relations among families living at Bajío estates.[80]

The evictions of the years before 1810 also made plain to the poor who was benefiting from their misery. When tenant families were evicted, they were repeatedly replaced not by other modest cultivators, but by wealthier tenants with outside sources of income who could afford to pay higher rents and finance the cultivation of commercial crops of wheat, fruits, and vegetables. The lands of families evicted from Bajío estates were often combined into larger units and taken over by tax collectors, town officials, gentry families seeking more lands, important textile producers, and merchants holding municipal meat monopolies.[81] Thus,

---

[80] Tutino, "Life and Labor," pp. 269-270; Brading, *Haciendas and Ranchos*, pp. 197-198; Morin, *Michoacán*, pp. 269-270, 278, 283.

[81] JSE, vol. 213, no. 88, 9 Dec. 1784; no. 91, 27 Dec. 1784; no. 340, 14 May 1789; no. 450, 9 July 1802; no. 452, 9 Aug. 1802; no. 459, 22 Aug. 1802; vol. 214, no. 102, 22 Apr. 1806.

while the agrarian majority suffered declining incomes, deepening insecurities, periodic famine, and painful evictions, they could plainly see the Bajío elites and other prosperous townspeople were reaping rewards from their suffering.

During the eighteenth century, Bajío elites retained control of the region's croplands, while fortified by infusions of wealth from the Guanajuato mining boom. That expansion of mining also favored the urban people of the Bajío and other regions, creating a rapidly expanding demand for the foods favored by Mexico's Hispanized upper classes. Bajío estate operators responded by alloting their best lands to raising wheat, fruits, and vegetables, shifting maize onto less fertile fields. The staple of the Mexican poor was no longer commercially attractive, and production did not keep pace with population growth.

Meanwhile, the continuing growth of the Bajío population allowed elites to undermine the once favorable living conditions of the rural poor. Permanent estate employees remained favored residents, retaining the security of year-round work plus maize rations. But they were forced to accept declining wages and declining debts—as overpayments became less necessary to attract and hold a work force. At the same time, rapidly increasing numbers of tenant families had to live by planting maize on dry, hilly lands on the fringes of Bajío estates, becoming a reservoir of seasonal workers paid minimally to plant and harvest commercial crops.

Estate residents thus faced a shift from lives of comfortable and secure dependence to situations of worsening poverty and insecurities, still linked to dependence. And the uncertainties of subsistence plaguing the rural poor of the Bajío became deadly during the recurrent famines that began in 1785 and 1786 and culminated in 1809 and 1810. The late colonial agrarian structure of the region produced substantial profits for financially strengthened elites. For the rural majority, that new environment brought only deepening poverty, new insecurity, and periodic famine.

### CRISIS AT DOLORES: CHARCO DE ARAUJO, 1796–1800

The Hidalgo revolt began in 1810 at the town of Dolores, located in the uplands on the northeastern fringe of the Bajío. Land was poor there, and irrigation was rarely possible. Because the region had long emphasized grazing, along with a precarious maize agriculture, Dolores was one of the last areas of the Bajío to undergo the transformation from grazing to cultivation—and from social relations of dependent and secure employment to dependent but insecure tenancies. Given the poor agricultural resources around Dolores, the transition after 1785 brought severe consequences.

The famine of 1785 and 1786 accelerated the shift from grazing to cultivation at Dolores. From 1740 through 1786, only 150 to 250 cultivators paid tithes on crops there each year. In 1787, 1,008 residents paid. The years of starvation pushed many families to rent lands from Dolores estates to plant subsistence maize. As better harvests returned, the number of maize growers fell. In 1789 there were 460—still more than double the number before the famine. And when another drought brought widespread hunger again in 1789 and 1790, the number of tenant cultivators at Dolores again rose dramatically. In 1792, 723 producers paid tithes on crops (mostly on maize).[82]

As in most of the Bajío, the countryside around Dolores was dominated by estates with resident communities. The rural areas of Dolores and nearby San Miguel included three haciendas with over 200 resident families. But most estate communities there at the end of the eighteenth cen-

---

[82] *Gazeta de México*, 27 Apr. 1790; Hurtado López, *Dolores Hidalgo*, Cuadro no. 4, p. 18.

tury had fewer than 70 families.[83] As these small communities of estate dependents faced worsening insecurities,
they increasingly resented their dependence. During the
decade after 1800, at least three groups of estate residents
from the northeast uplands of the Bajío went to court claiming legal rights as Indian communities. They sought independent control of the lands they cultivated and political
autonomy in local affairs. The claimants called themselves
Indians, although their use of Spanish surnames and easy
testimony in Spanish revealed much Hispanization—typical
of Bajío Indians. The courts were not impressed, and there
is no sign that any group of estate dependents successfully
won community status, thus independence from the Bajío
elite, before 1810.[84] However, the suits are direct evidence
of the growing resentment of dependence among Bajío estate residents.

The problems that plagued estate dependents around
Dolores before 1810 are detailed in the surviving accounts
of labor relations at the hacienda named Charco de Araujo.
The estate was owned by the Aldama family of San Miguel,
marginal members of the provincial gentry who later joined
Hidalgo in leading the insurrection. The lives of the residents of Charco de Araujo illustrate the problems of poverty, dependence, and insecurity that led many of the rural
poor around Dolores to join the uprising of 1810.

The survival of the Charco de Araujo accounts covering
the four years from 1796 to 1800 is fortunate. During those
years the estate underwent the classic transformation of the
eighteenth-century Bajío. A property in the marginal uplands, the estate had long specialized in sheep grazing. But
in 1796, as the demand for croplands and for maize increased among the rural poor, Charco de Araujo began to
turn lands over to maize and to settle a growing population
of tenants. During the four years covered by the accounts,

[83] Ibid., pp. 45-46; Galicia, *Precios y producción*, pp. 20-21.
[84] Tutino, "Life and Labor," pp. 377-378.

estate wool production was cut in half while maize planting increased proportionately. And the number of both employees and sharecroppers also increased, providing the larger work force needed for crop production. (The Charco de Araujo accounts are analyzed in detail in Appendix B. The following discussion is based on that analysis.)

Between 1796 and 1800, 74 men belonging to 40 extended families served as employees or sharecroppers, or both, at Charco de Araujo. Just over half of the families provided only employees, while the rest sharecropped, usually in conjunction with employment. And most families at the estate included more than one employee, or both employees and sharecroppers. Multiple activities were the only way that dependent families could increase earnings in hard times. Individual employees generally worked for the estate less than two years and then moved on. Their extended families, however, maintained ties with the property for longer periods—with different members undertaking employment or sharecropping at different times. Most employees at Charco de Araujo did not work year round. Only 40 percent were paid for working more than 90 percent of the time they were at the estate—approximating full employment. Another 40 percent were employed only 70 to 90 percent of the time. And 20 percent worked even less. The scarcity of truly year-round work at the estate surely contributed to the turnover of individual employees. The security long associated with estate employment in the Bajío was waning.

What did these employees earn for their efforts? Wages varied with age and experience, following the customary pattern of colonial Mexico. Boys began to labor seasonally around their eighth year, earning only one real daily for planting or harvesting estate crops. During adolescence, young men might obtain more permanent employment. When first hired, youths generally received only one peso each month, plus a small weekly ration of maize—a daily rate that was less than what they had received when

younger and working only seasonally. By offering a regular
income and secure maize rations, the estate could lower the
wage rate.

With increasing age and experience, the monthly wages
and weekly rations of estate employees increased. Established adult employees at Charco de Araujo generally
earned 3 pesos monthly, plus 2 almudes of maize each
week. Given an average of 10 months' work, most earned
about 30 pesos along with 8 fanegas of maize each year.
That would sustain a small family only minimally. Thus, the
sons of employees began to work as seasonal day laborers as
soon as possible. For the families living primarily from employment at Charco de Araujo, the necessities of subsistence forced multiple family members to serve the estate.

Those employees did not receive most of their earnings
in money. As was typical of Mexican estates located far from
town markets, workers obtained food, cloth, shoes, and a
variety of other goods from the estate during the course of
each year. The manager kept a record of their receipts,
along with an account of wages and days worked. Once each
year, more or less regularly, the accounts of earnings were
balanced against the value of goods and money received.
Some workers did not take goods valued as much as the
wages due them. Others had obtained more than their wage
incomes. They owed debts to the estate.

Such overpayments went to only a minority of the employees at Charco de Araujo at the end of the eighteenth
century. Nearly 45 percent of the estate's employees generally balanced accounts during the four years from 1796 to
1800. Only 35 percent obtained overpayments that ranged
from 20 to 60 percent of their wage allotments. A small minority built even larger debts, but most were workers who
received a few goods, worked only briefly, left the estate—
and repaid their debt.

In general, employees who worked at the estate for less
than two years received little more than the low wages allotted them. Those remaining two years or longer, however,

were rewarded with overpayments providing from 20 to 60 percent more in goods than their wages would buy. Clearly, overpayments were not being used to attract and hold workers—workers were no longer scarce in the Bajío around 1800. Instead, payments in excess of wages were given to employees who remained at the estate and proved to be valued workers. The resulting debts did not restrict mobility. Workers with small debts usually paid them when they left estate employment, or shortly afterward. Among those who had served longer and obtained larger overpayments, debts tended to accumulate without repayment, and many indebted workers eventually left the estate without clearing their accounts. In a few instances, their debts were charged to kinsmen who remained at the property, a bookkeeping shift that primarily served to keep the unpaid debts from appearing as losses in the manager's account. But over the long term, the remaining employees neither worked off nor paid their debts. When they left or died, the estate absorbed the overpayments as part of labor expenditures.

In sum, overpayments served primarily to reward the minority of employees at Charco de Araujo who became more permanent dependents. Most employees worked for shorter periods and received only their wages—wages low compared with those paid at other Bajío estates in the 1770s and 1780s. The Charco de Araujo accounts confirm that permanent estate employees in the Bajío faced declining incomes as well as reduced security toward the end of the eighteenth century. And a declining proportion of estate employees were truly permanent workers.

Meanwhile, the estate was settling a growing number of tenants on its land. Beginning in 1796, six men began to sow maize and frijol (the bean that was the protein of the Mexican poor) on lands allotted by Charco de Araujo. The estate provided land, seed, and the use of a plow team. The tenant family performed the labor. And then the estate and the tenant divided the harvest evenly. In 1796 and 1797, the estate planted twice as much maize and frijol as its sharecroppers. The tenants, however, achieved much higher yields. Because the estate was converting former pastures without irrigation to crop production, the yields of both the estate and its tenants were below Mexican averages. The tenants obtained higher yields most likely because they provided better care for their crops—their subsistence depended on it.

The manager of Charco de Araujo responded by settling ten additional sharecroppers in 1798. Estate cultivation was cut back, while tenant plantings nearly tripled. The results, however, proved disappointing for the estate and painful for the new sharecroppers. The yields of the second group of sharecroppers in 1798 and 1799 were much lower than those of the estates' six original tenants. Not surprisingly, the extension of maize cultivation onto less and less fertile lands brought declining yields. The tenants at Charco de Araujo suffered personally the deepening insecurities inherent in the agrarian transformation of the Bajío.

Given the declining earnings of estate employment and the declining yields of sharecropping, families at Charco de Araujo had to combine multiple jobs, or jobs with sharecropping, to sustain growing families. To evaluate the success or failures of their efforts, I have calculated an approximation of total family earnings from employment, maize rations, and the harvests retained from sharecropping.

The total earnings of extended families rose the longer they remained at the estate. Those at Charco de Araujo less than two years generally obtained less that 50 pesos' worth of total earnings each year. Those remaining two years or longer obtained from 50 to 80 pesos annually. In part, the increase resulted from the overpayments allowed families who worked for the estate two years or more. But much of the increased earnings of the families at Charco de Araujo for longer periods resulted from their sending more members to work as employees or sharecroppers.

The owners and manager of Charco de Araujo took advantage of the difficulties facing large families struggling to survive. As more family members went to work at the estate, total family earnings did not increase proportionally. In part, that resulted from the low wages customarily paid to youths first entering regular estate employment. The declining maize yields from the extension of sharecropping onto marginal lands also contributed to the small increases in earnings that families got from large increases in work. But in several instances, the estate management was more directly responsible. Often, when a son was hired for the minimal wage of one peso per month, his father was forced to take a pay cut of a half peso monthly. The total labor effort of the family thus doubled, while its income increased only minimally—a half peso monthly. By such machinations the estate forced struggling families to vastly increase their labor in order to obtain but small increases in earnings. Because additional earnings were essential to sustain growing families, the dependents of Charco de Araujo had little choice but to accept such unfavorable conditions. Insecure and living near the margins of subsistence, estate residents provided greatly increased work for a little more food.

To conclude, for the 40 families at Charco de Araujo between 1796 and 1800, life was a constant battle to subsist in the face of declining incomes, falling crop yields, and mounting insecurities. Among employees, both wage rates and overpayments were less than rates prevailing in the Bajío a few decades earlier. Even those with relatively steady work found that they were laid off for a few weeks or months each year. The end of the labor scarcity that had long favored the rural poor in the Bajío allowed elites to offer estate workers less permanent employment, lower wages, and reduced overpayments. The year-round, highly paid, and secure employment that had characterized rural life in the Bajío until the middle years of the eighteenth was increasingly rare by 1800.

Meanwhile, growing numbers of residents at Charco de Araujo—as at other estates across the Bajío—had to accept

life as insecure tenants or sharecroppers. As the gentry
gained increased profits by turning the region's best lands
over to wheat and other crops that fed the upper classes, the
maize that sustained the rural and poor masses was left to
marginal lands and struggling tenants. In the northeast uplands of the Bajío, where lands were best suited for grazing,
Charco de Araujo could not produce good harvests of
maize over the years. But as maize production declined in
more fertile regions, both estate owners and tenants were
ready to attempt cultivation on poor land. Estates might
earn new income. Tenants hoped to produce the staple that
sustained their families. But on poor soils with irregular
rainfall, harvests were small and inconsistent. When such
marginal lands were opened by tenants at Charco de
Araujo, the first year's yields were minimally adequate—
and then they declined as the poor soils wore out quickly.

As so often happens among families facing poverty and
insecurity, Bajío estate dependents had no choice but to increase their work. Fathers and sons took on multiple jobs,
and also often sharecropped estate lands. Mothers and
daughters rarely appear in estate accounts, but they labored
in sharecropped fields, tended gardens, made clothing,
reared children, and often raised a few chickens or hogs—
work essential to family sustenance. The regional gentry retained the upper hand and made sure that such expanding
labor efforts remained minimally rewarded. The best many
families could look forward to was an escalating struggle to
counteract the deepening cycle of poverty and insecurity.

Yet the people facing these difficulties at Charco de
Araujo, and across the Bajío, at the end of the eighteenth
century were not the poorest of rural Mexicans. By combining jobs and tenancies such families did manage to obtain
barely enough maize, frijol, and other foods (including
some meat protein), as well as the clothing and other goods
basic to a minimal subsistence. Many residents of peasant
communities in central and southern Mexico were poorer
and faced annually uncertain harvests. But peasants lived

with greater autonomy in the villages. Landed elites were not so clearly responsible for their difficulties. Because they cultivated community lands, their poverty seemed more the result of population growth and their insecurity appeared more the consequence of climatic inconsistencies. Free of social relations of personal dependence, villagers rarely perceived their poverty and insecurity as social problems— and showed little interest in rebellion in 1810.

The critical point, then, is not that the rural poor of the Bajío were poor and insecure, but that they were dependent while becoming increasingly poor and insecure. Their worsening problems had social causes apparent to all. Poverty resulted from the lowering of wages and the reduction of overpayments. Insecurity was caused by the lack of permanent employment and the expansion of tenancies that forced many to take on the risks of poor harvests. Bajío elites directly organized the agrarian transformation that forced worsening conditions onto the rural poor—and most rural families lived as dependents of those elites. That population of agrarian dependents forced to endure deepening poverty along with painful insecurities responded quickly to Hidalgo's call to arms in 1810.

## Industrial Crises Compound Agrarian Grievances, 1785–1810

The Hidalgo revolt began in the northeast uplands of the Bajío, and during its first month most insurgents were from rural areas. But the insurrection eventually recruited many participants in the Bajío's towns and cities. Agrarian grievances were crucial to the origins and the wide extension of the uprising, but other grievances contributed. The Bajío was unique within Mexico because of the integration of estate agriculture, textile production, and silver mining in the regional economy. The Hidalgo revolt was regionally intense because crises afflicting all three sectors converged in 1810.

The textile industry was concentrated in the cities of the eastern Bajío, especially in and around Querétaro. From the late sixteenth century, *obrajes* (workshops) using African slaves and other forced laborers had made cloth with wool from the large flocks of sheep then grazing in the Bajío. The industry expanded slowly through the seventeenth century, and then grew rapidly and diversified after 1700. Then, the growth of the Bajío population allowed textile entrepreneurs alternatives to organizing large workshops with forced labor. Obraje production expanded from 1700 to about 1780, but not nearly as rapidly as did the cloth production of *trapicheros* (artisan families). By the end of the eighteenth century, both the number of looms and the total workers linked to artisan family cloth production far exceeded those of obrajes. And while the large workshops still specialized in woolens, trapicheros made cloth of cotton as well.[85]

The growing predominance of artisan family cloth production was not a retreat from commercialism, nor a shift away from elite dominance of the industry. Rather, entrepreneurs found a new and presumably more profitable way to organize commercial production. Instead of owning and operating large workshops, and facing the persistent difficulties and high costs of recruiting and retaining a permanent labor force, textile entrepreneurs increasingly operated as merchant-financiers. They controlled supplies of cotton and wool, as well as access to markets. But they let poor artisan families bear the costs of owning looms and the burdens of providing labor. By the late eighteenth century, Bajío textile entrepreneurs were increasingly merchant-clothiers. They dominated the industry financially, while putting out the work to supposedly "independent" artisans. The problems of labor recruitment that had troubled the

[85] This analysis of the crisis of the Bajío textile industry is based on Tutino, "War, Colonial Trade, and Bajío Textiles"; see also, Super, "Querétaro Obrajes," and Brading, ed., "Noticias sobre la economía."

industry, and led to the expensive reliance on slaves and other coerced workers, were increasingly resolved by a structure that forced growing numbers of artisan families to exploit themselves by working long hours for little compensation.

The growing importance of merchant domination and putting-out production incorporated many rural families into the textile industry in the late eighteenth century. The most labor-intensive part of cloth production, the spinning of yarn, was increasingly put out to women in poor rural families. The deteriorating conditions facing those families after 1750 left many rural women in need of the earnings provided by such additional work. For entrepreneurs, rural women were a usefully flexible work force. They needed work when it was available, yet they could survive by their families' other activities when the textile market slumped. And they remained available to work again when demand increased.

The growing importance of the putting-out system in Bajío textile production during the eighteenth century brought a change in labor relations parallel to that in rural areas of the region. During most of the colonial era, while population was sparse and labor scarce, Bajío textile entrepreneurs had to offer permanent and secure employment to obtain and retain workers. They often had to coerce workers to accept such conditions. But the growing regional population of the eighteenth century, in the context of an expanding commercial economy, allowed textile entrepreneurs to offer less-permanent work and to use the efforts of growing numbers of workers through the flexible—yet for the workers, most insecure—putting-out relations. By the 1780s, dependent insecurity characterized labor relations in the Bajío textile industry, as among the region's estate workers.

That structure forced deepening problems upon the urban and rural families tied to textile production just as the industry began to face unprecedented hard times in the

1780s. The difficulties began as a consequence of the agrarian transformation of the Bajío. As former pastures were turned into croplands, livestock moved out of the region. The vast herds of sheep that once grazed in or near the Bajío, supplying wool easily and cheaply to local textile producers, moved far to the north. Increased shipping costs began to raise the price of wool in the Bajío. And drought struck more arid northern regions more often and more severely, repeatedly reducing wool supplies and further driving up prices. Often, what little wool was available in drought years could not be sent to the Bajío, as mules could not travel on parched trails. By 1780, then, wool prices had begun a steady rise, accentuated by recurrent years of drought.

Agrarian changes in the Bajío thus forced textile producers there to face higher costs and insecure supplies of wool. Were those the only problems, the price of cloth would have risen accordingly. But as Bajío cloth makers faced higher wool prices, they also encountered new competition from cheap, industrially produced imports.

Throughout most of the colonial era, the concentration of the Mexican population in the interior highlands and the persistent weakness of Spanish textile industries combined to protect the Mexican market for local producers. But by the late eighteenth century, the expansion and early mechanization of cotton production in the Catalan region around Barcelona, along with tax and trade concessions favoring Spanish industries within the empire, allowed imports to claim a growing share of the Mexican textile market. Bajío producers were caught between rising wool prices and competition from low-priced imports.

Many obrajes closed down and others curtailed production during the 1780s. Obraje operators thus cut their losses by forcing both obraje weavers and rural spinners to face unemployment. Many artisan families also lost work—but many more could not afford to stop production. They made cloth for subsistence, not for profit. They had no choice but to work longer hours to produce more cloth for less income—exploiting family labor more intensively to lower their costs in the face of cheaper imports. Unfortunately, this expanded production further flooded the market and kept prices low.

The outlook for families dependent on the Bajío textile industry was bleak in the early 1790s. They were absorbing the costs of an industry suddenly subjected to unfavorable forces from the international market. Then in 1793, international developments brought an unplanned and unexpected respite. Spain entered the wars set off by the French revolution. Catalan cloth production was disrupted and Atlantic trade often blocked. Imports all but disappeared from Mexican markets, and boom production suddenly developed in the Bajío (and elsewhere in Mexico).

The good times lasted from 1793 to 1802. Then peace returned to Europe. Textile imports immediately returned to flood the Mexican market—throwing many Bajío producers out of work, while forcing others once again to work extended hours for reduced earnings. And when war resumed after less than two years, the Spanish crown opened imperial trade to neutral (meaning North American) ships. After 1803, wartime no longer protected Mexican textile producers. Instead, imports arrived irregularly in large quantities, imposing painful uncertainties of employment and income on many Bajío families.

The Napoleonic capture of Madrid in 1808 brought no resolution for Mexican cloth makers. Spanish resistance centered in Seville and Cádiz—and allied with the British. In 1809 and 1810 a new wave of textile imports arrived in Mexico, many now from British mills. Once again, unemployment and worsening poverty afflicted Bajío cloth producers—this time in an era of imperial crisis and local drought and famine. The grievances of many spinners and weavers thus converged with those of rural estate dependents on the eve of Hidalgo's call for insurrection.

Difficulties similar to those plaguing textile workers also struck the miners in and around the city of Guanajuato by

1810. The men who dug ores and refined them into silver had long formed a regional labor aristocracy. According to the 1792 census, a group of about 6,000 workers, located mainly in Guanajuato, produced the silver that made Mexico the most valuable colony in the Spanish empire. For performing often dangerous work underground in the mines or with mercury in the refineries, mine workers received wages far above prevailing rates.[86] And they were aware of their pivotal role in the Spanish empire. Concentrated in mining centers such as Guanajuato, they were sensitive to changes in their employment and earnings—and ready to react vehemently, at times violently, to protect their interests.

During the eighteenth century, the mines at Guanajuato enjoyed two long eras of boom growth and prosperity, each ending in collapse. And each downturn caused massive unemployment that helped to stimulate rioting and violence among the mine workers. The first period of expansion ended abruptly in 1753, and the industry remained depressed until 1767. That midcentury collapse of mining did not immediately set off protests among the mine workers. But when in 1766 José de Gálvez imposed new taxes on basic foods such as maize, wheat, and meat; created a new monopoly that would raise tobacco prices; and called for enrollments in new militia units; an estimated 6,000 rioters took over the streets of Guanajuato. A year later, with mining production and employment still depressed, the mine workers of Guanajuato rioted again on learning that Gálvez had expelled the Jesuits from Mexico. This time, the protestors controlled the streets of Guanajuato for three days and aimed most of their violence at the offices of the royal treasury and the tobacco monopoly. They were crushed only after the mobilization of troops that had recently arrived from Spain.[87]

Soon after these two episodes, mining production re-

---

[86] Brading, *Miners and Merchants*, pp. 249-250.
[87] Ibid., pp. 233-234; Morin, *Michoacán*, pp. 135-137.

sumed its rapid growth. The resulting expansion of employment opportunities apparently moved the mine workers' grievances to the background. During the final years of the eighteenth century, wealthy mining entrepreneurs invested millions of pesos in driving old Guanajuato mines deeper into the mountains. Their investment paid for the massive labor costs of excavation and drainage. Such a labor-intensive expansion promised new gains for the workers at Guanajuato. But the rising costs of reviving and maintaining old mines deep underground soon began to threaten the profits expected by the mine owners, and they responded by attempting to reduce the customary high earnings of the mine workers of Guanajuato.

In addition to their high wages, workers at Mexican silver mines had traditionally received *partidos*—small shares of the ores they mined. They thus had an incentive to increase production. But when late in the eighteenth century the mine owners of Guanajuato began to fear that their workers' earnings would curtail profits, they moved to end the partidos. No doubt, the population growth that was then ending the labor scarcity in the Bajío led owners to expect that they could reduce workers' earnings without disrupting mining operations. The Rayas mine led the way, ending the partidos in the 1770s. When the workers protested, the newly created militia and police patrols forced compliance with the owners' new policies. Early in the 1790s, the largest mine at Guanajuato, the Valenciana, followed suit as rising labor costs again threatened profits. The workers responded with a production slowdown. The owners then called out the militia to force the resumption of full production.[88]

The Valenciana mine produced half of all the silver extracted at Guanajuato from 1780 to 1810. Detailed records of its finances illustrate the developing difficulties of the industry. The silver mined at Valenciana exceeded 1,500,000

[88] Brading, *Miners and Merchants*, pp. 277-278, 288.

pesos in 1788, 1789, 1791, 1795, 1798, and 1799. Production then declined modestly, exceeding that high level only once again, in 1808. Meanwhile, the costs of production rose rapidly. Averaging less than 800,000 pesos yearly in the late 1780s, they rose to exceed 1,200,000 pesos in both 1808 and 1809. Part of that increase resulted from the higher costs of agricultural goods—mules and the grains to feed them—caused by the agricultural transformation of the Bajío. Another part reflected the rising prices of mercury and imported tools caused by the trade disruptions of a war era. And part resulted from the rising costs of paying more than 3,000 workers to dig and drain mines descending ever deeper underground.

Only the costs of labor, however, were within the control of the mine operators. They thus forced the elimination of the partidos in the late 1790s. But that only slowed the increase of mining costs. At Valenciana, owners who had consistently made a profit of more than 1,000,000 pesos yearly in the late 1790s rarely gained over 200,000 pesos a year after 1805. The rising costs of operating aging mines in times of rising prices and wartime disruptions were threatening the profitability of the industry—and thus the employment of thousands of mine workers.[89]

When the drought of 1809 and 1810 struck an industry already reduced to that slim margin of profit, the results were devastating. Complaining of unbearably high costs of mules, other livestock, and the grains to feed them, the refiners at Guanajuato closed down 30 percent of their operations. Mining declined similarly. Massive unemployment followed, along with new insecurities among those still working—and wondering for how long. The local elite expressed its sympathies with the workers, emphasizing the drought as the cause of their miseries.[90] That "natural"

[89] Ibid., pp. 284-291.
[90] Ibid., p. 342.

calamity was but the last cause, however, in a structural decline of the mining industry at Guanajuato.

The elimination of the partidos at Guanajuato made the mine workers less participants in the profits of Mexico's most profitable industry, and more obviously dependent laborers. They suffered an obvious decline in earnings—although a decline that did not leave them impoverished as long as they worked. But when massive unemployment struck in 1809 and 1810, at the same time that drought made food scarce and expensive, poverty became a reality for many families accustomed to living as the aristocrats of the colony's labor force. The insecurities inherent in their lives as dependent laborers became painfully clear.

The Hidalgo revolt did not begin among the mine workers of Guanajuato nor among the textile producers of Querétaro. The insurrection began among the primarily agrarian people of the northeast uplands of the Bajío. Many rural families, however, had participated in both agricultural and textile employment—men working at estates while women spun yarn for obraje operators and merchant-clothiers. And soon after the uprising began, it was joined by rebels from the Bajío's cities and towns, including many textile workers and miners.

The massive insurrection that developed in the Bajío in the fall of 1810 derived primarily from the agrarian transformation that forced dependent, but comfortable and secure, rural families to suffer worsening poverty along with new insecurities. The development of parallel conditions in industrial employment contributed to the spread of the uprising into urban areas. Perhaps most important, the simultaneous development of deepening poverty and insecurity in both agriculture and industry created a social environment in the Bajío laden with new uncertainties of basic subsistence. The pervasive sense of injustice that resulted left many people ready to take the risks of insurrection when the opportunity arose.

# CHAPTER THREE

# Toward Insurrection: Provincial Elites, Political Conspiracies, and Drought, 1808–1810

THE MAJORITY OF THE RESIDENTS of the Mexican Bajío in the late eighteenth century were poor and suffering the effects of complex social changes that left them increasingly insecure. Their direct dependence on powerful elites made clear the social causes of their deepening difficulties. The grievances to fuel an insurrection were moving toward a climax in the first decade of the nineteenth century. But neither the agrarian nor the industrial poor of the Bajío were suicidal fools. However deep their sense of outrage, of injustice, they would not risk an uprising unless they saw an opportunity to rebel without provoking an immediate and overwhelming violent response by regional elites and the colonial state.

The irate residents of the Bajío would not take up arms against their rulers without evidence of weakness in the state and division among elites that might prevent a rapid and unified response by those in power. Elite divisions might also provide rebels with powerful allies. From the vantage of the Bajío poor, the essential opportunity for insurrection appeared in 1810. Since 1808 they had been hearing that the Spanish king was held captive. Mexican elites had begun to debate an uncertain political future. The weakness of the colonial state had engendered apparent divisions among Mexican elites. And the severe drought and famine of 1809 and 1810 had simultaneously brought agrarian and urban grievances to a peak of outrage.

Thus, when in 1810 Father Miguel Hidalgo called upon

his parishioners to take up arms, the breakdown of elite unity appeared confirmed. Was not the priest the former rector of the seminary at Valladolid (Morelia)? Was he not also an estate owner, as well as a friend of the Intendant at Guanajuato and of many elite families at Querétaro? When several young militia officers from prosperous trading and landed families at San Miguel emerged as Hidalgo's lieutenants, it confirmed to the angry poor that a segment of the Bajío elite was ready to revolt.

The appearance of these agitators calling the Bajío populace to arms, while debates over imperial legitimacy continued, created an image of deeply divided elites. The autumn of 1810 appeared an opportune time to attempt an insurrection. Tens of thousands of Bajío residents perceived that opportunity and joined Hidalgo. Their perception proved false. Hidalgo and his few elite allies did not represent a substantial fraction of the Bajío elite. The most powerful inhabitants of the region might complain about the uncertainties prevailing in the empire, but they had no reasons to rebel—and certainly no interest in calling to arms the masses they ruled.

Unfortunately, the insurgents of 1810 could not know that Hidalgo and the other rebel leaders were but marginal members of the provincial elite. They could not know that those agitators had turned to the masses for support only after they had failed to recruit insurgents among Bajío elites. Thus, they could not know that the apparent opportunity for insurrection in September of 1810 was but a deadly illusion. When faced with mass insurrection, the colonial state did not prove weak; when faced with mass insubordination that threatened their wealth and power, colonial elites were not divided. That absence of opportunity for sustained insurrection helps explain the calamitous failure of the uprising. Yet the clear appearance of that opportunity (however false) was essential to the outbreak of the Hidalgo revolt.

### Bajío Elite Adaptations, 1785–1810

Why were Bajío elites quick to debate imperial legitimacy, yet adamantly opposed to insurrection? Eric Wolf argues that Bajío elites were more entrepreneurial, perhaps more capitalist, than those elsewhere in Mexico. He concludes that unique provincial leaders led the Hidalgo revolt, hoping to end their subordination within a colonial order based on privilege and economic restrictions.[1] Wolf erred doubly. Established Bajío elites did not lead and rarely supported the revolt. And those elites differed little in economic goals and activities from other Mexican powerholders. The favored few who dominated life in the late colonial Bajío enjoyed the advantage of access to profitable commercial, textile, mining, and agricultural activities in one region. But those unique opportunities only facilitated the success of Bajío elites in pursuing patterns of activities common to powerful families across Mexico.

Since the sixteenth century, the ascent to elite status in Mexico was accomplished generation after generation by small numbers of immigrants from Spain, and even fewer natives of the colony. Ambitious newcomers to the colony repeatedly used their links with kin already in Mexico to enter the risky, but potentially profitable, world of imperial Spanish commerce. Many who became wealthy in such trade risked their fortunes again in silver mining, seeking ever greater riches. And the few who acquired great wealth in commerce and mining all but inevitably invested in landed estates. Commercial agriculture could not generate the large profits potentially possible in trade and mining. But estate operation in colonial Mexico was modestly profitable—and a much more secure investment. Throughout the colonial centuries, Spanish immigrants to Mexico who amassed wealth in risky commercial or mining ventures

---

[1] Wolf, "Mexican Bajío," p. 192.

later secured their wealth, and the elite status it might maintain, by investing in landed properties. Their Mexican-born heirs inherited those estates, married into more established landed families, and worked to maintain the family within the elite oligarchy that dominated colonial life. Of course, some families were more successful than others in pursuing and maintaining elite status. But this general pattern of elite ascent and family maintenance persisted through the colonial era and across Mexican regions—including the Bajío.[2]

What distinguished Bajío elites in the eighteenth century was their ability to achieve great success while following the established pattern. Bajío elites were probably second in wealth and power only to the great landed families of Mexico City at the end of the eighteenth century. Thanks to the regional combination of rich silver mines and expanding commercial development, Bajío elites were exceptionally successful in acquiring the wealth essential to elite life. And thanks to the availability of profitable commercial estates, they were favored in their persistent efforts to use commercial cultivation to maintain elite status. Once established as members of the regional elite, such landed families regularly ruled the political affairs of their cities and towns. Brading's analysis of the mining elites of Guanajuato emphasizes repeated cases of families making their fortunes in trade and mining, investing in landed estates, and then taking seats on the city council of that wealthiest of colonial cities.[3]

At Querétaro, the most prominent families followed a parallel track, gaining wealth in risky trade and textile activities and then securing their economic base by investing in landed estates. And the shift toward land ownership brought increased participation in Querétaro's political

[2] The pattern is evident in Brading, *Miners and Merchants*, and Ladd, *Mexican Nobility*, pp. 13-88. It is discussed in greater detail in Tutino, "Creole Mexico," pp. 15-192, and "Power, Class, and Family," pp. 359-381.

[3] Brading, *Miners and Merchants*, pp. 303-328.

life.[4] In the smaller towns of the region, locally powerful families ruled by similar means. In San Miguel, for example, the Canal family enjoyed local pre-eminence based on wealth acquired generations earlier by merchants who invested in numerous estates: five in the immediate vicinity of San Miguel and Dolores, plus several grazing properties farther to the north. Their neighbors and elite allies of the Lanzagorta y Landeta clan had similarly used the proceeds of trade earlier in the eighteenth century to acquire a landed base of at least four valuable estates.[5]

I shall not enter the debate over how capitalist were Bajío elites at the end of the colonial era. They were certainly entrepreneurial—seeking profit in market-oriented activities—yet they relied on labor relations that were diverse and often not reduced to a pure wage nexus. What is clear is that the most successful of Bajío elites were not more or less capitalist, or more or less entrepreneurial, than were the most powerful families of Mexico City or of other Mexican regions. All sought wealth and elite status in the more speculative activities of mining and trade, and then attempted to secure their gains by landed investment. Bajío elites were very successful followers of the pattern, thanks to the regional economic boom of the eighteenth century. But they followed a pattern common to those who sought wealth and power across colonial Mexico.

The power and visibility of the most successful elite families, however, should not overshadow the lives of the many who aspired to wealth and power, but failed to attain them. Domingo Allende arrived in San Miguel as a Spanish immigrant with commercial ambitions. He traded there during the last years of the eighteenth century, yet left his heirs but one modest estate.[6] The Aldama brothers, sons of the manager of a local textile obraje, operated a small store at

[4] See Appendix A, Table A.5.

[5] AGN, Padrones, vol. 24, fol. 3, 1793; vol. 36, pp. 2-4, 1792; Fernández de Recas, *Aspirantes americanos*, p. 184.

[6] AGN, Padrones, vol. 36, p. 3, 1793.

San Miguel and bought the Charco de Araujo estate in the 1790s. They never had great economic success.[7] Allende's son and the Aldama brothers later joined Hidalgo in leading the insurrection of 1810. Father Hidalgo also had a career that suggests the failed pursuit of elite status. The Mexican-born son of an estate manager, he supplemented his clerical income by organizing artisan workshops at Dolores and by operating one modest estate near Zitácuaro, just south of the Bajío.[8] These eventual insurgent leaders enjoyed wealth and power far greater than that allowed the majority of Bajío residents, but they lived well beneath the established elite families of Guanajuato, Querétaro, and other towns. They were but marginal elites.

The wealthy and powerful families of the eighteenth-century Bajío thus formed an internally stratified dominant class. Great landed clans, who were usually the beneficiaries of fortunes acquired earlier in trade and mining, dominated the region. Still favored in the larger social context, yet significantly less wealthy and powerful, were marginal elites who struggled to maintain the appearance of elite life on often fragile economic bases. During the years after 1750, the dominant families of the Bajío faced many challenges, but they never suffered losses sufficient to lead them to challenge the colonial regime. In contrast, the marginal elites of the region faced great difficulties and repeated frustrations during this period. It was they who led the insurrection of 1810.

There were three distinct, though related, economic transformations in the late colonial Bajío: one in agriculture that evolved steadily after 1750; another in the textile industry that began around 1780 and developed very inconsistently; and the third in mining that emerged and culminated suddenly after 1800. The results of all three trans-

---

[7] Morin, *Michoacán*, pp. 171-172.

[8] Hamill, *Hidalgo Revolt*, pp. 53-88; Brading, ed., "La situación económica," pp. 15-82.

formations were devastating for the working poor of the region. Their variable impact on Bajío elites helps explain the attitudes of powerholders toward the insurrection of 1810.

The crises of textile production and of silver mining produced economic difficulties for entrepreneurs as well as their employees. To the extent that both industrial crises were caused by developments external to the Bajío—foreign competition and wartime disruptions—they struck all classes. Mine operators and textile entrepreneurs saw profits vanish. They responded by denying work to many dependents. In such conditions, elites and workers could jointly lament the difficulties of their industries—although workers faced problems far more severe.

But the elites most hurt by the industrial crises of the late eighteenth and early nineteenth centuries were not the established members of the Bajío oligarchy. Instead, those who faced difficulties were commonly aspirants to elite status. John Super has shown that after 1785, the ownership of Querétaro obrajes turned over at a rate of once every two years.[9] Clearly, obraje operators were struggling. But those owners were rarely fully established in the Querétaro elite. Rather, they were mostly newcomers, operating textile workshops in the hope of acquiring the fortunes essential to elite life. The decline and uncertainties that plagued the industry primarily frustrated the ambitions of numerous families seeking elite membership. Similarly, the families that profited most from the eighteenth-century mining bonanza at Guanajuato had invested their wealth in secure landed properties by the 1790s.[10] Their wealth, power, and elite status were well established before the rising costs of excavation and drainage combined with the drought of 1809 and 1810 to undermine the industry. Thus, the late colonial crises of textiles and mining did not significantly

[9] Super, "Querétaro Obrajes," Table II, p. 211.
[10] Brading, *Miners and Merchants*, pp. 285-291; and *Haciendas and Ranchos*, pp. 135-141.

undermine the wealth and power of the core of established elite families in the Bajío.

Having avoided by landed investment the greatest losses caused by the industrial difficulties, Bajío elites reaped substantial benefits from the agrarian changes that forced severe difficulties onto the rural poor. The declining earnings, marginal tenancies, evictions, and general insecurity imposed on agrarian families were implemented directly by landed elites who aimed to claim rising profits during the long era of commercial expansion and population growth. The agrarian crisis of the eighteenth century in the Bajío was a crisis of the dependent poor. It was an economic triumph for landed elites. And the leading families of the Bajío were entrenched as landed elites by 1800. The difficulties then facing struggling entrepreneurs in mining and textile production served as one more reminder of the long-established wisdom that the only safe investment in colonial Mexico was landed investment. The great families who operated numerous estates that were large, economically diversified, and amply financed reaped the profits of the agrarian transformation of the Bajío during the years before 1810. That class would not produce many rebels.

The same agrarian changes, however, were not so advantageous for many marginal members of the provincial elite. Families operating single, small estates—often on the less fertile lands of the Bajío uplands, and often lacking financial resources—found profits scarce and inconsistent. The difficulties of the Aldama brothers at Charco de Araujo are evident in the earlier discussion of that estate's operations. Father Hidalgo faced similar problems trying to make a profit by letting out his small estate near Zitácuaro to numerous poor tenants. Marginal members of the Bajío elite generally operated economically weak estates, and they lacked the landed and financial resources to profit from the agrarian changes so beneficial to the wealthiest Bajío estate owners.

The crises of mining and textile production frustrated

many aspirants to elite status, while the agrarian transformation brought problems and few profits to lesser elites operating marginal estates. But those difficulties generally spared the wealthiest and most established landed clans of the Bajío—the core of the region's dominant class at the end of the colonial era. The result was that while marginal elites might protest and even plot rebellion, creating an appearance of elite divisions, the core of established powerholders remained economically strong and committed to the defense of the colonial regime.

Beginning in 1804, the Spanish regime attempted to place a new burden on Mexican landed elites. Facing the rising costs of the prolonged European wars, the monarchy enacted an emergency revenue measure called the *Consolidación de Vales*. Church institutions were required to call in all their outstanding capital. The royal treasury would receive the total receipts, and then was to pay annual interest to the Church to fund ecclesiastical activities. In colonial Mexico, numerous Church institutions functioned as mortgage bankers and many estate owners owed substantial sums—suddenly subject to immediate payment in full. In addition, throughout the colonial centuries, many landed families had assigned part of the value of their estates to the Church, paying annual interest to provide stipends to support selected churchmen—usually family members or retainers. This was capital that the Church had never loaned, but was suddenly demanded in full from elite families by a government facing a deepening financial crisis. Few of the affected landholders had the cash at hand to pay those obligations immediately. A chorus of protest quickly sounded—followed by much maneuvering to avoid payment. Many established elite families across Mexico were threatened by the Consolidation order.[11]

But were they so hurt, or so maddened, that they would risk their lives of wealth and positions of power in rebellion

[11] See Flores Caballero, *La contrarrevolución*, pp. 28-65.

against the colonial regime? Most were not. The reasons are clear when analysis shifts from the threat to the application of the Consolidation. First, not all great landed families in Mexico were affected. Many of the wealthiest clans who had acquired fortunes and bought estates with the wealth of the recent mining boom held their properties without large obligations to the Church.[12] But many other leading landed families, often those longest established on the land, did owe large sums to Church lenders. Most were eventually successful, however, in negotiating delayed payments in installments extended over a decade or more. Few had made more than one or two payments when the Consolidation was canceled in 1808.[13] Those payments imposed an immediate financial drain on some elite families, but also reduced their debts and thus their future obligations. Total losses were rarely excessive, and there is no evidence that the Consolidation undermined the landed base of any substantial segment of the great landed families of Mexico in the early nineteenth century.

The most powerful families of colonial Mexico used their political influence to negotiate a resolution of the Consolidation that deflected its demands away from their fortunes. Marginal elites paid more heavily. Less wealthy estate owners generally owed more—proportionally—to the Church and they were less able to acquire cash for immediate payment or to negotiate favorable terms of delayed payment. Almost too typical of such marginal elites facing the Consolidation was Father Hidalgo, whose only hacienda was embargoed for several years because he could not pay his debts to the Consolidation.[14] Thus, that emergency revenue program paralleled the economic developments of the period before 1810 in striking hard at marginal elites, while

---

[12] Tutino, "Creole Mexico," pp. 39-40.
[13] Lavrin, "The Execution," pp. 34-40, 46-47.
[14] Ibid., pp. 36-37; Brading, ed., "La situación económica," pp. 15-82.

sparing the more established landed families that ruled Mexican society.

In general, until 1810 the landed elite of the Bajío remained strong economically. There were over 500 estates in the Bajío (including both the Intendancy of Guanajuato as well as the regions around Querétaro) around 1800.[15] Yet only sixteen properties from that region were advertised for sale due to financial difficulties in the periodicals of Mexico City during the 1790s. And despite the financial crises of textile and mining, as well as the pressures of the Consolidation, only fifteen were offered from 1800 through 1809.[16] This was not a landed elite facing the loss of its landed base—or any other fundamental difficulties. When those powerful families faced an unprecedented crisis of imperial legitimacy beginning in 1808, they eagerly joined in often heated political debates. But they showed no interest in taking up arms against imperial rule—especially if rebellion included the mobilization of the masses they expected to rule.

## FAILED CONSPIRACIES, 1808–1810

When Napoleon captured the Spanish king and the imperial center of Madrid early in May of 1808, he touched off intense debates all across the Spanish empire. Colonial elites and imperial officials in distant regions, long accustomed to rule from Madrid, suddenly faced basic uncertainties of imperial legitimacy. Should colonials obey Napoleonic Spain? Should they look to one of the juntas emerging in Spain in opposition to French rule and claiming to represent national sovereignty? If so, which junta should they follow? Or should they proclaim continuing loyalty to the captured Ferdinand VII—and rule themselves until he might regain his throne? During the eventful

[15] Wolf, "Mexican Bajío," p. 188.
[16] See Appendix A, Table A.6.

summer of 1808, elites across Mexico—including those in the Bajío—publicly debated these basic questions of political life. The emergence of a powerful elite segment that pressed for substantial Mexican autonomy, always in the name of Ferdinand VII, created a widespread belief that many were ready to consider breaking away from the Spanish empire. In an era dominated by the independence of the United States and the French revolution, the emergence of such fundamental political debates created an impression that Mexican elites were ready to take up arms to claim national independence.

Such views were based on deep misperceptions of Mexican elite interests and goals. Established Mexican power-holders were conscious above all else of their position as a dominant class, sustained in wealth and power by ruling a subordinate agrarian majority. Such class-conscious elites would debate colonial political developments, as long as those debates remained the affairs of powerful gentlemen. But they would not take up arms against the colonial regime. Such action would begin conflicts that could threaten their favored positions. They could not imagine calling the poor to arms, for complicity in such violent insubordination would surely undermine the foundations of their power.

During the first decade of the nineteenth century, however, Mexicans of all classes were inexperienced in the ways of political debate—and of rebellion. Powerful elites believed that they could openly debate basic issues of colonial legitimacy without creating a perception of class division and regime weakness. Marginal elites and increasingly irate agrarian subordinates heard those debates and believed that the commotion among powerholders indicated a real opportunity for insurrection. That perception proved false—but the proof emerged only after the uprising had begun.

Beginning in June of 1808, Mexicans learned in rapid succession of the flight of the Portuguese court to Brazil in the face of Napoleon's armies; of the abdication of Charles

IV of Spain in favor of his son Ferdinand VII; of the deten-
tion of both Charles and Ferdinand in Bayone, and the abdication of the latter in favor of Napoleon's brother Joseph;
of the mass, violent protests of Spaniards against the French
takeover; of the creation of juntas claiming national sovereignty, first in Valencia, later in Seville.[17] The always incomplete news of such developments provoked deepening political debates among Mexican elites suddenly faced with
the breakdown of long-established imperial legitimacy.

Who should rule and who could rule in Mexico suddenly
became open questions. In that uncertain context, the Mexico City council led a movement seeking greater autonomy
for colonial elites. The great landed patriarchs and their allies who controlled that council called for a Mexican assembly to be selected by city councils across the colony—councils dominated by landed elites. The assembly would then
rule in the name of Ferdinand VII until he regained his
throne. The Viceroy, José de Iturrigaray, emphasized that
Spain was in "a state of anarchy" and seconded the call for
a Mexican assembly. The movement toward political autonomy for Mexican elites quickly found support in the Bajío.
The Querétaro council, led by Corregidor Miguel Domínguez and the landed patriarch Pedro Antonio de Septién,
joined in calling for a Mexican assembly to govern in the absence of Ferdinand VII.[18]

The movement for Mexican autonomy was directed by
established members of the Mexican elite, mostly great
landholders. Such a shift in colonial government, however,
appeared a threat to the interests of many elite aspirants
linked to imperial commerce—especially merchants who
had yet to consolidate their elite position within Mexico.
Their chances to acquire wealth depended on the continuation of the existing channels of trade within the Spanish
empire. They preferred to declare loyalty to the junta dom-

[17] Anna, *Fall of Royal Government*, pp. 37-38.
[18] Ibid., p. 48; Hamnett, *Revolución y contrarrevolución*, pp. 157-158.

inated by the merchant interests of Seville, the center of colonial commerce. The leaders of the Mexico City Consulado, the merchants' guild, thus joined with members of the colonial administration and judiciary in opposing the proposed Mexican assembly—and any increased autonomy for Mexican landed elites. The dispute broke into open conflict when on the night of September 15, 1808, Gabriel Yermo led the Consulado's militia in ousting Viceroy Iturrigaray in order to crush the autonomist faction of the Mexican elite. It was the first of many coups in nineteenth-century Mexico. Its goal was to confirm the colony's close dependence on Spain. But by using force to overthrow the legitimate Spanish Viceroy, the merchants and their bureaucratic allies further undermined the legitimacy of the colonial regime they hoped to defend.

The Mexican elites whose aspirations for greater autonomy were thwarted by Yermo's coup chose not to retaliate. Such a response could easily lead to prolonged conflict that would endanger both life and property—and the autonomists had much property to protect. If political debate engendered violence, they would bow out. But they had opened a debate that others with less to lose would continue.

In the fall of 1809, a conspiracy seeking Mexican independence was discovered among provincial elites at Valladolid (Morelia). The leaders were captured and detained for a time. But colonial officials saw their threat as so limited that they later released the participants with minor reprimands.[19] Only a few months later, another conspiracy—perhaps linked to the first—developed at Querétaro. It too was exposed and foiled. But the failure of the Querétaro conspiracy touched off the Hidalgo revolt.

The Querétaro conspiracy has been portrayed as representing the grievances of provincial elites, especially those of Mexican birth known as Creoles. They formed a group

[19] Hamill, *Hidalgo Revolt*, pp. 95-97.

that resented the many preferences that favored newcomers from Spain in colonial economic affairs and especially within the colonial administration.[20] Their grievances were real, and several conspirators joined out of such resentments. But it is equally important to emphasize that the conspiracy failed—that the majority of Bajío elites, including most Creole elites, refused to participate in the planned movement for independence.

Only two of the Querétaro conspirators belonged to the highest level of the regional elite, and only one of them led an established landed family. The Corregidor of Querétaro, Miguel Domínguez, held the second most powerful colonial office in the Bajío—second only to the Intendant of Guanajuato. Not part of a landed family of note, Domínguez had worked his way up in the colonial bureaucracy. As a native Mexican, he surely resented the advantages enjoyed by Spaniards within the administration. From 1808 on, he was a prominent advocate of Mexican autonomy. Pedro Antonio de Septién was the son of a wealthy immigrant Spaniard who had amassed a fortune in commerce and mining at Guanajuato. The son inherited the rich estates purchased by his merchant father, briefly held colonial office as Subdelegado at Celaya, married into the Querétaro landed elite and assumed the senior position on the city council there.[21] The very visible roles of Domínguez and Septién in leading the Querétaro conspiracy have led observers to presume that they represented the larger regional elite. But their participation was unique. Others of their high political and economic position would not join them.

Perhaps Domínguez' and Septién's experience in the colonial bureaucracy had made them more sensitive to the liabilities faced by Creoles in government service since the Galvez reforms begun in the 1760s had brought clear pref-

[20] Ibid., pp. 18-52; Brading, *Miners and Merchants*, pp. 345-347.
[21] Ibid., pp. 312-313; *Gazeta de México*, 17 Feb. 1789, 30 Jan. 1808.

erences favoring Spanish-born bureaucrats.[22] More immediately, they were certainly alienated by the year-long investigation that followed their leadership of the 1808 autonomist movement in Querétaro. No action was taken
against them, but during the course of the judicial investigation, Domínguez and Septién were forced to present
themselves before their political opponents on the High
Court of Mexico City, defend their actions as ultimately loy-
alist, and abjectly swear their devotion to the Spanish empire.[23] As provincials, Domínguez and Septién were apparently selected for exemplary humiliation, presumably to
discourage any further autonomist organization.

That ordeal may have discouraged others, but it only confirmed the opposition of Domínguez and Septién to the regime in power after the 1808 coup. They were ready to lead
another conspiracy in 1810. But they quickly discovered
that few of their peers among leading officeholders and established landed elites would join them. They thus were
forced to plot with a Querétaro grocer, an estate administrator, plus several marginal elites from the outlying towns
of San Miguel and Dolores. Such conspirators were locally
prominent, but they could not approach the wealth and
power of the dominant Bajío elites.

The majority of the Querétaro conspirators were neither
heirs to great fortunes nor owners of important landed
properties, nor holders of important colonial offices. Most
were marginal elites, often the sons of men who had come
to Mexico from Spain seeking elite status—but had failed to
attain it. Ignacio Allende's father was such an immigrant
who traded at San Miguel, purchased one modest estate,
but died bankrupt shortly before 1810. The immigrant father of Juan and Ignacio Aldama had managed the obraje
owned by the Canal family at San Miguel. The brothers ran
a small store there and struggled to operate Charco de

[22] See Burkholder and Chandler, *From Impotence to Authority*, pp. 83-135.
[23] Septién y Septién, ed., *Precursores de la independencia.*

Araujo. Mariano Abasolo's father held the royal tobacco monopoly at Dolores. He profited enough to leave his son three estates in that marginal region of the Bajío uplands. Mariano married into another locally prominent family. But in early 1810, Abasolo faced bankruptcy and failed to escape it when the head of the Canal family refused to loan him 2,000 pesos.[24]

Father Miguel Hidalgo y Costilla was also a marginal member of the Bajío elite. As the son of an estate manager, he spent his early years in close contact with the agrarian poor of the region, an experience he would repeat later in life as parish priest, first at San Felipe and then at Dolores. Such experiences perhaps brought Hidalgo closer to the rural poor than many of his fellow conspirators. Yet between his childhood on a Bajío hacienda and his later years as pastor in poor rural parishes, Hidalgo enjoyed a remarkable career as an independent intellectual within the Church. He was sent to study with the Jesuits at Valladolid and was present when his teachers were expelled by order of the Spanish Crown. He later returned to his studies at the College of San Nicolas at Valladolid, where he advanced from student to teacher and finally to rector. But his financial probity, personal integrity, and theological conformity were questioned. He resigned under a cloud as rector in 1792, leaving to become a parish priest for reasons never explained. He remained active intellectually, reading French and keeping in touch with the ideas of the Enlightenment. His combination of intellectual independence and resentment of the conservative Church hierarchy, his knowledge of revolutionary intellectual and political developments in Europe, and his long ties with the Bajío poor all moved Hidalgo toward his role as insurgent leader.

And surely the cleric's readiness to agitate was heightened by his long, varied, but minimally successful career as

[24] Alamán, *Historia de Méjico*, I, 228-229; Brading, *Miners and Merchants*, p. 344; JSE, vol. 215, no. 172, 12 Aug. 1810.

entrepreneur. Using his clerical salary as a base, Hidalgo purchased several estates, but only kept one for any length of time. He tried his hand at mining on a small scale. And after taking up residence at Dolores in 1803, he established several workshops. He attempted tanning, silk raising, olive growing and oil production, grape cultivation and wine making, and most successfully, pottery. Hidalgo's economic efforts were as varied as they were constant, and often he attempted to produce goods that imperial restrictions envisioned as Spanish monopolies. Hidalgo never profited substantially from all these activities. Not that he was poor; he always enjoyed wealth far greater than most of his parishioners. But he never attained the secure economic base that would have gained him a place in the Bajío elite. His economic life was one of constant struggle to maintain but marginal elite status. Here was the perfect agitator: a man of extensive and independent learning, with close ties to the rural poor, whose ambitions had been frustrated in both his ecclesiastical career and economic endeavors.[25]

Father Hidalgo and the other men of Querétaro, San Miguel, and Dolores who participated in the conspiracy of 1810 neither belonged to the established elite, nor represented that dominant class. They were frustrated, marginal elites, understandably opposed to the imperial regime during a time of disruptions and uncertainties. But their opposition was not a major threat to that regime. They lacked the economic resources, the political experience, and the social linkages to organize an effective assault on the colonial power structure.

Such conspirators were unlikely to gain much support among the wealthiest and most powerful Bajío families who had not endured substantial losses during recent years. Yet the plotters began with just such expectations. They aimed to recruit conspirators among Bajío elites, and they espe-

[25] This section summarizes the fine discussion of Hidalgo's interwoven intellectual and economic careers in Hamill, *Hidalgo Revolt*, pp. 53-88.

cially hoped to gain adherents among the region's militia officers. Septién, Aldama, Allende, and Abasolo were officers. Had many more joined, the rebellion might have included most of the region's armed forces—precluding any quick defense of the regime. But few militia officers, and even fewer powerful elites, responded positively to the conspirators' plans. And it was the failure to elicit support among Bajío elites that turned the rebels' attention toward the agrarian masses.[26]

The plotters apparently believed that they could use the grievances of the Bajío populace for their own purposes. A letter written by Allende, reporting conversations with Septién, referred to the masses as Indians who were ignorant, but surely ready to respond to any call to arms from the conspirators. And as plans turned more toward calling the populace to arms, Father Hidalgo acquired a more central role. He had long known the Bajío poor and was generally viewed favorably by those who knew him.[27] His assistant at Dolores had recently testified in support of one group of estate residents who had gone to court to try to gain community status and independent land rights.[28]

Hidalgo certainly knew the Bajío poor far better than did his fellow conspirators. He knew that they were not very "Indian," not wholly ignorant, and not lacking in a clear conception of their own difficulties. He thus knew that the plotters' complaints of injustices to Creole elites were not compatible with the grievances of the agrarian poor—grievances against Bajío elites, including many Creole landholders. Yet he remained willing to lead the Bajío populace in armed insurrection, perhaps expecting that he could bridge the gap between marginal elite conspirators and outraged agrarian masses.

The failure of the Querétaro conspiracy to recruit sub-

[26] Ibid., pp. 111-113.
[27] Ibid.
[28] Tutino, "Life and Labor," pp. 377-378.

stantial support, or even minimal assistance, among Bajío elites is revealed by the flood of denunciations received by the authorities between September 9 and 15, 1810. Many who knew of the conspiracy, most likely because they had been invited to join, not only refused to participate, but quickly wrote to inform the authorities.[29] Officials acted promptly, detaining the conspirators living at Querétaro. When Hidalgo, Allende, and the others at San Miguel and Dolores learned of the arrests, they immediately turned to the masses and precipitated the insurrection. On the morning of September 16, 1810, Hidalgo called his parishioners to revolt. He quickly discovered that while Bajío elites were reluctant to even plot rebellion, thousands among the rural poor were ready to join in a violent insurrection against the colonial regime—in their view a regime that included landed elites.

The Querétaro conspiracy did not fail because it was revealed; it was revealed many times because it failed to elicit support among established Creole elites. The conspirators' turn toward the masses, and Hidalgo's move toward leadership, came in response to the failure to gain elite support. Clearly, no substantial segment of the powerful Bajío elite was ready to risk wealth and power by challenging the colonial regime in 1810. Only frustrated marginal elites were ready to call the masses to arms. Among the most powerful Mexicans, there were no major divisions when faced with the question of insurrection in 1810. The dominant class of the Bajío was solidly united in opposition to any violent rebellion that might upset the social structure they ruled—whatever their political disabilities.

Yet a very different perception of elite attitudes developed among the rural poor of the Bajío. After all, a prominent local clergyman, assisted by several militia officers, called them to arms. The agrarian poor were not students of fine distinctions of elite class stratification. They could

[29] Hamill, *Hidalgo Revolt*, pp. 117-118.

not know that those calling them to rebellion were local leaders, politically isolated marginal elites in the larger regional and colonial context. The rural poor of the eastern Bajío saw local elites in rebellion and inviting mass participation. They concluded that powerholders were divided over the basic question of loyalty to Spain. Thus developed the critical paradox of the Hidalgo revolt: the actions of marginal elites as agitators created sufficient perception of elite division to convince many among the outraged poor that an opportunity for insurrection existed in 1810. Yet actual elite division was minimal. When the insurrection proved massive enough to threaten elite power, even the political division within the dominant class vanished. Thus developed the deadly illusion of opportunity that helped precipitate the insurrection, and then contributed to its devastating defeat.

## DROUGHT, 1808–1810

Hidalgo's call for rebellion was not the only precipitant of insurrection in the Bajío in 1810. The rush of thousands of people to join the uprising was also an immediate response to two years of extreme drought and famine. The famine did not cause the revolt, just as Hidalgo's proclamations did not cause it. Causes were more complex and extended far back into the social transformations that had forced worsening difficulties on the agrarian poor for decades. Drought did produce a sudden worsening of the poverty and insecurity already plaguing the rural residents of the Bajío. And it made the social bases of those difficulties plainly visible. The drought and famine years of 1809 and 1810 brought the emerging sense of outrage and injustice among the Bajío poor to a peak. Thus, many long-struggling agrarian families were uniquely ready to respond when Hidalgo called them to arms in the fall of 1810.

The summers of 1808 and 1809 brought little rain. Maize became increasingly scarce and expensive during 1809 and the first eight months of 1810. Those two years of dearth struck a rural population in the Bajío already suffering from declining earnings, declining maize yields, and deepening insecurities. At the same time, the spread of unemployment in textile production and silver mining, in part caused by the drought, forced many urban families to face extreme difficulties. Bajío observers began to foresee a repeat of the deadly famine years of 1785 and 1786.

One of the first reports of difficulties from 1808 reveals that the severity of the famine resulted not merely from drought, but from the impact of drought on an ever more fragile structure of subsistence production. The manager of the Puerto de Nieto estate, just east of San Miguel, wrote in April of 1808 that he had just finished clearing lands long used for pasture in the estate's uplands. He planned to begin maize cultivation there. But these marginal croplands would produce good harvests only if well manured and only with ample rains. The rains had yet to begin and the lands newly cleared in response to the regional scarcities of maize could not be planted.[30]

The entire summer of 1808 brought only sporadic and insufficient rains, and thus Bajío crops that relied on natural precipitation were poor. The recent agrarian transformation of the region had reserved most irrigated fields for the wheat, fruits, and vegetables consumed by the wealthier, more urban segments of Mexican society. The maize that sustained the rural poor was relegated to marginal uplands that were rarely irrigated, and those lands produced little in 1808. The maize on marginal upland fields was also cultivated primarily by poor tenants and sharecroppers. The rural poor thus faced double burdens when the drought began in 1808.

Many of the great landholders of the Bajío fared better, often profiting from the scarcities of 1808. Having stored maize from previous years' harvests, many had grain to sell.

[30] JSE, vol. 214, no. 91, 1 Apr. 1808; CPP, no. 33, 18 Apr. 1808.

Puerto de Nieto held over 16,000 fanegas in early 1809,
stored from four previous harvests. The owner, José Sánchez Espinosa of Mexico City, however, expected prices
would continue to climb. He ordered his manager to stop all
sales, which undoubtedly accelerated the rapid rise in maize
prices.[31]

Unfortunately for the Bajío poor, Sánchez Espinosa was
right, and he gained ample profits for his economic fore-
sight. Following the poor harvest of 1808, the summer of
1809 brought almost no rain. By August of that year it was
clear that extreme scarcities faced all of central and north
central Mexico. The colonial authorities began to gather information. Reports repeated the same story: little rain,
withering crops, rising prices, and worsening food shortages. Hardest hit were the interior uplands ranging from
Oaxaca in the south, through the central highlands around
Mexico City, across the Bajío, and north into San Luis Potosí and Zacatecas. Regions nearer to the coasts fared better.
In Veracruz, Puebla, Valladolid, and Guadalajara, officials
expected only modestly reduced harvests in August of
1809.[32]

The drought and resulting scarcities of 1809 thus focused on the highland regions that had historically relied on
the Bajío to provide reserve maize. But by the early nineteenth century, the agrarian transformation of the basin
had eliminated that role. Rather than providing reserve
grains to feed people in drier regions of the Mexican highlands, the Bajío now faced its own shortage.[33]

Since the great famine of 1785 and 1786, when the Bajío
first failed to serve as a reserve granary for central Mexico,
there had been a search for an alternative. The lowlands
nearer the Mexican coasts seemed promising. Rains there

[31] CPP, no. 38, 9 Sept. 1808; no. 39, 20 Sept. 1808; no. 43, 18 Oct. 1808;
JSE, vol. 214, no. 96, 25 Oct. 1808; CPP, no. 49, 1 Nov. 1808; no. 52, 31 Mar.
1809; no. 53, 1 Apr. 1809.
[32] AGN, Intendencias, vol. 73, exp. 7, fol. 14, 1809.
[33] AGN, Intendencias, vol. 73, exp. 7, fols. 9-11, 19 Sept. 1809.

were more plentiful and regular. With sparse local populations, coastal regions could raise ample surpluses that might feed the densely populated highlands when rains failed periodically. Economic difficulties intervened, however. The high humidity of the lowlands precluded the long-term storage of maize there. Stored grain would soon rot. For the lowlands to serve as a reserve granary, then, maize would have to be shipped to the highlands after each harvest and stored there until times of scarcity. Either landed elites or the colonial authorities would have to pay substantial shipping costs well before they might reap the profits of dearth. Neither was ready to make that investment in the security of the Mexican poor. When severe scarcity returned to the Bajío in 1809, the populace had no place to turn.

In early September, reports from Querétaro indicated that a third of the crop was already lost. By the end of the month, two thirds had withered. When local authorities, led by Corregidor Domínguez, inquired of nearby estate owners about maize held in storage, the responses were dismal. Many reported that they had sold their limited reserves earlier to buyers in other regions where prices had peaked more rapidly.[34] In such cases, Bajío estates were continuing to provide reserves to other regions—now to the detriment of the local population.

As famine loomed over the region, Bajío elites once again attempted to ameliorate the situation. And again, relief focused on urban centers. City councils feared that the drought would kill enough livestock to prevent the movement of available grain and limit the cultivation of future crops. The authorities at Querétaro and San Miguel legislated against the worst abuses. They prohibited the further storage of grain, ordering all maize into town markets immediately. They insisted that all employees customarily given maize rations continue to receive them. Employers

[34] AGN, Intendencias, vol. 73, exp. 9, fol. 69, 2 Sept. 1809; exp. 7, fols. 9-11, 19 Sept. 1809.

were not allowed to fire workers as a means of lessening the amount of maize they needed. Such enactments all too clearly reflected the abuses then facing the Bajío poor.[35] They had little effect in preventing their continuation.

The responses at Puerto de Nieto, outside San Miguel, and La Griega, near Querétaro, were typical. Both estates held maize stocks throughout 1809. Some was held in reserve to provide food rations for permanent employees as well as seed for the next planting. Thousands of fanegas were shipped north to San Luis Potosí to fulfill similar needs at estates operated there by the same family. There were still important securities for permanent estate employees. The starving multitudes around San Miguel and Querétaro who did not receive rations were allowed to purchase maize at the estates. But they could buy only in minute quantities and by appearing personally at the estate granaries. When pressed to send maize to town markets, the estate managers bluntly stated that such shipments would only serve to bring down prices. Sales limited to small quantities at estate granaries placed the burden of transportation literally on the backs of the hungry poor. And prices remained high. After repeated inquiries, the managers at Puerto de Nieto and La Griega finally admitted to holding nearly 8,000 fanegas of maize late in 1809. But only 500 fanegas were delivered for sale at San Miguel—a token to stop continuing pressures. None went to Querétaro.[36] These were hard times—except for profiteering landed elites.

The scarcity and high price of maize hit the urban poor of the Bajío hard. They were completely dependent on purchased maize, and as the staple became more costly, more and more of family earnings went to obtain basic food. Meanwhile, the drought helped to worsen urban unemployment. The costs of operating the mines at Guanajuato

[35] AGN, Intendencias, vol. 73, exp. 7, fols. 9-11, 19 Sept. 1809; JSE, vol. 215, no. 167, 28 Oct. 1809.

[36] JSE, vol. 214, no. 108, 24 Nov. 1809; no. 113, 3 Jan. 1810; vol. 215, no. 170, 25 Jan. 1810; vol. 214, no. 118, 14 July 1810.

had been rising steadily in recent years, and the drought sent them to new heights. Mines and refineries closed, leaving many without work just as food became most expensive.[37] In the textile industry of the region, already facing a crisis based on rising wool prices and foreign competition, the drought made fiber supplies even more scarce and expensive. And 1809 and 1810 brought another wave of imported cloth to Mexico. Mass unemployment thus struck many textile workers just as food became scarce.[38]

The impact of the drought on the rural population of the Bajío varied with the economic positions of agrarian families. Those with members who retained permanent estate employment that guaranteed maize rations faced few difficulties, as long as they kept their jobs and the estate provided the rations. These were secure dependents—once again reminded that security was the reason that they had accepted lives of dependence.

But the agrarian transformation that had swept the Bajío since 1750 left fewer and fewer families protected by such security. Expanding numbers of rural families were increasingly dependent on tenancies or sharecropping for subsistence. Tenancies did give rural families increased autonomy—they did control production of basic subsistence goods. But it was a limited autonomy—dependent on lands allotted them by landed elites. And Bajío elites generally allowed tenants to cultivate only marginal lands that produced declining yields—and no yields at all when the rains failed. Thus, the modestly increased autonomy of tenant production brought greatly increased insecurity. When drought occurred in 1809 and 1810, that deepening insecurity became painfully apparent. Sharecroppers planted their crops, expended months of effort in cultivation, and reaped little or nothing at harvest time. Their only income

[37] AGN, Intendencias, vol. 73, exp. 4, 25 Aug. 1809; Brading, *Miners and Merchants*, p. 342.

[38] JSE, vol. 214, no. 88, 8 Mar. 1808; no. 90, 28 Mar. 1808; no. 97, 12 Nov. 1808; no. 107, 21 Nov. 1809.

would come from seasonal day labor at the estates' irrigated fields. But such work paid little and provided no maize rations. Instead, the meager wages received for planting or harvesting estate crops had to buy maize at inflated prices.

Tenants owing cash rents might face even greater difficulties. They too planted crops, labored long to cultivate them, and harvested little. They too might earn a little cash in estate fields and purchase some high-priced maize. But cash tenants, unlike sharecroppers, still owed rents to landlords, even after their crops had failed. In the summer of 1810, the tenants at La Griega still owed their rents for 1809. The estate manager agreed to a proposal that allowed them to delay payment until after the harvest of 1810. They would then sell their oxen to pay their back rents.[39] The elite landlord would thus claim his due, if a year late. But how were the tenants to raise crops in the coming years without their plow teams?

As the agrarian transformation of the Bajío made insecure cash earnings and share tenancies on marginal lands increasingly prevalent, the costs of periodic drought were primarily borne by the rural poor. They faced not only poverty, but the specter of starvation when drought was prolonged. And the outrage sure to develop among those facing such crises easily focused on the owners and managers of Bajío estates. Had they not kept irrigated fields for their own profitable cultivation of the foods of the rich? Had they not allotted their tenants only lands of marginal fertility that were subject to the vagaries of natural rainfall? Had they not forced the hungry poor to undertake long treks to buy but small amounts of maize at painfully high prices?

To the rural poor of the Bajío, the causes of poverty and insecurity were clearly social—not natural. The famine of 1809 and 1810 made that apparent. They knew that their repeated encounters with famine were generating rising profits for landed elites with vast estates and irrigated fields.

[39] JSE, vol. 214, no. 118, 14 July 1810; no. 120, 28 July 1810.

The outrage of the agrarian poor in the Bajío was surely heightened because of the recent appearance of their difficulties. Decades earlier, their parents and grandparents had enjoyed higher earnings, guaranteed maize rations, and thus substantial security as estate dependents. The trials of subsistence facing the Bajío poor in 1810 were not old, established problems. They were recent developments, forced upon them by powerful elites. The agrarian poor of the Bajío were thus outraged by the injustice of their lives. Many were ready to lash out violently when Father Hidalgo called them to insurrection in September of 1810.

## INSURRECTION, 1810

When, on the evening of September 15, 1810, Hidalgo and the other conspirators living at San Miguel and Dolores learned that their plot had been revealed and their allies at Querétaro apprehended, they faced critical decisions. The landed patriarch of San Miguel, Narciso María de la Canal, offered to provide Ignacio Allende with the funds to flee into exile. Allende, however, refused the offer and went on to Dolores to meet with Hidalgo and other conspirators. They knew that Mariano Abasolo could mobilize the small militia detachment there. A few other local residents were also ready to join. And during the night, Luis Gutiérrez raised about 200 mounted men from the Hacienda Santa Barbara. Deciding to proceed immediately with the revolt, the conspirators rounded up and jailed all the native Spaniards living at Dolores.

The next morning was Sunday, September 16. The residents of Dolores, as well as many families from the surrounding countryside, would converge early in the morning for Mass and the weekly market that followed. Hidalgo resolved to call the assembled multitude to insurrection. He proclaimed his opposition to European Spaniards and to the French rulers of Spain, while proclaiming loyalty to Ferdinand VII, then held captive in France. He said nothing about the actual Spanish imperial regime based in Seville, opposed to France and ruling in Mexico via the victors in the coup of 1808. Avoiding such complex details, Hidalgo proclaimed his readiness to lead an insurrection demanding more local autonomy in Mexico, while sustaining traditional loyalty to the Spanish monarch. He uttered not a word of independence at the beginning. Instead, the priest called for insurrection in support of a Spanish king deposed by alien, perhaps godless, Frenchmen. Could a rebellion appear more legitimate? By noon of that first day, Hidalgo had recruited numerous rebels around Dolores, variously estimated from several hundred to a few thousand.[40]

The insurgents headed south toward San Miguel that afternoon. Large numbers of rural people joined as the rebels passed. At the settlement of Atotonilco, Hidalgo acquired a banner devoted to the Virgin of Guadalupe. The rebel priest quickly added that religious symbol of Mexican nationalism to the ideological apparatus of his insurrection. The image of national unity and religious legitimacy was enhanced by the symbolic place of honor afforded the Virgin early on. The insurgent leader began by skillfully using the symbols of monarchy and religion to suggest that the revolt aimed only to preserve the traditional core of colonial Mexican life.

Arriving in San Miguel on the evening of the sixteenth, the insurgents quickly claimed control. The local militia was led into the uprising by Lieutenants Allende and Aldama. The commander, Narciso María de la Canal, refused to join. He was also careful not to oppose the rebels. He could only watch while insurgents captured several immigrant Spanish merchants, which rebel leaders supported, and looted several stores, which the leaders opposed but could not stop.[41] The response of the patriarch of the Canal fam-

[40] Alamán, *Historia de Méjico*, I, 242; Hamill, *Hidalgo Revolt*, pp. 118-123; García, *Con el cura Hidalgo*, pp. 36, 40-42, 44-45.

[41] Hamill, *Hidalgo Revolt*, pp. 123-124, 132-134; Alamán, *Historia de Méjico*, I, 246; García, *Con el cura Hidalgo*, pp. 45-46, 50-53.

ily presaged the reaction of most established elites across the Bajío. When first faced with the insurrection, they had no forces to use in opposition, and thus they prudently offered no resistance. But with substantial property interests to defend, they would not join the uprising.

After a few days at San Miguel, the insurgent forces, which had grown to 6,000, headed south toward Celaya—in the heartland of the Bajío plain. Negotiations for a peaceful capitulation failed, and the rebels soon entered, looted, and captured the town. Once again, established elites stood back. They could not fight the rebels, but they also refused to support or collaborate with them. Their apprehension turned to horror as Hidalgo assembled a rebel mass of nearly 25,000 by September 23, shortly after capturing Celaya.[42]

In less than two weeks, Hidalgo had recruited thousands of rebels and now controlled a wide swath of the Bajío from the uplands near Dolores to the rich bottomlands around Celaya. The agrarian families there had endured years of worsening poverty and deepening insecurities. The past two years of famine had aggravated those problems and made their social origins clear. The call to arms by a prominent local clergyman, seconded by several young local leaders, created an appearance of divided elites. And the rebel leaders' emphasis of loyalty to the monarchy and homage to the Virgin of Guadalupe suggested a movement of traditional legitimacy—an insurrection whose goal was to return Mexico to better times recently lost. The people of the eastern Bajío and the northeast uplands responded by joining in large numbers.

One final factor was crucial to the origins of this first of many regional agrarian uprisings in nineteenth-century Mexico. After two years of severe drought and food shortages, the summer of 1810 brought ample rains. By the mid-

[42] Hamill, *Hidalgo Revolt*, p. 124; Alamán, *Historia de Méjico*, 1, 246; García, *Con el cura Hidalgo*, p. 59.

dle of September there stood in Bajío fields ample supplies of maize—the first good crop in two years.[43] Prevailing practices would leave that crop standing in the fields until December to dry on the stalks. But it was mature and edible in September when the insurrection began. Hidalgo and the Querétaro conspirators had first scheduled their uprising for December, when the regional harvest would be nearly completed. Because they had expected to recruit landed elites to the uprisings, they decided to await the completion of estate harvests before beginning the movement. When they failed to elicit elite support and turned toward the masses, early autumn became an ideal time to rebel. The crops that would stand in the field during the next three months would provide essential sustenance for the insurgents—and the rebels proved eager to claim those crops as the movement swept across the region. Many years of grievances were brought to a peak by two years of famine; the ample harvest of 1810 provided the food that made mass insurrection possible.

During the early weeks, it became clear to rebel leaders that they had precipitated an insurrection that was more social and more agrarian than they expected or desired. Hidalgo directed his followers to attack only the estates of immigrant Spaniards. Most insurgents had little use for such niceties of elite birthplace. They sacked haciendas regardless of ownership to obtain food and livestock, and to recruit new rebels. The insurgents were asserting their vengeance against the landed elites who ruled the agrarian structure that had brought them worsening poverty and painful insecurities in recent years.[44]

By the time Celaya was captured, Hidalgo was at the head of a massive insurrection deeply rooted in the agrarian population of the Bajío. From Celaya, it was essential to capture

[43] Alamán, *Historia de Méjico*, I, 246.

[44] Ibid.; JSE, vol. 214, no. 121, 10 Oct. 1810; no. 122, 18 Nov. 1810; no. 127, 3 Feb. 1811; no. 130, 4 May 1811; no. 131, 2 Dec. 1811.

one of the two pivotal urban centers that dominated the region politically and economically. The insurgents had to decide whether to turn east to the commercial and textile center of Querétaro or west to the mining city of Guanajuato. The recent difficulties of the textile industry probably left many workers at Querétaro favorably inclined toward the insurrection. But the rebel leaders knew that their conspiracy was foiled there, and that authorities were already mobilizing the local militia. Hidalgo thus decided to turn away from that commercial city and to focus the insurrection next on Guanajuato.[45]

Marching from Celaya to Guanajuato, the insurgents passed through the agrarian heartland of the Bajío basin. Rebels joined in large numbers every day. Most came armed only with their machetes.[46] It was a large, undisciplined, angry, and undefeated insurgent mass that approached Guanajuato in late September, intent on capturing the richest prize in the Spanish empire.

Lying in rugged mountains just north of the Bajío plain, Guanajuato would be difficult to defend and almost impossible to reinforce. Its capture would prove the insurrection a threat to colonial prosperity, if not to the colonial regime. After all, Guanajuato's silver had made Mexico the richest of New World colonies during the eighteenth century. Its capture would strike at the core of the colonial economy.

The people of Guanajuato responded to the insurgents just as had the residents of San Miguel and Celaya. Among the wealthy, only two marginal elites, both Creoles, joined the rebels.[47] The poorer majority, including many mine workers, however, received the insurgents more favorably. Despairing of support from the local populace, the Intendant Juan Antonio de Riaño led colonial officials, local elites, and the small militia unit into the massive municipal gran-

45 García, *Con el cura Hidalgo*, pp. 51-52, 58.
46 Ibid., pp. 58, 64.
47 Brading, *Miners and Merchants*, p. 344.

ary—the *alhóndiga*. With ample food supplies, the Guanajuato elite hoped to hold out for weeks. Assisted by the retreat of the elites, Hidalgo quickly gained massive support.
The manager of the Valenciana mine, facing economic decline, organized several thousand rebel mine workers,
many of whom had recently faced unemployment and famine simultaneously. Thus reinforced with local rebels, the
insurgents assaulted the granary on September 28. The expected long siege became a short, murderous rout. About
300 of those inside the granary, along with other Spaniards
in the city, were killed. Widespread looting followed.[48] Guanajuato was captured and Hidalgo recruited even more urban rebels. During the next two weeks, rebel numbers approached 60,000.[49]

In less than a month, the insurgents had taken over all of
the Bajío except for the eastern areas around Querétaro.
Tens of thousands of rebels were mobilized. And they had
yet to face significant opposition. Such developments had
no precedent in central Mexico in the centuries since the
Spanish conquest.

The causes of the insurrection that began the era of
agrarian violence in Mexico are complex. Most fundamental was the agrarian transformation that forced rural families in the Bajío, long accustomed to lives of secure dependence, to suddenly face worsening poverty, new insecurities,
and recurring years of famine. The grievances caused by
these agrarian developments were heightened by the later
crises in the region's textile and mining industries. The difficulties plaguing textile workers were especially important
because they struck not only urban workers, but many
agrarian families in which women had turned to spinning as
a means to supplement declining support from agriculture.
The political debates that began in 1808 were important because they created the appearance of a deeply divided elite,

[48] Hamill, *Hidalgo Revolt*, pp. 139-140.
[49] Ibid., p. 124.

and because they produced a small core of insurgent leaders among frustrated, marginal elites. Finally, the drought and famine of 1809 and 1810 pushed agrarian grievances to a peak, deepened the crises of textile and silver production, and focused mounting discontent on regional elites—many of whom profited while the poor faced starvation.

This explanation of insurrection, emphasizing the worsening poverty and most especially the insecurity among the dependent agrarian population of the Bajío, should not be stretched to illogical extremes. There is no evidence, for example, that families who suffered most severely from the agrarian or industrial crises were in the forefront of the insurrection. Personal decisions rarely mirror social developments in a simple way. And the evidence presently available does not allow analysis of personal decisions about joining the insurrection.

My argument is social, not personal. It emphasizes that the deepening poverty and insecurity that struck the Bajío poor after 1750 created a social context in which these mounting difficulties became pervasive concerns. They were felt painfully by those directly affected. Yet even among families still favored with permanent employment and good security, satisfaction was surely tempered by the experiences of less fortunate kin, neighbors, and friends. By the early 1800s, none among the Bajío poor knew who would be next to lose a permanent, secure job or to face eviction from a plot of estate land. All knew how suddenly they could face a search for a new means of life—a search that generally meant taking on tenant cultivation of poor lands in the marginal uplands of another estate, while laboring seasonally in irrigated fields. And none among the Bajío poor knew when drought would again trigger famine—but all knew that it would be soon. Such pervasive insecurities of subsistence, but recently forced on the Bajío poor, led thousands to join the Hidalgo revolt in 1810.

The rapid rising of so many rebels during the first month of the revolt brought early success in the Bajío. But the euphoria of early victories masked important signs of weakness within the insurrection. Most important was the emerging isolation of the leaders. They continued to hope that once the rebellion showed strength, at least some of Mexico's elites would join them. The actual result was just the opposite. Elites divided by political squabbles since 1808 quickly discovered their more fundamental class unity when faced with the mass insurrection in the Bajío. The questions of colonial elite autonomy they had so recently debated paled in importance when the defense of elite wealth and power became immediate concerns. The political divisions among Mexican powerholders in 1810 did not provide an opportunity for sustained insurrection. Instead, insurrection was the stimulus that re-established elite solidarity.[50]

The rapid reconstruction of Mexican elite unity in defense of power and privilege was typified by the stance of most of the former Querétaro conspirators. When confronted with the insurrection's violent assaults against the established social structure, Corregidor Domínguez led his fellow conspirators in offering their services against the uprising their plotting had helped to begin. The authorities responded favorably. All but a few minor conspirators from Querétaro were released without penalties and allowed to turn their energies against the revolt. A few Querétaro elites, along with several less-prominent allies, might consider rebellion to achieve greater political autonomy for themselves. They might ponder calling the masses to arms, as long as they believed that those masses would obediently serve elite political interests. But when the realities of insurrection made plain the uprising's inherent threat to elite power, former conspirators quickly joined the majority of elites in their deep loyalty to the colonial regime.[51]

---

[50] Brading, *Miners and Merchants*, pp. 244, 319; Hamill, *Hidalgo Revolt*, p. 170; Anna, *Fall of Royal Government*, p. 65.

[51] Alamán, *Historia de Méjico*, I, 258-259; Hamnett, *Revolución y contrarrevolución*, pp. 152-168.

The few marginal Creole elites who led the insurrection thus failed to gain substantial support among powerful Mexicans, whether born in the colony or in Spain. Rebel leadership arose only among marginal, provincial elites. Estate administrators, mine managers, and others of intermediate social status joined in substantial numbers. Rural clergy were particularly prominent as insurgent leaders.[52] In one fundamental way, estate and mine managers and rural clergy held similar positions in colonial Mexican society. Most were Mexican Creoles who were not wealthy, but enjoyed comforts well beyond those available to the majority. And they lived as favored dependents of powerful elites, whom they served by dealing directly with the Indian, mestizo, and mulatto people who performed the colony's work. These marginal elites were thus pivotal intermediaries between Mexico's dominant families and the subordinate masses. Many were descendants of men who had sought elite status, but failed to attain it. And many had apparently begun to resent being asked to manage the masses for the benefit of more-powerful elites. In their position as pivotal intermediaries, they knew both elite and masses well. Once they developed their own grievances against the colonial regime and the elites they served, they were strategically placed to lead an insurrection.

Yet these marginal elites could not identify with the grievances that drove the angry populace to violence. Later, after facing defeat outside the Bajío, Hidalgo began to address the concerns of the mass of rebels—as he perceived them. He proclaimed the abolition of slavery and called for the end of tributes—the head tax paid yearly by Indian and mulatto men. But slavery was no longer a major part of labor relations in Mexico. Only a few slaves, mostly elderly, remained to be emancipated. And the end of tributes would not begin to resolve the difficulties that had pushed the Bajío masses toward insurrection. The tribute was a long-es-

[52] See Farriss, *Crown and Clergy*, pp. 197-203, 254-265.

tablished head tax that rarely claimed even 7 percent of a poor family's annual earnings. Although its abolition would provide some financial relief, it would do little to correct the problems of declining wages, rising rents, falling crop yields, persistent famines, and mounting evictions that afflicted the agrarian poor in the Bajío. Hidalgo would even later decree that the lands that Indian communities rented out to Spaniards and other outsiders were to be reclaimed for use by community residents. That order perhaps helped to recruit rebels elsewhere in Mexico, but it meant little to Bajío insurgents who had long lived as estate dependents without community land or other rights.[53]

Hidalgo focused his limited social reform proposals on problems directly linked to the colonial regime. He avoided questions about wages, rents, tenant security, food supplies, and other issues closer to the lives of thousands of his followers. Such difficulties could be blamed on the regime only indirectly. They had developed as part of the agrarian transformation engineered by Mexican elites. Early on, while Hidalgo and other leaders still hoped for elite support, the avoidance of such social issues was politically sensible. But long after it became clear that Mexican elites would not join the movement, the rebel priest refrained from raising issues linked to the inequalities and insecurities inherent in the emerging agrarian structure of the Bajío. Hidalgo and his allies among the rebel leaders were only marginal elites, but they retained elite perspectives. They would not propose changes that might threaten the established structure of Mexico's economy and society.

The leaders of the insurrection were trapped in an impasse. They had hoped for substantial support among Mexican elites. But when that failed to develop, they could not turn and identify with the grievances of the poor who had risen en masse. Hidalgo and the other insurgent leaders were marginal elites who retained elite values. By calling the

---

[53] Hamill, *Hidalgo Revolt*, p. 136; Mejía Fernández, *Política agraria*, p. 44.

populace to arms, they alienated established powerholders. Without such elite support, the prospects of achieving political autonomy in Mexico were limited. Yet even after they had precipitated a massive agrarian insurrection, marginal elite leaders could not propose a program of fundamental socio-economic change. Their own elite values and goals precluded that.

The dilemma seemed minor during the early weeks of insurrection, while the rebels enjoyed nearly unopposed success in the Bajío and thousands joined the uprisings without inquiring into the leaders' programs. There was no program of social change. In 1810, there had never been such a program addressed to the Mexican masses. Outraged rebels attacked and looted rural estates and town centers, venting rage without clear ideological concerns.

Meanwhile, the leaders could debate among themselves whether to maintain the pretense of loyalty to Ferdinand VII, or to make an open declaration of independence. They could try with little success to focus insurgent anger on Spanish officials and immigrant merchants. And both leaders and followers among the rebels could agree on a vague hatred of distant but heretical Frenchmen who had captured their king.[54] That veneer of religious nationalism held the insurrection together during the early weeks of unchallenged victories.

But shielded from the view of most insurgents were squabbles among the leaders that were becoming increasingly intense. Hidalgo would not consider a program of truly radical change, but he was ready to proclaim minimal reforms and to allow his followers to avenge grievances through looting. Allende was repulsed. He demanded a more disciplined uprising that would work under his control to attain limited political ends.[55] Given the leaders' primary goal of gaining Mexican autonomy, Allende's argu-

[54] Hamill, *Hidalgo Revolt*, pp. 132-134.
[55] Ibid., pp. 141-143.

ments made good sense. But Hidalgo's inclinations more closely reflected the realities of the insurrection. The revolt had gained its early successes not because of political victories, but thanks to the readiness of thousands of long subordinate residents of the Bajío to use the insurrection to take vengeance against regional elites. If such rebels were held in check by insurgent leaders, why should they participate in the uprising at all? Perhaps a clear program of reforms that addressed the insurgents' grievances might have allowed rebel leaders to exert greater control. But such a program was not offered—and insurrection could be sustained only by allowing a free reign for retaliatory violence.

The early gains of the revolt in the Bajío were startling to long-time observers of colonial social stability in Mexico. But those successes were limited. Only the lower classes had risen in force, led by a minority of disgruntled marginal elites. They quickly dominated the Bajío, but alienated the most powerful elites there and elsewhere in Mexico. An insurrection without the support of at least a major segment of the dominant class was doomed to failure—unless the agrarian masses in many other regions would join a class-based revolt. Then, perhaps, colonial rulers and elites could be swept into submission—or more likely into exile. The response of the rural poor in other Mexican regions remained unknown in October of 1810, just after the capture of Guanajuato. On that response hinged the outcome of the first mass insurrection in modern Mexican history.

# CHAPTER FOUR

# The Limits of Insurrection: Regional Reactions to the Hidalgo Revolt, 1810

An uprising limited to the Bajío poor could not triumph. Following the victory at Guanajuato, Hidalgo led the insurgents southeast toward Mexico City. Capture of that colonial administrative and economic center was essential to the success of the revolt. And control of the capital would hinge on the attitudes and actions of the peasant villagers who populated the highland valleys surrounding Mexico City. If Hidalgo could stimulate insurrection in the central valleys as intense as that in the Bajío, he might capture the colonial capital and perhaps eventually triumph in the face of staunch elite opposition.

But few central highland villagers joined. The insurgents failed to take Mexico City. The demise of the uprising became a matter of time. The Hidalgo revolt collapsed four months after it began, primarily because it failed to stimulate massive insurrection outside the Bajío and adjacent areas. Most central highland villagers refused to rebel. A similar attitude prevailed among most estate residents in regions north of the Bajío such as San Luis Potosí. There, many estate employees remained in the ranks of the militia that would eventually defeat the insurrection. Only in Jalisco, just west of Bajío, did the revolt recruit numerous additional adherents in 1810. The uprisings thus remained isolated among the lower classes in an important, but limited, region of north central Mexico. The opposition of unified elites and the passivity of the agrarian and urban masses across most of Mexico left regionally isolated insur-

gents to face the regime and its militia alone. Such an insurrection could not prevail.

To understand the failure of the Hidalgo revolt, then, it
is not enough to acknowledge the strength and organization of the royalist opposition. It is equally important to understand why the majority of subordinate Mexicans outside
the Bajío and Jalisco chose to remain aloof from the uprising. Comparative analysis of the conditions of agrarian life
in the central highlands and more northerly regions such as
San Luis Potosí, where insurrection was minimal, and in Jalisco, where rebellion was substantial, should help refine
our understanding of the social bases of loyalty and rebellion in 1810—and also help explain the failure of the revolt
begun by Hidalgo with such success in the Bajío.

## The Central Highlands: Loyalist Community Peasants

The response of the peasant villagers in the central valleys
surrounding Mexico City was crucial to the success or failure of the insurrection. The Valley of Mexico, including the
capital, plus the adjacent basins of Cuernavaca to the south,
Toluca to the west, and the Mezquital to the north, have
dominated Mexico for centuries. At least since the rise of
the imperial city of Teotihuacan over a thousand years before the Spanish conquest, every regime that has ruled
Mexico has ruled from these central valleys.[1] The reasons
are evident. From time immemorial to the end of the colonial era and beyond, the central highlands were home to the
more dense populations in Mexico, as well as the site of the
most intense cultivation and the largest urban centers.[2] Indigenous conquerors such as the Aztecs, as well as the Spaniards with Cortés, knew that to rule Mexico they had to con-

[1] See Sanders and Price, *Mesoamerica*.

[2] Humboldt, "Tablas geográficas políticas," pp. 148-149, emphasizes the
concentration of the Mexican population around Mexico in the 1790s.

quer the central valleys. Father Hidalgo and the insurgents from the Bajío faced the same task in 1810.

Marching from the Bajío toward Mexico, the insurgents passed through Michoacán. There they recruited numerous rebels among marginal provincial elites and rancheros, including part of two militia units, one from Valladolid and another from Zitácuaro.[3] But as the insurgents began to enter the regions densely settled by peasant communities, there was no sign of mass rural support. The results were the same as the rebels from the Bajío approached the colonial capital through the valley of Toluca. In the pivotal central highlands, where nearly 90 percent of the rural population were peasant villagers, Hidalgo found only minimal support.[4]

The villagers of central Mexico retained important landholdings and local political rights to the end of the colonial era. Most villagers continued to speak indigenous languages and to live as peasant cultivators, thus remaining far more "Indian" than the rural people who joined Hidalgo in the Bajío. And the vast majority of central highland villagers showed little inclination to join or support the revolt, even when 80,000 rebels camped near their communities late in October of 1810.

The minimal level of insurrection in the central highlands cannot be attributed to either comfortable material conditions or to any lack of recent tensions. The villagers of central Mexico were in most cases at least as poor, and probably poorer, than many of the residents of the Bajío who had flocked to join Hidalgo. William Taylor has shown that during the late eighteenth century, the central highlands experienced a marked increase in local protests, riots, and sporadic violence. Villagers were protesting increasing encroachments against village landholding and political

[3] García, *Con el cura Hidalgo*, p. 79.

[4] Tutino, "Creole Mexico," pp. 348-350; see Appendix C, Tables c.2 and c.3 for the concentration of Indios de Pueblo in the Intendancy of Mexico.

rights. But the majority of the disputes resulted in brief, demonstrative violence and were eventually resolved in the colonial courts.[5] One large and lengthy conflict began in the valley of Toluca in the 1790s. It pitted several villages against the Condes de Santiago, one of the greatest landed families of colonial Mexico. There were several riots, numerous injuries, a few fatalities, and interminable court battles. The conflict remained unresolved in the fall of 1810.[6] Yet Hidalgo recruited few rebels even while his insurgents camped next to the villages involved in that dispute during the days prior to the crucial battle for Mexico City. The villagers of the Toluca valley were even reluctant to provide supplies to the rebels, and many insurgents from the Bajío felt the opposition of the central highland villagers in the shortages of provisions during their brief stay in the Toluca region.[7]

The villagers of central Mexico responded to Hidalgo as communities more than as individuals or families. Most communities reacted in unison under local leaders—and most remained loyal to the regime. The leaders of several villages went so far as to place notices in the *Gazeta de México* proclaiming their loyalty to the colonial order. A few communities threatened to join the insurrection, primarily to gain leverage in old local conflicts. At Amecameca, near Chalco, villagers threatened to join Hidalgo if a long-standing labor dispute was not resolved in their favor. It was settled quickly and the villagers did not rebel. In the rare instances when communities did not act in unity, when villagers defied local leaders, it was usually because local notables were leaning toward joining the uprising, and villagers refused to follow—and then turned in their leaders. There were exceptions, but the vast majority of villagers in

---

[5] Taylor, *Drinking, Homicide, and Rebellion*, pp. 113-151.

[6] Tutino, "Creole Mexico," pp. 348-352.

[7] García, *Con el Cura Hidalgo*, p. 85.

the central highlands refused to join or support the crucial battle for the colonial capital late in October of 1810.[8]

This quiet but staunch loyalty to the colonial regime in the face of Hidalgo's insurrection calls for an explanation. The agrarian social structure of the central highlands was radically different from that of the Bajío. And that distinct agrarian structure, built around corporate peasant communities, sustained more acquiescent attitudes toward the colonial order, which in turn resulted in firm inaction among central highlanders when Hidalgo called for insurrection in 1810.[9]

During the period before the Spanish conquest, millions of Mexican peasants lived scattered across the central highlands, cultivating the soil and paying homage and tributes to the indigenous nobility. After the conquest, Old World diseases plus social disruptions produced a catastrophic decline in the peasant population. In response, after 1550 the colonial regime moved to congregate the surviving peasants in villages. The communities were allotted lands at least minimally sufficient for their residents' subsistence, and local notables were granted limited, but important, rights to local rule.

Meanwhile, much of the land vacated by the combination of depopulation, which reached 90 percent after 1600, and congregation was given by the regime to wealthy and well-connected Spanish colonists who set about building commercial estates. They aimed to produce and sell the food and other products demanded by the growing Hispanic populations of urban centers and mining towns—and thus to generate the profits essential to maintaining lives of elite wealth and power. By 1650, a century of transition had established an enduring colonial agrarian structure in the

[8] Burke, "Peasant Responses," pp. 7-9, 13 (I thank the author for making this essay available to me); see also, Alamán, *Historia de Méjico*, I, 255-256.

[9] The general analysis of agrarian stability in the central highlands reflects the conclusions reached in my dissertation, "Creole Mexico," as well as my continuing work on that pivotal region.    —

central highlands. Elite Spanish families owned estates that controlled the majority of the basins' best lands. Interspersed among the estates, however, were more numerous peasant communities that retained at least minimal lands, local self-government, and the majority of the rural popu-lation.

The colonial regime had favored colonial elites with extensive land grants. But Spanish officials also feared the excessive economic power of those same elites. By providing lands, legal privileges, and a general guarantee of survival to the peasant communities, the colonial authorities showed concern for the Mexican peasantry—while curtailing the power of emerging landed elites. Mexican aristocrats might control vast areas of land in the densely settled central highlands, but they did not rule the peasant population directly. Thus, the population that could provide the workers essential to profitable estate operations remained in the landed communities, subject first to local leaders, and protected by the colonial regime. And that regime retained the power to mediate the relations between the two primary constituents of the central highlands' agrarian structure: estates and peasant villages.

The result was a relationship of symbiotic exploitation. The peasants were exploited. Their villages held lands but minimally sufficient to their subsistence. Given the tradition of unequal distribution of community lands (Mexican peas-ant communities have never been internally egalitarian), lo-cal leaders generally held large shares, leaving many vil-lagers with lands less than adequate to production of a minimal family subsistence. But the vast majority of central highland villagers retained through the colonial era access to lands that allowed most of them to produce a critical part of their subsistence. Meanwhile, most had no option but to also provide seasonal labor for low wages at nearby estates. Given the scarcity of land resources, villagers could not subsist without the work and wages available at the estates. And landed elites could not operate estates profitably without access to the labor services of the villagers. Thus were estates and villagers linked in relations of clear inequality that were essential to the survival of both. Such relations of symbiotic exploitation proved enduring and remarkably stable in the face of mounting social tensions—and even insurrection.

The peasant population of the central highlands began to expand again in the second half of the seventeenth century. By the later eighteenth century, village populations began to press hard against landed resources that could not expand. Internal village inequalities increased. A landless minority appeared in many communities. And most peasants retained landholdings that were becoming progressively less adequate to subsistence production. Peasant autonomy waned—but did not vanish. Villagers had to work more of each year at nearby estates. And tensions mounted, resulting in sporadic violence within families, within communities, between communities, and between communities and estates that increased steadily in the central highlands during the late colonial period.

Yet the entrenched agrarian structure of village autonomy, coupled with the relations of symbiotic exploitation that linked central highland estates and villages, proved able to absorb these growing pressures. Village land became less adequate to peasant subsistence, but the process was slow to develop and resulted most immediately from population growth within an established agrarian structure. No recent actions of elites nor policies of the colonial regime visibly caused the decline of the villagers' autonomy. Meanwhile, nearby estates could increase production of subsistence crops and offer the villagers expanded opportunities for seasonal labor. Given the agrarian structure of the central highlands, village population growth automatically triggered increased estate production, and thus increased incorporation of peasants into the estate economy. Peasant autonomy declined while elite profits rose. But the shift was slow rather than a radical departure from long-prevailing agrarian social relations. The peasants remained residents of their communities; they still cultivated their remaining subsistence plots and lived directly subject to community notables—not landed elites. Thus, while central highland peasants faced a loss of autonomy during the later eighteenth century, they retained an important base of autonomy in food production and local government.

Within that agrarian structure, landed elites did not always appear as the causes of peasant problems. Villagers were, of course, quick to protest against landlords who tried to appropriate community lands or otherwise challenge village prerogatives. But central highland communities often found both monetary and legal assistance from one elite estate owner when village lands were threatened by another. Many estate operators were aware of the importance of community land retention in sustaining a work force that could be employed at the estates seasonally, when the crop cycle demanded numerous hands. Such landlords were eager to help preserve the villagers' base of partial autonomy.[10] More generally, as village population pressures made subsistence lands ever more scarce, the increasing seasonal labor available at nearby estates often appeared to the villagers as a solution, or at least a compensation, more than a problem.

The stabilizing characteristics of the agrarian structure of the central highlands became most evident in times of famine, as recurrent there as elsewhere in Mexico. The great famines of 1785 and 1786 and of 1809 and 1810 struck the central highlanders as well as Bajío residents. But when subsistence crops withered and died in the central highlands, it happened on lands that had long been cultivated by members of the community. The resulting hunger was perceived as an act of God—a subsistence calamity, not a social crisis. The crops were lost because of frost, or drought, or some

---

[10] Tutino, "Creole Mexico," p. 345.

other "natural" cause—not because an estate owner had allowed the villagers to cultivate only marginal lands.

And while lamenting the loss of crops due to the unstable Mexican environment, central highland villagers could turn to nearby estates for work and maize. Estate crops were rarely lost until late in the growing season. Villagers could thus earn some wages during the years that crops failed. Irrigated estate fields rarely lost their crops and thus provided work for the villagers throughout years of crisis. And central highland estates customarily sold maize, if at inflated prices in times of crises, to the villagers they employed. Thus an estate operator could appear as a benefactor to central highland villagers in times of subsistence crisis—even while the elite landlord reaped handsome profits from the villagers' hunger. Herein lay the basic stabilizing effect of the structure of symbiotic exploitation that linked elite landlords and peasant villagers in the central valleys—profiteering appeared as a favor to the poor rather than as the cause of their misery.

Other aspects of the agrarian structure based on peasant villages also worked to deflect discontent away from landed elites and the colonial regime. When famine occurred, as in 1785 and 1786, community notables could organize expeditions to the warmer and wetter low country to the south to obtain maize. Should they encounter obstruction or excess profiteering there, they were experienced in the ways of protesting to colonial officials.[11] In addition, the larger central highland communities included a priest, a royal official or his lieutenant, and often several local traders who were interested in helping villagers through hard times—and in preventing local conflict. Village priests organized local relief efforts, while preaching obedience to the established order.[12] Clerics, officials, and traders all supported villagers' petitions for relief from tributes and other taxes in times of

[11] FCA, pp. 448-449, 482.
[12] FCA, pp. 438-441.

subsistence crises—petitions that were often successful.[13] The colonial regime, along with village priests, officials, and traders, appeared most concerned for the villagers' welfare in times of crisis.

The contrast with the situation of the Bajío estate dependents is marked. There, the agrarian poor faced only the blatant profiteering of landlords, with neither community notables nor local priests, officials, or traders to speak for their survival. In the Bajío, the agrarian structure that left the agrarian poor as direct dependents of elite landlords served to focus discontent onto those who profited while the majority suffered. In the central highlands, the actual suffering was similar, but community notables, along with the local representatives of the colonial church and state as well as petty rural merchants all mediated between elites and the rural poor. As those mediators actively sought to alleviate the hunger of the central highlanders, discontent shifted away from landed elites and the colonial regime.

Thus, when subsistence crises struck the central highlands in the late eighteenth and early nineteenth centuries, great landlords might appear as benefactors of villagers. Their estates, after all, offered wage labor and maize for sale at a time when the villagers' crops had failed. Meanwhile, rural priests, officials, and merchants worked visibly to ameliorate the suffering of community peasants. And should any doubt remain that their suffering resulted from a "natural" calamity, the villagers' attention was drawn to the religious rituals of relief supplication that were organized in central highland communities by priests, local officials, and even estate managers.[14]

It is, of course, easy for the historian to note that the lands held by landed elites limited the villagers' access to resources and lay at the root of their difficulties. But by the

[13] FCA, pp. 715-745.
[14] Tutino, "Creole Mexico," pp. 362-363.

late eighteenth century, the structure of land distribution between estates and villages in the central highlands had been entrenched for nearly two centuries. Late colonial elites had done little to create the prevailing agrarian situation. They had inherited it. They also profited from it. Yet their estates often appeared as benefactors to villagers by offering wage labor and maize for sale when village production failed. No recent transformation of the agrarian structure, such as that engineered by Bajío elites, had struck the central highland villagers in ways that would focus grievances on the most powerful of colonial Mexicans—the great landed families of Mexico City.

The hindsight of the historian also sees easily the self-interest of the rural clerics, officials, and merchants who worked for the survival of the villagers in times of crisis. After all, the villagers paid the fees that supported the rural priest, the taxes that sustained the rural official, and bought the good that brought small profits to the village merchant. That self-interest in the villagers' survival was basic to the social stability of the central highlands. Because priests, officials, and petty traders cared for the survival of the villagers—however selfishly—the villagers did not develop the outrage against the regime and the agrarian structure that might have led them toward insurrection when subsistence crises struck repeatedly in the years before 1810. Instead, they perceived a succession of unfortunate climatic crises which destroyed their crops on village lands, and during which estates offered labor and maize to purchase, and local priests, officials, and traders offered varied assistance. Despair surely plagued the villagers in the worst of crises, but they did not develop acute social greviances against the agrarian structure and the colonial regime. Because they perceived natural disasters, not social crises, few villagers would join the insurrection when it entered their region in 1810.

While villagers formed the great majority of rural residents of the central highlands around 1800, they were not

alone. Most estates there employed a core of permanent
workers as supervisors and for a few skilled and specialized
tasks. They were generally called *sirvientes*, and were primarily mestizos, mulattoes, and even poor Spaniards. They
received monthly wages, a weekly cash supplement, and
weekly maize rations. They thus enjoyed both substantial
pay and ample security. They were also quite mobile. Few
remained estate dependents for life in the central highlands. Instead, most regular estate employees were young
men from ranchero families—the minority of middling
farmers in rural Mexico. They would work as estate dependents for a few years, gaining a regular income plus security, perhaps while they had young children or awaited a
landed inheritance. Most eventually left the estates to operate ranchos, often while also working mule trains to gain
additional income.[15] Such estate dependents who were part
of more independent ranchero families were not apt to oppose the agrarian structure in which they remained a favored minority.

Facing greater difficulties were the estate residents
classed as Indians and generally called *gañanes*. They had
left the villages, more or less permanently, to work for
wages at the estates. Many central highland properties located near large villages employed no gañanes. Estates less
able to count on the seasonal work of villagers might maintain perhaps 25 resident Indian families. They earned daily
wages, generally lower than those paid to villagers who
came only seasonally, and were employed about 30 weeks
each year. The gañanes were not usually allotted maize rations, but they could purchase the staple from the estates at
whatever price the market would bear—the same privilege
afforded the villagers who worked more seasonally for
higher wages.

Gañanes apparently derived from the unfortunate minority of central highland villagers who lacked access to

[15] Ibid., pp. 306-312.

community lands. Those facing such difficulties found the availability of wage labor for just over half of each year, even at low pay, along with the opportunity to buy maize, a minimally viable means of survival. Even in times of famine, most central highland estates maintained stocks of maize to sell to both gañanes and villagers.[16] Gañanes in the valleys of Mexico, Toluca, and the Mezquital were the poorest, most dependent, and most insecure of the rural poor in the central highlands. They seemed good candidates for insurrection. But they formed only a small minority of the regional agrarian population. They were isolated in small groups at estates, surrounded by far more numerous villagers. And the gañanes did retain a limited security in 1810. There is no evidence that they responded in large numbers to Hidalgo's call to arms.

Thus, when tens of thousands of insurgents from the Bajío arrived in the valley of Toluca, the rural poor of the central highlands had just experienced two years of famine—without a sharpening of grievances against landed elites or the colonial regime. Hidalgo's emphasis on attacking the regime could not find great favor among villagers whose landed communities had been created and sustained through centuries by regime support. When villagers had problems, they might protest with brief violent outbursts, but they repeatedly went to the colonial courts for resolutions. And while the communities did not always win, they won or gained acceptable compromise often enough to retain an abiding belief in the legitimacy of colonial justice.[17] Such peasant villagers, retaining substantial subsistence autonomy, symbiotic if exploitative relations with landed elites, and a persistent belief in the efficacy of colonial justice, found little reason to risk life and join Hidalgo. At the same time the minorities of more permanent estate de-

---

[16] Ibid., pp. 312-319; FCA, pp. 466-467.
[17] On colonial justice for Indians, see Borah, *Justice by Insurance*.

pendents in the central highlands retained enough security to blunt any grievances. They too would not rebel.

Thus, when Hidalgo faced the small but determined detachment of 2,500 militiamen sent to protect Mexico City at Monte de las Cruces, in the pass between the valleys of Mexico and Toluca, his forces included almost exclusively the rebels who had arrived with him from the Bajío. The battle pitted a small but trained and well-armed force against an untrained and minimally armed rebel mass—an insurgent crowd that was not supported by the surrounding population of peasant villagers. The battle proved a bloody stalemate. Hidalgo judiciously decided not to advance on the capital.[18] He might have occupied the great city—the largest in the New World. But he would have difficulty holding it for long without the backing of the local population. The rebel priest failed to rally the central highland peasants to his banner—even though that banner proclaimed his devotion to the Virgin of Guadalupe. Devotion to the Mexican Virgin and opposition to Spaniards and Frenchmen would not raise insurrection among agrarian people who had not developed acute social grievances. After the unsuccessful battle just west of Mexico City, Hidalgo did proclaim his goal of having the lands rented out by villages returned for use by their residents.[19] That proclamation came too late. When the insurgents turned back toward the Bajío, Hidalgo's movement was clearly in decline, if not yet defeated.

## San Luis Potosí: Royalist Militiamen and Rebel Villagers

Having failed to raise revolt among the central highland villagers and having failed to take the colonial capital, early in November Hidalgo led his remaining followers in retreat toward the Bajío. Defeat and demoralization reduced the

[18] Hamill, *Hidalgo Revolt*, pp. 126, 149-150.
[19] Mejía, *Política agraria*, p. 44.

insurgents to an estimated 40,000. Their line of march suggests the goal of taking Querétaro and thus consolidating rebel control over the Bajío. But before the insurgents could reach that pivotal commercial center, they were intercepted by royalist forces at Aculco. On November 7, the Intendant of Puebla, Manuel de Flon, and General Felix Callega led 7,000 trained militiamen against the rebels. The insurgents suffered a deadly defeat.[20]

By all accounts, the core of the forces that defeated Hidalgo at Aculco, and would continue to dog him elsewhere, were militiamen from San Luis Potosí.[21] That militia was composed primarily of estate residents from the more arid region just north of the Bajío, led by estate administrators, and trained by General Calleja. Why did the estate dependents of San Luis Potosí choose not to rebel and to remain in the ranks of the royalist militia that was most responsible for crushing the insurrection?

Large estates predominated in the agrarian structure of San Luis Potosí, as they did in the Bajío. In the dry, northerly regions of large grazing properties, over 70 percent of the rural population lived as estate residents.[22] But while Bajío estate dependents had suffered the agrarian transformation that forced them to endure worsening poverty and insecurity, those in San Luis Potosí and other northerly regions generally retained permanent employment, guaranteed maize rations, and thus the security basic to social stability.

With vast, semiarid open spaces and few towns, northern Mexico was dominated by great estates. Most rural families depended on estates for all aspects of life—subsistence, social relations, religion, etc. Their material survival depended on a system of annual provisioning (*avíos*). Once

---

[20] Hamill, *Hidalgo Revolt*, pp. 178-180.

[21] García, *Con el cura Hidalgo*, p. 78, provides the insurgents' perspective; for a view from San Luis Potosí, see Barragán, "La provincia," pp. 320-321.

[22] For estate life in San Luis Potosí, see Tutino, "Life and Labor."

each year, the estate owner assembled a shipment of cloth, shoes, hats, and assorted other goods for his northern estates. The goods were distributed among estate residents as partial payment for their work during the year to come. In the course of the year, the workers were allotted weekly maize rations and they obtained other foods on account from the estate. The management also paid their tributes and ecclesiastical fees and charged them to their continuing accounts. At the end of each year, the residents' work was accounted against the goods and payments they had obtained. Most found that they had received a bit more than their work would allot, leaving small debts of from 5 to 10 pesos.[23]

Such estate residents were especially dependent—and exceptionally secure. The estates provided all their material necessities, often in advance of the performance of the year's work. The persistence of modest debts indicates payments beyond wage levels. Yet the substantial annual movement of workers between estates reveals important mobility among estate dependents in the dry regions north of the Bajío. Such agrarian conditions appear as favorable for workers as was possible in a structure dominated by estate dependence.

The exceptional security, and the ample mobility retained by the estate residents of San Luis Potosí, resulted from two conditions that were distinct from those in the Bajío—where estate dependence also predominated, but security was vanishing around 1800. First, San Luis Potosí, Zacatecas, and other northerly regions were more arid and thus were devoted more to stock grazing than to crop cultivation. These were the regions that expanded stock raising as herds were displaced from the Bajío during the eighteenth century. Herding, however, required much less labor

---

[23] See ibid. and Velázquez, *Cuentas de sirvientes*. The latter publishes and comments upon a set of extremely revealing estate accounts.

than crop production—and it required that labor year-round. Thus, northern estates generally offered more permanent and less seasonal employment than those in the Bajío.

Second, the regions north of the Bajío remained sparsely settled. Alexander von Humboldt calculated that around 1800, the Intendancy of Guanajuato, including most of the Bajío, had 1,093 inhabitants per square league (1 league equals 5,573 meters). At the same time, the province of San Luis Potosí had only 303 persons per square league—and it was the most densely settled area of northern Mexico.[24] Such sparse populations persisted north of the Bajío, despite exceptionally rapid increases in the late eighteenth century.[25] The late colonial period brought much migration into San Luis Potosí and other northerly regions, as the mines boomed at Zacatecas, Catorce, and elsewhere. The growth of mining also rapidly increased the demand for estate produce in the north, while grazing estates there became the primary suppliers of wool to the Bajío, and of mutton, leather, and other livestock products to Mexico City and much of the central highlands.

The growing demand for northern estate products and the sparse northern populations maintained a situation of continued labor scarcities—a situation favorable to estate residents. Around 1800, there were attempts to reduce the earnings of some estate employees in San Luis Potosí. But the attempts were only partly successful and fell short of undermining the basic security of families of estate dependents.[26] And into the decade after 1800, should financial or transportation problems delay the arrival of the annual shipment of provisions to a northern estate, or should provisions arrive that did not meet the residents' expectations, the estate quickly faced a shortage of workers.[27]

[24] Humboldt, "Tablas geográficas políticas," pp. 146-148.
[25] Tutino, "Life and Labor," p. 343.
[26] Ibid., pp. 364-365.
[27] Ibid., pp. 345-355.

Regions such as San Luis Potosí did experience agrarian changes during the late eighteenth century, but those changes reinforced the prevailing social relations of secure dependence. Much of the change in northerly areas was in response to changes in the Bajío. The expansion of stock grazing in the north reflected the completion of the shift to cultivation in the Bajío and led to a demand for growing numbers of cowboys, shepherds, and goatherds who obtained year-round employment with good security at northern grazing estates.

After the failure of the Bajío to sustain its own population in the famine of 1785 and 1786, northerly regions could no longer rely on obtaining reserve grains there. Thus, there followed a movement to increase cultivation in San Luis Potosí and elsewhere in the north. In 1783, the estate named San Agustín de los Amoles, located near Guadalcázar in San Luis Potosí, and its related properties employed 120 dependents but rented lands to only 12 tenants. By 1804, the same estate employed at least 250 residents, while renting lands to 59 tenants. Similar developments occurred at the estate called San Ignacio del Buey, situated near Villa de Valles in the more easterly regions of San Luis Potosí. This was an area of warmer and wetter lowlands that increasingly raised crops for northern Mexico as the Bajío failed in that role. And at San Ignacio del Buey, the 75 employees and 49 tenants of 1783 increased to 150 employees and 89 tenants by 1804. Between 1803 and 1804 alone, the Amoles estate hired 20 new employees classed as *labradores*—men employed year round and receiving maize rations to cultivate estate crops. The number of employees caring for livestock held steady. And there was a parallel increase in the number of permanent employees raising crops at the Buey estate in the same years.[28]

[28] The figures for 1783 derived from ibid., pp. 359, 367; those for 1803 and 1804 are my calculations from materials in Velázquez, *Cuentas de sirvientes*. Totals for 1803 are scattered throughout the work; additions for 1804 are on pp. 133-139.

The expansion of crop production at these estates in San Luis Potosí did not undermine the prevailing social relations of dependence compensated by security. Crop cultivation might demand only seasonal workers, but the labor scarcities in the north forced estate operators there to continue to offer permanent employment along with maize rations to those they hired for field work. The contrast with the recent shift to tenancies and widening insecurities in the Bajío is clear.

The security of northern estate residents became most evident when drought struck—an occurrence more common there than in the Bajío and other regions farther south. When the famine of 1785 and 1786 hit the arid north, maize became as scarce and expensive as elsewhere in Mexico. But the residents of northern estates could shift to consuming more meat, thanks to the presence of large herds of livestock that could neither survive nor be moved due to the parched conditions.[29]

The agrarian social structure of the region provided another buffer against the effects of the drought. Like the estate dependents of the Bajío, those in the north lacked the community leaders, village priests, rural officials, and petty merchants who might organize relief and petition for tax exemptions. But the estate dependents of the arid north had more powerful allies. The great landlords of the region worked actively to cushion the impact of scarcities on their rural dependents. In the autumn of 1785, at the onset of the great famine, a suit was begun by the Conde de Medina y Torres, one of the wealthiest landlords in the colony with multiple estates around Zacatecas and San Luis Potosí. He was supported by other powerful men, including the Marqués de Rivascacho and Antonio de Bassoco. The latter was perhaps the wealthiest merchant of late colonial Mexico. He owned no estates, but depended on properties around San Luis Potosí to supply meat to Mexico City, a business he con-

[29] FCA, p. 155.

trolled through a monopoly (*abasto*) contract. The suit lamented the preferences given urban populations over the rural poor in the allocation of relief supplies of maize. It emphasized the dependence of all urban activities as well as silver mining on the sustenance produced by the agrarian poor. The specific request was for permission to extract maize from the Bajío and elsewhere to provide rations for estate dependents around Zacatecas and San Luis Potosí.[30]

Such solicitation by the most powerful elites for the wellbeing of estate dependents was not heard in the Bajío in the late colonial period. But the labor scarcities in the more arid regions to the north forced elites to maintain the security of their dependents. Great landlords and merchants thus worked at the highest levels in the colonial government to obtain the maize necessary to provide sustenance for estate residents around San Luis Potosí. They imported maize into the region during the great famine of 1785 and 1786, during the local scarcities of 1804, and again during the famine of 1809 and 1810.[31]

When Hidalgo called for insurrection in September of 1810, the estate residents in the dry regions north of Dolores showed little inclination to join. For them, the years of scarcity just ending were reminders of the security they gained by living as estate dependents. Given that security, estate residents in San Luis Potosí were not only opposed to the insurrection—they were ready to fight in their militia units to defend the colonial regime and the agrarian society in which they lived. Among estate dependents, security made the critical difference.

And it was because of this security that the residents of the Bocas estate near San Luis Potosí followed their administrator, Captain Juan Nepomuceno Oviedo, into battle against Hidalgo's rebels. Oviedo had managed those vast

[30] FCA, pp. 111-136.
[31] Velázquez, *Cuentas de sirvientes*, p. 141; JSE, vol. 214, no. 108, 24 Nov. 1809; no. 113, 5 Jan. 1810; vol. 215, no. 170, 25 Jan. 1810; vol. 214, no. 118, 14 July 1810.

grazing estates for years, and his militia unit was recruited primarily among his dependents at Bocas and those at other estates nearby. They became famous as the feared Tamarindos, allowing Oviedo to attain the rank of Colonel, before he died a royalist martyr at the siege of Cuautla.[32] His fame rested ultimately on his ability to mobilize the secure estate dependents of San Luis Potosí to defend the colonial order.

The loyalty of the estate residents of San Luis Potosí, the majority of rural families there, was basic to the defeat of the Hidalgo revolt. Others in the region, however, were more sympathetic to the insurrection and took up arms when an opportunity appeared. In the city of San Luis Potosí, the provincial capital, a group of disaffected provincial elites wisely waited until Calleja's militia had marched south to face Hidalgo before they rose and took over the city early in November of 1810.[33] Why might the leading citizens of this provincial city of only 11,000 inhabitants join the insurrection?[34] A memorial written to the restored King Ferdinand VII in 1814 by a local representative is suggestive.

The disaffected were provincial leaders in a region dominated by vast estates, generally owned by more powerful elites from Mexico City or the Bajío. Ecclesiastically, their province was divided between the Archbishopric of Mexico and the Bishopric of Michoacán, both based far to the south. Commercially, what little trade was not controlled by the region's great landlords was ruled by the great merchants of Mexico City. The mining and estate economies of San Luis Potosí expanded rapidly during the late colonial era, but provincial elites gained little. They remained locally prominent, but dependent and marginal elites in the larger colonial order.

They thus worked to establish a local bishopric, to allow

[32] Alamán, *Historia de Méjico*, II, 320; Bazant, *Cinco haciendas*, p. 175.
[33] Alamán, *Historia de Méjico*, II, 21-23.
[34] Humboldt, "Tablas geográficas políticas," p. 155.

church affairs to be organized locally. They sought the opening of a port along the northern Gulf coast, preferably at Soto la Marina. Such reforms would help break the province's dependence on powerful outsiders. But the most radical reforms proposed by local leaders from San Luis Potosí aimed to break the stranglehold the elites of Mexico City and the Bajío had on the agrarian economy and society of the region. The memorial proposed that estate lands be distributed among estate residents in emphyteusis—an arrangement that would give cultivators permanent rights of use in exchange for an annual fee to the landlord. In theory, estate owners would lose no wealth, but they would lose control of much of estate production. In addition, there would be an increase in the number of relatively independent small farmers and grazers—rancheros. One result would be an expansion of provincial commerce, surely benefitting the provincial leaders behind the proposal.[35]

With such grievances and goals, the rebellion of a few provincial elites at San Luis Potosí is understandable. They sought greater regional independence. They knew, however, that they could not expect support from the agrarian majority of estate dependents. They also knew that they could not confront Calleja's militia. But their revolt did find support in the nearby Indian community of San Miguel Mezquitic.

Landed communities included only 30 percent of the agrarian population of San Luis Potosí around 1800.[36] Most villages in these northern regions were founded by the Spanish late in the sixteenth century, when colonists were brought in from Tlaxcala and other more southerly regions. They were expected to serve as buffers against the warrior nomads still in the north. To attract and hold the native colonists, these new northern communities received extensive land grants and enjoyed local political independ-

---

[35] Barragán, "La provincia," pp. 319-353.
[36] See Appendix C, Table c.2.

ence. By the eighteenth century, most of these transplanted communities still retained large areas of land. They were not closely linked to the agrarian economy focused on the great estates, although some communities did provide organized work gangs during a few weeks of each year. The Indians of Venado, in northern San Luis Potosí, specialized in shearing sheep and moved from estate to estate during the shearing season, obtaining both wages and food rations for their efforts.[37] But overall, estates obtained nearly all their labor from their resident dependents. Northern villagers provided only a small supplement.

During most of the colonial era, estates and communities in San Luis Potosí coexisted easily. They often shared their less fertile resources: villagers were allowed to use the maguey, nopal, and tuna cactus on estate lands and estate livestock might graze on village pastures. But in the eighteenth century, as the economic pace of the region quickened, disputes over resources became more common. More-established elites generally worked to maintain good relations with villagers near their estates, but newcomers to estate operations began to seek advantages by denying villagers customary benefits. The new owner of the Hacienda Gogorrón, Juan Antonio de Jauregui y Villanueva of Querétaro, denied the villagers of Valle de San Francisco all access to estate lands. He began to demand fees for what had customarily been free use. And he imposed his demands in 1786, amidst the depths of famine. The local priest backed the villagers and the courts ordered open access to the estate's uplands.[38]

The conflict that developed at San Miguel Mezquitic was more complex and less easily resolved. Throughout most of the colonial era, the community had faced few economic problems. Village landholdings substantially exceeded the

[37] Velázquez, *Cuentas de sirvientes*, p. 140; Tutino, "Life and Labor," p. 365.

[38] FCA, pp. 342-347.

subsistence needs of its population.[39] Community leaders, with the encouragement of colonial authorities, had let out lands to the adjacent Jesuit estate called La Parada. This was not a sale, but a delegation of rights of use in exchange for a yearly fee—a *censo*.[40] That cession of town lands produced an enduring dispute, as the estate owners claimed property rights, while the villagers insisted on their original claims. The courts were kept busy. Such disputes were endemic to colonial Mexico; they cannot explain insurrections.

By the late eighteenth century, Mezquitic had nearly 10,000 inhabitants, almost as many as the provincial capital. In the 1780s, one José Ygnacio Lozano became parish priest. During the 1790s, he began a program of economic development in Mezquitic, much like that led by Hidalgo at Dolores. The cleric perceived a community with substantial resources that were underutilized. Extensive lands produced little more than subsistence for the villagers. Lozano saw opportunities for profit. He began to offer community lands for cash rents to the highest bidders. A few favored village leaders obtained large plots, but most of the rentals went to outsiders from the city of San Luis Potosí. The priest took over lands on which he planted 100 fanegas of maize, often harvesting over 6,000 fanegas. He boasted that his harvests were better than those at any hacienda. He built new dams and expanded local irrigation. But the water primarily went to the fields of the new renters, not those cultivated by poorer villagers. The priest also boasted that where once there were only 6 looms, now there were 100. When textile markets were strong (an irregular occurrence after 1785), over 400 residents of Mezquitic participated in the expanded industry. Lozano also helped develop substantial rope production in Mezquitic, using fibers from the large stands of maguey cactus on town lands. By the early

[39] AGN, Tierras, vol. 1,385, exp. 7, 1807.
[40] Bazant, *Cinco haciendas*, pp. 10-16.

1800s, the community of Mezquitic and the priest Lozano appeared to be enjoying a new commercial success.

Lozano consolidated his power in the community by favoring one group of residents with land rentals. He worked to insure his allies' control of local government. But the priest's combination of economic success and political power also created a faction vehemently opposed to him. Its members used access to the colonial courts to accuse the cleric of improperly alienating town lands, improperly controlling local elections, and most grievously, of refusing to allow the defense of community resources against the encroachments by several nearby estates. The cleric's opponents claimed that he acted in collusion with the new owner of La Parada who had bought the estate after the expulsion of the Jesuits and now claimed ownership of the lands earlier ceded by Mezquitic.

The dispute split the community deeply. The priest's opponents accused him not only of violating community rights, but also of living licentiously while neglecting his religious duties. They claimed that he profited by running a store that primarily sold liquor to local residents. He replied that all his actions aimed only to benefit the community—and that his detractors were no more than a gang of insubordinate drunkards. The truth cannot be ascertained in testimony filled with such invective. That nearly all the witnesses supporting the priest were merchants and officials from San Luis Potosí and the managers of nearby estates suggests that there was some truth in the claims of those who opposed the cleric's power.

The cura of Mezquitic had a vision of community development. He believed that the town's vast resources would be used more profitably in the hands of local leaders, merchants from San Luis Potosí, and himself. But shifting the town's land to more profitable uses also forced many residents long sustained by subsistence production to seek other means of support. Many would have to labor for major tenant cultivators, or for Lozano. Many would spend increased time making firewood, charcoal, and pulque for sale locally and in San Luis Potosí. Many would have to work in the expanded textile production. And many would work in the new rope works the priest had developed. In little more than a decade, Lozano had engineered a rapid shift in the economy of Mezquitic from peasant subsistence activities to primarily commercial production. Many residents began to face insecure dependence on wage labor and the commercial economy.

That transformation divided the community. Some residents gained from the changes. Local leaders backed by Lozano held large areas of land, and they controlled a town treasury newly filled with the income of land rentals. Several textile makers and rope workers found their new activities profitable enough to place them squarely in the priest's group of supporters. But another group had lost community leadership. And many others had lost access to community lands. They became increasingly irate. Eventually, they went to Mexico City and hired an attorney to press their suit. But the High Court favored the priest's vision of community development. The judges saw the protestors as mere troublemakers, jailing them for a time in the capital in 1807. Nothing was resolved locally, tempers remained short, and the land disputes with nearby estates as well as the internal political fights festered until the news of Hidalgo's insurrection arrived in 1810.[41]

Like other agrarian people with grievances, the villagers of Mezquitic awaited an opportunity to rebel. They waited until Calleja and the militia left the region, and until local rebels took over the city of San Luis Potosí. Then, in November of 1810, the faction at Mezquitic that had fought the priest Lozano proclaimed allegiance to Hidalgo, forced existing local leaders out, and took over the lands disputed

[41] This dispute is reconstructed from testimony in AGN, Tierras, vol. 1,335, exp. 6, fols. 1-6, 1802; vol. 1,363, exp. 1, fols. 1-48, 1805-1807; vol. 1,385, exp. 7, fols. 1-15, 1807; vol. 1,402, exp. 2, fols. 1-151, 1806-1809.

with nearby estates. The rebels controlled Mezquitic until March of 1811 when part of the local militia returned—a detachment under the command of the manager of La Parada. The rebels were subdued, the leaders ousted by the uprising were returned to office, and disputed lands returned to estate control. Old local officials, back in power, claimed that the rebels were but a small minority, now all dead or departed. They hoped that the community would not be punished for its months of insubordination.[42]

As institutions, the village communities of San Luis Potosí differed little from those in the central highlands. But their roles in the provincial agrarian structures were very different. While central highland villages provided the mass of seasonal labor essential to estate operations there, in San Luis Potosí estates relied overwhelmingly on resident workers. Thus, villagers in such northerly regions faced less direct exploitation by landed elites—and less symbiotic ties with landed estates. As a result, San Luis Potosí elites had less incentive to preserve the landed autonomy of villages. In times of economic expansion, it was easy for them to covet community lands. The result at Mezquitic was an assault on community autonomy led by the local priest in alliance with local merchants and the owners of nearby estates. And that attack on community autonomy generated the grievances behind the village revolt in support of Hidalgo in 1810. But that revolt was a marginal event in a region dominated by great estates—whose residents remained loyal militiamen, thanks to their retention of a critical base of security.

## JALISCO: SECOND HOME OF INSURRECTION

The loyal militia of San Luis Potosí defeated Hidalgo's insurgents at Aculco, a defeat that prevented the rebels from reclaiming their base in the eastern Bajío. Following quickly

[42] AGN, Tierras, vol. 1,412, exp. 4, fols. 1-11, 1813.

upon the bloody stalemate at Monte de los Cruces, the defeat at Aculco disheartened many insurgents, who quietly left for home.[43] The remnants of the rebel forces turned west. Allende took one group to Guanajuato. Hidalgo led the others through Valladolid and eventually to Guadalajara.

Allende failed to hold Guanajuato. At the end of November, Calleja and the San Luis Potosí militia began the second siege of that mining city in less than a month. Allende escaped, but the royalists reclaimed the city and publicly executed more than 50 people accused of complicity with the rebels. This was exemplary justice, intended to discourage future thoughts of insubordination. Calleja even arrested Narciso María de la Canal, the Creole patriarch of San Miguel. He was imprisoned for the crime of not opposing the insurgents, and soon died in a Querétaro jail. Others arrested were marginal elites, mostly clerics, suspected of sympathizing with the rebels. Following two bloody waves of battles and persecutions, the once rich mining city approached ruin. One day early in December, a caravan of eighteen carriages took an equal number of wealthy families out of the city toward refuge in Querétaro. Guanajuato was again held by royalists. But the battles provoked there by the Hidalgo revolt hastened the demise of a city already facing the economic decline of its mines.[44]

Unable to hold Guanajuato, the main insurgent forces were expelled from their home base in the Bajío. But the insurrection found new life among thousands of recruits in Jalisco, to the west. Earlier in the insurrection, as Hidalgo led the main force toward Mexico City, a rebel band led by José Antonio Torres, a Bajío estate administrator, marched toward Guadalajara, the urban center of Jalisco and the capital of all of northwestern Mexico, known as New Galicia

[43] JSE, vol. 214, no. 122, 18 Nov. 1810.
[44] Alamán, *Historia de Méjico*, II, 34-48; JSE, vol. 214, no. 125, 11 Dec. 1810.

in the colonial era. Passing through a region of peasant towns and villages around Zacoalco, south of Guadalajara, Torres found substantial local support. The Creole elites of Guadalajara, like their peers elsewhere, remained loyal to the regime and sent their militia to face the insurgents outside Zacoalco. But the rebels, bolstered by local agrarian support, defeated the militia, killing over 250 loyalists on November 4, 1810. That victory allowed Torres to recruit additional support in rural central Jalisco and to capture the city of Guadalajara.[45]

When Hidalgo, Allende, and the original Bajío rebels faced defeat and expulsion from their home territory, Jalisco appeared a safe haven. By late December, the consolidation of insurgent forces at Guadalajara brought rebel numbers to about 40,000. And by mid-January, continuing recruitment returned rebel strength to its earlier peak level of about 80,000.[46] Central Jalisco proved the only region outside the Bajío where the Hidalgo revolt elicited mass agrarian support. Having suggested explanations for the mass insurrection in the Bajío, for the passivity of most central highland villagers, for the loyalty of most estate dependents in San Luis Potosí, and for the rebellion of one group of villagers there, I will now analyze the social bases of insurrection among the villagers of central Jalisco.

The agrarian structure of the countryside around Guadalajara was most complex. Large numbers of villagers lived near large numbers of estate dependents—with neither way of agrarian life singularly predominant. Thanks to a comprehensive analysis of the estate economy in the eighteenth century by Eric Van Young,[47] and a detailed study of the role of villagers in the insurrections of 1810 by William Taylor,[48] the agrarian origins of rural conflict in central Jalisco can be incorporated into this comparative inquiry.

[45] Hamill, *Hidalgo Revolt*, pp. 197-198; Taylor, "Rural Unrest," p. 15.
[46] Hamill, *Hidalgo Revolt*, pp. 197-198.
[47] Van Young, *Hacienda and Market*.
[48] Taylor, "Rural Unrest."

Throughout most of the early colonial era, the city of Guadalajara remained small. The surrounding rural regions were sparsely populated and little incorporated into the commercial economy. This was a region settled by sedentary peasants before the conquest, but they were few in number when compared with the dense peasant population of the central highlands. With few Indian peasants to rule and no valuable mines to develop, central Jalisco was slow to attract Spanish colonists. Although the capital of New Galicia and thus seat of a high court, Guadalajara developed slowly as an urban center.

With but modest populations of peasants and Spaniards, and with ample agricultural resources, the commercial estate economy was limited before the eighteenth century. Estates in central Jalisco found only weak markets for grain and few workers available for estate labor. During the seventeenth century, then, many estates emphasized stock grazing, for it required few laborers. To create a work force for at least limited estate cultivation, the labor draft known as the *repartimiento* continued in Jalisco into the eighteenth century—a century longer than such forced work systems endured in the more densely settled central highlands.[49] The persistence of the labor draft around Guadalajara reflected the retention of ample lands by most villagers there. Throughout most of the colonial era, most villagers in central Jalisco lived by raising crops on village lands and engaging in craft production. With such substantial subsistence autonomy, along with active involvement in local and regional markets, most Jalisco villagers would labor at estates only when the state forced them—and then they obtained both wages and food rations for their services.

A transformation that accelerated in the middle of the eighteenth century, however, brought rapid deterioration to the lives of many Jalisco villagers. In many economic aspects that transformation paralleled the changes occurring

---

[49] Van Young, *Hacienda and Market*, pp. 216-219, 238-245.

simultaneously in the Bajío just to the east. The rural population expanded rapidly, abruptly ending a long era of rural labor scarcities. The urban market of Guadalajara grew even more rapidly. With new markets for estate produce and with labor increasingly available, rural estates became more attractive investments. Elite families with wealth from commerce and mining began to buy estates and invest in improvements such as new or expanded irrigation systems. The landed elite of central Jalisco was thus reinforced and became an increasingly stable landed class.[50]

Increasingly prosperous elites were responsible for the shift in estate activities. With new irrigation, cultivation expanded at the expense of grazing. Wheat production expanded more rapidly than maize, responding to the wealthier consumers of Guadalajara—although maize remained the predominant crop in the region. By the late eighteenth century, especially after the famine of 1785 and 1786, the failure of the agrarian economy to increase maize production in pace with population growth led to a sudden and sustained rise in the price of the staple of the poor. Here, too, developments in Jalisco paralleled those in the Bajío.[51]

But if the changes in the agrarian economy of Jalisco followed those in the Bajío, the related social adaptations did not. The rural regions around Guadalajara included too many landholding villages for developments there to mirror those in the Bajío exactly. And Jalisco had too many estate residents for its social relations to parallel those of the central highlands. What made rural Jalisco unique, and uniquely volatile outside the Bajío, was the mix of landed villages and estates with large resident populations. Neither institution could predominate. Nor did estates and villages become linked in relations of symbiosis essential to both. Instead, they disputed increasingly scarce resources, producing situations in many Jalisco villages similar to those that

[50] Ibid., pp. 117, 142-168.
[51] Ibid., pp. 59, 82, 207-220; FHEM, III, 112-115.

led to insurrection in the more isolated community of Mezquitic in San Luis Potosí.

As the commercial estate economy expanded quickly after 1750, estates in Jalisco continued to depend primarily on resident workers. Perhaps the long era in which villagers performed seasonal labor only when forced by state drafts left estate operators reluctant to turn to the communities. Most permanent estate employees, *sirvientes*, earned 4 pesos monthly, plus ample maize rations. They were provisioned with other goods annually in advance of service—and most would not work without prior compensation. Most closed their annual accounts owing one or two months' wages to the estates—that is, they had obtained goods and money worth 5 to 10 pesos more than their work had earned. However, those debts did little to hinder the mobility of Jalisco estate employees. They moved regularly, often leaving estates to absorb the costs of unpaid debts. Modest estates around Guadalajara generally had populations of about 200 persons, providing from 50 to 70 regular workers. Larger properties might have from 600 to 1,000 residents, providing from 150 to 400 permanent employees.[52]

The persistence of high wages and ample security among estate dependents in Jalisco suggests conditions more like those of estate residents in San Luis Potosí than in the Bajío. Not surprisingly, there is no evidence of mass insurrection among the secure estate dependents of Jalisco in 1810.

There was an expansion of small tenancies on estate lands around Guadalajara after 1750. Estate accounts report growing numbers of renters, subrenters, sharecroppers, and even squatters, who were responsible for an increase in the production of maize on marginal estate lands. Although evidence remains sketchy, it appears that the shift toward insecure tenancies was only a secondary development in Jalisco.[53] Thus, no shift toward social insecurity characterized

[52] Van Young, *Hacienda and Market*, pp. 245-269.
[53] Ibid., pp. 232-233.

the life of estate dependents, a clear contrast with developments in the Bajío. The growing number of tenants in Jalisco surely faced difficulties, but their insecurities did not become pervasive grievances affecting large numbers of estate residents and potentially leading to mass insurrection.

The villagers of central Jalisco also provided labor to estates, but they did so on a limited scale. Community residents formed only about 20 percent of the entire province of Guadalajara around 1800, though they were concentrated in the central areas near the capital city, where they perhaps approached half of the rural population.[54] Villagers provided seasonal labor for a few weeks each year to assist in estate harvests and other labor-intensive activities. But seasonal workers generally provided only a small part of estate labor in Jalisco, usually less than 10 percent.[55] And some of those few seasonal workers were from families of estate employees and tenants. The role of villagers in estate labor around Guadalajara was thus minimal. In contrast, at the Hacienda de Pilares, near Acolman northeast of Mexico City in the central highlands, seasonal workers from nearby villages obtained wages that totaled 55 percent of all estate expenses from 1791 to 1795.[56] Clearly, the villagers of Jalisco were much less important as workers in the estate economy, and estate labor was much less important to the villagers of Jalisco. Relations between villages and estates around Guadalajara did not approach the level of symbiosis, and thus the potential for conflict between the two pivotal institutions of rural life there was heightened.

During the years of agrarian change in the late eighteenth century, Jalisco villagers faced major and often destabilizing difficulties. Long accustomed to substantial autonomy—and deeply devoted to that autonomy—they saw the rapid growth in their own numbers leave community lands

[54] See Appendix C, Table c.2.
[55] Van Young, *Hacienda and Market*, pp. 261-264.
[56] Tutino, "Creole Mexico," Table 3.9, p. 164, and Table 6.4, p. 327.

ever less adequate after 1750. Towns and villages sought new lands, and new villages were created from old towns strained beyond their resources. But the availability of land for such expansion was limited. After 1750, land disputes proliferated within villages, between villages, and between villages and estates—all indicating worsening shortages of community resources. Before 1750, villages had regularly sold surplus maize in Guadalajara. After that date, the surplus vanished as local consumption demanded all the maize community lands could produce. Population growth was undermining the autonomy of villagers with limited resources.[57]

One result was a rapid polarization of the internal structure of many villages. Local notables took large areas of scarce resources for themselves, often claiming rights of personal property. They rented other community lands to outsiders, or non-Indians living in the community, who could pay ample rents into town treasuries. The expanding agricultural economy provided new opportunities for village leaders with favored access to local resources.[58] Meanwhile, late colonial reforms forced many Jalisco villagers to face the departure of their Franciscan pastors, clerics who had long favored community cohesion and local autonomy. They were replaced with secular clergy who were often more likely to view their parishes as opportunities for economic activities—much like Father Lozano at Mezquitic.[59] The arrival of clerics more interested in development than devotion furthered the commercialization of community economies and the polarization of their social relations as population growth made subsistence autonomy less possible for most villagers.

With community lands failing to provide for their sustenance, how might villagers gain new income? The agrarian

[57] Van Young, *Hacienda and Market*, pp. 88, 278, 345.
[58] Ibid., pp. 290-291.
[59] Taylor, "Rural Unrest," pp. 37-38.

structure of Jalisco precluded a compensating increase of seasonal labor at estates, such as developed in the central highlands. Some villagers turned to full-time estate employment, relinquishing autonomy already in decline for the security of dependence. And many villagers around Guadalajara turned to increasing craft production. Villagers there, as elsewhere in Mexico, had combined craft activities with subsistence cultivation since before the Spanish conquest. Household production of pottery, cloth, and other goods maintained family control of production, while sales depended on local markets. After 1750, with the decline of subsistence autonomy, increased craft activities might compensate for lost sustenance while allowing peasant families to maintain a limited independence. The making of pottery had long been a tradition in towns such as Tlaquepaque and Tonalá. More an innovation of the late eighteenth century was the rapid expansion of household textile production in the communities of central Jalisco, a development that reflected not only the villagers' quest for new income, but also the expansion of the market in an era of rapid population growth. And as the Intendant of Guadalajara, José Fernando Abascal y Sousa, emphasized in a report of 1804, the expansion of villagers' textile production also resulted from the restriction of imports during the wars of the 1790s.[60]

Such increased textile production brought new earnings to villagers much in need. It also subjected them to increasing dependence on markets they could not control. They thus faced new insecurities. They made mostly cotton goods. The raw fiber had to be obtained from merchants who brought it in from the Pacific lowlands to the south. Villagers surely also depended on merchants to sell cloth outside local markets. Detailed information is lacking, but it is probable that merchants controlled much of the new textile production among Jalisco villagers through a putting-out system. In addition, the predominance of cotton goods

[60] FHEM, III, 121-122, 131-132.

left the spinners and weavers in Jalisco villages most susceptible to the volatile changes in the market caused by the
rapid shifts from war to peace, and from protection to open
ports, that recurred in Mexico from 1785 to 1810.

Jalisco villagers thus found declining subsistence autonomy, increasing social polarization, and increased dependence along with new insecurities during the later part of the
eighteenth century. They also faced growing numbers of
conflicts with estates. Many suits were brought by villagers
claiming lands. Others were begun by estate owners seeking
new resources for expanded production. And those disputes became increasingly violent, as invasions, expulsions,
and retributions became more common. Estates and villages disputed land use as well as ownership. Hispanic land
law had given villagers—and others—free access to estate
uplands for pasturing animals and gathering wood. But as
land use became more intensive in Jalisco, estate operators
began to try by means legal and illegal to enclose their lands
and to deny access to villagers.[61]

Again, there is a clear contrast with developments in the
central highlands. There, estate owners recognized the
need to preserve the villagers' access to both community resources and estate uplands—to preserve their estates' essential seasonal work forces.[62] There were land disputes between estates and villages in the central highlands in the late
eighteenth century, but there was no general assault on
community resources and resource use as developed in Jalisco. And central highland landed elites periodically defended the landed interests of the communities from which
they drew workers.

In both regions, the colonial courts worked to mediate between estates and villages.[63] In the central highlands, where
labor relations of symbiotic exploitation linked estates and

[61] Van Young, *Hacienda and Market*, pp. 332-338.
[62] Tutino, "Creole Mexico," pp. 343-346.
[63] Van Young, *Hacienda and Market*, pp. 315, 342.

villages, however unequally, state mediation was reinforced and agrarian stability entrenched. But in central Jalisco, links between estates and villages were but marginally important to estate profits and villagers' subsistence. Conflict over scarce resources characterized estate-village relations there. The courts attempted to meditate and achieved some success in times of peace. But when the Hidalgo revolt came to Jalisco late in 1810, many villagers remembered the mounting tide of conflicts more than the state's attempts to mediate. Not surprisingly, large numbers of villagers became rebels in Jalisco.

Drought struck Jalisco villagers periodically, as it did the rural poor across all of highland Mexico. The calamity of 1785 and 1786 was as intense there as elsewhere. Local harvests were lost, and many villagers were reduced to eating roots and whatever else they could scavenge. Disease ravaged a nutritionally weakened population. In one group of villages around Sayula, the local priest estimated that one third of the Indian population died. Mortality was highest among women and children.[64] Even in the few villages fortunate enough to harvest some maize, supplies quickly vanished as local residents and outsiders used up the scarce food.[65]

Most organized relief efforts focused on supplying the city of Guadalajara. Urban officials scoured the countryside near the city for maize, while also importing large amounts from the hot country to the south. Their efforts were but partially successful. It is estimated that 20 to 25 percent of the urban population died in 1785 and 1786—a death rate parallel to that in the city of Guanajuato and no doubt inflated by the deaths in the city of rural people who fled there in a desperate search for sustenance.[66]

Village priests sought and often obtained tribute exemp-

---

[64] FCA, pp. 682-687.
[65] FCA, pp. 679-681.
[66] Van Young, *Hacienda and Market*, pp. 94-101; FCA, 78-83, 87-96.

tions for Jalisco villagers during the crisis.[67] But such relief of monetary burdens was small compensation to villagers without food. And the villagers of Jalisco could not count on income from estate labor and access to estate maize to at least partially compensate for the loss of village crops. They were not a large enough part of the estates' labor forces to gain the work that helped central highland villagers through times of scarcity. Instead, when crops failed, Jalisco villagers could only turn to their craft production for income. But in all likelihood the markets for pottery, cloth, and other goods shrank drastically in times of famine because most Mexicans then used all their income to buy food. When famine struck the villagers of Jalisco, it struck them doubly.

In the later part of the eighteenth century, hunger plagued those villagers amidst escalating conflicts with estates over resource controls. Villages that had lost land disputes, or that had lost access to estate uplands, could easily conclude that landed elites were in large part responsible for their suffering. The disastrous famine of 1785 and 1786 would thus appear to many Jalisco villagers as much a social crisis as a natural disaster. Their grievances against elites surely mounted.

The famine of 1809 and 1810, so important to precipitating insurrection in the Bajío, spared Jalisco. Both a report of the Intendant at Guadalajara and the records of maize entries into the city granary indicate years of at least average harvests.[68] Clearly, famine was not an essential precipitant of insurrection in Mexico at the end of the colonial era. In the Bajío, famine focused the attention of the agrarian poor on the social origins of their misery and brought grievances that had developed over many years to a peak; thus, it was a pivotal precipitant of the mass uprising there. But

[67] FCA, pp. 663-675, 689-692.

[68] AGN, Intendentes, vol. 73, exp. 17, fol. 14, 1809; Van Young, *Hacienda and Market*, Table 8, pp. 78-79.

in the central highlands, the same famine of 1809 and 1810 reminded villagers of the importance of their links with estates. And in San Luis Potosí it made the security afforded estate residents most evident. Famine could also reinforce social stability. And in Jalisco, villagers who escaped the famine of 1809 and 1810 rebelled without that precipitant. The role of the famine in heightening grievances or reinforcing stability varied with the social relations prevailing among the rural poor. Eventual decisions about rebellion reflected underlying social conditions primarily. Famine might make the impact of those conditions on the rural poor more blatantly obvious. But famine did not cause insurrections.

The primary precipitant of insurrection in Jalisco in 1810 was the prior insurrection in the Bajío. When José Antonio Torres approached central Jalisco via Sayula and Zacoalco late in October, he found substantial support among villagers who had suffered the worst of recent agrarian changes. Zacoalco was the core of the Jalisco uprising. The town had lost numerous land disputes and had developed a local tradition of revolt in the late eighteenth century. Along with other nearby communities, Zacoalco had seen the departure of the Franciscans and the arrival of many non-Indian traders. Community life became increasingly polarized and commercialized. Community cohesion declined as subsistence autonomy waned. And prolonged disputes with landed elites gave the villagers' grievances a clear social target.[69]

When Torres and his band of rebels from the Bajío arrived among such villagers, they found massive—though never universal—support. However, enough villagers joined the insurrection to overwhelm the militia detachment sent out from Guadalajara early in November. After the insurgents' clear victory at Zacoalco, local merchants

[69] Taylor, "Rural Unrest," pp. 15, 28-29, 33; Van Young, *Hacienda and Market*, pp. 81, 281-282.

were killed and haciendas looted. And Torres amassed a force estimated at 20,000 insurgents. They easily occupied Guadalajara, much to the chagrin of local elites who opposed and feared the insurrection.[70]

Rebels were not recruited from all Jalisco villages, of course. At Tlajomulco, the community had engaged in many conflicts during the eighteenth century, yet it retained much land and solid local cohesion. A few weavers there did join the uprising, but most of the community remained passive—neither joining nor opposing the insurgents. At Tonalá, the most litigious of Jalisco communities, residents retained ample good lands while also producing pottery sold across Mexico. There, too, there was no insurrection in 1810. Insurrection is never universal. Local developments and personal decisions regularly lead some to rebel while others do not.[71] But in Jalisco, in contrast with the central highlands, agrarian social changes engendered grievances that led thousands of villagers to join the Hidalgo revolt.

With such widespread revolt among villagers, Jalisco became the second home of the forces remaining with Hidalgo and Allende after the defeat at Aculco and the expulsion from Guanajuato. By early January of 1811, the combined insurgent forces in Jalisco—including Bajío rebels, local villagers, and others of diverse origins—again approached 80,000. But having recaptured the Bajío, General Calleja and Intendant Flon came to Jalisco with their militia forces. The untrained and poorly armed mass of insurgents proved incapable of facing 6,000 experienced militiamen who were well armed, backed by artillery, and now battle tested. The battle at Puente de Calderón proved no contest. Over a thousand insurgents died, as thousands more fled in disarray in the face of disciplined troops.[72]

[70] Taylor, "Rural Unrest," pp. 15-19.
[71] Ibid., pp. 42-51.
[72] Hamill, *Hidalgo Revolt*, pp. 198-202.

The insurgent leaders fled north, where they were captured, tried, and executed a few months later. Most of their followers tried to return home as inconspicuously as possible. Others turned to guerrilla tactics and remained in rebellion. But the battle of Puente de Calderón, the battle for Jalisco, ended the Hidalgo revolt as a large-scale threat to colonial rule in Mexico. Insurrection limited to the Bajío and Jalisco, however intense there, could not survive in the face of the unified opposition of elites, a mobilized militia loyal to the regime, and the passivity of the agrarian majority in the central highlands and elsewhere.

## SOCIAL BASES OF AGRARIAN INSURRECTION, 1810

There was no single cause of agrarian insurrections in early nineteenth-century Mexico. The grievances that led thousands of Bajío estate residents to rebel with Hidalgo in September of 1810 were distinct from the difficulties that led villagers in Jalisco to join the movement in later months. Similarly, the social conditions that held the loyalty of the central highland villagers were radically different from the conditions that kept the estate dependents of San Luis Potosí not only loyal, but ready to fight for the colonial regime.

The social bases of rural loyalty or rebellion in Mexico in 1810 depended first on whether agrarian families lived as peasant villagers or as estate dependents. These were radically different ways of rural life, structured by different relations with landed elites and the colonial regime—and resulting in distinct means of attaining subsistence. Villagers lived in communities founded by the colonial state and long sustained by the colonial courts. While ultimately dependent on the state, villagers held lands and were delegated political rights that gave them substantial, if always incomplete, autonomy of subsistence and government. Villagers provided labor services at estates held by elites, but they did not become permanent dependents of those powerholders.

In contrast, estate residents lived in communities

founded by landed elites. Such rural families had no rights
to lands and no independent political organization. They
gained subsistence by laboring for elites, or by cultivating
lands allowed them by those landholders. Their subsistence
autonomy was thus limited. And while they could go to the
colonial courts seeking redress of grievances, they lacked
formal institutions of local government to organize and
fund such efforts. Estate residents lived as direct dependents of landed elites, and were only secondarily linked to
the colonial state.

Around 1800, neither village life nor estate dependence
was inherently more or less likely to stimulate insurrection.
The villagers of the central highlands remained passive in
1810, while many in Jalisco rebelled. And estate residents in
the Bajío took up arms against the regime, while those in
San Luis Potosí fought to sustain it. Rather, it was particular
social changes affecting villagers, and distinct changes
among estate dependents, that pressed some toward insurrection while others remained loyal, or at least passive.

Given the dependence fundamental to the lives of estate
residents, security was their primary concern. Where labor
scarcities existed due to sparse populations and local economic conditions, estate dependents generally retained security and showed little interest in insurrection. Such security held the loyalty of the agrarian majority of San Luis
Potosí, as well as the segments of the rural population living
as estate dependents in Jalisco and the central highlands.
In contrast, where demographic growth and changes in the
estate economy forced estate dependents to endure worsening insecurities accompanied by deepening poverty, insurrection could become massive. Such deteriorating conditions pervaded estate life in the Bajío after 1750 and
generated the grievances underlying the origins of the
Hidalgo revolt there in 1810.

When villagers joined the insurrection later in 1810, their
grievances were distinct. Their lives were structured by a
basic autonomy—an autonomy they cherished despite its

limitations. Their loyalty or insurrection depended on the extent that their autonomy endured, or, if it were declining, on the speed of the decline as well as on its immediate, perceived causes. In the central highlands, villagers had faced a long, progressive loss of autonomy as their numbers grew while their lands did not. The agrarian structure of the region, however, kept the majority of rural families in the villages, leaving estates dependent on villagers for most labor services. Thus, as villagers slowly lost autonomy, they simultaneously increased their labor at nearby estates. And with such consolidated relations of symbiotic exploitation essential to the profits of estates and the survival of villagers, elites refrained from a pervasive assault on village resources. Thus, the declining autonomy of central highland villagers was a long, slow process that was far from complete by 1810. Neither local landed elites nor the colonial regime appeared responsible for the losses of autonomy that did occur. Retaining substantial autonomy and lacking clear grievances against elites and the state, the villagers of the densely settled valleys around Mexico City remained loyal in 1810. Their passivity doomed the Hidalgo revolt.

The villagers of Mezquitic in San Luis Potosí and Zacoalco and others in Jalisco, in contrast, faced rapid losses of autonomy in the late eighteenth century that were attributable to offending powerholders. These were communities in regions long sparsely settled and minimally involved in the commercial agrarian economy. Villagers there had retained lands more than ample to local needs well into the eighteenth century. Then, after 1750 in both regions, rapid population growth made village resources less adequate while rapid commercial development brought new inequalities and insecurities to village life. And because the villagers of San Luis Potosí and Jalisco were but minimally important as laborers at local estates, they found no compensating increases in estate labor. Without relations of symbiotic exploitation, in times of population growth and commercial expansion, estates and villages easily began to dispute increasingly scarce and valuable resources. And as villagers lost resources in those disputes, they were quick to blame their lost autonomy on landed elites, or others such as local priests or officials who were clearly profiting. Thus did the rapid loss of autonomy that struck the villagers of Jalisco and Mezquitic after 1750 generate acute social grievances, resulting in substantial insurrections after Hidalgo broke the colonial peace in 1810.

While the grievances underlying the mass agrarian insurrections within the Hidalgo revolt differed among estate dependents and villagers, two general characteristics were shared by all who rebelled in 1810. First, they suffered social deteriorations that, though different, were rapid and of recent origin. People have long shown an ability to adapt to and endure the most perverse conditions—but such adaptation takes time. Where social deterioration developed as a long, slow, and steady process, adaptation could develop to blunt the grievances that might lead to insurrection. The centuries-long decline of autonomy among central highland villagers allowed such adaptation, helping to curtail grievances there. But where the loss of autonomy developed suddenly and rapidly after 1750, as in many Jalisco villages, adaptations could not keep pace. Grievances mounted and insurrection followed.

The second general characteristic of social developments underlying insurrections in Mexico at the end of the colonial era was that the rapid deteriorations of agrarian life had evident social, that is human, causes. Estate residents were so directly dependent on landed elites that whatever benefits they gained or losses they suffered were clearly attributable to those powerholders. When deterioration struck estate dependents, usually as a loss of security, the resulting grievances automatically focused on elite landlords. Among the villagers, the development of social grievances was more complex. Their fundamental autonomy, based on the use of community resources and direct dependence primarily on village governments, made the role of landed elites appear more distant and less direct. Thus, when the autonomy of central highland villagers declined in the eighteenth century due to the impact of population growth on an agrarian structure nearly two centuries old, the responsibility of elites for the villagers' difficulties was veiled. In contrast, when landed elites engaged in a direct assault on village resources during times of population growth, as occurred in Jalisco, grievances easily focused on elite actions. Such developments made insurrection much more probable. Direct evidence of elite powerholders' responsibility for deteriorating agrarian conditions was thus a pivotal factor in provoking agrarian insurrections.

The rapid and clearly elite-caused loss of security by estate dependents in the Bajío generated the acute social grievances that led to mass insurrection there in 1810. The rapid loss of autonomy, clearly worsened by elite land annexation, produced the grievances behind the insurrection of many Jalisco villagers soon afterward. But those grievances and the resulting insurrections proved limited to those areas. In the far more densely settled central highlands, as in other regions to the south, insurrection was minimal in 1810. And among estate dependents in San Luis Potosí and similar regions to the north of the Bajío and Jalisco, not only was insurrection limited, but many among the rural poor retained enough loyalty to the regime to fight in its defense. The combined weight of the passively loyal villagers of central Mexico and the actively loyal estate residents of northerly regions far exceeded that of the insurgents of 1810. Given the firm unity of elites in opposition to the insurrection, the Hidalgo revolt was fated to be a large, destructive, but failed, attempt to challenge the colonial regime and its agrarian structure.

# CHAPTER FIVE

# Agrarian Guerrillas Continue the Insurrection, 1811–1816

THE DEFEAT AT Puente de Calderón in January of 1811 ended the Hidalgo revolt as a threat to the colonial regime. The attempt to combine a political movement for Mexican autonomy with mass insurrection had failed, due in part to unified elite opposition, in part to contradictions within the insurrection, and in large part to the absence of mass support outside the Bajío and Jalisco. But the collapse of Hidalgo's movement did not end insurrection in Mexico. The uprising begun by the rebel priest provided both an example and an opportunity for other insurgents. And Hidalgo's failures taught important lessons in insurgent tactics. Agrarian rebels would fight on in numerous Mexican regions for several years after 1810. They abandoned thoughts of quick victory with massed forces, turning instead to guerrilla tactics. They would operate in smaller, more mobile units in regions where the terrain and the sympathies of the rural populace shielded rebels from easy repression.

Such guerrilla insurgents could not overthrow the colonial regime directly, but they helped undermine the foundations of colonial society. They repeatedly sacked the stores of merchants in rural towns. They pillaged haciendas, taking grain, livestock, and profits from landed elites. They plagued roadways away from the larger cities and towns, making travel and trade increasingly risky. Not surprisingly, guerrilla activities faced solid elite opposition and violent reactions from colonial authorities. But the agrarian guerrillas proved elusive and difficult to defeat. In regions of sustained guerrilla insurrection, the agrarian economy collapsed for years after 1810. The colonial agrarian structure could not long endure such conflict. The brief but massive Hidalgo revolt had failed in its primary goal of quickly toppling the colonial regime. But the agrarian guerrillas who carried on the insurrection were more successful in damaging the colonial economic structure—thus striking at the base of the colonial order.

## MORELOS AND THE HOT-COUNTRY REBELS: POLITICAL REVOLT FAILS AGAIN

José Maria Morelos led the insurgent movement in Mexico following Hidalgo's defeat and execution. A man of mixed race and modest means, Morelos had worked as a youth at the estate of an uncle in the hot country of Michoacán, near Apatzingan. He later studied and became a priest under Hidalgo's tutelage at the Valladolid Seminary. But with neither family wealth nor powerful allies, Morelos had difficulty gaining a stipend to support him and a parish to serve. From the 1790s, he ministered to poor congregations isolated in the hot country near the Pacific coast of Michoacán. He hoped for a more favorable placement, but never obtained one before 1810.[1]

Morelos joined Hidalgo at Valladolid (now named in his honor as Morelia) in October of 1810. After protesting that he sought only a chaplain's role in the insurrection, Morelos accepted the command to raise insurrection in the Pacific hot country he knew so well. He quickly recruited several estate owners as rebel leaders and raised a band of mobile, mostly mulatto, insurgents who became an effective force under his leadership.[2] The hot-country revolt led by Morelos included members of all classes from those isolated regions. Lowland elites often led their estate dependents into

---

[1] Timmons, *Morelos*, pp. 1-29.
[2] Ibid., pp. 40-46; see also Díaz Díaz, *Caudillos y caciques*, pp. 28-31.

the rebellion. And additional troops were recruited among peasant villagers.[3] Why was such a multiclass revolt possible in the Pacific hot country in 1810?

The lowland basins of Mexico's Pacific slopes remained sparsely populated throughout the colonial era. Indigenous populations were small when compared to the dense concentrations of peasants in the central highlands. Early Spanish colonists sought peasants to rule and mines to develop, and when the low country proved to have neither, they were slow to enter the region. But crops with commercial potential such as sugar, cacao, cotton, indigo, and rice required a climate more tropical than the central highlands. Thus, late in the sixteenth century, Spaniards began to claim lands and build estates in the hot and humid Pacific low country. But those early developments were limited. In the Tepalcatepec basin of lowland Michoacán, Spaniards had claimed only 25 percent of the land by 1650, and would increase their holdings to only 36 percent by 1715. Given the sparse local population, the lands not claimed by Spaniards were adequate to sustain the lowland peasantry. The local population thus had little incentive to labor at Spaniards' estates, forcing commercial producers of tropical crops to rely heavily on expensive African slaves. As those slaves followed the Mexican pattern of mixing with indigenous peasants, their offspring became a growing population of free mulattoes.[4]

To the end of the colonial era, the hot country remained sparsely settled. Resources remained relatively plentiful for both estates and peasants. But during the late eighteenth century, the population increased rapidly as migrants moved in growing numbers into the Pacific lowlands. As the Bajío became increasingly crowded and characterized by deteriorating agrarian conditions, growing numbers of Mexicans seeking new opportunities turned toward the hot

[3] Timmons, *Morelos*, p. 50.
[4] Barrett, *Cuenca de Tepalcatepec*, I, 78-87, 94, 105, 126-127, 154-168.

country. The region was far from crowded, but most new-comers soon learned that only the wealthy could buy or build estates there. And only established families could claim lands as members of village communities.

Thus, the majority of immigrants had no choice but to live as estate dependents. A minority found permanent employment—secure dependence. Many more became tenants, facing both the opportunities and insecurities inherent in such lives. And others only survived as *arrimados*, squatters allowed to live on estate lands in exchange for offering seasonal labor services. Such marginal families had neither autonomy of subsistence production nor security of regular employment. They faced an extreme combination of dependence and insecurity, living only by seasonal day labor.[5]

During the eighteenth century, then, the growing numbers of tenants and squatters at hot-country estates brought about the expansion of social relations of insecure dependence. Those difficulties were compounded by several changes in the markets for tropical estate produce. During the eighteenth century, the sugar industry of the Pacific lowlands declined in the face of competition from regions closer to the highland markets. Early in the century, the decline of sugar was in part compensated by the expansion of cotton and indigo production—both essential for the growing Mexican textile industry. But after 1785, the decline and uncertainties of cloth production in the Bajío and elsewhere led to problems for low-country estates that supplied raw materials. When imported cloth displaced Mexican products in highland markets, lowland elites found profits falling—and their estate dependents faced reduced opportunities for secure employment and declining conditions for tenancies.[6]

Meanwhile, the residents of hot-country communities

[5] Morin, *Michoacán*, pp. 66-69, 228-234.
[6] Barrett, *Cuenca de Tepalcatepec*, I, 169-172.

faced transformations that left many families with minimal lands for subsistence, even while total community resources remained ample. Community leaders looked to fill local treasuries by renting land to outsiders—perhaps immigrants unhappy with the prospect of living as estate dependents.[7] Details are scant, but late colonial changes within low-country communities appear to parallel the developments at Mezquitic in San Luis Potosí. Profit-oriented community notables were using their power to allocate community resources in ways that generated increased commercial production and more community revenue, but that also threatened the subsistence production of many less fortunate villagers.

During the later eighteenth century, the hot country of the Pacific lowlands experienced rapid population growth coupled with volatile economic changes. Elites developed and expanded estates, but found that changing market conditions made profits inconsistent. Estate dependents were increasingly forced to accept insecure tenancies—or to rely on seasonal wage labor alone. Villagers faced worsening inequalities and reduced access to land, as community resources were let out to commercial producers. And all these complex changes occurred in regions still isolated by distance and rugged terrain from the highland centers of colonial life. Morelos could tap the discontent of low-country elites, estate dependents, and villagers by focusing opposition on the colonial regime—a regime that seemed distant and little concerned with such isolated areas.

Morelos understood the agrarian base of his rebellion. Late in 1810 he proclaimed the end of slavery, as well as the end of tributes and of community treasuries. Villagers were to keep the proceeds of their production.[8] In 1811, he proclaimed that community lands were to be allotted only to local residents, and no longer rented to outsiders. But More-

7 Ibid., pp. 154-172.
8 Timmons, *Morelos*, p. 51.

los followed Hidalgo in not addressing the problems of estate depedents. Several of Morelos' lieutenants were low-country estate owners, and their importance in the insurrection apparently precluded reforms to alleviate the insecurities facing estate residents.[9] Hidalgo could not lead a radical social revolt because of his own frustrated aspirations to landed elite status. Morelos perhaps understood agrarian concerns more fully, but his political links with provincial elites precluded all but the most limited reform proposals. Neither of the principal political leaders of the insurrection that began in 1810 addressed the agrarian grievances of estate dependents—grievances that led so many of their supporters to rebel. That separation between the leaders' programs and the rebels' grievances proved a basic weakness of the more political insurrections of the independence era.

Late in 1811, with his base in the hot country established, though having failed to capture the key Pacific port of Acapulco, Morelos headed toward the central highlands and the colonial capital.[10] Like Hidalgo, he knew that only success there could bring political victory. Like Hidalgo, he entered the central regions through the valley of Toluca, first capturing the town of Tenango. And like Hidalgo, Morelos found little support among the villagers there. He was quickly dislodged by royalist forces.[11]

Persisting in his political goals and aided by the mobility of his core of about 5,500 lowland rebels, Morelos turned toward the sugar-producing basin just south of Mexico City that now bears his name. There, amidst numerous village communities and the valuable sugar estates owned by some of the richest families of Mexico City, the second battle for control of the stategic central highlands was fought early in 1812 at the prolonged siege of Cuautla. This battle was

[9] Díaz Díaz, *Caudillos y caciques*, p. 33.

[10] Timmons, *Morelos*, pp. 44-46.

[11] Alamán, *Historia de Méjico*, II, 294-299.

more contested than Hidalgo's earlier confrontation at Monte de las Cruces. But the results were similar. The insurgents found insufficient local support to sustain a challenge to the regime in the pivotal central highlands.

The region now known as Morelos was like the rest of the central highlands in being populated primarily by peasant villagers, in having developed estates owned by Mexico City elites and supplying that urban market, and in maintaining important labor relations that tied villagers to estates. But Morelos was unique within the central highlands because of its lower altitude and warmer and wetter climate. Sugar production predominated at estates there, production that required not only cane cultivation but also the refining of sugar. Capital investment in sugar estates was thus greater than at most Mexican properties. Labor demands were also much larger. The cultivation of cane and sugar production required more workers during more of each year than did the cultivation of grains that predominated in most of the central highlands.

During the sixteenth and seventeenth centuries, the great demand for more permanent labor at Morelos sugar estates led to the large-scale use of African slaves. As the slaves mixed with the local peasants, the populations of both estates and villages became increasingly mulatto. And throughout the colonial era, estates there maintained large populations of resident workers. At the end of the eighteenth century, the residents of Morelos estates could provide over half of annual labor needs. Meanwhile, seasonal workers for cutting cane were annually drawn from villages near the estates, from communities in the surrounding mountains, and from the small but growing population of estate tenants.[12]

As a result, relations between estates and villagers in Morelos developed a locally unique mix of conflict and sym-

[12] Barrett, "Morelos and Its Sugar Industry," pp. 168-171; Martin, "Haciendas and Villages," pp. 410-419.

biosis. Symbiosis remained strong because the estates depended on the seasonal labor of villagers for the crucial harvesting of cane. That need was important enough to lead Morelos estates to schedule sugar harvests so as not to compete with villagers' maize production. And even with such scheduling, estate operators complained that they could not count on villagers to be available when estates needed them.

The symbiotic labor relations between Morelos estates and villages, however, were challenged in the late eighteenth century by widening conflicts. As the market for sugar expanded after 1750, estates began to covet the land and water resources held by villages in the lowland basin. With seasonal workers available among estate tenants, and especially from nearby highland villagers, many sugar growers began to pursue the most fertile of village resources. The result was a proliferation of land conflicts between estates and villages in the Morelos lowlands. Most were resolved in the courts, though some villagers resorted to breaking estate dams and irrigation canals when decisions went against them. Around 1800, conflict was becoming more pervasive in Morelos, but it was conflict tempered by relations of symbiosis between estates and villages.[13]

Famine rarely struck the residents of this climatically favored lowland basin in the midst of the central highlands. The catastrophe of 1785 and 1786 spared Morelos. Crops there were nearly normal. When villagers in other central highland regions searched for maize, they often went to Morelos. And the colonial authorities paid ample bounties to Morelos estate operators to plant irrigated maize during the winter of 1786.[14] Thus, while Morelos villagers faced increasing conflicts with expansive sugar estates, they also continued to obtain seasonal work there. And the absence of intense famine in the region helped keep the grievances

[13] My interpretation is based on materials in Martin, "Haciendas and Villages," pp. 413-419, 423-426.

[14] Ibid., pp. 409, 412, 421-422.

that did develop from becoming more intense. Developments in Jalisco proved that famine was not essential to insurrection. Developments elsewhere in Mexico, however, emphasize that famine could bring emerging agrarian grievances to the acute levels essential to insurrection. In Morelos, where grievances were emerging in escalating disputes over land and water resources, the absence of famine moderated those developing grievances.

When José María Morelos and the low-country rebels captured the town of Cuautla, in the heart of the sugar basin, they found some local support. A few local priests, estate managers, estate laborers, and villagers joined the rebels.[15] Local elites, as usual, supported the royalists and tried to mobilize estate dependents against the insurgents. Villagers and rancheros were said to sympathize with the insurgents.[16] But estate dependents in Morelos proved reluctant defenders of the colonial regime, and the villagers there proved reticent rebels at best. No mass insurrection of villagers distracted Calleja and his troops, including the San Luis Potosí militia, under the leadership of Juan Nepomuceno Oviedo, when they besieged Cuautla during the spring of 1812. Morelos and those who arrived with him from the low country faced the siege all but alone.[17] Without massive local support, the rebels could not withstand the siege, and their only alternative was to escape. The Morelos region that in 1910 would begin and sustain the most adamant of agrarian insurrections under Zapata, generated only limited rebellion in 1810.

Morelos and those who escaped with him retreated south toward Oaxaca. As they traveled the way through the rugged highlands of the Mixteca, they found some support among a populace that had just weathered the insecurities of boom and bust while producing cochineal dye for export.

[15] *Morelos: Documentos*, pp. 304-349, 378-379.
[16] Ibid., pp. 260-262.
[17] Alamán, *Historia de Méjico*, II, 313.

But when the insurgents entered the more strategic and densely settled central valleys of Oaxaca, they again encountered passivity among the agrarian majority. In another region where established communities retained substantial landholdings, peasants saw no gain in taking up arms against the colonial regime.[18]

Morelos carried on for several years. Fighting in isolated, mountainous regions, he and his troops long eluded defeat. True to his political goals, he called a congress that met at Chilpancingo in the summer of 1813. Unable to remain there, his government became a guerrilla regime, eventually proclaiming a constitution for an independent Mexico at Apatzingán in October of 1814. But unable to elicit substantial elite support, and unwilling to propose radical reforms that might have tapped more agrarian discontent, Morelos could not triumph.[19] He was captured and executed in 1815, and the movement he had led then fragmented. One remnant, led by Vicente Guerrero, held out in the mountains of the hot country, and in 1821 joined in the more conservative independence movement led successfully by Agustín Iturbide.[20]

During five years, Morelos proved that guerrilla tactics could sustain insurrection longer than the mass mobilization attempted by Hidalgo. He also learned that extended rebellion, even with regional agrarian support, depended greatly on geographic isolation. But the guerrilla tactics and regional isolation that allowed Morelos' insurrection to endure also precluded victory over the colonial regime. Morelos' failure to recruit numerous rebels in his sallies into the central highlands proved again that in 1810 most rural

[18] Taylor, "Town and Country," pp. 90-94.

[19] Some of Morelos' supporters, the famous Guadalupes who were mostly middle-sector professionals from Mexico City, did propose the breakup of Mexican haciendas, surely as a frontal assault on landed elite power. It is not clear that Morelos ever endorsed their proposal. See Timmons, *Morelos*, pp. 97-108.

[20] Ibid., p. 154; Díaz Díaz, *Caudillos y caciques*, pp. 34-37.

Mexicans were not ready to take up arms in insurrection. And it was because the great majority of agrarian Mexicans refused to rebel that the insurgents had to fight the colonial regime as guerrillas in isolated regions.

## Jalisco and the Bajío: Agrarian Insurgents without Hidalgo

Morelos' efforts to continue Hidalgo's political movement toward independence have overshadowed the simultaneous existence of numerous agrarian rebel movements in several Mexican regions. Morelos helped these insurgents primarily by keeping the main royalist forces occupied for nearly five years. Because their leaders were less politically and ideologically oriented, these rebels have often been portrayed as mere bandits. Mexican elites certainly portrayed them as such at the time—which is not surprising. The agrarian guerrillas that roamed numerous Mexican regions after 1810 cost elite landowners and merchants substantial profits. Yet while elites viewed them as bandits assaulting the rights of legitimate property, insurgents viewed themselves as taking just revenge against social structures of injustice. They survived for years by adopting mobile guerrilla tactics, remaining close to isolated highland strongholds, and operating in regions where they found sympathy and support among the agrarian population.

Hidalgo's defeat near Guadalajara and the shift of the political center of insurrection to the hot country under Morelos did not extinguish the agrarian uprisings in Jalisco and the Bajío. The grievances of Jalisco villagers and Bajío estate dependents were not linked to the goals of insurgent leaders, and many carried on their insurrections long after the defeat and death of those leaders. Hidalgo, Allende, and other marginal elites may have participated in the insurrections in the Bajío and Jalisco, but they neither created nor fully controlled the movement among the agrarian populace.

In Jalisco, the villagers of Zacoalco and surrounding communities maintained their insubordination for several months after the defeat at Puente de Calderón. Even more enduring was the rebellion along the north shore of Lake Chapala, not far to the east. The villagers there had participated in the uprising of 1810 to some extent. They became even more rebellious, however, as they faced persistent royalist repression after Hidalgo's defeat. Their insubordination focused on the island of Mescala. As late as 1814, over 1,000 rebels held out on that former prison island—sustained by the residents of the shore villages.[21]

Elsewhere in Jalisco, many of the bandits that had been plaguing the region during the years of economic change and escalating conflict since 1785, after 1810 declared their participation in the insurrection against Spain. Bandits, after all, possessed the skills of the guerrilla and surely resented the regime that had outlawed them. Led most prominently by Pedro Moreno of Lagos, they infested the region northeast of Guadalajara known as the Altos de Jalisco—the uplands inhabited by fiercely independent rancheros.[22]

In the Bajío, insurrection continued through 1811 and into 1812, led by Albino García. García was a mestizo from Valle de Santiago, a former estate cowboy and foreman, said also to specialize in smuggling and other illegal activities. He joined Hidalgo early in the revolt. And from early 1811, he recruited rebels to continue the insurrection in the center of the Bajío basin. García maintained a mobile core of about 800 mounted insurgents that long kept the royalists at bay. They were sustained by the local agrarian population, which provided additional fighters when needed. Controlling the central core of the Bajío, García's rebels broke estate dams, cut irrigation ditches, and generally obstructed local estate operations. They disrupted transportation on the major route linking Querétaro and Guanajuato. And they periodically ranged far from their home base near Valle de Santiago, asserting their power at the fringes of the Bajío region. García was a frustrating embarrassment to authorities trying to make much of the victory over Hidalgo. Early in 1812, three columns of troops were sent to stop García, but his mobility combined with local support enabled him to continue his guerrilla activities. Finally, after nearly six months of pursuit, the troops captured and executed Albino García in June of 1812.[23] In a region of open country offering little geographical refuge, García used guerrilla tactics and agrarian support to sustain insurrection for a year and a half after the defeat of Hidalgo.

In the northeast uplands of the Bajío around Dolores and San Miguel, the birthplace of the insurrection of 1810, agrarian revolt continued even longer. Large numbers of estate residents there had joined Hidalgo early on, and had quickly turned to sacking the haciendas that ruled their lives. With the defeat of the mass political movement early in 1811, the agrarian rebels of the northeast Bajío again concentrated their revolt on the estates of their home region. They repeatedly attacked large properties, taking livestock, foodstuffs, and any other portable valuables. They captured estate managers when they could, holding some for ransom and killing others. Several times in 1811, estate owners and managers assembled forces of loyal dependents to join small detachments of royalist troops in attacking the rebels. Although the defenders of the regime won every battle, the rebels would disappear into nearby highlands, to appear again once the troops had gone. During the summer of 1811, several estates in the northeast Ba-

---

[23] Osorno, *Insurgente Albino García*, pp. 18-20, 25-33, 41, 201-210; Díaz Díaz, *Caudillos y caciques*, pp. 21-28; also, Hamnett, "Royalist Counterinsurgency."

jío attempted to raise crops—often with the manager away at the royalist sanctuary of Querétaro. Apparently loyal dependents harvested modest crops late in 1811—and insurgents appropriated them. Elites then generally abandoned estate operations around San Miguel and Dolores, and for the next several years estate residents who were left to themselves had to deal with the local insurgents.

The manager of Puerto de Nieto did not dare to return to that property just east of San Miguel until 1816. When he attempted to resume estate operations, he concluded that the residents had become insubordinate, even insolent, and would not work as he expected. With rebellion then waning across most of Mexico, the landowners with estates in the countryside around San Miguel obtained a detachment of 200 experienced royalist troops to protect their properties—and to intimidate their dependents. Early in 1817, 30 soldiers were stationed at Puerto de Nieto. Their presence subdued the residents enough to allow the manager to begin to resume estate operations. That rebuilding would prove a long, difficult, and not always profitable process.[24]

## The Sierra Gorda: Bastion of Agrarian Rebels

The persistence of agrarian revolt around San Miguel and Dolores in the northeast uplands of the Bajío resulted primarily from the depth of the rebels' grievances. Their enduring insurrection was facilitated by proximity to the Sierra Gorda, the rugged, almost forbidding mountain enclave just east of the Bajío. The Sierra provided a haven for rebels pursued by royalist troops, because it too was home to mass insurrection beginning early in 1811. The combination of local discontent and impenetrable terrain made

[24] See the reports of estate managers in JSE, vol. 214, no. 121, 10 Oct. 1810; no. 122, 18 Nov. 1810; no. 127, 3 Feb. 1811; no. 130, 4 May 1811; no. 131, 3 Dec. 1811; CPP, no. 79, 1 Jan. 1815; JSE, vol. 214, no. 152, 28 Aug. 1816; no. 153, 23 Nov. 1816; no. 155, 27 Mar. 1817; no. 157, 8 May 1817.

the Sierra Gorda a bastion for agrarian rebels during the years after 1810. That region would persist as a hotbed of rural violence throughout the nineteenth century.

Despite their proximity, the Sierra Gorda and the Bajío were as different as two Mexican regions could be. The Bajío had few indigenous communities and had developed from the late sixteenth century as an Hispanic agricultural region. The Sierra, in marked contrast, remained an enclave of indigenous refuge, but minimally incorporated into colonial society before the middle of the eighteenth century. The rugged geography of the Sierra accounts for most of the difference. After the wars between Spaniards and nomadic Indians in the later sixteenth century, the Sierra Gorda was left as a predominantly Indian region of little economic interest to Spaniards. Missionaries periodically entered, aiming to convert the natives, to congregate them into settlements, and to teach them to work like "civilized" Europeans. Those attempts continued throughout the seventeenth century and continually failed. While some of the inhabitants of the Sierra acquired a veneer of Christianity, most disliked life subject to mission regulations. They repeatedly returned to their isolated highland homes, where they lived independent of colonial society. They were the most autonomous of Mexicans during the colonial era.

By the late seventeenth century, it was clear that the residents of the Sierra Gorda would not be incorporated into colonial society by the efforts of missionaries alone. There followed a series of attempts to back missionary preaching with armed force. The Sierrans would be made to congregate, convert, and work. But into the early years of the eighteenth century, these attempts to colonize the Sierra had little success. When their liberty was restricted, the residents of the region retreated again and again into the back country. When faced with armed force, they rebelled with famed ferocity—as in 1703. In the 1720s, another approach was attempted. A group of Spanish families was settled in the Sierra, allotted lands, and told that they were to serve as a permanent militia to control the indigenous majority. They were to set an example of settled cultivation, and to enforce the authorities' will when asked. Again, their success was minimal.[25]

The residents of the Sierra Gorda were strongly attached to lives of isolated autonomy. They resisted the missionaries not only because they disliked the regulations imposed by mission life, but also because the missionaries were repeatedly followed into the Sierra by colonists with more economic interests. Many planned to build estates on the lands vacated by the converted and congregated residents of the region. And they expected to use the mission residents as seasonal workers. The response of the independent Sierrans was flight whenever possible—and violent protest when necessary.

The one partially successful attempt to convert and congregate the residents of the Sierra Gorda began in 1744 under Franciscan missionaries, including Junipero Serra who would later become famous for his work in California. The new Franciscan effort encouraged the Indians to settle in mission congregations, to convert to Christianity, and to live by utilizing mission resources. Estate operators were kept at a distance, the Franciscans insisting that they were not creating a new reservoir of seasonal laborers. By permitting mission residents to live as peasants on mission resources, the Franciscans allowed the survival of a basic sense of community autonomy. Meanwhile, the military colonists remained in place, ready to respond in case of resistance. And in 1748, José de Escandón led a large military expedition into the Sierra Gorda, crushing the remnants of indigenous opposition—and sentencing many captives to labor in the Querétaro obrajes.[26] Responding to the combination of incentives and repression, hundreds of Sierrans remained at

[25] For the early missions, see Galaviz, *Sierra Gorda*, pp. 19-63. For the military colonists, see AGN, Tierras, vol. 1,872, exp. 5, 1769; vol. 1,019, exp. 5, 1777.

[26] Super, *Vida en Querétaro*, p. 136.

the new missions for several decades, even while the resulting exposure to epidemic diseases diminished their numbers.

In 1770, however, the new missions were taken from
Franciscan control and turned over to Mexican parish
clergy. The change resulted from the expulsion of the Jesuits from Spanish dominions, leaving the colonial authorities in need of experienced missionaries on the strategic
frontier of the northwest—California and adjacent areas.
The Franciscans were thus removed from the Sierra Gorda.
The results were devastating to the prospects of peaceful
colonization there. The secular clergy who replaced the
Franciscans came without missionary training and without
the financial backing of a missionary order. They appeared
more interested in collecting fees and developing economic
enterprises than in ministering to their charges or protect-
ing them from the demands of nearby estate operators.[27]
After 1770, then, there began in the Sierra Gorda a period
of escalating conflict both within mission communities, and
between communities and the growing number of outside
migrants entering the region.

The secularization of the missions coincided with and facilitated a wave of estate development in the Sierra Gorda
in the late eighteenth century. The continuing agrarian
transformation of the Bajío, just to the west, stimulated new
interest in colonizing the Sierra. Rising prices of food and
livestock products led elites to seek new regions for estate
development. The Sierra Gorda was a unique region—near
major colonial markets, yet little developed as part of the estate economy. Elites from Mexico City and Querétaro led in
developing new estates in the Sierra Gorda. And numerous,
less fortunate mestizos and mulattoes, facing declining
agrarian conditions in the Bajío, were willing to take the
risks of opening new tenancies in the Sierra. The direct result of the rapid incursion of estates and tenants was a series

[27] Galaviz de Capdeveille, "Descripción y pacificación," pp. 132-143;
Gómez Cañedo, *Sierra Gorda*, pp. 65-115.

of land disputes that began in the 1780s, continued into the 1790s, and intensified in the early 1800s. The issues were similar in most of the conflicts: indigenous residents of Sierra communities would accuse estates or their tenants of usurping lands. The estate owner would reply that the inhabitants of the region were barbarous savages, living without civilization, and now engaged in a brazen assault on legitimate rights of property. The natives at times won in the courts, but their repeated protests indicate that they rarely gained control of the lands they had won. The colonial courts could not mediate effectively between Indians and Spaniards amidst this scramble for land in the rugged and isolated Sierra. Rioting became endemic to relations between the indigenous Sierrans and the residents of expanding estates.[28]

During the years before 1810, the fiercely independent inhabitants of the Sierra Gorda felt invaded by waves of missionaries, soldiers, secular priests, estate developers, and tenant cultivators. Some families but recently enticed into the congregations again returned to their isolated lives in the Sierra's uplands. Those who had become accustomed to community life pursued court actions against those who would take their lands, undermining community autonomy. And as many Sierrans faced diminished resources, they would join labor gangs organized to provide seasonal labor at estates in the nearby Bajío.[29] Agrarian life in the Bajío and the Sierra Gorda differed fundamentally in 1810, but the transformation of the Bajío was forcing radical

[28] Agrarian conflicts in the Cadereita region of the Sierra Gorda are recorded in AGN, Tierras, vol. 610, exp. 1, 1742; vol. 1,742, exp. 4, 1769; vol. 998, exp. 1, 1776; vol. 1,053, exp. 1, 1781; vol. 1,290, exp. 3, 1797; vol. 1,098, exp. 6, 1783; vol. 1,873, exp. 9, 1795; vol. 1,267, exp. 17, 1796; vol. 1,373, exp. 3, 1806; also in INAH, Serie Querétaro, roll 27, 1806. See also Super, *Vida en Querétaro*, pp. 190-192. On conflicts around Xichú, see AGN, Tierras, vol. 447, exp. 1, 1744-1798; vol. 1,098, exp. 6, 1783; vol. 1,290, exp. 3, 1797; Bienes Nacionales, vol. 550, 1801; Tierras, vol. 1,341, exp. 5, 1801-1805; vol. 1,373, exp. 3, 1806; and *Gazeta de México*, 7 May 1808.

[29] Tutino, "Life and Labor," p. 365.

changes onto the residents of the Sierra. The demographic growth and economic changes that brought worsening insecurities to Bajío estate dependents also stimulated the explosion of estate development that assaulted the long-entrenched independence and subsistence autonomy of the natives of the Sierra Gorda. The Sierrans were quick to join their neighbors in insurrection.

Had Hidalgo turned east from Dolores toward the Sierra Gorda in September of 1810, he would have found ample support for his insurrection there. He might then have led the "Indian" revolt his detractors perceived. But Hidalgo's political goals led him toward the Bajío basin, Guanajuato, and Mexico City. The increasingly irate residents of the Sierra Gorda, however, did not need Hidalgo to call them to insurrection. Once they knew that a sustained uprising was underway and occupying royalist forces, they rose under local leaders, seeking redress of local agrarian grievances.

Exactly when the Sierra Gorda insurrection began is unclear. But once Hidalgo was defeated early in 1811, the authorities began to take notice of the continuing defiance of the inhabitants of the Sierra around Xichú as well as Cadereita. The rebels' agrarian goals were apparent in their attacks on haciendas, whether owned by Spaniards or Mexicans. They took livestock as well as crops. Estate managers, the local agents of landed elites, were the primary targets of personal violence. These agrarian rebels controlled the Sierra Gorda for years after 1811. They made transportation between central Mexico and San Luis Potosí and other northern regions possible only in armed convoys. And they helped shield many neighboring insurgents from royalist repression. The adjacent rebels of the northeast Bajío and the Sierra Gorda kept one strategic region of north central Mexico out of royalist control until 1816.[30]

[30] Alamán, *Historia de Méjico*, II, 162; JSE, vol. 214, no. 126, 18 Jan. 1811;

## Toward the Capital: Guerrillas in the Mezquital and Apan

The enduring insurrection in the Sierra Gorda also helped sustain another uprising that occurred in regions closer to the colonial capital beginning in 1811. Both Hidalgo and Morelos had approached Mexico City through the valley of Toluca, found little support there, and eventually retreated from the strategic center of the colony. But other rebel leaders with less political goals were able to sustain insurrection for years near the capital when they approached via the Mezquital and the plains of Apan. The bastion of the Sierra Gorda lay just north of the Mezquital, and the Sierra de Puebla provided a refuge east of Apan. Insurgents who maintained guerrilla mobility in such regions were difficult to defeat. And many rural residents of the Mezquital and Apan proved receptive to the rebels. The guerrillas operating north and east of the colonial capital could not attempt to capture Mexico City, but they could long sustain a rebellion that imposed costly economic losses on the landed elites of the capital. Given the more agrarian and less political goals of the guerrillas, such destruction may be judged a substantial rebel success.

Royalists blamed Julian Villagrán for the guerrilla agitation in the Mezquital. A modest trader and muleteer from Huichapan, where the Mezquital met the Sierra Gorda, Villagrán held a captain's commission in the militia regiment based at Tula. In 1810, his son was a fugitive from murder charges. That November, rebels loyal to Hidalgo came to Huichapan and Villagrán joined, claiming control of his home region for the insurrection. Early on, however, it became clear that Villagrán was more concerned with ruling Huichapan and the Mezquital than with aiding Hidalgo and

---

no. 127, 3 Feb. 1811; no. 130, 4 May 1811; no. 131, 2 Dec. 1811; and Galaviz de Capdeveille, "Descripción y pacificación," pp. 143-144.

his political quest. Beyond this drive for local power, Villa-grán's goals are not clear. But he recruited numerous followers among the agrarian poor of the Mezquital and used guerrilla tactics to elude the royalists for nearly three years. His insurrection kept communications uncertain along the route linking Mexico City with Querétaro and the north. And guerrilla bands claiming loyalty to Villagrán repeatedly attacked the haciendas of the Mezquital throughout 1811 and 1812.[31]

Beginning late in 1810, the decidedly royalist manager of the Tulancalco estate in the southern Mezquital, one Manuel Olguín, wrote a series of letters that reveal much about the agrarian base and destructive consequences of Villa-grán's insurrection. Although the active rebels were still far north of Tulancalco, Olguín expressed mounting fears. He had learned that haciendas and their managers were the favorite targets of insurgent violence. Many estate managers, as well as priests and traders from nearby towns, were fleeing from the rebels. And as more and more rebels were recruited in the Mezquital, Olguín feared that the harvest scheduled to begin in December of 1810 would be interrupted by labor shortages, if not by insurgent attacks.[32]

Such early reactions of fear and flight by the defenders of the colonial regime in the Mezquital are revealing. No insurrection existed in the southern reaches of that dry basin in the fall of 1810, yet those who served the landed elites and the colonial state there presumed that rebellion would soon begin—and that they would be its targets. Their expectations proved correct. By early 1811, haciendas across the Mezquital, including those in its southern areas not far from Mexico City, were under attack from agrarian guerrillas.

Why did the Mezquital basin and the nearby plains of Apan generate the only sustained insurrections in the rural

---

[31] Alamán, *Historia de Méjico*, I, 303; II, 51-53, 231; III, 220-222.
[32] PCR, no. 141, 10 Nov. 1810; 24 Nov. 1810.

regions surrounding Mexico City during the years after 1810? These areas to the north and northeast of the colonial capital mixed peasant villages with great estates, like other areas of the central highlands. But as its name suggests, the Mezquital was the most arid of the central basins. Fields there produced more maguey cactus for pulque fermentation than grains—which were limited to a few irrigated plains. The aridity of the Mezquital and adjacent areas led estates there to emphasize stock grazing and pulque production, in turn generating agrarian social relations distinct from those in the grain-producing regions of the central valleys.

The peasant communities of the Mezquital faced severe difficulties and insecurities of subsistence. Although a few larger towns such as Atitlaquía and Ixmiquilpan held some irrigated croplands, most villagers in the Mezquital lived in smaller communities with lands suitable only for grazing goats and raising maguey. Few Mezquital villagers could use community resources to raise the maize essential to an autonomous subsistence. Instead, they raised maguey and fermented pulque from its sap, while making rope and other products from its fibers. They engaged in diverse other crafts. And they labored periodically at nearby estates or the mines of Pachuca or Real del Monte.

But the mines relied primarily on permanent, skilled workers. And so, too, did the estates of the Mezquital. Given their arid lands, estates there primarily grazed livestock and produced pulque. Neither activity required large numbers of workers. The care of estate livestock occupied a small core of permanent estate dependents, mostly Hispanized mestizos and mulattoes. Pulque production required larger numbers of temporary and unskilled workers only when the young plants were transplanted for cultivation—a process that occurred only once each year. Tapping the sap and the fermentation of pulque required only a few skilled workers—mostly Indians, for this was an indigenous product but recently commercialized as an estate activity. Given such limited but regular labor demands, the arid pulque regions northeast of Mexico City, including the Mezquital and Apan, had mestizo and mulatto populations proportionally twice as large as those in the regions of the central highlands.[33]

Yet villagers still formed the great majority, totaling nearly 80 percent in the pulque regions, compared to nearly 90 percent in the grain-producing zones. As community populations expanded rapidly in the late eighteenth century, villagers faced a painful dilemma. Arid village lands made autonomous subsistence production impossible, while arid estate lands kept labor demands low. The symbiosis that partially compensated for the declining autonomy of villagers in the grain-producing regions of the central highlands could not develop in the Mezquital.

Villagers there faced lives characterized by relatively autonomous poverty, plagued by insecurities. From such positions, they viewed neighboring estates with growing hostility. And estate managers perceived Mezquital villagers as unreliable workers. Apparently because labor relations between estates and villagers were irregular, villagers were not always available when estates needed them. Managers responded by locking in village labor gangs they feared would depart. Such coercion only heightened the villagers' resentments. They had no wish to become dependent on estates that offered work only infrequently—and then became coercive. Sporadic violence became common. During the drought years of 1809 and 1810, which struck such arid regions very hard, villagers survived by stealing estate livestock. Managers knew that the thefts were acts of desperate people. Yet they pursued those who challenged property rights, and jailed those who were caught. Conflict heightened by famine thus characterized relations between Mezquital estates and villagers in 1810.[34]

[33] See Appendix C, Table c.3.
[34] Tutino, "Creole Mexico," pp. 134-141, 217, 346-347; PCR, no. 141, 12 Mar. 1810.

It was that recent escalation of conflict that led estate managers, priests, and merchants in the Mezquital to expect many villagers to join or at least support the insurrection. And by early 1811, those expectations became realities. Numerous bands of mounted guerrillas claiming allegiance to Villagrán marauded through the southern Mezquital, attacking estates owned by Spaniards and Mexicans alike. The rebels recruited a few allies among estate employees, but primarily found assistance among the Mezquital villagers. And as elsewhere, estate managers were the first targets of insurgent violence. The one estate owner found at his property was summarily executed. As such depredations escalated, more estate managers, priests, and traders fled for the safety of the larger towns. Estate operations continued at a greatly reduced level, subject to repeated guerrilla attacks. Profits vanished.[35]

The principal force opposing the insurgents in the Mezquital was organized by the Conde de Cortina, owner of the large Tlahuelilpan estate. Most of the soldiers were estate dependents who—under the command of Cortina's manager—pursued the rebels vigorously; but the guerrillas' mobility and the support of the village populace precluded many direct confrontations. When battles did occur, the royalists always claimed victory and many rebel casualties. But most guerrillas escaped to nearby highlands, to appear again elsewhere as a plague upon the estates of the Mezquital during 1811 and 1812.[36] As long as Villagrán dominated the region from the Sierra Gorda through the Mezquital, the agrarian guerrillas roamed freely. Only in May and June of 1813 did a concerted royalist drive lead to the capture and execution of Villagrán. There followed a royalist

[35] PCR, vol. 143, 19 Jan., 26 Jan., 2 Mar., 30 Mar., 26 Apr., 4 May, 18 May, 24 May, 1 June, 8 July, 13 July, 30 July, 31 Aug., 5 Sept., 2 Nov., 15 Nov., 16 Nov., 7 Dec., 14 Dec. 1811; PCR uncatalogued materials, "Autos . . . 1810," 13 Jan., 10 April 1812.

[36] Alamán, *Historia de Méjico*, II, 262; PCR, vol. 143, 24 Mar., 1 June, 2 Nov. 1811.

sweep that returned colonial rule to the regions he and the guerrillas had dominated.[37]

While Villagrán ruled and agrarian rebels pillaged, the great estates of the Mezquital suffered substantial losses. Livestock was requisitioned by guerrillas and royalists alike. Food stocks were taken by loyal troops in exchange for promises of future payment. Rebels took what they could with no such formalities. Production was limited by labor shortages and uncertainties, as well as by the prolonged absences of managers. And access to markets was always questionable. Thus, the great landed families of Mexico City who owned most of the large estates in the Mezquital lost the profits of two years of operations. Agrarian guerrillas like those in the Mezquital could not threaten the regime directly, but they imposed severe economic losses on the landed elites whose economic power was fundamental to the structure of colonial society.

A similar agrarian insurrection developed six months later yet lasted years longer on the plains of Apan, to the southeast of the Mezquital and northeast of Mexico City. This was another arid region where estates primarily raised hogs and produced pulque. Large estates dominated the region, outnumbering villages,[38] yet villagers still constituted more than over 60 percent of the population at Apan.[39] Those villagers shared the problems of their neighbors in the Mezquital. Arid community resources were a poor base for subsistence production, while pulque and grazing estates provided few opportunities for even seasonal employment. Such difficulties were worsened by late colonial population growth, and made periodically deadly in years of famine. The villagers at Apan were not among the first to rebel. But when they finally seized the opportunity to take revenge for their grievances, their insurrection proved vi-

[37] Alamán, *Historia de Méjico*, II 51-53, 231; III, 220-222, 290-295.

[38] Tutino, "Creole Mexico," pp. 303-305; AGN, Padrones, vol. 5, fols. 315-316, 1792.

[39] See Appendix C, Table C.3.

olent and enduring, forcing great losses on many elite families of the colonial capital.

The uprising at Apan began in August of 1811. It was led by José Francisco Osorno, called a highway bandit by the royalists. Whatever his personal shortcomings, Osorno quickly recruited support among the villagers of Apan and nearby Calpulalpan, and dominated the entire region—including the Otumba area of the valley of Mexico. Having lost control of many valuable estates, Mexico City elites pressed for a rapid royalist response. A force of newly arrived Spanish marines was sent to end the uprising. They were unable to defeat the rebels, while persecuting much of the village population—thereby creating even greater support for the insurgents. From the autumn of 1811, Mexico City elites lost control of their estates in a large area around Apan.[40] Even the great pulque estate called Ojo de Agua, located no more than 30 kilometers from Mexico City, and one of the two properties sustaining the family of the Marqueses de Vivanco, was subject to enough insurgent interference to eliminate all profits from 1812 through 1815.[41]

For several years after 1811, because estate managers dared not enter the region from Otumba to Calpulalpan and Apan, the local populace was left to use estate resources as it pleased. Every time Osorno's control of the region was challenged by royalists, he fought a few skirmishes and then retreated into the Puebla highlands to the east around Zacatlán. Once the troops left to pursue rebels elsewhere, Osorno returned to Apan. Early in 1814, he flaunted his strength by leading 600 insurgents across the valley of Mexico to sack the town of Texcoco and then the great Chapingo estate, the other property of the Vivanco clan. The rebels returned to Apan so quickly that they eluded the expedition sent to punish them. It was not until the summer

[40] Alamán, *Historia de Méjico*, II, 264-268; JSE, vol. 214, no. 124, n.d. (c. 1811).

[41] Tutino, "Creole Mexico," pp. 170-173.

of 1816 that the pacification of other regions allowed a concentration of royalist troops at Apan. Osorno was defeated
and colonial officials and elites reclaimed the region. In August, estate managers began to return and assume the task
of rebuilding estates held by insurgents for six years.[42] Like
the agrarian rebels of the northeast Bajío, the Sierra Gorda,
and the Mezquital, the insurgents around Apan had no
chance to overthrow the colonial government. But they succeeded in attacking the wealth of landed elites in their regions, and that, too, struck at the core of the colonial regime.[43]

## THE LESSONS OF AGRARIAN INSURRECTION, 1810–1816

Among the tens of thousands of rural Mexicans who participated in the conflicts touched off by the Hidalgo revolt,
deadly failures as well as limited successes taught important
lessons. The early mass revolt led by Hidalgo provided
mostly negative lessons. Rural rebels learned that political
debates among elites, however heated, did not necessarily
stem from deep divisions within the dominant class, especially when that class saw its power threatened from below.
They learned that provincial leaders, however prominent
locally, did not necessarily represent an important, alienated segment of the colonial elite. They learned that tens of
thousands of massed and angry rebels were no match for a

[42] Alamán, *Historia de Méjico*, IV, 169, 245-246, 259-264; JSE, vol. 214, no.
134, 16 Feb. 1812; no. 144, 2 Sept. 1814; no. 151, 28 Aug. 1816.

[43] The extent of insurgent damage to estates and elite fortunes is debated. Brian Hamnett sees only "sporadic and temporary losses" (see
Hamnett, "Economic and Social Dimension," p. 25). Doris Ladd views elite
estate problems as significant, but regionally restricted (Ladd, *Mexican Nobility*, pp. 133-161). I find Ladd's emphasis more persuasive. Direct damage to estates was widespread from 1810 to 1816, while transportation
problems disrupted the entire economy. The financial problems experienced by landed elites after independence were in part due to the lasting
impact of the insurgents' depredations (see Chapter 6 below).

few thousand trained and well-armed militiamen in open combat. And the first agrarian insurgents from the Bajío learned that the rural poor of other Mexican regions faced different economic structures and social relations. However poor and exploited, the inhabitants of those other regions might choose not to support an insurrection. These were all negative lessons of Hidalgo's failed attempt to mobilize the discontent of the rural populace for political ends—goals not equally important to the insurgent masses.

After the collapse of the Hidalgo revolt, however, the long survival of the agrarian guerrilla movements provided rural Mexicans with more positive lessons. They learned the importance of guerrilla mobility, and that such mobility worked best when nearby highlands provided easy refuge. They saw that guerrilla success was also concentrated where the rural population offered firm support. And perhaps most important, the agrarian poor of many Mexican regions learned during the years after 1810 that guerrilla actions could inflict great losses on landed elites. If Hidalgo's dream of quickly seizing the colonial government through mass insurrection proved a fantasy, insurgents such as Villagrán, Osorno, and many others proved that sustained rebellion could weaken the estate economy and thus the colonial structure.

The Hidalgo revolt and the subsequent guerrilla conflicts marked the beginning of more than a century of agrarian violence in Mexico. Rural Mexicans learned much about insurrection from these early conflicts. But they remained novice insurgents. Their movements lacked any explicit ideology of agrarian justice. They proposed no structural reforms to correct the wrongs they felt so deeply. There were several reasons for the absence of a unifying and potentially constructive ideology. First, many of the earliest and most ideological of the insurgent leaders, such as Hidalgo, only partially perceived or shared the grievances of the mass of insurgents. Second, as rebellion developed in various Mexican regions, rural people took up arms to protest distinct grievances. The radically different agrarian crises of the adjacent Bajío and the Sierra Gorda highlight the more general situation of regionally specific rural grievances generating regionally isolated insurrections. Rebels from many regions might agree that recent changes had imposed or worsened injustices. All could oppose landed elites and the colonial regime. But there was little shared basis for a unifying vision of agrarian change. And radical agrarian ideologies, so common to the twentieth century, were scarce around 1800. Such a vision could not be imported in 1810; it would have to develop amidst Mexican conflicts—a process that would take much of the next century. The lack of unifying goals guaranteed that the rebels of the independence era would be known merely as *insurgentes*—insurgents. That designation made clear their opposition to the colonial order—and their lack of a shared program for a more just Mexican future.

The absence of an ideology of agrarian justice is understandable. Yet the lack of such clear goals kept the rural rebels of the independence era a primarily destructive force. They inflicted vengeful damage upon great estates and their managers. But they could not begin to work toward a new agrarian structure more just in the eyes of the rural majority.

Disunity and ideological weakness hurt the insurgents' cause, but did not ultimately cause their defeat. Their failures had more basic roots in the agrarian structures of Mexico at the end of the colonial era. Beginning in 1810, large numbers of estate residents, suddenly forced to endure worsening insecurities, rebelled with Hidalgo in the Bajío. Soon afterward, peasant villagers whose autonomy had been threatened or undermined joined the uprising in Jalisco, the Sierra Gorda, and elsewhere. Later, villagers in conflict with estates in more arid regions of the central highlands, such as the Mezquital and Apan, saw an opportunity and joined the insurrection. But far larger numbers of agrarian families remained passively loyal to the colonial order. The majority of peasant villagers in the central highlands and Oaxaca retained substantial autonomy, as well as symbiotic if exploitative links with nearby estates, and refused to rebel. The majority of estate dependents in northerly regions such as San Luis Potosí retained security sufficient to sustain their loyalty to the regime. It was the predominant passivity of the majority of rural Mexicans, coupled with the firm opposition of the most powerful colonial elites, that guaranteed the failure of insurgent attempts to overthrow the colonial regime. But in the process, agrarian Mexicans learned much about insurrection, and those lessons proved useful as they continued to experiment with opposition to the agrarian structure during the nineteenth century, and into the revolutionary era that began in 1910.

# PART TWO

# TOWARD AGRARIAN REVOLUTION, 1810–1940

# CHAPTER SIX

# Independence, Disintegration, and Agrarian Decompression, 1810–1880

HAVING DEFEATED the Hidalgo revolt and the guerrilla insurrections it spawned, Mexican elites led by Agustín Iturbide brought their own independence movement to a successful conclusion in 1821. Their goals were conservative. They declared national sovereignty, in an attempt to preserve their own power from the challenges of Mexican insurgents and Spanish liberal reformers.[1] Mexican elites saw independence as a means to claim control of the state to serve their class interests. They quickly faced a series of dilemmas. Could they integrate the vast territories and diverse peoples they claimed to rule into a coherent nation? Could they rebuild an economy damaged by years of international disruptions and local insurrections—and suddenly wrenched out of the Spanish imperial system? Could they build a national regime that would serve their interests, preserve their powers, and achieve enduring stability? And could they implement their economic and political goals and still hold the agrarian majority in subordination?

Mexican elites generally failed to achieve these goals during the period after 1821. Andrés Molina Enríquez characterized the era as one of national disintegration.[2] The national economy floundered from 1810 to 1880. Politics was characterized by sharp divisions, recurrent armed conflicts, and periodic foreign interventions—including two major

---

[1] See Villoro, *Proceso ideológico*, pp. 199-265; Anna, *Fall of Royal Government*, pp. 191-226; and Ladd, *Mexican Nobility*, pp. 121-131; on events in Spain, see Fontana, *La quiebra de la monarquía*.

[2] Molina Enríquez, *Los grandes problemas*, p. 111.

invasions. And the rural poor became very insubordinate, pressing new demands and from the 1840s joining in increasing numbers of violent insurrections.

Rather than resolving the conflicts that underlay the agrarian revolts that began in 1810, independence apparently worsened them. This chapter explores the agrarian social consequences of independence. The next examines the recurrent insurrections that exploded across Mexico from the 1840s through the 1870s. Unfortunately, we know less about rural life after independence than during the late colonial era. But recent studies suggest that the early national years brought basic changes to agrarian social relations across Mexico.

Although disintegration raises images of destruction, the loss of unity, of cohesion, often includes more creative elements. Socially, disintegration is most destructive in the eyes of economic elites and political leaders accustomed to preference and predominance. But others may use or even promote disintegration to challenge, escape, or evade the powers of dominant groups. For them, disintegration may be creative as well as beneficial. In Mexico, the combination of economic decline and political instability after 1821 did diminish the wealth and power of the heirs of colonial elites—who expected to rule the new nation. But the same disintegration brought new opportunities to provincial elites who began to vie for power. And for the majority of Mexicans with no pretentions to wealth or predominance, the era of disintegration allowed some to escape and others to alter old roles of subordination. The era of national disintegration was also an era of decompression for the agrarian poor. Many of the social pressures they had faced during the late colonial period were relieved. And they found new means to challenge the powers of those who ruled.

## THE EMERGENCE OF THE PERIPHERIES

As soon as they had claimed national independence, the great families of Mexico City faced challenges to their power. Perhaps the first and most enduring of those challenges came from the leaders of outlying provinces who had often supported independence movements, not only to oppose Spanish rule, but also to oppose the dominance of Mexico City. After 1821, the leaders of many peripheral regions gained new strength and were increasingly effective in blocking attempts of central Mexican elites to rule the nation alone.

The core areas of colonial Mexico—regions that included substantial Hispanic and Hispanized populations, were integrated into the commercial economy, and subject to the power of Mexico City elites—formed but a small yet central part of the territory claimed by the Mexican nation after 1821. The colonial core focused on Mexico City and encompassed the central valleys around the capital, the Puebla basin to the east, the highlands of Michoacán to the west, as well as the Bajío and the mining and grazing areas of Zacatecas and San Luis Potosí. It was in and near these central regions that the conflicts of the independence era were fought.

Other regions of Mexico were nominally part of the colony and at least superficially ruled by colonial officials. But for centuries after 1521, they received few Spanish settlers and were little involved in the colonial economy. In the far north, aridity and the continuing opposition of native peoples defending their territories kept Spaniards few and generally concentrated in isolated mining centers such as Parral and later Chihuahua.[3] In the southeast, in Oaxaca, Chiapas, and Yucatán, dense populations of indigenous peasants were long spared intense Spanish penetration by the lack of silver and other economic incentives in their regions. There, a few officials and less than opulent colonial elites lived amidst exceptionally autonomous peasant majorities until the end of the colonial era.[4] Along the hot and

---

[3] See West, *Mining Community*; and Hadley, *Minería y sociedad*.

[4] See Taylor, *Landlord and Peasant*, and "Landed Society"; and Farriss, *Maya Society*.

humid coasts of the Gulf and the Pacific, sparse populations of peasants encountered only small numbers of Spaniards and African slaves during most of the colonial era.[5] All these regions, very different among themselves, remained peripheral to the heartland of colonial Mexico. There were also internal peripheries—regions like the Sierra Gorda that were geographically adjacent to the colonial core, but barely incorporated into its economic life and sociopolitical structures before the end of the eighteenth century.

The movement of growing numbers of Europeans and their commercial economies into these peripheral regions began in the late eighteenth century. Bourbon reformers in Spain then aimed to extend both administrative controls and commercial activities into regions long marginal to colonial affairs. The simultaneous growth of population and worsening social pressures in the colonial core also stimulated the emergence of the peripheries. After 1760, the production of basic foods lagged ever farther behind the growth of population in central Mexico, as evidenced by rapidly rising prices.[6] The resulting social deterioration, made deadly in the famine years of 1785 and 1786 and again in 1809 and 1810, contributed to the grievances underlying the Hidalgo revolt of 1810. Another result was the accelerating movement of people and production toward regions previously marginal to colonial life. Those with the means sought lands for new estate development, hoping to profit from scarcities and rising prices. The more numerous poor migrated in search of a plot of land to rent or sharecrop, regular wages, or a combination of both. That expansion of commercial activities into the peripheral areas, along with the rush of migrants there, contributed to the conflicts that underlay the uprisings in Jalisco, the Sierra Gorda, and the Pacific hot country beginning in 1810.

[5] See Barrett, *Cuenca de Tepalcatepec*, 1.
[6] Garner, "Price Trends," makes this clear.

Other peripheral regions, farther from the conflicts set off by Father Hidalgo, also experienced changes during the late eighteenth century. Along the Gulf coast, Veracruz was little settled or exploited by Spaniards until the rise of the sugar industry there in the eighteenth century—a development viewed as still limited by Alexander von Humboldt around 1800.[7] In Yucatán, small numbers of Spaniards had long lived without great riches by demanding tributes and labor services from entrenched Maya peasants. There, a new trade in livestock products, food, and cordage for the expanding shipyards of Havana, combined with local population growth, created a new demand for estate production. A small but dynamic commercial economy developed in Yucatán after 1780.[8] In general, then, the Mexican peripheries increased their Hispanic populations, their commercial activities, and the conflicts over lands and other resources during the years after 1760. Regional elites began to consolidate new powers in developing peripheral societies.

As long as the colonial regime and economy remained strong in central Mexico, the emergence of the peripheries was a secondary development. The migration toward outlying areas and the increased production there probably helped relieve the social pressures mounting in the core highlands. But from 1810, as economic difficulties, insurrections, and political conflicts wracked the colonial core, peripheral elites found new independence, and their regions received more and more migrants often fleeing the disruptions on the central plateau.

Regional elites often joined the political debates of the independence era with an eye to consolidating their regional power. That was evident in the support the leaders of the city of San Luis Potosí gave to the Hidalgo revolt—a deci-

---

[7] Humboldt, *Ensayo político*, pp. 176-177.

[8] Farriss, *Maya Society*, pp. 355-377; Patch, "Agrarian Change," pp. 30-36.

sion based on the frustration of regional leaders in a province dominated by landed and commercial elites from the
Bajío and Mexico City. Similar concerns for local predominance guided the leaders of far northern Nuevo León as
they faced the difficult choices of the independence conflicts.[9] And while provincial elites looked for advantages,
many among the rural poor sought refuge. Upland regions
on the fringes of the colonial core received an influx of new
settlers beginning in 1810. Growing numbers of families
took on the burdens of building new lives as isolated rancheros to escape the disruptions and dangers of insurrections—and the penalties of suppression.[10]

These developments became politically manifest in the
rising demands of assertive provincial elites. The liberal regime ruling Spain in 1814 established Provincial Deputations in Mexico to represent the elites of colonial urban centers. Seven Deputations were seen as sufficient to represent
Mexico's diverse regions. When they were reestablished in
1821, fourteen Deputations provided greater regional rep-
resentation. And the number increased to eighteen by late
1822. Much of the expansion was to allow a political voice to
emerging peripheral elites.[11] Regional elite power and self-
consciousness quickly demanded recognition as independence opened the political arena in 1821. There were early
tangible results. Following the collapse of Iturbide's ill-fated
experiment in empire, the nation adopted a federalist constitution in 1824, granting substantial autonomy to twenty
states. And ports such as Tampico, Soto la Marina, and Ma-
tamoros along the Gulf, and San Blas on the Pacific, opened
and allowed peripheral regions direct access to international trade during the 1820s.[12]

[9] Vizcaya Canales, *En los albores.*

[10] González y González, *Pueblo en vilo,* pp. 69-76; Schryer, "Sierra de Jacala," pp. 150-151.

[11] See Benson, *La diputación provincial,* especially the maps, pp. 42, 66,
69.

[12] See Herrera Canales, *Estadística,* Cuadro 197, p. 237.

Perhaps the most significant result of the emergence of peripheral regions in Mexico during the late colonial and independence eras was the persistence of political conflict for half a century after 1821. The rising demands for federalism and liberalism came in large part from peripheral elites—seeking guarantees of regional autonomy via political federalism and the power to assault the dominant institutions of colonial life through a liberalism that focused on limiting the powers of the Church and the rights of peasant communities. Not surprisingly, the elites of the old colonial core generally clung steadfastly to centralism and conservatism—centralism in defense of their presumed right to rule the nation and conservatism in defense of the Church and traditional privilege.

Political battle lines, of course, were never neatly drawn. There were always conservatives and even a few centralists among provincial elites. And there were liberals and even federalists in the central core—generally drawn from emerging professional and political groups hoping to challenge the heirs of the colonial aristocracy in their home regions.[13] But the strength of centralism and conservatism was in the colonial core, while the lasting impetus toward federalism and liberalism came from the rising peripheries. From 1821 until 1867, that conflict was not resolved. Emerging peripheral elites were still consolidating their powers in rapidly changing provincial societies—and often engaged in local factional disputes.[14] And while the elites of numerous peripheral areas all opposed the centralism of Mexico City, they had little else in common. The elites of Sonora, Oaxaca, and Yucatán defined themselves in terms of local interests—their only unity was opposition to outside domination. At the same time, as we shall see, the elites of the old colonial core were being weakened. They could not mount a successful effort to drive their diverse and dis-

[13] See, for example, Tutino, "Hacienda Social Relations," pp. 503-515.
[14] See Voss, On the Periphery.

united opponents from the political arena. Persistent conflict and political instability resulted.

Amidst the seeming chaos, long-term developments favored the peripheries. If economic expansion occurred anywhere in Mexico from 1810 to 1880, it was in peripheral regions where new ports opened, new lands were brought into commercial production, and new export markets tested—however tentatively.[15] Population growth also concentrated in the peripheries during the first three quarters of the nineteenth century. While the populations of the central highlands around Mexico City and Puebla, as well as the Bajío, grew little if at all from 1800 to 1877, expansion was rapid in regions to the north and south, and along both coasts.[16] There was apparently a steady migration from the central plateau core toward the developing peripheries during the years after independence.

The emergence of the Mexican peripheries between 1780 and 1880 deserves further analysis. We have barely begun to probe the economic processes that drew people into regions long considered undesirable. We know little of the relations between newcomers and established residents, and of the resulting social configurations. But it is clear that the rise of the peripheries was a fundamental development of nineteenth-century Mexico, underlying much of the instability of the era.

## THE DECLINE OF THE CENTER

Developments in the core regions of central Mexico after independence prove the inseparability of economics and politics. The elites who led in the declaration of national sovereignty aimed to impose that fundamental political change; but at the same time, they wanted to maintain the

[15] For example, see Rus, "Whose Caste War?" pp. 129-131; Chávez Orozco and Florescano, *Agricultura e industria*; and Weimers, "Agriculture and Credit."

[16] See Appendix C, Table c.4.

economic and social systems that had long served their interests. Building a national state to replace the colonial regime was a slow, difficult, and contested process. Maintaining the colonial economy proved impossible, in part because of political instability. And persistent economic difficulties hindered the stabilization of national politics. The power of the center—the dominance of the great families of Mexico City and the economy they ruled—eroded substantially after 1821.

The colonial economy that had served central Mexican elites so well during the eighteenth century seemed to vanish after 1821. Most obvious was the decline of silver mining. The great mines of Guanajuato and elsewhere were facing difficulties caused by declining ores and rising costs when insurrection broke out in 1810. The decade of conflict that followed forced many mines to close and others to curtail operations. Deep shafts flooded, making the revival of mining a difficult and expensive process. After 1821, it appeared that only the introduction of steam pumps could restore Mexican mining. The new technology came along with the entry of British mining companies into Mexico. Yet even British investment and technology only slowly revived Mexican silver mining. Most mines were eventually drained and resumed production, but the costs were high and the British found few profits. Mining generally returned to Mexican control by the middle of the nineteenth century.[17]

Silver production had peaked in the late colonial era, exceeding 5.5 million kilograms from 1801 to 1810. Decline set in during the decade of insurrections, and output fell again to only 2.6 million kilograms during the 1820s—less than half the level of the the last decade of colonial prosperity. From that depression, silver production began to expand slowly during the 1830s and had reached 75 percent of the late colonial level by the 1840s. But it was not until the 1870s that silver mining again matched the production of

[17] For example, Randall, *Real del Monte.*

the late colonial era.[18] Given the role of silver as the leading sector of the central Mexican economy, driving both international trade and much internal commerce, the decline of mining was a blow to the economy—and to the wealth and power of central Mexican elites.

The collapse of silver mining was the primary cause of Mexico's postindependence difficulties in international trade. Production of the new nation's primary export product fell precipitously just as external trade had to be reoriented outside the Spanish imperial system. And that difficult reorganization of commerce had to occur without many of the leading merchants of the late colonial era. Most of those established traders had been immigrants from Spain, and as the conflicts of the independence era escalated, many left Mexico, taking their often ample capital with them.[19] With little silver to export, without the capital accumulated by leading colonial merchants, and facing new patterns of trade, the commercial segment of the central Mexican elite was weakened after independence.

The decline of silver mining and the weakness of commercial elites combined to threaten the power of the dominant class of central Mexico—the great families that during the late colonial era had integrated commercial, mining, and landed activities to rule the core regions of the colony. The entrenched colonial pattern of ascent to elite status and family maintenance is well known. Generation after generation, a favored few accumulated wealth in commerce and mining and then secured their positions by investing in landed estates. Successful miners and merchants repeatedly married into established landed families. And the continuous infusions of wealth from trade and mining into landed families financed the operation of the great estates—the basis of elite family maintenance.[20]

[18] Urrutía and Nava, "La minería," p. 128.

[19] Flores Caballero, *La contrarrevolución*, pp. 78-79.

[20] Brading, *Miners and Merchants*; Van Young, *Hacienda and Market*, pp. 139-175; and Tutino, "Power, Class, and Family."

Independence interrupted this pattern of elite integration. The departure of most of a generation of immigrant merchants after 1810 precluded their eventually joining and reinforcing established landed families. The decline of mining and of international trade limited the wealth available to those who remained and might join the landed oligarchy. The opening of the ports of peripheral regions decentralized Mexican commerce, shifting profits away from the Mexico City merchants most likely to join the old oligarchy. And the arrival of traders from England, France, the United States, and elsewhere also altered the flow of wealth in postindependence Mexico. Many of these newcomers entered commerce in the cities of the core and the ports of the developing peripheries—and they were less certain to invest in Mexican estates and to marry into Mexican elite families than their Hispanic predecessors of the colonial era. Together, these developments combined to financially weaken the long-dominant elite families of central Mexico after 1821—just when they needed capital to restore the estate economy after nearly a decade of insurrections.[21]

Struggling landed families found little help from the Church, the other source of estate financing during the colonial era.[22] During the years of insurrections, many estate operators could not or would not pay their obligations to ecclesiastical creditors. Following pacification, Church lenders pressed for back payments. Facing their own financial difficulties, landowners petitioned the new national government for a debt cancellation. But the fledgling state was not ready to take on the economic power of the Church. Struggling estate owners and clerical creditors were left to confront each other, and the shortage of capital for estate financing persisted.[23] Independence left a financially weak-

[21] This analysis is developed in Tutino, "Hacienda Social Relations," pp. 503-515.

[22] Bauer, "The Church in the Economy," emphasizes the secondary role of Church lending.

[23] Lavrin, "Problems and Policies"; Costeloe, *Church Wealth*; and Díaz-

ened central Mexican elite facing increasingly scarce and expensive credit.

That long-dominant class began to lose unity as well as power. The integration of mining, commercial, and landed activities within great colonial families had sustained a unified late colonial elite. But with newcomers, often foreigners, dominant in mining and trade, Mexican elites became primarily landed elites. Politicians and generals, who might bring important political connections but usually little wealth, became the leading aspirants to elite family membership after 1821.[24] It was thus a financially weakened and increasingly divided elite that presumed to rule Mexico from Mexico City after independence.

Without ample financial resources, Mexican elites could not extract consistent profits from their estates. As large producers in an economy that included many small cultivators, colonial elites had generally profited not by supplying basic foodstuffs on a regular basis, but by holding essential goods until recurrent years of poor harvests made food scarce and expensive.[25] Such estate operations could be profitable—if elite families had the financial means to fund large-scale cultivation and then to store the produce until prices peaked, often two to four years later. The great families of late colonial Mexico City commanded such resources, due in large part to their close ties with commerce and mining. Their estate operations were modestly but consistently profitable.[26]

After independence, elite families short of funds found estate profits inconsistent at best. Many could no longer afford to hold crops, but had to sell just after the harvest when

---

Polanco, *Formación regional*, p. 40; on a rising coastal area, see Weimers, "Agriculture and Credit."

[24] See Ladd, *Mexican Nobility*, p. 212; and Tutino, "Hacienda Social Relations," pp. 503-515.

[25] See Florescano, *Precios del maíz*.

[26] Tutino, "Creole Mexico," pp. 167-178; Van Young, *Hacienda and Market*, pp. 224-235; and Maya, "Estructura y funcionamiento."

prices were lowest. Others had to use credit to finance cultivation—often paying high rates of interest and agreeing to sell their harvests to creditors at low prices.[27] In such situations, estate production was not generally profitable—estates that had to pay for labor could not compete with small producers relying on unpaid family workers. Meanwhile, the decline of mining was cutting into the markets for estate products.

The operation of landed estates ceased to serve as a secure base to support elite families after 1821. Mexico City elites operating grain-producing estates as well as sugar properties in the central highlands faced reduced profits interrupted by recurring years of losses. Properties changed hands rapidly as old families lost estates while others attempted to join the landed aristocracy—often without sufficient financial backing, and thus with little success.[28] In the Bajío, nearly every estate around Valle de Santiago that was not owned by a church institution changed hands at least once between 1830 and 1850. At León, estate ownership became similarly unstable after independence. Even the Obregón family, principal beneficiaries of the late colonial mining bonanza at Guanajuato, lost valuable properties there.[29]

The decline of central Mexican elites often benefited their competitors on the peripheries. During the late colonial years, the family of the Marqueses de San Miguel de Aguayo, based in Mexico City, held a vast landed empire in far northern Coahuila. The disruptions of the decade after 1810 surely contributed to the financial difficulties that led the titled colonial family to lose its landed patrimony to creditors in the 1820s. A group of British investors tried to operate the properties through the 1830s, with little suc-

[27] See Tutino, "Hacienda Social Relations," pp. 509-512.

[28] Ibid., pp. 518-528; Maya, "Estructura y funcionamiento"; and Bazant, "La hacienda azucarera."

[29] Díaz-Polanco, *Formación regional*, pp. 40-41; Brading, *Haciendas and Ranchos*, pp. 98-99, 108-113, 201, 204.

cess. In 1840, they were bought by the Sánchez Navarro family—a rising clan based in Coahuila that had first gained wealth in provincial commerce and then begun to acquire estates, often by taking advantage of the financial difficulties facing others during the early national years. The acquisition of the Aguayo properties left the Sánchez Navarros dominant in an immense region of northeastern Mexico.[30]

The spectacular rise of families such as the Sánchez Navarros in peripheral Coahuila should not blind us to the fundamental difficulties facing the more established elites of central Mexico during the years after independence. Those difficulties led to the disintegration of much of the commercial estate economy that had been so vital during the late colonial period, and to a major realignment of agrarian social relations.

## THE EXPANSION OF PEASANT AND RANCHERO PRODUCTION

Historians have asserted repeatedly that Mexican independence brought political chaos but little social change. Certainly the leaders of the new nation hoped to minimize social alterations. But persistent economic difficulties, coupled with political instability, undermined elite attempts to maintain social stability after 1821. The formal institutions of agrarian society—haciendas, peasant villages, ranchos—changed little after independence, but the social relations among landed elites, rancheros, peasant villagers, and estate dependents changed substantially. Although information about these postindependence agrarian transformations remains limited, it appears that social changes after 1821 often benefited rancheros and the agrarian poor at the expense of struggling elites. The years following inde-

[30] Altman, "Family and Region"; and Harris, *Mexican Family Empire*, pp. 155-172.

pendence brought economic decline to landed powerholders and an expansion of peasant and ranchero production.

The collapse of silver mining, the decline and disorgani-
zation of international trade, and the financial difficulties
plaguing established elites all contributed to Mexico's economic malaise between 1810 and 1880. John Coatsworth es-
timates that total national income in Mexico fell below the
level of 1800 and remained there at least into the 1860s. In
an era of population growth, per capita income remained
below late colonial levels through the 1870s.[31] Yet we know
of no calamitous famines afflicting wide areas of Mexico
from 1821 to 1868. The sources for the history of famine
after 1821 are limited, but it seems unlikely that scarcities of
the magnitude of 1785 and 1786 and of 1809 and 1810
would escape the attention of observers of the postindependence period.[32]

The decline of national income, combined with the apparent relief from devastating famine, suggests that the
economic collapse of the postindependence years was primarily a reduction of commercial production—activities
most likely to be captured in national accounting. There
was apparently an increase in the production of foodstuffs
for family consumption outside the commercial economy.
If that is true, then while the commercial economy collapsed, the subsistence economy strengthened—reversing
trends of the late colonial years. By the 1840s, landed elites
in central Mexico were complaining of surplus production—and shortages of consumers.[33]

In the Bajío and more northerly regions long dominated
by great estates, weak markets for estate produce and elite
financial difficulties led to a dramatic shift away from large-
scale estate production after independence. Increasing
areas of estate lands were turned over to tenants, ranging

[31] Coatsworth, "Obstacles," Table 1, p. 82.
[32] Florescano, ed., *Análisis histórico*, pp. 39-45.
[33] González Navarro, *Anatomía del poder*, p. 132.

from a few large producers, to more numerous rancheros, to multitudes of poor peasant sharecroppers. In the Bajío, this shift toward tenant production may appear a continuation of late colonial developments. But there was a critical difference. During the late colonial years, Bajío elites were economically strong and their estate operations were increasingly profitable. Estate operators then settled expanding numbers of poor tenants on marginal estate lands in order to have a source of seasonal labor for growing estate production. After independence, tenant cultivation in the Bajío expanded at the expense of estate production. Elites turned lands over to tenants in order to gain at least some income in times of financial constraints and weak markets. The postindependence acceleration of the shift toward tenant production in the Bajío reflected the economic decline of elites and led to an expansion of peasant and ranchero production.[34]

Parallel developments occurred across most of northern Mexico after 1821. In these more arid regions of sparse population, estate landholding had long predominated and most rural families lived as permanent, secure estate employees. Where northern estates continued to maintain large numbers of permanent employees, security persisted after independence. The residents of one large property near Zacatecas in the 1840s and the 1860s still obtained combinations of wages, guaranteed maize rations, and other benefits that allowed a minimally comfortable and secure subsistence. In more sparsely settled Coahuila, workers remained so scarce that estates could only attract them with large advances, plus the standard combinations of wages and rations. Elites there devoted great efforts to holding workers accountable for working off the resulting debts.[35]

[34] Ibid., p. 140; Brading, *Haciendas and Ranchos*, pp. 108-113, 201; Miller, "The Mexican Hacienda," pp. 312-314, 316-319.

[35] Cross, "Living Standards"; Harris, *Mexican Family Empire*, pp. 205-206, 218, 225-230; González Navarro, *Anatomía del poder*, pp. 150-155.

After independence, however, such secure dependents were increasingly outnumbered at northern estates by growing populations of tenants. In Aguascalientes, weak markets in the mining centers of Zacatecas and San Luis Potosí cut into estate profits. A few elites with ample financial resources responded by expanding irrigation and experimenting with new crops such as cotton. But more generally, estate profits were few and growing populations of tenants were settled on estate lands. New congregations called *rancherías* appeared on many Aguascalientes properties after 1821.[36]

In Coahuila, the vast estates of the Sánchez Navarros faced persistent difficulties in marketing their principal products, sheep and wool, during the early independence era. Market relations with Mexico City and central highlands were broken. The continuation of substantial textile imports after 1821 limited the outlets for wool. The exceptionally wealthy Sánchez Navarros sought new markets in northern Mexico. They experimented with new crops such as cotton and sugar cane, as well as fruits and vegetables. And they, too, turned increasing areas of their properties over to tenants. Some large estates were leased entirely to major tenants, who took on the risks of commercial production in unstable markets. And both the Sánchez Navarros and their major tenants turned over much of estate production to numerous small renters. When the Sánchez Navarros acquired the Aguayo holdings in the Laguna region of western Coahuila, numerous tenants were working the lands there—tenants who had become very independent during the previous years of unstable and financially weakened ownership. They attempted to preserve that independence through a rent strike against the Sánchez Navarros in 1841.[37]

A transition from secure employment toward increasing

[36] Rojas, *Destrucción de la hacienda*, pp. 24-28.
[37] Harris, *Mexican Family Empire*, pp. 183-185, 201, 231-239.

tenant production also occurred in San Luis Potosí after independence. By the late 1820s, over 40 percent of estate crops were raised by tenants.[38] At the hacienda named Cárdenas in 1831, 1,366 tenants far outnumbered the 641 employees.[39] By the 1850s, over 400 permanent employees remained at the Bocas estates, but they, too, were outnumbered by 800 tenants, including about 200 poor sharecroppers. Many of the tenants were newcomers who lived in over a dozen small settlements scattered across the estate property. Many had cleared marginal lands to try to raise maize in a region of scarce and inconsistent rains. Their crops often failed and rents were not always paid. By 1853, tenants owed the Bocas estate nearly 15,000 pesos in back rents. When the owner demanded recompense in labor, backed by a threat to confiscate the tenants' livestock, they rioted.[40]

The evident weakening of landed elites and the rapid expansion of tenant production encouraged the residents of several northern estates to petition for status as independent communities. Although such transformations of estate dependents into autonomous landholders were rare, at least one group successfully gained such independent control of lands they leased. The settlement called San Juan de Salinillas, on the Cruces estate in San Luis Potosí, became the independent community of Concordia in 1850. Its 800 residents won 17 square kilometers of land, most of it arid, from the estate.[41] The people of Concordia were but an extreme example of a common postindependence development across northern Mexico: the decline of estate production and of social relations of secure employment, and the rise of ranchero and peasant family production on estate lands.

[38] González Navarro, *Anatomía del poder*, p. 140.
[39] Márquez and Sánchez, "Fraccionamiento de las tierras," p. 53.
[40] Bazant, *Cinco haciendas*, pp. 104, 110-119.
[41] Ibid., p. 121.

Most of the emerging rancheros and peasants of northern Mexico remained tenants. They gained increased control over production, yet remained dependent on elites for access to land. They perhaps gained the maximum autonomy possible in arid regions dominated by large estate landholdings. Among the more substantial tenants, the rancheros, subsistence production was combined with active participation in regional markets. They may be classified as dependent peasant-farmers. Among smaller tenants, subsistence production was generally coupled with seasonal labor on estate fields. They may be categorized as poor peasant-laborers. Of course, the division between rancheros and peasants was not precise. What is clear is that both groups gained in autonomy, while facing the insecurities inherent in raising crops and grazing livestock in dry regions.

As long as elites remained weak, it appears that the gains in autonomy overshadowed the insecurities facing the growing numbers of estate tenants in northern Mexico. The best evidence of this is the flood of migrants that brought large numbers of families from central regions into the north to take up tenancies. North central states such as San Luis Potosí saw their populations nearly triple during the first three quarters of the nineteenth century. Some regions farther north grew even more rapidly. During the same period, the more densely settled regions such as Guanajuato and Jalisco experienced much smaller population increases.[42] The availability of lands for tenant production was drawing people into the arid north after independence.

The expansion of tenant production also increased the potential for agrarian violence across regions that had remained stable in 1810. Elites still kept the best, irrigated lands for estate production and allotted less fertile fields to their tenants. The conflicts in the Laguna region and at Bocas reveal the potential results. But during the first half-century after independence, confrontations between northern

[42] See Appendix C, Table c.4.

elites and their growing numbers of tenants remained sporadic. Landlords facing persistent economic difficulties could not press demands for higher rents onto tenants, nor threaten mass evictions. This was an era of agrarian decompression—of elites seeking tenants in order to keep estate production going during hard times in the commercial economy.

Agrarian social relations based on tenancies, incorporating dependence with insecurity into the lives of the rural poor, came to predominate across northern Mexico between 1821 and 1880. Should the commercial economy revive, should elites find new prosperity and power, tenants might begin to face new demands—making the dependence and insecurity of their lives more painfully evident. The Díaz era of the late nineteenth century brought just such developments—with explosive consequences, as we shall see.

In central Mexico, where most agrarian families continued to live in landed communities, postindependence developments also worked to entrench and even expand peasant production—and to raise the potential for agrarian tensions. In the highland basins around Mexico City, relations between estates and villages had long reflected delicate negotiations that attempted to balance the estates' needs for seasonal workers against the villagers' subsistence production and their needs for supplemental income. During the eighteenth century, villagers often enjoyed access to estate pastures and woodlands as long as they continued to provide labor services. They gained both cash earnings and access to important resources for their seasonal labor at nearby estates.[43]

After independence, this relationship of symbiotic exploitation began to break down. Many estate operators in central Mexico were chronically short of cash, making payment for villagers' labor difficult. Many peasants began to

[43] See Tutino, "Creole Mexico," pp. 303-368.

refuse to work at estates without immediate cash payment. Some landlords responded by threatening to deny access to estate resources to those who did not labor. But many villagers would not give in. Most retained at least minimal subsistence lands. And population growth was minimal in the central highlands during the first three quarters of the nineteenth century.[44] With migration toward the north and other peripheral regions relieving population pressures in the central highlands, villagers could drive hard bargains with estates seeking their services as laborers.

They persistently refused to labor except for immediate cash payment. Thus, only the minority of elites with ample cash resources could count on regular labor supplies during the postindependence period in central Mexico. In some regions, villagers successfully pressured estates into bidding up the wages offered to scarce workers at harvest times.[45] Other estates tried offering advance payments when funds were available, hoping to attract needed workers.[46] The emergence of such bidding for villagers' labor services is one more indication of the relative weakening of landed elites in their relations with landed peasants after 1821.

With elites facing economic difficulties while villagers held onto important resources, the relations between them shifted modestly—but importantly—in favor of the villagers. The chinampa cultivators in the communities just south of Mexico City not only retained their most valuable lands but maintained a strong community cohesion after independence, despite continuing attempts by city dwellers to gain access to their exceptionally fertile lands so close to the nation's largest market.[47] In an extreme example of village

[44] See Appendix C, Table c.4.
[45] Tutino, "Hacienda Social Relations," pp. 521-524.
[46] Maya, "Estructura y funcionamiento," p. 341.
[47] Lira, *Comunidades indígenas*, pp. 21, 77-78, 117-119. Chinampas are exceptionally fertile and well-watered garden plots built as islands in the lake beds south of Mexico City. They are erroneously called "floating gardens."

strength, the community of Ocoyoacac in the valley of Toluca purchased in 1850 lands it had long disputed with a
neighboring estate.[48]

Many more communities perceived the prevailing weakness of landed elites and the new national state and went to
the courts claiming title to lands previously held by estates.
The suits repeatedly asserted that the estates were utilizing
lands stolen from the villagers. Estate owners would respond by showing legally validated titles. The truth of such
competing claims is rarely evident. Mexican elites and villagers were equally capable of fabricating land claims. Each
also held a different definition of justice—elites relied on
colonial land titles, while villagers looked to ancestral possession. In most instances, the courts backed the elites, but
persistent villagers did make some notable gains. In the
1840s, a group of communities in the valley of Toluca won
title to lands long held by the Condes de Santiago, one of
Mexico's oldest and most landed families. The news of that
victory leaped from village to village across central Mexico,
and elites braced themselves for another barrage of village
land claims. Community leaders began to examine the documents carefully, seeking a basis for such claims.[49] With villagers increasingly reluctant to perform estate labor, and
with land disputes proliferating, the relations between elites
and villagers in the central highlands became less symbiotic
and more overtly conflictive during the years after independence. Landed elites convinced themselves that they
were being besieged by insubordinate peasants.

As long as their financial problems continued and their
state remained fragile and contested, elites could do little to
effectively subordinate such villagers. Instead, around the
middle of the nineteenth century, estates began to offer
portions of their fields to villagers who would become

[48] Menegus Bornemann, "Ocoyoacac," p. 97.
[49] These developments are detailed in Tutino, "Agrarian Social
Change."

sharecroppers. The shift to such tenancies helped relieve elites' pressing needs for cash. Sharecroppers raised maize on estate lands without demanding cash payment. And access to lands to grow maize, even if half the harvest went to the landlord, was one offer that attracted growing numbers to work estate lands. Elites also hoped that villagers who were tenants on estate fields would not challenge for title to those resources. The beginning of any such claim would surely bring quick eviction. And villagers who were also sharecroppers might be pressed more easily to labor seasonally.

For villagers, sharecropping was acceptable because it would allow them to increase maize production. For elites, the system was appealing because it would resolve pressing financial and labor difficulties. Yet while each participant expected to benefit, the shift toward sharecropping also increased the potential for agrarian conflict in the central highlands. A growing part of villagers' subsistence production became dependent on access to estate lands. When harvests were ample, peasant production expanded and estates appeared as benefactors. But when crops periodically failed, central Mexican estates more easily became the targets of peasant grievances. During the colonial era, when central Mexican villagers produced maize almost exclusively on village lands, crop failures appeared as calamitous acts of nature. But when crops failed on sharecropped lands, villagers blamed their hunger on the estates' insistence on allotting them only marginal, nonirrigated fields. Sharecropping made peasant subsistence production more dependent on elites, and thus, as crop failure became more of a social issue in central Mexico, villagers might begin to seek more social solutions.

The timing, magnitude, and immediate consequences of the shift toward sharecropping in the central highlands remain uncertain. Share tenancies were common at Chalco by the 1850s, and were the predominant means of raising maize at the Jalpa estate in the northern valley of Mexico in the 1860s. At Chalco, sharecropping was at times arranged between estates and communities, organized by village leaders. At Jalpa, individuals contracted to sharecrop estate lands. A few were modest commercial producers, probably rancheros, while many more were poor peasant families combining sharecropping with labor on estate fields.[50] After 1880, sharecropping was the primary means of cultivating maize on estate land across Mexico.[51] But just when sharecropping became the predominant link between estates and villages in the central highlands is unknown. This much, however, is clear: sharecropping was an expanding part of agrarian social relations in the central highlands by the 1850s. Growing numbers of villagers became dependent on access to estate lands for subsistence production. Peasant cultivation there was shifting from relatively autonomous insecurity toward increasingly dependent insecurity—heightening the potential for agrarian conflicts in the central highlands that had remained so stable in 1810.

Dependent production by peasant families using estate lands thus expanded in both northern and central Mexico during the half-century after independence. At the same time, there was also a rapid expansion of ranchero production across Mexico. Rancheros had lived in small numbers almost everywhere in Mexico during the colonial era. They produced much of their own subsistence, while marketing larger surpluses than most peasants. During the colonial centuries, rancheros remained marginal participants in Mexican agrarian life, overshadowed in most regions by great estates and peasant communities.[52] The years after independence, however, brought rapid increases in the numbers and importance of rancheros in Mexico. As estates shifted to tenant production, many families of modest means established themselves as rancheros on rented lands.

[50] See ibid., and Tutino, "Family Economies."

[51] Miller, "The Mexican Hacienda," pp. 329-331.

[52] See Brading, *Haciendas and Ranchos*; Tutino, "Creole Mexico," pp. 264-270; and "Life and Labor," pp. 246-350.

Most remained tenants. But a growing number of these rancheros became landowners. As financial difficulties continued to plague landlords, a surprising number of estates were subdivided and sold in fractions during the middle decades of the nineteenth century.[53]

While rancheros became more important across all of Mexico after 1821, they came to predominate in several upland regions on the fringes of the old colonial core areas of central Mexico. In the Huasteca of eastern San Luis Potosí, by 1854 nearly 70 percent of the agrarian population was clasified as *labradores*—family cultivators who were primarily rancheros rather than impoverished peasants. Subsistence was said to be cheap there.[54] Upland sections of Michoacán and Jalisco became famous as regions of rancheros during the nineteenth century. In these regions of western Mexico, landed elites faced difficult dilemmas after independence, according to Jean Meyer. They could either let their lands to poor sharecroppers, or sell off their estates in fractions. The result was the decline of the hacienda and the triumph of the rancheros.[55]

The emergence and development of ranchero societies after independence await broad investigation. But two detailed case studies, one of a ranchero community in Michoacán and the other from Hidalgo, suggest some general trends. Ranchero societies flourished during the nineteenth century in regions little populated and minimally integrated into the commercial economy during the colonial era. The lands settled by rancheros were often part of large but undeveloped estates. During the eighteenth and early nineteenth centuries, landowners allowed tenants to settle, seeking income from unused resources. Through the first half of the nineteenth century, the ranchero communities expanded through both local reproduction and the arrival

[53] Brading, *Haciendas and Ranchos*, p. 203; Bazant, "La división," pp. 33-41.

[54] González Navarro, *Anatomía del poder*, p. 71.

[55] Meyer, *Esperando a Lozada*, pp. 25, 33.

of newcomers—often fleeing the disruptions of the era. In some instances, estates were eventually subdivided and the rancheros became landowners. Elsewhere they remained tenants. In general, by the middle of the nineteenth century, ranchero communities had expanded and become more complex. Many prosperous rancheros let out lands to small tenants and sharecroppers—often also employing them at harvest time. The expanding ranchero communities were not egalitarian societies, but most rancheros worked the land along with family members, and lived alongside their dependents.[56] Their communities remained closely integrated. The expansion of ranchero production after independence was another element in the declining dominance of landed elites and their great estates in Mexico.

The expansion of peasant and ranchero production brought new similarities to agrarian social relations across Mexico during the nineteenth century. Rancheros seemed to appear everywhere, though their importance varied by region. Among the agrarian poor of the arid north, the permanent employment that had provided security to estate dependents during the late colonial era gave way to increasing tenant production. Estate residents remained dependent, gained limited autonomy, and faced new insecurities. In the central highlands, the relations of symbiotic exploitation that had linked relatively autonomous villagers to great estates in the eighteenth century began to break down. Villagers might increase subsistence production by sharecropping estate lands, thus also increasing their dependence on landed elites.

After 1821, then, social relations of dependent insecurity—based on expanding tenant production—became increasingly common to agrarian life in both central and northern Mexico. Regions strikingly different in 1810 were

[56] González y González, *Pueblo en vilo*, pp. 64-113; and Schryer, "Ranchero Economy," pp. 419-426.

becoming increasingly similar after 1850. As long as elites remained weak, and the era of decompression persisted, the potential for social conflict inherent in these developments remained muted. But should elites attempt to press demands upon rural families facing lives of dependent insecurity, agrarian grievances would mount. Beginning in the 1840s, while economic crisis and general decompression persisted, frustrated powerholders attempted to use political means to make gains at the expense of the rural poor. They set off waves of regional insurrections across Mexico from then until the early 1880s. Then, three decades of apparent peace brought both political and economic pressures down hard upon rural people facing dependent insecurity. That period of renewed compression set off the national revolutionary conflicts that began in 1910.

# CHAPTER SEVEN

# Politics and Agrarian Conflicts, 1840–1880

THE EMERGENCE OF the peripheries, the decline of the commercial economy and the power of elites in the central highlands, and the shift toward peasant and ranchero production all contributed to the destabilization of agrarian life in Mexico during the long era of decompression that followed independence. The outbreak of violent insurrections in that context, however, resulted repeatedly from the intrusion of another new element of Mexican life after independence: politics. During the colonial era, there were officially no politics—only administration and justice. After independence, however, politics became a central part of Mexican society. The elites—and those who aspired to join them—began to jockey for control of the state and for the power to define its policies. Two aspects of the emerging political life of newly independent Mexico became fundamental provocations of agrarian conflicts: the new role of the state as an instrument of elite class power, and the political liberals' goal of denying peasant communities the right to hold land. As liberals gained in political power, agrarian insurrections proliferated.

## THE NATIONAL STATE, LIBERALISM, AND AGRARIAN POLITICS

Before 1821, the Mexican state was but part of a colonial regime, based in Spain, whose primary concern in Mexico was to control a colony that generated immense wealth in silver. From the early colonial years, Spanish authorities had feared the independent power of Mexican elites. Thus, while allowing them extensive lands and great wealth, the colonial regime worked to curb their power. Sustaining the landed resources and political independence of peasant communities was one means of limiting elite power in central Mexico. The persistence of such communities denied Mexican elites direct power over the agrarian population of the most densely settled regions of the colony. One result was the survival of substantial autonomy among the villagers of central and southern regions—autonomy that was the basis of the relations of symbiotic exploitation that linked many estates and villagers and sustained rural stability there. When conflicts did pit villagers against elites and their estates, the colonial courts served as accepted mediators—at times favoring the villagers and often forcing compromise onto elites.[1]

The mediating role of the colonial state disappeared with independence. With the defeat of the Hidalgo revolt and subsequent insurrections, Mexican independence was an affair of the elites—powerholders who claimed control of the state and aimed to make it an instrument of their interests. Had those elites been economically strong and had their state achieved unity and stability, the years after 1821 might have brought unmitigated disaster upon the agrarian poor. But elites' persistent economic difficulties and political conflicts kept their new state factionalized and unstable. The result was a lengthy period in which economically struggling and politically divided elites attempted to use unstable state powers to pursue class interests against an entrenched agrarian population that was actually increasing its control over rural production. As economic developments and social decompression began to favor peasants and rancheros and weaken elites, the latter claimed state

[1] See Tutino, "Creole Mexico," pp. 343-368; Taylor, *Drinking, Homicide, and Rebellion*; Van Young, *Hacienda and Market*, pp. 315-342; and Borah, *Justice by Insurance*.

powers and attempted to use them as means to salvage their waning positions. Before 1880, they provoked insurrections more often than they gained any clear advantages.[2]

In the seemingly endless conflicts over control of the new Mexican state, those who challenged the power of the heirs to the colonial oligarchy, and who often envisioned a new structure for Mexican society, identified with liberalism. The political philosophy of individual equality provided a platform for attacks on the privileges of landed aristocrats, the Church, and the military—and on the corporate rights of peasant communities. The foundations of Hispanic liberalism developed in the Spanish enlightenment of the eighteenth century. Liberalism first permeated legislation affecting agrarian Mexico during the era of Spanish liberal opposition to Napoleon. The established elites of central Mexico led their independence movement, in part, to escape the application of liberal principles to the society they ruled. They would soon face equally threatening liberalism and assaults on their powers and privileges within the new nation they created.[3]

The earliest success of liberalism in Mexico both reflected and reinforced the waning power of the old colonial elite. The Spanish liberal Cortes had abolished entails in 1820, legislation confirmed in Mexico by 1823. Entails had provided a state guarantee against the division or loss of the landed patrimonies that sustained the greatest colonial families. Liberalism opposed entails as bulwarks of privilege and brakes on innovation and social mobility. By the early 1820s, many of the aristocratic clans long favored by entails were ready to acquiesce to their abolition. The economic disruptions of the previous decade had left many in precarious circumstances; they owed large debts and lacked the funds to finance estate operations. The end of entails would allow them to sell off lands or entire estates, and use

---

[2] This thesis is developed in Tutino, "Agrarian Social Change."

[3] See Hale, *Mexican Liberalism*, especially pp. 108-147, 215-247.

the proceeds to pay debts and revive their remaining properties. The end of entails allowed established elite families to salvage at least a portion of their power.[4]

The first victory of liberalism in Mexico came easily because most elites expected to gain—old aristocratic families could free themselves of debts, while aspirants to landed status foresaw easier access to estate properties. Liberal opposition to the corporate powers of the Church and the military, in contrast, engendered long conflicts that need not detain us here. Liberal attacks on the rights of peasant communities also provoked persistent debates and escalating conflicts. Combined with the new role of the state as an instrument of elite class power, liberal opposition to peasant community "privileges" helped provoke much of the agrarian violence of the nineteenth century.

Since the eighteenth century, Hispanic liberals had envisioned great economic gains if the lands held by peasant communities were mobilized—that is, converted to private property that could be bought and sold, as well as mortgaged. They argued that peasants who became owners of their lands would have new incentives to increase production. But in Mexico, the poor peasants who relied most on community lands already used them very intensively for subsistence production. The real gains of a shift from community to private ownership would go to those who might benefit from a mobilization of peasant holdings. Formerly inalienable village lands might be sold or lost for debt once they became private property. Villagers would thus lose the underlying guarantee of subsistence autonomy that community property had long provided. Few Mexican villagers shared the liberals' vision that the privatization of community lands would bring them benefits.

The liberal Spanish Cortes of 1812 and 1813 passed constitutional provisions and enabling legislation to end community landholding. Those enactments were known in

[4] Ladd, *Mexican Nobility*, pp. 153-158.

Mexico, but not widely implemented—prudent restraint in an era of continuing rural insurrections.[5] The abolition of community landholding was proposed and hotly debated in the constitutional and regular congresses of both national and state governments during the 1820s. The national regime reached no clear decision, leaving the states to approach the issue from their regional perspectives—a wise recognition of the regional variations of rural life in Mexico.[6]

In the 1820s, two pivotal states resolved the issue in opposite decisions. The state of Mexico allowed community landholding to persist, while Jalisco declared its abolition. There were proponents of the end of peasant community "privileges" in the state of Mexico, then encompassing most of the central highlands as well as adjacent areas. (The states of Morelos, Hidalgo, and most of Guerrero were later created from sectors of the larger state of Mexico.) But no measure was enacted, perhaps out of fear of disruptions.[7] In the central valleys, the colonial agrarian structure was based upon peasant communities, their landholdings, and their provision of seasonal laborers to nearby estates. In the 1820s, the colonial system of symbiotic exploitation was expected to revive. The immediate privatization of community lands there would disrupt an agrarian economic and social structure that had held stable in 1810. Central Mexican elites chose not to undermine that structure—and perhaps provoke vehement peasant opposition—during the uncertain first years of nationhood.

The state of Jalisco, in contrast, passed laws in 1825 and 1828 calling for the privatization of community lands. Liberalism was stronger in this region nearer the periphery. And agrarian conditions differed from those in the central highlands. In Jalisco the estate economy had developed

---

[5] Orozco, *Los ejidos*, pp. 175-180.

[6] Hale, *Mexican Liberalism*, pp. 225-228.

[7] Ibid., pp. 226-232.

only late in the colonial era—and more in conflict with peasant communities than symbiotically linked to them. Many Jalisco villagers had joined the insurrections of 1810. Thus could Jalisco legislators more easily abolish community landholding. Much village land was subsequently privatized, with many communities complaining that they did not receive full payment for their properties. Such developments surely heightened many villagers' opposition to privatization, and the process in Jalisco was disputed and delayed for decades.[8]

The liberals' goal of ending community landholding became evident shortly after independence. The wisdom of implementing that goal, however, would be debated long afterward. And the ability to enforce such a radical alteration of the rural social structure would await the return of general economic prosperity and political stability late in the century. In the meantime, the debates and the attempts to implement such changes would set off escalating agrarian conflicts.

The insurrections of 1810 through 1816 revealed two patterns of grievances underlying rural revolts in Mexico. The Hidalgo revolt arose primarily among estate residents from the Bajío forced to endure worsening conditions of dependence and insecurity. Secondarily, other uprisings in Jalisco, the Sierra Gorda, and elsewhere resulted from the grievances of peasant villagers facing attacks on their autonomy. During the period after independence, there was little sustained rebellious activity among estate dependents. The era of decompression in which estate production was turned over to many tenants—who gained autonomy that apparently compensated for persisting insecurities—relieved, or at least cushioned, the grievances of many estate dependents.

It was assaults on peasant autonomy, the secondary pat-

---

[8] Meyer, *Esperando a Lozada*, pp. 36, 98; González Navarro, *Anatomía del poder*, pp. 139, 142-143.

tern of insurrection in 1810, that increasingly generated the grievances that led to rural uprisings after 1821. The development of the economies of peripheral regions led to waves of encroachments on village resources—with predictable results. The liberalism that opposed all rights of community landholding often justified the encroachments in the peripheries, and would eventually legitimate a direct attack on peasant village properties in the central highlands as well.

Yet agrarian conflicts did not engulf Mexico immediately after independence. The defeats suffered by the insurgents of 1810 were still fresh memories. The financial difficulties of elites, along with the collapse of the commercial economy, certainly relieved some pressures on the rural poor in the 1820s and 1830s. And the proposals of liberals to abolish community landholding remained tentative, and if legislated, often not implemented—limiting the political pressures on villagers in the first years after 1821.

One conflict, presaging many later insurrections, did develop in the 1820s in Sonora on the far northwestern periphery. Spanish occupation had been minimal there during the colonial era, mostly missionaries and a few garrison outposts. The Yaqui and other indigenous peoples had retained their lands and much political independence. They considered themselves nations. The late eighteenth century brought increased Spanish settlement and economic activity, and independence handed emerging local elites the power to rule regional politics and economic developments. They quickly began to use that power to encroach on Yaqui lands, while also denying that nation any separate political recognition. Such postindependence attacks on the political and economic autonomy of the Yaqui led to violent uprisings in 1826 and 1827, and again in 1831 and 1832, each led by Juan de la Cruz Banderas.[9]

The revolts led by Banderas were defeated militarily. But

[9] Voss, *On the Periphery*, pp. 2-32, 41-42, 48-61, 66-67; Hu-Dehart, *Yaqui Resistance*, pp. 15-55.

pacification during the following years depended as much on the emergence of a local political faction led by Manuel Gándara that called itself conservative and opposed the local liberals. Gándara accepted the Yaqui's claims to lands and local autonomy, and used Yaqui support to rule Sonora from the late 1830s to 1856. And the Gándara-conservative-Yaqui alliance persisted as an opposition movement into the 1860s—keeping the Yaqui working within the political arena to preserve their autonomy.[10] The revolts of the 1820s and early 1830s, although defeated, made Yaqui power evident to regional political actors. They might accept that power, as did Gándara, and preserve a tenuous agrarian peace. Or they might work to undermine it, as did later liberals, and provoke escalating agrarian conflicts.

## THE CRISES OF THE 1840S

The first of several rounds of agrarian insurrections that followed Mexican independence began in the 1840s. By then, the economic weakness of elites and the fragility of their new state were obvious. The war with the United States in 1846 and 1847 cost the nation large areas of little-occupied territory along its far northern frontiers. And during the war, several massive rural insurrections challenged the powers of elites and their state within Mexico. In Yucatán, tens of thousands of Maya took arms and nearly drove the Hispanic population into the sea. The Sierra Gorda exploded into another insurrection. The residents of the towns and villages of the southern Isthmus of Tehuantepec also rebelled during the war years. And soon after the end of international hostilities, villagers in the core central highlands began to challenge the power of those who had long ruled them. Defeated in war and confronted with multiple internal insurrections, Mexican elites faced their greatest crisis since independence in the late 1840s.

[10] Voss, *On the Periphery*, p. 99; Hu-Dehart, *Yaqui Resistance*, pp. 56-59.

The famous insurrection known as the caste war of Yucatán resulted from the grievances generated among Maya peasants by regional elites attempting to use state powers to compensate for the economic difficulties of the postindependence era. Yucatán had remained peripheral to the colonial economy. The majority of the population were Maya who retained substantial autonomy as peasants. Their primary contacts with Spaniards were mediated by Franciscans and other clerics. A small and modestly wealthy regional elite lived mostly in Mérida, sustaining aristocratic pretensions by collecting tributes and labor services from a conquered population still entrenched on the land.

The late eighteenth century brought new trade with Cuba—livestock and other products were exported to Havana. Combined with population growth in Yucatán, that commercial expansion led the development of a modest estate economy in the regions near Mérida and Campeche after 1780, incorporating a growing number of Maya as tenants and laborers. But independence cut off trade with Cuba, because the sugar island remained a Spanish colony. The end of livestock exports crippled the already weak economic base of Yucatecan elites, and they were forced to search for new ways to make profits. But with limited financial resources, poor lands in an arid region, and no new markets, the prospects for commercial revival seemed bleak. Some estates tried sugar production, with little success. Others looked to exports of cordage made from the henequen cactus—but found only small markets until much later in the century. Between 1821 and 1845, the only new "resource" available to Yucatecan elites was their state government. With old exports failing and new ones showing little promise, they began to use the powers of government to take control of resources long left to the Maya majority.

Strong regional population growth continued through the 1830s and helped push an expansion of Hispanic commercial activities into the interior of the peninsula. Lands long used by Maya peasants—and often owned as titled property by no one—were claimed by those who could gain state approval. Meanwhile, the Franciscans who had at least partially shielded the peasants from such expropriations were replaced with secular clerics, who were primarily interested in collecting fees for their services. In the early 1840s, Yucatecan liberals then in power culminated the assault on Mayan resources by ordering the congregation of many scattered and partially nomadic peasants into villages—and then limiting the lands available to those communities. The postindependence state in Yucatán had clearly become the agent of regional elites working to expropriate resources from the Maya majority.

But that state was newly organized, poorly funded, and often factionalized. It could serve only as an unstable agent of elite power. Competing regional factions fought to control the state government at Mérida, their disputes heightened by involvement in equally unstable Mexican national politics. Civil wars among elite factions persisted while elites claimed resources essential to Maya autonomy. As Maya grievances mounted and political conflicts created potential opportunities for insurrection, elites began to arm groups of Maya and to involve them in political wars. When in 1847 the Mexican war with the United States coincided with another political conflict in Yucatán, nearly 100,000 Maya took the opportunity to strike back at those who presumed to rule them.

Not all Maya, of course, became insurgents. Most of those who lived near the cities of Mérida and Campeche were accustomed to close involvement with Spaniards and their commercial economy. Since the late eighteenth century, growing numbers had lived as tenants or worked as seasonal laborers at developing estates. Able to combine subsistence production with estate labor, they lived under a regional variant of the symbiotic exploitation that had maintained the stability of the central highlands in 1810. Thus, the Maya most linked with the commercial economy of Yucatán generally remained passive in 1847, with many fighting in the armies that defended elite interests.

In the interior regions of the peninsula, Maya peasants, who formed a larger majority of the population, were accustomed to living all but independent of Spanish rule. It was not until after independence that these Maya of the interior faced the encroachments of Yucatecan elites attempting to use their new agent, the state, to usurp resources and to impose new rules of peasant life. The Maya of the interior of Yucatán now faced new and sudden threats to their entrenched autonomy—and they rebelled en masse.

Elite political conflicts amidst the war against the United States provided ample opportunity for insurrection. The insurgents almost conquered—or better, reconquered—the entire Yucatán peninsula, and it took a decade of fighting and substantial help from central Mexico before the rebels were finally forced to retreat to the backlands. Then, trade relations and munitions supplies from the British at Belice, enabled a large remnant of Maya insurgents to hold out until early in the twentieth century.[11]

The other major regional insurrection of the late 1840s, in the Sierra Gorda, awaits social analysis. Long a peripheral enclave in the central Mexican heartland, the Sierra experienced the late penetration of Hispanic society and its commercial economy during the eighteenth century. Sporadic protests had culminated in sustained insurrection during the years after the Hidalgo revolt. Developments in the region after independence are little known, but the movement of outsiders into the region and the expansion of their commercial interests seem probable. The uprising of the later 1840s began amidst the political conflicts set off by Mexico's impending defeat in the war against the United States. What began as a conflict among local elites was sus-

[11] This analysis of the caste war reflects my reading of Reed, *Caste War*; González Navarro, *Raza y tierra*, pp. 43-75; Farriss, *Maya Society*; Patch, "Agrarian Change"; and Lapointe, *Los mayas rebeldes*.

tained by thousands of agrarian rebels recruited among the tenants of the region's estates as well as among the indigenous peoples still demanding free access to the resources of the Sierra's rugged uplands. The uprising of the Sierra Gorda brought together—or attempted to bring together—peasants facing threats to their autonomy and estate dependents demanding more favorable conditions in the Sierra Gorda as well as in adjacent areas such as the Río Verde region of San Luis Potosí. A proclamation issued in 1849 by one rebel leader, Eleuterio Quieroz, called not only for rights of self-government and landholding for peasant communities, but also demanded limitations on rents and improved labor relations for estate dependents—as well as the rights of estate resident communities of over 1,500 people to become independent, landholding communities. The agrarian insurrection in the Sierra Gorda, adjacent to the core regions of central Mexico, endured for three years before facing defeat.[12]

The smaller but regionally intense conflict at the Isthmus of Tehuantepec during the war with the United States resulted from developments parallel to those that provoked the caste war in Yucatán. After independence, regional elites facing the decline of the colonial export economy, there based on indigo, began to use their control of the state of Oaxaca to claim property rights over coastal salt beds long used freely by the inhabitants of the southern Isthmus. Salt was basic to the Mexican diet, and Isthmus residents not only supplied themselves but also traded salt to distant regions. The sudden loss of access to the beds cut into local autonomy and also curtailed regional trade. That loss at the hands of elites favored by the state occurred during escalating conflicts over land rights. Those disputes pitted Isthmus villagers against landlords generally based in the city of

[12] See Reina, *Las rebeliones campesinas*, pp. 291-302; González Navarro, *Anatomía del poder*, pp. 38-48; and Reina, "La rebelión campesina de Sierra Gorda."

Oaxaca and repeatedly favored by the state government there. Similar disputes caused by the encroachments of elites onto peasant resources in the peripheral regions near the Pacific coasts of southwestern Mexico set off sporadic uprisings beginning in the early 1840s.[13]

The conflict at Tehuantepec escalated in the early 1840s as villagers repeatedly "stole" salt, and both estates and villagers sequestered livestock grazing on disputed lands. When the war against the United States claimed the attention of state leaders and armed forces in 1846, Isthmus villagers were free to utilize the disputed resources. Late in 1847, as the war ended, the Governor of Oaxaca, the liberal Benito Juárez, confronted an Isthmus population led by the people of Juchitán, a village that was ignoring state regulations in matters of property. In Juárez' definition, that was insurrection. He sent an army to restore the rule of his state—and provoked a violent conflict that endured several years.[14] Once again, weak regional elites attempted to use new and poorly established powers of state to gain control of resources from long-entrenched peasants. The result was another violent conflict, precipitated by the opportunity provided by the war against the United States.

These sustained regional insurrections tested the powers of the Mexican state in the late 1840s. Once the international war ended, with Mexico accepting defeat and great losses of territory, these uprisings on the peripheries were eventually subdued. But before they were finally contained, uprisings also began to threaten the agrarian peace in the central highlands. Beginning in 1848, the regions forming the modern states of Mexico, Hidalgo, and Morelos produced numerous rural protests, including many violent confrontations. For the first time since the Spanish conquest, widespread agrarian conflict developed across the core of the central highlands. The villagers of the grain-

[13] See Hart, "The 1840s."
[14] Tutino, "Rebelión indígena."

producing regions whose passivity was fundamental to agrarian stability in 1810, in the late 1840s became increasingly ready to strike against landed elites and their state.

This era of nascent agrarian conflict in central Mexico deserves comprehensive analysis. At present, only the developments leading to the emergence of rural violence in the Chalco region, just southeast of Mexico City, are known in detail.[15] During the period after independence, Chalco elites had faced repeated difficulties financing estate operations and recruiting workers. The turnover of estate ownership was rapid. After the war with the United States, however, Chalco elites showed a remarkable resolve to seek new means of reviving their estate economy. They built new dams and canals to expand irrigation. They sought new sources of water by drilling artesian wells. They experimented with seeds to increase production of wheat and maize. And they tried new products, especially dairying on cultivated alfalfa pastures.

Many of these innovations, however, led to confrontations with Chalco villagers. Since independence, estate financial difficulties had strained labor relations. The links of symbiotic exploitation that had long united estates and villagers began to break downs as villagers were reluctant to work for estates that could not pay cash. When in the late 1840s the construction of dams and canals caused encroachments on village lands, conflict became more overt. When elites claimed village fields because they were more easily irrigated by new water works, the villagers became adamant. They went first to the courts to seek redress—their tradition since colonial times. But now the courts repeatedly backed elite claims, whatever their merits. Chalco villagers concluded that the courts no longer served as even minimally impartial mediators. They had become agents of elite

[15] On the extent of these uprisings, see Reina, *Las rebeliones campesinas*, pp. 61-63, 123-126, 157-177; on Chalco, see Tutino, "Agrarian Social Change."

interests. With the old symbiosis of labor relations disappearing and the mediating role of the colonial courts gone, villagers began to take their protests into the fields. They obstructed estate operations. They blocked construction projects. They confiscated estate tools and construction materials. When most frustrated, they assaulted estate managers—the owners usually remained safely away in Mexico City. In response to the villagers' obstructions and increasing violence at Chalco, the state of Mexico sanctioned the use of whatever force was available to landowners. That usually meant arming the small groups of permanent estate employees from several properties to suppress the villagers' revolts.

The uprisings at Chalco in the late 1840s were not sustained mass insurrections such as those in the peripheral areas. They were lengthy protests, punctuated by sporadic violence, that continued for several years. The simultaneous conflicts in the Morelos basin, just south of Chalco, and in the Mezquital to the north, were of similar dimensions.[16] They may appear minor when compared with Yucatán's caste war, but they were larger and more sustained than any previous agrarian protests in the central highlands. Late colonial conflicts almost always were confined to single villages and usually lasted but a day—and rarely more than a week. Suddenly in the late 1840s and extending in to the early 1850s, peasants from multiple villages were coordinating protests that were at least sporadically violent and endured for months—at times years. And such protests were occurring simultaneously in several regions of the pivotal central highlands. By 1850, the stability that had held through the colonial centuries in central Mexico was vanishing. The confrontations that began in the late 1840s would escalate in the coming years.

With relations of symbiotic exploitation strained and con-

---

[16] González Navarro, *Anatomía del poder*, pp. 160-168; Reina, *Las rebeliones campesinas*, pp. 61-63, 123-126, 157-177.

flict ever more prevalent in estate-village relations, those who ruled the state of Mexico began to find the liberals' program for ending community landholding more attractive. A survey of village properties was ordered by the governor in 1848. Most villages refused to respond. Then in the autumn of 1849, amidst a rising tide of agrarian conflicts, the state of Mexico declared the end of community property rights. Several other states, including Jalisco and Michoacán, passed or reenacted similar legislation almost simultaneously.[17] Mexican elites from the core as well as the periphery were moving toward agreement on the goal of ending community property rights—the ultimate base of peasant autonomy.

But how were weak and often divided state governments going to implement such a radical and deeply unpopular change in land tenure? To the struggling leaders of the late 1840s, the only solution was the creation of rural police. Legislation calling for rural constabularies, to be funded and led by landed elites or their dependents, almost everywhere followed the enactments abolishing community landholding in the late 1840s. But in the state of Mexico, the economic problems of elites and their state government precluded the founding of effective police in rural areas. The new units appeared slowly and were chronically underfunded, undermanned, and undersupplied. Thus, although numerous state governments decreed the end of community property rights and the creation of rural police, they remained incapable of imposing such fundamental changes on entrenched peasant communities. Elites made clear their goal of using state powers to undermine community strength and peasant autonomy—as well as their inability to do so. Such attempts to use state powers to com-

[17] Tutino, "Agrarian Social Change"; Menegus Bornemann, "Ocoyoacac"; and González Navarro, *Anatomía del poder*, pp. 143-144. The national legislature considered in 1849 a law that would end community landholding in the Federal District, but did not enact it. See Lira, *Communidades indígenas*, pp. 134, 159-162.

pensate for fundamental economic weakness could only lead to the escalation of agrarian conflicts.[18]

## LIBERAL POLITICS AND AGRARIAN INSURRECTIONS, 1855–1880

The political forces provoking the escalating agrarian violence in Mexico began to operate on a national scale in 1855. A faction holding staunch liberal principles claimed control of the national state, ousting the last conservative government of Antonio López de Santa Ana. On June 25, 1856, the new regime proclaimed the Ley Lerdo, named for Finance Minister Miguel Lerdo de Tejada, abolishing nationally the property rights of all corporate organizations. Henceforth, only individuals would own properties. Liberal principles of economic individualism were served. Not incidentally, the landed wealth of the Church, a leading supporter of the opposition conservatives, would be alienated. And the landed bases of peasant community autonomy and cohesion would be undermined. The Lerdo law would radically restructure landholding—and agrarian social relations—across Mexico.

Who were the liberal reformers? Who supported their rise to power? And why were they so intent on crippling Mexico's peasant communities? The triumphant liberals of 1855 were led by Juan Alvarez, political strongman of the regions around Acapulco along the Pacific. His most visible allies were Finance Minister Lerdo, from Veracruz, and Justice Minister Benito Juárez, from Oaxaca. The rising regions of the peripheries were well represented in liberal leadership. In general, liberal officeholders were lawyers and other professionals. Their reforms aimed to solidify a coherent and stable national state.[19]

[18] Tutino, "Agrarian Social Change"; and González Navarro, *Anatomía del poder*, pp. 123-125.
[19] Sinkin, *The Mexican Reform*.

Was the liberal triumph of the 1850s thus primarily a movement of provincial leaders and their middle-class allies seeking political stability in times of turmoil? It was that—and much more. The liberal leaders of nineteenth-century Mexico were provincials and middle-sector professionals who represented particular interests and worked toward a political stability that would favor those interests. Unfortunately, we know little about the liberals' bases of political support. But their goals are evident, and we may consider their political foundations from that perspective.

The liberals certainly did not represent the remnants of the colonial elite, a group in decline since 1810 but still powerful and generally a bulwark of conservative politicians.[20] Nor did the liberals represent the agrarian poor. While Juan Alvarez periodically defended peasant interests in his home region—usually against his political enemies—few other liberals had links with the rural poor.[21] During the liberals' fight against the conservative regime of Santa Ana, a few peasant communities did proclaim their support, but their allegiance was more a protest of the conservatives' taxes than an endorsement of liberal programs.[22] Given the liberals' well-known goal of ending community landholding, the absence of agrarian support, especially in the central highlands and other regions of peasant villages, is understandable.[23]

Where did the liberals find political support if not among establish landed elites or the rural poor? Urban professionals and provincial elites provided the core of the liberals' base.[24] Andrés Molina Enríquez suggested that they also represented the rapidly expanding population of mestizo

[20] Such an interpretation emerges from a close reading of Calderón de la Barca, *Life in Mexico*.

[21] Díaz Díaz, *Caudillos y caciques*, pp. 96, 171-175.

[22] Reina, *Las rebeliones campesinas*, pp. 127-128.

[23] Fraser, "La política de desamortización," pp. 622-627; Tutino, "Agrarian Social Change."

[24] Leal, *La burguesía*, pp. 8, 61-62.

rancheros.[25] There is evidence from Jalisco that rancheros there were ready to fight for the liberal cause in 1856 and 1857 to contain the protests of villagers who opposed the privatization of their community lands.[26]

Provincial elites, urban professionals, and rural rancheros might all gain from the abolition of corporate landholding. Only the Church and the peasant communities would suffer directly. Landed elites outside the Church would lose no property to the liberals' reforms. They might well benefit. Estate operations might become more profitable as the waning strength and declining landholdings of peasant communities made laborers more available. Liberal leaders were not established landed elites—but many aspired to that status.[27] They had no quarrel with policies that served the class interests of great landholders.

The alienation law of 1856 did not directly expropriate the lands of the Church or peasant communities. Rather, their holdings were to be sold to the current tenants or occupants, with prices based on existing rents and payments extended over twenty years. Only properties not claimed by their occupants would be auctioned. The former owners, whether Church institutions or community governments, would receive the income from these forced sales. The state gained only a tax on each transaction.

Most of the properties still held by the Church in the middle of the nineteenth century were urban houses. Many members of the urban middle sectors would thus become homeowners, thanks to the liberals. Church estates in rural regions might become the property of single large tenants, more numerous modest tenants, or the wealthy elites who alone could buy at auction the large properties that the Church still operated directly. The alienation of ecclesiastical properties would thus serve elites, urban professionals,

[25] Molina Enríquez, *Los grandes problemas*, pp. 115, 130.
[26] Meyer, *Esperando a Lozada*, p. 90.
[27] See the career of Mariano Riva Palacio in Tutino, "Hacienda Social Relations," pp. 512-515.

and rural rancheros—allowing all an opportunity to gain or increase property holdings.[28]

Who might benefit from the privatization of peasant community lands? Village properties generally divided into three types: lands used to support local governments and religious festivals; lands used communally as pastures and woodlands; and lands held as subsistence plots by peasant families. Community income properties were often leased to mestizo rancheros, and the liberal reform would allow many to become landowners. Community pastures and woodlands might be auctioned, allowing both elites and rancheros to expand holdings.[29] Community-owned but family-held subsistence lands would become the property of the villagers who cultivated them. They, too, would become property owners, thanks to the liberals.

The majority of peasant villagers, however, opposed these radical reforms. They would gain no lands they did not already hold. They might lose access to pastures and woodlands. And the forced sale of community-income properties might bring new cash to local governments, but those alienations would also strike at community independence. Village governments had traditionally served two vital functions: the protection of community lands and the organization of community festivals—the two bases of community cohesion. The loss of village-income properties would strip communities of the means to pay for legal defense. And local governments would have no legal obligation, and little interest, in defending the rights of peasant families to small family properties. The alienation of village income properties would also make the funding of community festivals, the social and religious celebrations that held peasant villagers together, increasingly difficult. Instead of using community moneys to cover expenses, vil-

[28] See Bazant, *Alienation of Church Wealth*; and Berry, *The Reform in Oaxaca*.

[29] See, for example, Schryer, "Ranchero Economy," pp. 421, 427-428.

lagers would have to pay as individuals. The liberals' reforms would strike doubly at the heart of peasant community cohesion and autonomy.

Most villagers would emerge as owners of small plots of land, without access to pastures and woodlands, and without the protection of strong and independent local governments. Not surprisingly, as soon as the liberals announced their reforms in 1856, villagers across central Mexico protested vehemently. Armed resistance blocked reform in several areas, and violence was repeatedly threatened if the alienation law was implemented.[30] Perhaps the greatest resistance in 1856 and 1857 was in Jalisco. With the privatization of community lands there already underway based on state legislation, the liberals' national policies might lead to a quick completion of the process. Violent uprisings, aimed at blocking such a development, occurred in the regions around Zacoalco and Laka Chapala, which had earlier joined the Hidalgo revolt, as well as to the northwest around Tepic. There, Manuel Lozada emerged as a strong defender of community rights—becoming a force frustrating the liberals for nearly two decades.[31]

Such staunch and often violent opposition led the liberals to alter their program as applied to villages in October of 1856. They decreed that lands valued at less than 200 pesos would automatically become the property of the occupants. There would be no payment for sale or taxes. And no titles would be issued for these new small properties. The liberals claimed that peasants had been misled by their priests in opposing the reforms. Arguing that only the costs of the transaction could possibly harm peasant villagers, the liberals abolished those costs and decreed the automatic implementation of the privatization—without records. The October

[30] Molina Enríquez, *Los grandes problemas*, pp. 122-123; Tutino, "Agrarian Social Change"; Lira, *Comunidades indígenas*, p. 241; Powell, *El liberalismo y el campesinado*, pp. 83-84.

[31] Meyer, *Esperando a Lozada*, pp. 40, 49-59, 61-67, 78-88, 124-126, 134, 141-170.

decree resolved little. The reformers could claim that their reform was implemented, while acquiescing in the indefinite postponement of the privatization of community lands. Staunch peasant opposition once again had frustrated the plans of Mexican leaders.[32]

The liberals' reforms were also blocked by the emergence of violent political opposition. Among elites of all political hues, there was little public protest against the alienation of community lands. If implemented, that reform would serve the interests of the entire landed class by weakening the peasant communities. But the privatization of Church properties divided Mexican elites deeply. The demise of the economic power of the Church, steadily waning since the Spanish expropriation of the vast Jesuit estates in 1767, would cripple the conservative faction. Conservative elites thus rallied the defend the temporal wealth of the Church, opening another political war that wracked Mexico from 1858 to 1860. When the liberals won that test, a conservative remnant conspired with European interests and brought on the French occupation of 1863 to 1867, symbolized by the ill-fated empire of Maximilian of Hapsburg. The anticlerical reforms of the liberals thus provoked a decade of civil conflicts. Amidst those violent struggles, in 1859, the liberal President Benito Juárez decreed the nationalization of Church properties not yet privatized. They would be auctioned to the highest bidders, with the proceeds shoring up the liberal treasury. The combination of political warfare and peasant protest, however, blocked any general alienation of community properties during the decade after 1857.

The French abandoned Mexico in 1867, and Maximilian was captured, tried, and executed shortly afterward. Their conservative Mexican allies were left ultimately descredited. The liberals, led by the unflinching President Juárez, re-

[32] See Tutino, "Agrarian Social Change"; Lerdo de Tejada, *Memoria, 1857,* pp. 58-59.

claimed national power and quickly announced their intention of completing the privatization of village lands. Once again, Mexican elites but weakly in power and still facing economic difficulties attempted to use the powers of state—backed by liberal ideology—to attack the landed base of still-entrenched peasant communities. By the late 1860s, the expansion of sharecropping, of agrarian relations of dependent insecurity, also contributed to the heightening of grievances across the central highlands. And in 1868, the first generalized period of drought and famine since independence brought those grievances to a peak. The result was another round of widespread rural insurrections.

In the central highlands, rebellion began at Chalco early in 1868 and lasted into the summer. Local villagers not only opposed the privatization of their lands, but now demanded the redistribution of estate holdings. Numerous villages provided fighters and support to a guerrilla band that was not defeated until massive state forces were marshaled in Chalco six months later. The next year, agrarian revolts broke out in several other regions of central Mexico, becoming most violent in the Mezquital region of the state of Hidalgo. All these uprisings were eventually put down by the troops of the liberal regime. But the rebels achieved important successes. They often postponed indefinitely the privatization of community lands in their home regions. They inflicted substantial economic losses on still-struggling landed elites. And it was during the uprisings in the central highlands late in the 1860s that an ideology of agrarian rights developed, along with a small group of radical intellectuals ready to organize insurrections around that ideology.

The emerging agrarian leaders proclaimed the right of peasants to adequate subsistence lands linked to autonomous communities. Such ideology was only a clear proclamation of traditional peasant values. What was new was the appearance of intellectuals holding such values—and especially the willingness of many villagers to work with such

leaders. Why were Mexican villagers, so completely absorbed in limited local worlds for centuries, suddenly in the
late 1860s ready to deal with outsiders proclaiming a general ideology of peasant rights? The question deserves detailed consideration, but two developments appear important: first, the demise of the conservatives deprived peasant
villagers of their only potential allies in the political arena.
And surely more important, once the liberals made the destruction of community landholding a national policy, villagers began to see a need to work with leaders who placed
their problems in a national political context.[33]

Agrarian uprisings also broke out in the late 1860s in several regions of the Mexican periphery. The Yaqui of Sonora
had for years defended their lands and autonomy politically, via their alliance with Manuel Gándara's conservatives. Their strong opposition to the liberals led them to join
the conservatives in support of Maximilian's French-im-
posed regime. But with the ouster of that last conservative
government and the liberals' return to national power, the
Yaqui had no political allies to aid them against the liberals'
policies of opening their lands to commercial development.
In 1867 and 1868 they took up arms again to defend their
autonomy—only to be defeated by a combination of liberal
armies and local floods. The uprising did slow the commercial penetration of Yaqui lands. It also convinced the now-
dominant liberals that only force would subdue the Yaqui
and open their homeland for development.[34]

In 1868, far to the southeast, the Tzotzil Maya of Chamula and other highland communities of Chiapas also engaged in armed conflicts with those who would rule them.
This peripheral region had been part of Central America
and linked primarily to Guatemala during the colonial era.
A few Spanish officials and provincial elites then tried to ex-

[33] Tutino, "Agrarian Social Change"; Reina, *Las rebeliones campesinas*, pp.
45-47, 64-82, 132-135; see also Hart, *Anarchism*.

[34] Voss, *On the Periphery*, pp. 136-138, 158, 172, 191-192, 212; Hu-Dehart, *Yaqui Resistance*, pp. 56-59, 74-80, 86-89.

tract taxes and other tributes from a still-entrenched peasant economy. In 1712, a radical increase in those exactions,
caused by the pastoral visit of an entrepreneurial bishop,
provoked a massive insurrection with messianic religious
overtones. The Spaniards eventually crushed the rebellion
militarily—and then the colonial state looked to moderate
the level of tribute demands. The Chiapas insurrection of
1712 made plain the entrenched power of the peasant villagers there and the limits of the tribute exactions they
would bear. To the end of the colonial era, the Maya of
highland Chiapas remained in possession of ample lands
and the commercial economy of their region was minimal.
Land was generally available for both villagers and the few
Spaniards who operated estates. Few land titles were issued,
as was common in such peripheral areas of Central America.

After independence and annexation to Mexico in 1824,
the elites of the old colonial capital (newly renamed San
Cristóbal de las Casas) faced a spurt of population growth[35]
as well as rising political competition from the liberal elites
of the emerging commercial center at Tuxtla. Both groups
were willing to use state powers to claim lands long held by
Maya communities—a process that accelerated in the 1850s
and 1860s as liberals took national power and backed their
allies in Chiapas. With the ouster of the French, the final defeat of the conservatives, and the definitive victory of liberalism, in 1867 numerous Maya from Chamula and neighboring villages joined a movement of social and religious
separation—an attempt to withdraw from the Hispanic society and commercial economy that were now in the nineteenth century threatening to undermine their base of autonomy. Refusing to countenance such a withdrawal, .
Chiapas elites used state forces to block the Maya's separa-

[35] See Appendix C, Table c.4.

tism——and provoked a bloody confrontation not finally quieted until the state emerged vicotrious in 1870.[36]

Perhaps the largest and certainly the longest lived of the insurrections begun in 1868 was led by Manuel Lozada in the regions around Tepic. Beginning with his opposition to the liberal legislation of 1856, Lozada became the dominant political actor in his home region. His hostility to the liberals led him, like the Yaqui, to support the French-backed empire of Maximilian during the 1860s. When Juárez returned to power in 1867, Lozada first offered his allegiance—expecting local autonomy in return. But by 1868 it was clear that Juárez and his allies were intent on privatizing the lands that sustained both community governments and religious activities, as well as peasant subsistence production, in Lozada's domain. Enraged, he took up arms and recruited supporters among the villagers around Tepic as well as among the less Hispanized natives of the adjacent Sierra Madre. With support from villagers defending community autonomy and highlanders fighting to preserve their more isolated independence, Lozada held off the forces of the liberal state until 1873 when he was defeated, captured, and executed.[37]

The uprisings that began in the late 1860s were barely quieted when another round of agrarian insurrections developed in the mid-1870s. Once again, liberal politics and policies helped provoke rebellions. Again, drought that was both widespread and severe compounded agrarian grievances. For the first time, a national program of economic development added to the provocations that set many among the rural poor to challenge their rulers. And the politicization of agrarian protests continued to develop.

[36] Favre, *Cambio y continuidad*, pp. 25-79, 287-307; Reina, *Las rebeliones campesinas*, pp. 45-57; Rus, "Whose Caste War?" pp. 131-156.

[37] Meyer, *Esperando a Lozada*, pp. 231-232, 235-256; Reina, *Las rebeliones campesinas*, pp. 193-228.

In July of 1872, shortly after beginning a new term as president, Benito Juárez died. He was succeeded by his vice president, Sebastián Lerdo de Tejada—brother of the late Miguel who was so famous for his laws attacking Church and peasant community lands. But Porfirio Díaz, a Oaxacan like Juárez and a general famed for his efforts against the French, expected to assume liberal leadership. He had challenged Juárez in 1871, but failed to oust the hero of Mexican liberalism. When Lerdo, however, aspired to retain the presidency through a new term to begin in 1876, Díaz rebelled again—this time with success.

The divisions among liberal leaders in 1875 and 1876 helped both to provoke and to provide opportunities for insurrections. As factions competed for political support, Díaz issued his Plan of Tuxtepec early in 1876. Among his goals, he called for effective democracy and municipal autonomy. In revisions issued at Palo Blanco in March, Díaz promised to curb state centralization, judicial improprieties, and favoritism toward foreign interests.[38] Díaz did not address agrarian questions directly in these formal proclamations. But his calls for local autonomy and judicial probity allowed many to conclude that he would favor community interests. Informally, Díaz reputedly claimed that he would always side with the villagers in their continuing struggles with landed elites.[39] And was he not in revolt against Sebastián Lerdo and the liberal faction most identified with the privatization of village lands? Such developments raised expectations that Díaz would pursue policies more favorable to peasant villagers and others among the rural poor.

Once in office, however, Díaz could not become a champion of the agrarian majority. In part, he shared policy goals with other liberals. As military commander in Oaxaca in the late 1860s, Díaz had worked to accelerate the priva-

[38] López Portillo, *Elevación y caída*, pp. 105-108.
[39] Stevens, "Agrarian Policy," p. 153.

tization of community lands.[40] Díaz opposed not privatization—only the abuses which made privatization a pretext for expropriations. Díaz maintained the laws calling for the privatization of village lands and after 1885 oversaw their increasing implementation. He worked to prevent some abuses—and acknowledged his inability to prevent or correct many more.[41]

Meanwhile, Díaz' programs to accelerate commercial development in Mexico worked against many peasant villagers. Once in office as president, Díaz pressed forward with the planning and construction of a rail network that would both integrate the Mexican economy and link it more closely with the United States. Long-struggling landed elites expected new opportunities for profit; but to gain those profits, they had to control the lands best served by the new transit lines. Lands held by villagers and small holders became targets of usurpation. And the courts repeatedly backed the claims of the powerful, whatever their legality. Thus, the first consequence of the development of Mexico's expanded rail network was to help provoke one more wave of agrarian uprisings.[42]

The divisions among Mexico's liberal rulers in 1875 and 1876, Díaz' apparent calls for agrarian justice, the simultaneous wave of land usurpations set off by rail projects, and the two years of extensive and severe drought in 1875 and again in 1877[43] combined to generate another round of widespread and often enduring rural insurrections. Uprisings broke out again in several regions where they had occurred earlier. Since their defeat in 1868, the Yaqui of Sonora had watched as liberal state regimes pressed on with development projects that encroached on their homelands. José María Leyva, called Cajeme, had in 1868 fought with the Sonoran liberals to subdue his people and he was re-

[40] Berry, *Reform in Oaxaca*, pp. 172-182.
[41] Stevens, "Agrarian Policy," pp. 160-166.
[42] Coatsworth, *El impacto*, ii, 54.
[43] Florescano, ed., *Análisis histórico*, Cuadro 6, p. 40.

warded with the post of state agent among the Yaqui. By 1875 he had become a staunch defender of Yaqui autonomy. Taking advantage of political divisions among Sonora's liberal factions, Cajeme announced that he and the Yaqui would support only those who accepted their autonomy and protected their lands. No liberal faction would accept such terms. So Cajeme led his people in another mass revolt—a violent protest against encroachments on Yaqui autonomy that was not subdued until he was captured and executed in 1887. And Yaqui guerrilla protest continued, along with increasingly violent repression, until Díaz undertook mass deportations to Yucatán after 1900.[44]

Insurrections also developed, beginning in 1877, among the peasants of the arid Mezquital as well as the Sierra Gorda—regions of repeated uprisings since the era of the Hidalgo revolt. In the highlands around Tepic, the isolated indigenous peoples who had earlier joined Manuel Lozada's larger agrarian movement rose again, this time turning their outrage into a protest of messianic religious salvation.[45]

In the Huasteca, the lowland regions of eastern San Luis Potosí, villagers took up arms in sustained rebellion for the first time early in the Díaz era. In a region marginal to the commercial economy, proposed rail lines led to a flurry of land conflicts. Beginning in 1876, village leaders sought land titles in the archive of Mexico City while local protest was led by a rebel priest, Mauricio Zavala. When President Díaz attempted to negotiate a settlement by recognizing the villagers' titles and offering a judicial review of all claims, local officials and courts blocked the implementation of such a policy of mediation. Local elites pressed their land claims, effectively subverting the resolution proposed by the Díaz government. Violent conflict thus spread, and became

[44] Voss, *On the Periphery*, pp. 272-287; Hu-Dehart, *Yaqui Resistance*, pp. 94-100.

[45] Reina, *Las rebeliones campesinas*, pp. 136-139, 200-204, 306-312, 317-321; Meyer, *Esperando a Lozada*, p. 246.

more ideological and politicized with the renewed activity of the rebel priest in 1881. Now there were calls for the division of estate lands among villagers. Such an uprising could not be countenanced by the Mexican state, and in 1883, troops led by General Bernardo Reyes crushed the Huasteca rebels, on orders from then President Manuel González.[46]

These insurrections of the early Díaz era remained regional movements, but they did bring agrarian conflicts another step closer to national political developments. From 1875 to 1880 there was an explosion of radical journalism and political activity. Intellectuals holding anarchist and socialist ideals worked to link mounting peasant protests to political ideologies and goals. A congress of representatives of rural communities met with many radical intellectuals in Mexico City in 1878 and 1879. Some of the participants then turned directly to organizing village revolts at Huexozingo and San Martín Texmelucan in the Puebla basin. And at least one political actor of national prominence, General Miguel Negrete, linked his political revolt against Díaz with the agrarian insurrection in the Sierra Gorda.[47] The uprisings of the late 1870s accelerated the politicization of agrarian violence that would culminate in the revolution of 1910.

The recurring waves of agrarian insurrections in the late 1840s, the mid-1850s, the late 1860s, and the 1870s all developed in response to the emergence of the Mexican state, first regionally and then nationally, as an agent of elite class interests, along with the liberals' policy of using that instrument to attack the landholding rights of peasant communities. Sooner or later, all the uprisings collapsed in the face of military force. But military defeat does not always mean failure. The insurgents of the middle decades of the nineteenth century prolonged the economic difficulties of those

[46] Stevens, "Agrarian Policy," pp. 155-160; Reina, *Las rebeliones campesinas*, pp. 271-288.

[47] Coatsworth, *El impacto*, II, 62; Reina, *Las rebeliones campesinas*, pp. 255-265, 271-279; Meyer, *Problemas campesinas*, pp. 165-220.

who aimed to rule. They slowed the consolidation of the liberals' political power. And they delayed significantly the implementation of the laws that would privatize community lands.

Immediately after the proclamation of the Lerdo Law in 1856, there was a flurry of privatizations in communities adjacent to larger cities. There, many community leaders acquiesced in rapid sales of income properties, surely pressured by powerful tenants with political backers. Once these early sales were negotiated, however, many communities faced continuing difficulties in collecting the payments due. Liberal leaders appeared more concerned with mobilizing community properties than with insuring that the villages obtained the payments owed them. The resulting loss of community wealth no doubt confirmed many villagers' opposition to the privatization program.[48]

Away from urban centers, such early implementation was rare. During the decade of political turmoil from 1858 to 1867, the alienation of community lands all but ceased. Beginning in 1868, however, the liberals used their unopposed political power to press again for implementation of the Lerdo Law. Villagers in several regions rebelled, as we have seen. Elsewhere, implementation began slowly. In the state of Mexico in 1870, nearly 65,000 claimants obtained title to lands worth nearly 1,000,000 pesos, primarily around Zumpango, Tenango del Valle, and Tenancingo. Other areas of the central highlands had little privatization then. The community of Ocoyoacac, in the valley of Toluca, has been studied in detail. Privatization began there in 1867 when 24 local residents claimed lands worth about 60 pesos each. In 1875, the state of Mexico pressed village officials for a more complete alienation. They responded by pointing to the decree of October 1856 that left all properties worth less than 200 pesos automatically privatized. That

[48] Lira, *Comunidades indígenas*, pp. 244-258, 265, 323, 325; Berry, *Reform in Oaxaca*, pp. 172-182.

ploy helped to delay the final resolution, and it was not until the years between 1887 to 1889 that the subsistence lands of most Ocoyoacac families were converted to private, titled property. That long-delayed alienation of community lands at Ocoyoacac typified developments across the state of Mexico, where the majority of community properties were not privatized until after 1885.[49]

The implementation of the Lerdo Law was similarly delayed elsewhere. In Oaxaca, the only activity in 1856 was in the immediate vicinity of the state capital. Despite continuing pressures from liberal state governments—backed by Oaxacan liberal Presidents Juárez and Díaz—alienations were still underway in Oaxaca in the early 1900s.[50] In Michoacán, the privatization of lands held by the village of Churumuco was also long delayed, hotly disputed and resulted in an enduring local conflict. Liberal state officials began to press local leaders to distribute village lands in 1868. Community leaders refused, foreseeing the ruin of the community. Then in 1872, the villagers split into factions over the issue. A local minority joined liberal state officials in demanding full privatization. The debate raged until 1878 when the lands of Churumuco were alienated. Over 200 local residents received title to former community properties. Later, the villagers learned that the commissioners brought in to implement the privatization had sold off lands worth 3,000 pesos to pay for their work. The faction that had opposed the alienation then protested the sale as illegal, and attempted to cancel the entire proceeding in the courts. The authorities upheld the commissioners, however. There followed a period of endemic local conflict that erupted into several violent clashes that continued into the twentieth century.[51]

It appears that the alienation of community properties—

[49] Menegus Bornemann, "Ocoyoacac," pp. 91-95.
[50] Berry, *Reform in Oaxaca*, pp. 172-182.
[51] Sánchez Díaz, "La transformación," pp. 63-78.

discussed in Mexico since the 1820s, widely legislated by state governments from the late 1840s, and made national law in 1856—was implemented but slowly and incompletely. Many villagers remained determined, and often violent, opponents throughout the years after independence. Ultimately, they did not object to owning the subsistence plots they had long cultivated. But they resented deeply the loss of village pastures and woodlands. And they objected strongly to the alienation of community income properties—the bases of local government and religious life. Without those properties, villagers would have to pay for religious services and community festivals. Village governments would lose their independent revenues—and thus their ability to defend the community from outside pressures.[52]

Because local governments and community religion had depended on the same system of community property as peasant cultivators, village notables and poor peasants had long shared an interest in defending that system. Local leaders repeatedly used community revenues to defend village lands. The privatization of community properties, even if all were retained as personal property by villagers, threatened the links uniting community leaders and peasants—the ultimate base of peasant community autonomy.[53] Village festivals would become an expense as much as a source of pride and cohesion. Village officials would have little reason to defend the subsistence lands of peasant families. And the majority of poor villagers would find it hard to defend their properties—their autonomy—alone.

It was the defense of basic peasant values that underlay many of the insurrections of nineteenth-century Mexico. And those uprisings often helped delay or deflect the privatization of community lands. The relationship between

[52] Powell, *El liberalismo y el campesinado*, pp. 76-77; Berry, *Reform in Oaxaca*, pp. 186-187.

[53] See Lira, *Comunidades indígenas*, pp. 283-284.

insurrection and the delay and limitation of the privatization policy is clear in the case of Tamazunchale and the
nearby villagers of the Huasteca region of eastern San Luis
Potosí. After their long and violent uprising from 1876 to
1883, there was little immediate thought of privatization.
Díaz began to discuss the possible implementation of the
Lerdo Law there with the governor of San Luis Potosí only
in 1894. And Díaz emphasized that privatization would
have to proceed there with neither cost nor loss of lands
among the villagers.

Local officials, apparently ignoring the president's ad-
vice, instead offered to sell the lands to the villagers. When
the villagers protested that they lacked funds to purchase
lands they already owned, the officials then began to offer
lands to the highest bidders. In 1897, the villagers protested
to Díaz. The president—remembering Tamazunchale's recent history of insurrection and taking advantage of political divisions among elites of San Luis Potosí—successfully
imposed a privatization that left the lands in the hands of
the villagers. The insurrection of Tamazunchale did not
prevent the privatization of community lands, but it did delay it for over a decade and prevented it from becoming a
pretext for simple expropriation.[54]

While Díaz intervened to protect the land rights of the
peasants of Tamazunchale, he was aware that in other areas
of the Huasteca and San Luis Potosí, in Veracruz, in Chiapas, and elsewhere, privatization had been a pretext for the
expropriation of village lands. He was also aware of the
long history of agrarian violence among villagers stripped
of their autonomy. After 1900, Díaz began to take legal
steps to slow the assault on village lands. In 1901, he
amended Article 27 of the Constitution of 1857 to allow
non-Church corporations to hold lands.[55] The battle fought
by peasant villagers since the late 1840s against the liberals'

[54] Stevens, "Agrarian Policy," pp. 160-166.
[55] Ibid., pp. 162-163.

policy of privatizing lands was thus legally won. Many community properties survived to 1910 and afterward. But by 1900, the combination of peasant population growth and earlier privatizations and expropriations had already gone a long way toward stripping Mexican villagers of their cherished autonomy. As we shall see in the next chapter, that loss of autonomy combined with complex economic changes during the Díaz era to deepen the agrarian grievances that would drive the revolutionary conflicts that began in 1910.

The decades from the 1840s to the early 1880s brought recurring waves of agrarian violence to widespread areas of Mexico. At base, the causes of that conflict were the attempts by struggling elites to use their new and often unstable powers of state to compensate for economic difficulties and to impose their will on the rural poor. Elite factionalism kept their governments unstable, and economic difficulties kept their governments poor. In desperation, they repeatedly attempted to use such poor and unstable instruments of state power to undermine the landed bases of agrarian communities. They simultaneously provoked and provided the opportunities for mass insurrections. Violence became the norm in relations between elites and the agrarian poor in Mexico. And rural people facing political attacks on their autonomy began to consider political responses. From the 1840s to the 1880s, increasingly politicized violence became endemic to agrarian life in Mexico.

# CHAPTER EIGHT

# Political Consolidation, Dependent Development, and Agrarian Compression, 1880–1910

AGRARIAN MEXICO experienced endemic conflict and escalating violence during the era of decompression from 1810 to 1880. Rural insurrections were numerous and increasingly widespread. But most remained regionally isolated. And while politics was important in provoking agrarian uprisings, insurgents were just beginning to become politicized. Rebels timed their uprisings to take advantage of state and elite divisions and weaknesses. Peasants reacted vehemently against state efforts to undermine community autonomy. Yet these increasingly rebellious agrarian people rarely took active roles in political conflicts, leaving affairs of state to elites.

Elite factions contending for national power rarely sought agrarian support. Agrarian rebels rarely tried to forge alliances with political actors. Political conflicts thus remained within the dominant class, while agrarian conflicts pitted elite powerholders against the rural poor. Political and agrarian conflicts proliferated simultaneously in nineteenth-century Mexico, each helping to stimulate the other, and together fueling the chaotic combination of political disintegration and social instability. But at base, political and agrarian conflicts remained separate before 1880. Agrarian rebels could express their abhorrence for political developments, and prevent or delay the implementation of policies such as the privatization of community lands which they found intolerable. But they could not influence political developments more positively. Throughout the nineteenth century, they could not press elites toward policies more favorable to the rural poor.

By 1910, however, the separation of political and agrarian conflicts had ended. Contenders for national political power then began to court agrarian support, and agrarian insurgents actively pressed demands for land and justice upon political leaders. The result was a national political war so infused with agrarian insurrection that it became a social revolution. What happened between 1880 and 1910 to turn conditions of endemic agrarian conflict into a national agrarian revolution?

In 1876, in what appeared but one more political revolt, Porfirio Díaz claimed the presidency. That proved to be the last successful coup of nineteenth-century Mexico. Díaz left the office to his ally Manuel González from 1880 to 1884, and then returned to dominate the nation politically until 1910. Under his rule, Mexico achieved its first long period of political stability since 1808. Díaz' regime also oversaw the nation's first extended era of economic expansion. The problems that had plagued Mexican elites for over half a century appeared resolved under Díaz. Elites became richer, the state stronger and more stable, and together they ruled the nation more effectively.

The era of political stabilization and economic development at the end of the nineteenth century was also an era of agrarian compression. Population expanded rapidly while the liberal laws against community landholding were implemented, undermining the subsistence autonomy of many villagers. Tenant production, especially sharecropping, continued to expand after 1880. But under Díaz, increasingly powerful elites, backed by a unified state, could turn those relations of agrarian dependence to advantage. A rapidly expanding tenant population thus faced impoverization with worsening insecurities. Estate employees found less and less permanent work and had to rely on more seasonal employment. The pressures on the agrarian population intensified during the Díaz era. Yet the newly stabilized state proved strong enough to contain the discontent for three decades. The grievances, the outrage, of the rural poor mounted, while the state prevented or contained rebellious expressions. But when Mexican elites became deeply divided after 1900, a situation that led to the collapse of Díaz' state beginning in 1910, those compressed agrarian grievances exploded with revolutionary force.

## POLITICAL CONSOLIDATION, DEPENDENT DEVELOPMENT, AND LANDED ELITES

The famous peace of Porfirio was not established immediately in 1876. The Díaz era began, as we have seen, with another round of regional insurrections. Díaz and González, like their predecessors, eventually mustered the military force to defeat those who challenged their rule. And while they were suppressing agrarian insurgents, Díaz and González worked effectively to consolidate political stability and to stimulate economic growth. As a result, they secured a long era of agrarian stability. That stability, however, resulted primarily from the consolidation of state power—represented in rural areas by Díaz' much feared, if overrated, *rurales*.[1] Agrarian protest was contained under Díaz, while underlying grievances often deepened. That compression would eventually burst into revolution.

By the early years of his second term that began in 1884, Díaz was able to consolidate his rule. How he and González succeeded where so many of their nineteenth-century predecessors had failed remains an important question. Díaz' basic policy of political consolidation was simple—he aimed to remove local oligarchs from high political offices across the nation and to replace them with politically loyal agents. In the northern borderlands in the mid-1880s, Díaz ousted from political power the Maderos of Coahuila, the Terrazas of Chihuahua, and the Maytorenas of Sonora.[2]

[1] Vanderwood, *Disorder and Progress*.

[2] Langston, "Coahuila," p. 57; Wasserman, "Chihuahua," pp. 33-39; Hu-Dehart, "Sonora," pp. 182-184.

But how did Díaz convince elites who expected to rule their home regions to give up political power? Two factors converged in Díaz' political subordination of Mexican elites in the late 1870s and the 1880s. First, those elites still faced financial difficulties. The rapid turnover of landed properties that began after independence continued into the 1870s.[3] In central Mexico, a heavily indebted Mariano Riva Palacio lost in 1870 the estates he had worked to acquire since the 1830s, and that had provided the economic base at Chalco that underlay his political dominance of the state of Mexico for years.[4] Between 1855 and 1881, Isidoro de la Torre acquired five grain-producing and grazing estates in the state of Mexico and four sugar properties in Morelos. De la Torre's access to capital from his dealings with foreign financiers and government finance allowed him to acquire properties at the expense of others then struggling to hang onto estates burdened with mounting debts.[5]

Elite instability also continued in the far north. The Sánchez Navarros of Coahuila lost their vast properties in 1866 for collaborating with the French.[6] That political expropriation probably only hastened what economic difficulties would soon have accomplished. In the Laguna region of western Coahuila and adjacent Durango, the three great estates that had controlled nearly all the land were broken up and sold off for debts during the late 1870s and early 1880s.[7] And the rise of great landed families such as the Terrazas of Chihuahua during these years often came at the expense of struggling elites facing decline. Luis Terrazas acquired his largest property, half of the Encinillas estate extending over 386,000 hectares, in 1868 for only 4,000 pesos. That was at least a one-third reduction of the estate's value based on rents Terrazas had paid earlier as

---

[3] Beato, "La casa Martínez," p. 101.
[4] Tutino, "Agrarian Social Change."
[5] Huerta, "Isidoro de la Torre," pp. 174-181.
[6] Harris, *Mexican Family Empire*, p. 301.
[7] Vargas-Lobsinger, *La hacienda*, pp. 26-29, 44-45.

lessee of the property. The estate was available so cheaply because it had been taken from the Martínez del Río family of Mexico City, also for collaboration with the French.[8]

When Díaz came to power in 1876, then, the Mexican elite was still in a state of weakness and flux. Many who had struggled to operate landed properties during the long period of economic uncertainty and political instability were losing them to insurmountable debts, or to political opponents. A fortunate few were acquiring properties cheaply, while others were taking the chance of buying estates still burdened with debts. Such an unstable elite would have difficulty fending off the political assault mounted by Díaz. And perhaps some understood that they had acquired estates because others had lost them to political instability. They might prosper and keep their properties longer if they allowed political stabilization by ceding political prerogatives to the state being consolidated by Díaz.

And second, Díaz had new means to effect political peace. During the Díaz and González presidencies of 1876 to 1884, while still contending with the last round of nineteenth-century agrarian insurrections, the regime planned and saw constructed, primarily by foreign capitalists, the skeleton of the railroad network that would integrate the Mexican national market and bind it to the United States. When he returned to office in 1884, Díaz found that rail system sufficiently complete to allow the movement of administrators, as well as police and military forces, across Mexico with a speed unavailable to his predecessors. More important, the rail network created expectations of economic opportunities that dazzled the landed elites. They could step back from direct political power and leave it to Díaz and his allies. They would profit from the new economic opportunities of Mexico during the railroad era. It was a Mexican version of the classic trade-off of political power for economic opportunity that stabilized the national state in the 1880s.

[8] Fuentas Mares, . . . Y Mexico se refugió, pp. 157-177.

Viewed in the light of the preceding half century, the years from 1876 to 1910 brought new state strength and political stability. Yet Díaz never institutionalized his power. No national political system sustained his regime. Instead, he ruled personally for over three decades by manipulating "a delicate and volatile balance of forces."[9] Díaz could maintain his political power only by allowing regional elites to gain the economic rewards they expected. But that often led to difficulties for the rural poor. Díaz perhaps preferred to mediate social relations in rural Mexico, allowing elites to benefit while his state provided at least minimal justice for the poor. But to survive politically he could not block the economic ambitions of elites—who often saw gain based on expropriating peasant lands and exploiting rural labor. Thus, the rural poor faced numerous abuses perpetrated by elites, and by those who aspired to become elites—while the Díaz state provided effective justice only sporadically.[10] Díaz' political skills maintained that precarious balance from the mid-1880s until after 1900.

Such agrarian issues were part of a larger balancing act that was fundamental to Díaz' relations with landed and other elites across Mexico. He might rule as long as the economic and other interests of powerholders were generally served. Even during his heyday, Díaz' political success varied by region. In the northern borderlands he effectively ruled in Nuevo León, Chihuahua, and Sonora through competent political agents who kept local elites economically rewarded. But in Coahuila, a highly factionalized state elite was never easily subordinated by Díaz, and he had to intervene repeatedly to stabilize the local government. And Coahuilan elites would produce two of the foremost leaders of the revolutionary era after 1910: Francisco Madero and Venustiano Carranza.[11] The political peace of Porfirio was

---

[9] Langston, "Coahuila," p. 70.

[10] This is evident in Stevens, "Agrarian Policy."

[11] See Cerutti, "Poder estatal"; Wasserman, "Chihuahua"; Hu-Dehart, "Sonora"; and Langston, "Coahuila."

real, and remarkable after a half century of conflict and instability. But it was a fragile peace.

From the first years of his rule, Díaz found ready support from landed elites for policies of rapid railroad construction through concessions to foreign investors. Estate operators expected boom profits from the expanded markets that would be opened. And if foreign investors would finance the railroads in return for government guarantees of minimum profitability, then Mexican elites could look forward to new profits without bearing the costs of rail construction. They expected great benefits for little expense. But the financing, construction, and operation of Mexican railroads by foreigners also meant that the new national transportation system was designed primarily to facilitate export shipments and operated to favor export producers.[12]

Because of the railroads, for the first time in its history Mexico became a major exporter of livestock and agricultural produce. Stock grazers along the northern border regions could sell their cattle in the expanding markets of the United States. Railroads and steamships allowed the growers of tropical crops along the coastal lowlands of the south to gain access to United States markets. The famed expansion of agricultural production under Díaz occurred primarily in regions oriented to export. Maize production for Mexican consumption barely kept pace with population growth.[13]

The primary expansion of commercial agriculture in regions oriented toward exports is reflected in the results of Díaz' most famous agrarian policy—the massive distribution of *baldíos* (unclaimed lands) to facilitate new estate development.[14] Export production occurred primarily in the northern borderlands and the southern coastal lowlands,

[12] This is the primary conclusion of Coatsworth, *El impacto.*
[13] See Coatsworth, "Anotaciones."
[14] The following discussion is based on Appendix D, Tables D.1 and D.2.

sparsely settled regions long peripheral to national life. Over 90 percent of the area and 97 percent of the value of the lands distributed under Díaz lay in these emerging export zones. In the northern border states, the number of haciendas nearly doubled between 1877 and 1910, while smaller ranchos increased five times over. In southern coastal states, the number of haciendas also nearly doubled, while ranchos tripled. The growth of export production in these developing regions brought clear gains to landed elites, accompanied by a rapid expansion of the ranchero population.

In central and north central Mexico, the old colonial core regions, export production was limited and agrarian elites fared less well. Few lands were claimed there under Díaz' distribution program, because nearly all had been taken centuries earlier. In the central states, the number of estates classified as haciendas declined by 10 percent between 1877 and 1910, while the number of ranchos almost tripled. In the north central states, haciendas increased by only 30 percent, while the number of ranchos more than tripled. Under Díaz, agrarian elites with estates in central and north central Mexico, oriented primarily to internal markets, made few gains in landholding. In fact, large estates lost ground there to the rapid expansion of ranchero production.

The railroads that brought new markets to export producers often imposed new difficulties on landed elites linked to internal Mexican markets. For centuries, estates producing maize, wheat, pulque, and other crops basic to Mexicans' diets had supplied nearby urban centers. Central highland estates sold their produce in Mexico City or Puebla; those in the Bajío sustained the many cities there, as well as the mining centers just to the north; those in Jalisco provisioned Guadalajara. Only during years of extreme scarcity and peak prices could maize be shipped profitably over long distances—and then local authorities worked to prevent such shipments.

Under Díaz, the railroads opened the possibility of long-distance shipments of bulk produce. Urban markets could be supplied by more distant estates, generally increasing competition. Properties with exceptionally fertile resources might prosper; others less favored (but formerly protected by monopolies in local markets) could suffer losses. And with such increasing competition, there were new incentives for elites to limit the costs of production. For many, that meant investing in new, labor-saving technology. For most, it meant working to reduce the earnings of estate workers.

Among Mexican estates facing new competition during the late nineteenth century, those raising maize confronted especially damaging competition from a new region of supply—the United States. During the colonial era, the economic power of many landed elite families derived from their ability to produce large crops and then hold them until scarcity drove prices up. After independence, financial problems limited the ability of many estate operators to fund estate production and hold crops for long periods. Estate profitability thus declined. The economic revival of the Díaz era generated the financial resources to make estate operations profitable again. But the railroads that facilitated export production also allowed the import of agricultural produce. By the 1890s, when maize crops in Mexico failed in years of drought, imports from the United States began to meet the demand. Table 8.1 indicates that maize imports amounted to less than 1 percent of Mexican consumption in most years. But when crops failed across wide areas and prices peaked, as in 1892, 1896, and 1910, imports quickly rose to over 10 percent of national consumption. These imports eliminated the profit in holding estate crops in Mexico. In the face of such foreign competition, large-estate maize producers had no advantage over small growers. As a result, elites in central and north central Mexico rapidly turned maize production over to poor tenants, mostly sharecroppers, after 1880.[15]

[15] In *Los grandes problemas*, pp. 174, 306, 309, 320, Molina Enríquez

TABLE 8.1

Mexican Maize Production and Imports (in metric tons), 1892–1910

| Year | Mexican Production | Imports | Total | Percent Imports |
|------|------|------|------|------|
| 1892 | 1,383,715 | 219,759 | 1,603,474 | 13.7 |
| 1893 | 1,775,177 | 10,527 | 1,785,644 | 0.6 |
| 1894 | 1,920,278 | 4,078 | 1,924,356 | 0.2 |
| 1895 | 1,831,911 | 39,886 | 1,871,797 | 2.1 |
| 1896 | 1,821,341 | 227,616 | 2,048,957 | 11.1 |
| 1897 | 2,398,764 | 3,115 | 2,401,879 | 0.1 |
| 1898 | 2,313,570 | 7,042 | 2,320,612 | 0.3 |
| 1899 | 2,369,224 | 14,237 | 2,383,461 | 0.6 |
| 1900 | 2,099,775 | 38,027 | 2,137,802 | 1.8 |
| 1901 | 2,378,053 | 24,463 | 2,402,516 | 1.0 |
| 1902 | 2,329,780 | 3,610 | 2,333,390 | 0.2 |
| 1903 | 2,256,539 | 12,600 | 2,269,139 | 0.6 |
| 1904 | 2,060,025 | 12,096 | 2,072,121 | 0.6 |
| 1905 | 2,167,383 | 36,942 | 2,204,325 | 1.7 |
| 1906 | 2,338,926 | 52,823 | 2,391,749 | 2.2 |
| 1907 | 2,127,868 | 17,788 | 2,145,656 | 0.8 |
| 1908 | — | — | — | — |
| 1909 | — | 97,778 | — | — |
| 1910 | — | 229,874 | — | — |

SOURCE: Mexican production from *Estadísticas económicas: fuerza de trabajo*, p. 67; imports from *Estadísticas económicas: comercio exterior*, p. 180.

Under Díaz, then, landed elites tied to internal markets in the densely settled regions of central and north central Mexico faced new uncertainties. Their power as a class declined—at least in relation to the favored export producers. The increasingly numerous rancheros appear to have been a more dynamic element in the agrarian economy of the regions that were once the colonial heartland. And the struggling landed elites of central Mexico also faced during the

· noted the disruptive impact of maize imports and the decline of many haciendas as business enterprises, but not the link between the two developments.

Díaz era the rising power of emerging bankers and industrialists. The persistent weakness of central Mexican landed elites has been masked by the general commercial prosperity and political stability of the Díaz era. Not all Mexican elites prospered equally.

Developments during the Díaz era completed and consolidated the restructuring of the Mexican elite that had begun during the late colonial era and accelerated during the chaotic postindependence years. The established elites of central Mexico saw their powers erode in periods of alternating decline and stagnation. Meanwhile, elites of long-peripheral regions were gaining from the expansion of their emerging commercial economies. By the Díaz era, the old colonial peripheries were peripheral only geographically. The export economies of the northern borderlands and the southern coastal lowlands became core participants in the new and expanding economy focused on foreign markets. The importance of those once marginal regions and their rising elites was symbolized by Díaz' inclusion of Chihuahua's Enrique Creel and Yucatán's Olegario Molina in pivotal positions in the national regime after 1900. Thanks to the railroads and the dynamic process of export-oriented dependent development, the geographic peripheries became the economic core of Mexico. Meanwhile, the elites of central Mexico grappled with changing circumstances that seemed to favor only the exceptionally wealthy and those with estates linked to export production.

How did these complex developments affect the agrarian majority? That pivotal question can be approached only in regional contexts. And nineteenth-century changes had left Mexico much more regionally complex by the Díaz era. Although the distinction between northern regions dominated by great estates and central and southern regions where communities coexisted with estates remained, it no longer could describe adequately the major divisions of agrarian Mexico after 1880. Under Díaz, the development of export production led to four primary regional pat-

terns—with numerous subdivisions. The north divided into
the borderlands that were increasingly linked to the United
States and the north central states still oriented to Mexican
markets. The center-south split into highland regions, still
organized around estates and villages, still focused on internal markets, and the coastal lowlands developing rapidly
around estates raising tropical crops for export. Analysis of
agrarian social changes under Díaz must differentiate, at
least, among these four primary regions.

## THE COASTAL LOWLANDS: EXPORT PRODUCTION, LABOR COERCION, AND AGRARIAN STABILITY

In the southern coastal states of Veracruz, Tabasco, Yucatán, and Chiapas, large areas of land were claimed under
Díaz and thousands of new estates developed. Coffee, tobacco, and sugar led export production in Veracruz, as well
as in lowland regions of Chiapas and Oaxaca. Henequen,
the cactus fiber for hemp production, drove export development in Yucatán. While each export crop had particular
labor requirements and each coastal region had unique social characteristics, all shared one fundamental condition—
labor shortages. The rapid growth of export production in
regions still sparsely populated and long marginal to commercial development created demands for workers that
were not met by local people. Except in Yucatán where the
caste war had left a depopulation that was barely regained
by 1910, the populations of southern coastal Mexico grew
rapidly during the nineteenth century, testifying to the regions' rapid development. But populations remained
sparse to 1910.[16] And many residents of the coastal lowlands retained subsistence lands, making them reluctant to
work at new plantations for minimal wages.[17]

[16] See Appendix C, Table c.4.

[17] This general view of the coastal lowlands is based on Katz, *La servidumbre*, pp. 29-39; Cossío Silva, "La agricultura," pp. 83, 98-103; Cardoso
et al., *México en el siglo XIX*, pp. 316, 321, 324; and Leal, *La burguesía*, p. 98.

How, then, could export elites obtain workers? To a limited extent they offered higher wages. They also offered advances to those who promised to work. As a result, permanent estate employees, as well as the seasonal workers often recruited from nearby highlands, became indebted to estates. Typical of situations of labor scarcity in Mexican history, the workers at the export plantations of the coastal lowlands began to obtain earnings beyond their wage levels. But under Díaz, the boom profits of export production, the new efficiency of police forces, and the readiness of the state to serve elite economic interests combined to make more effective the enforcement of indebted workers' labor obligations. Debts thus became the pretexts for labor coercion in the export regions of southern Mexico during the late nineteenth century.

By the early twentieth century, the plantations of southern Mexico were infamous for the cruel, coercive labor relations described in John Kenneth Turner's *Barbarous Mexico*.[18] Workers' debts were bought and sold by estate owners—effectively buying and selling the indebted workers. The situation approached chattel slavery, as the state enforced the requirement that workers discharge debts before leaving an estate. Yet the agrarian poor of these coastal export zones proved the least rebellious of rural Mexico after 1910. The entrenched regional structures of elite power and labor coercion no doubt inhibited any early outbreak of insurrection, but once Díaz' state had collapsed and insurgent bands roamed Mexico, such constraints weakened. Still, there was little insurrection in the coastal lowlands. When revolution developed there, it came either from the outside or from reforming elites.[19]

The inhabitants of these regions were not uniquely averse to insurrection. The caste war of the mid-nineteenth

[18] Perceptions of rural Mexico before the 1910 revolution have been more influenced by Turner's graphic portrayals than any other work.

[19] See Joseph, *Revolution from Without*.

century showed the rebellious potential of the Yucatecan Maya, and those of Chiapas had fought their rulers as recently as 1868. Villagers around Papantla, Veracruz, sustained sporadic armed conflicts in the 1890s against those who came to survey lands for estate development. Díaz first tried to mediate these disputes. But unwilling to block promising commercial developments, he twice sent his troops to crush the Papantla rebels.[20] Like most Mexican peasants with lands vital to subsistence, the residents of the coastal lowlands were quick to rebel when that base of autonomy was threatened.

Yet as export estates developed across the coastal lowlands and labor coercion proliferated, the grievances essential to rebellion apparently moderated. From a liberal perspective that considers freedom, unfettered mobility, the crucial question in labor relations, plantation conditions in southern Mexico were abhorrent. But for the agrarian poor of Mexico, the evaluation of labor relations, and adaptation to them, was more complex. Most preferred autonomy, the ability to produce their own subsistence. Where such autonomy was not possible, and survival came to depend on access to lands and work controlled by elites, the critical concern became security. Mobility was important, but rarely as important as autonomy and security. And close scrutiny of labor relations in two major export regions of southern Mexico during the Díaz era indicates that while agrarian families lost autonomy and faced coercion—they gained security.

In Yucatán, the export demand for henequen boomed as binder twine became part of mechanized harvesting in the Midwestern United States. Estates usurped additional lands, aided by the post-caste war depopulation as well as by favorable state policies. Estate labor demands escalated. Henequen was unique among Mexican agricultural exports in that the cactus were perennial plants whose fibers could

[20] Reina, *Las rebeliones campesinas*, p. 359; Vanderwood, *Disorder and Progress*, p. 90.

be extracted year round. Labor demands in Yucatán were thus less seasonal and more permanent that elsewhere, further worsening the labor shortage that inhibited export production.[21]

The expansion of henequen plantations brought the expropriation and destruction of many Maya communities. But early on, the displaced peasants forced to become estate dependents were usually set up as tenants cultivating subsistence maize on estate lands—and required to provide a stipulated number of days' labor to the owners. As henequen demand rose, however, the use of estate lands for maize limited profits. From the 1880s, then, plantations began to limit tenancies and to convert their residents into fully dependent laborers. At this point the loss of autonomy was complete. But Yucatecan estates—still facing labor shortages—began to devote a portion of their export earnings to buying imported maize for their workers. Not only did this provide a basic security to plantation residents, it became an attraction to others. When drought or pests destroyed villagers' maize, as often happened in arid Yucatán, peasants fled to henequen estates where for their labor they could obtain the staple necessary for their survival. Many became permanent estate dependents. Others remained villagers, but labored part of each year at the plantations to gain access to imported maize. They often saw their debts build—as they were charged for maize and other goods they could not cover with the poor wages allotted them. They lost mobility as the state sanctioned their retention, as well as the work of the bounty hunters who chased them when they fled. But they found security—access to the maize that kept them alive. "The hacendado's ample supply of corn, water, and firewood furnished the campesinos with three commodities needed for survival."[22]

Recent explanations for the combination of intense labor

[21] Joseph, *Revolution from Without*, pp. 29, 76; Wells, "Yucatán," pp. 216-217, 219.

[22] Joseph, *Revolution from Without*, pp. 73, 83; Wells, "Yucatán," pp. 220-222, 224; quote from Wells, p. 222.

coercion and exploitation with the lack of mass revolutionary mobilization after 1910 in Yucatán have focused on two
factors: the power and repressive capacity of the region's
henequen elites and their state; and the lack of unity and
leadership among the rural poor.[23] The regional oligarchy
headed by Olegario Molina, with close links to International
Harvester and the Díaz regime, was exceptionally wealthy
and well connected. It could withstand substantial challenges to its rule. Yet Molina's power, based on a monopolistic arrangement with International Harvester that had
driven down henequen prices since 1902, might as well
have divided Yucatecan elites. Surely the power of Molina
in Yucatán was no greater that that of the Terrazas-Creel
clan in Chihuahua. Yet the latter collapsed in the face of a
revolutionary insurrection in 1911, as we shall see.

The question becomes this: why was there no mass agrarian mobilization in Yucatán in 1910 or the following years
to challenge the regional oligarchy and exploit its potential
divisions? The isolation of the Maya as estate dependents
and the lack of local agrarian leadership are not persuasive
arguments. Estate dependents without community organization had risen by the tens of thousands in the Bajío in
1810, and across northern Mexico many would join the Villista movement in the years after 1910. And if this study has
made any point, it is that leaders do not make agrarian uprisings in Mexico. Rather, leaders have repeatedly risen
wherever agrarian grievances have peaked and opportunities for insurrection developed.

There was no lack of opportunity for insurrection in Yucatán during the revolutionary era. In 1911, after Díaz fell
and left the country, local sympathizers with Francisco
Madero began to challenge the Yucatecan oligarchy. None,
apparently thought of calling the rural masses to revolt—as
happened elsewhere in Mexico. Perhaps memories of the

    [23] Joseph, *Revolution from Without*, pp. 37-41, 71, 88; Wells, "Yucatán," p.
236.

caste war still lived in Yucatán. But the local elite was clearly divided, and the national regime was in question. Insurrections had developed with lesser opportunities more than once in the past century. In 1915, Salvador Alvarado arrived in Mérida as representative of Venustiano Carranza's Constitutionalist faction—then in mortal combat with the more radical revolutionaries led by Zapata and Villa. Alvarado announced the triumph of the revolution in Yucatán and "systematically dismantled the old repressive mechanism that had supported the oligarchical regime."[24] What better opportunity for the rural poor to express their discontent, using violence to avenge old wrongs and to press the new rulers of the peninsula toward policies in the interest of the agrarian majority. Yet no mobilization occurred.

Were the residents of Yucatán's henequen plantations so broken that they were incapable of insurrection after 1910? That, too, was not the case. The Maya who produced the region's henequen never meekly accepted their lot. With the downturn of the export economy after 1907, there were escalating local protests. Remaining villagers challenged estates over questions of land and labor. Estate residents challenged henequen properties over questions of wages and working conditions. And those movements peaked in 1911—as the Díaz regime fell in Mexico City. But the protests remained local and concerned with correcting particular complaints—not with seeking violence transformations of plantation conditions. All were contained or repressed by local elites just as revolutionary mobilizations were developing out of similar agrarian protests elsewhere in Mexico.[25]

Ultimately, it appears that no revolutionary mobilization developed after 1910 in Yucatán because henequen workers there, however coerced and exploited, retained a fundamental security of subsistence. The decline of the hene-

[24] Joseph, *Revolution from Without*, pp. 88, 93-99; quote from p. 96.
[25] Wells, "Yucatán," pp. 234-236.

quen economy after 1902 was a decline of prices, not production—which reached its highest level of the Díaz era in 1910-1911.[26] That surge of production brought increased labor demands. In order to recover the earnings lost to falling fiber prices, Yucatecan elites expanded henequen production. They thus needed more workers. They also reduced wage levels. But for the majority of estate resident workers, that was only a bookkeeping alteration. They still obtained maize and the other minimal necessities of life from estate stores. Their wage earnings were accounted against those supplies. A wage reduction thus meant rising debts,[27] but most were already indebted beyond their capacity to repay. As long as henequen exports held strong and labor remained scarce, the plantations of Yucatán provided their workers with minimal housing, water, and maize—the basis of security.

Such security came with coercion and allowed an extreme exploitation of the Maya's labor. Conditions were often cruel. But insurrection in rural Mexico has not developed in response to coercion, exploitation, or even cruelty. Insurrections have emerged when peasants faced losses of subsistence autonomy and when estate dependents faced losses of security. In Yucatán, the henequen boom was constrained by labor shortages (in part a result of the caste war), leading local elites to provide minimal security to their workers. Neither kindness nor patriarchal concern produced those conditions—security was necessary to obtain and retain the labor force essential to henequen profits. And it was that security that kept the grievances of the rural poor of Yucatán in check. Conditions were bad, at times appalling, but they were not so extreme that the mass of Maya would take the deadly risks of insurrection. They never tested the power and repressive capacity of the Yucatecan

[26] Joseph, *Revolution from Without*, Table 3, p. 44; *Estadísticas económicas . . . comercio exterior*, p. 309.

[27] Wells, "Yucatán," p. 231.

regime after 1910—allowing the revolution to proceed there with little mass participation.

There was little mass mobilization after 1910 in Chiapas, too—another region where agricultural exports led to labor coercion, compensated by a minimal security. The development of coffee export production along the Soconusco hills of the Pacific coast of Chiapas was part of the larger coffee boom of the late nineteenth century that extended from El Salvador, through Guatemala, into Chiapas. Díaz' public land distribution program, along with the privatization of community properties, made lands available to the Germans, North Americans, and others who built coffee plantations to profit from the rise in coffee prices from 1880 to 1894. In a region of few people and little prior commercial development, the coffee planters of Chiapas found land easy to obtain—and workers scarce.

Few laborers emerged from the privatization of lands in the few communities in Soconusco because even the poorest of villagers were to retain five hectares. Substantial wage advances were offered to entice workers from the more densely settled Chiapas highlands, but such incentives still did not recruit sufficient workers. Coffee planters thus began to use the workers' debts as pretexts for coercion— holding at their estates workers who perhaps intended to stay only brief periods. They bought and sold workers' debts—and thus the rights to their labor. When coffee prices began to decline after 1894, however, Soconusco planters found the forced maintenance of a permanent labor force too costly. Coffee labor, after all, was concentrated in the fall harvest months. After 1900, they began to employ fewer permanent dependents, and turned to labor brokers who went to the peasant communities of the Chiapas highlands and offered wage advances to those who would agree to work the coffee harvests. Those advances created debts that allowed the planters to force workers to remain through the harvest season, and perhaps to return the following year. The fact that the Chiapas highlanders would go to the coffee harvests only if paid in advance indicates that they retained subsistence lands and were not desperate for the additional work. And perhaps most revealing, Chiapas coffee planters, like the henequen growers of Yucatán, used a portion of their export earnings to buy imported maize, thereby guaranteeing the subsistence base of those who worked their harvests.

The laborers picking Chiapas coffee were coerced and exploited, but they retained important subsistence lands in their highland communities—and they were guaranteed maize while they worked the coffee harvests of the coastal lowlands. They retained a base of community autonomy while they worked seasonally as estate laborers. As such, they were coerced, but were provided a basic security. And Chiapas did not experience a downturn of export production in the years prior to 1910. In 1908, a rail line opened between Soconusco and Tehuantepec, tying the region into the larger Mexican rail network and allowing exports to Europe and North America from Gulf ports. During the three years prior to 1910, with shipping costs reduced, coffee exports from Chiapas doubled in weight and tripled in value. Labor demands could only increase and labor scarcities persisted—preventing any assault on the security of Chiapas coffee workers. Because Chiapas highlanders retained important autonomy and coastal coffee workers were given basic security (and seasonally they were often the same people, or members of the same families), there was little base for mass revolutionary mobilization in Chiapas.[28]

Agrarian developments in Yucatán and Chiapas suggest that where the most radical economic changes of the Díaz era occurred, where established peasant societies were suddenly incorporated into the international economy as export producers, there was little revolutionary insurrection after 1910. Ultimately, that stability in the export regions of the coastal lowlands of southern Mexico resulted from the

[28] This discussion of Chiapas is based on Spenser, "Soconusco."

combinations of sparse populations with growing export profits. Export plantations needed workers, and their profits were sufficient to allow them to purchase often imported maize to provide that basic security to those who would work for them—even those they forced to work. And estate dependents with security might be coerced and exploited, but they rarely took the risks of insurrection.

## The Northern Borderlands: Export Production, Labor Mobility, and Revolution

In the far northern border regions of Mexico, the completion of rail links with central Mexico and the United States in the 1880s brought rapid development in mining, stock grazing, and where irrigation permitted, cotton cultivation and other agriculture. Across the region, large areas of land were claimed under Díaz' land distribution programs. Many new estates were built, and old ones became more commercial operations tied to national and international markets. Such developments led to conflicts that pitted elites of the borderlands against rancheros already established on lands suddenly coveted for commercial development, as well as against the many families who became estate dependents in these booming frontier regions. Revolution would explode across the northern borderlands after 1910.

Both the southern coastal lowlands and the northern borderlands were regions of sparse population, suddenly incorporated into growing commercial export economies during the Díaz era. Both regions' elites complained that labor shortages inhibited commercial development. In the southern lowlands, coercion accompanied by minimal security became the prevailing means for export producers to obtain and retain workers. And there was little mass insurrection there after 1910. In contrast, no system of coercion developed to control workers in the northern borderlands—and there, revolutionary mobilization was massive.

The differences reflected regional social characteristics. In the south, there were established indigenous populations living by peasant production. The challenge facing export producers in Yucatán and Chiapas was to move villagers out of their communities and onto estates for labor service—in adjacent regions. In contrast, the northern borderlands were far from population centers. To gain workers for export development, elites there had to convince workers to move hundreds of kilometers from their homes. It was apparently possible to use wage advances and debt coercion to entice and/or force peasants to become estate workers—if they also obtained minimal security, and if they moved only short distances within still-isolated home regions.

Such coercion could not organize the migrations of tens of thousands of workers and their families across the vast spaces from central Mexico to the northern borderlands. That mass movement could be stimulated only by the promises of work and higher earnings—which were offered by northern estate developers. Once workers arrived in the north, the open spaces of that dry region, along with the accessibility of the long and unpatrolled border with the United States, made any system of labor coercion improbable. Thus, the northern export regions that developed during the Díaz era were characterized by social relations of mobility, accompanied by insecurity.[29]

After 1910, the borderlands generated the massive agrarian mobilization that made Pancho Villa one of the most powerful contenders in the era of revolution. The agrarian base of Villa's northern revolution focused on two regions: Chihuahua and the Laguna, just to the south where Coahuila and Durango converge. Analysis of agrarian social developments there during the Díaz years reveals important contrasts with the southern coastal plantation re-

[29] Katz, *La servidumbre*, pp. 52-62.

gions—and helps to explain the revolutionary insurrections of the north after 1910.

In Chihuahua, agrarian grievances escalated when estate development assaulted the land rights of an established ranchero population. These were not indigenous peoples like the Yaqui of Sonora, who also fought for their landed autonomy. Rather, the agrarian population of Chihuahua descended from military colonists sent into the region in the late colonial era, and again the middle of the nineteenth century. They had received lands sufficient to live as modest rancheros. And they were expected to defend their communities, and thus Chihuahua, from the reprisals of nomadic Indians who resented the Spanish and Mexican settlement of their homelands. Early in the Díaz era, however, the nomads were crushed as the railroads opened new economic opportunities. Chihuahua elites no longer needed the colonists as buffers against the Indians, while the colonists' lands became attractive as export production boomed.

Two bursts of rapid rail construction, one between 1880 and 1884 and the other from 1897 to 1906, led to assaults on the lands of the colonists, their communities, and other rancheros in Chihuahua. Estate development for export production was led by the family headed by Luis Terrazas and his son-in-law Enrique Creel. The clan was ousted from political power by Díaz in 1884. But in the following years, they concentrated on economic affairs, profiting massively from the opening of export markets and financial relations with the United States. The family made political amends with Díaz after 1900, and Luis Terrazas returned to office as governor in 1903. The family had both economic hegemony and political control of Chihuahua, while Creel held national posts, until 1910.

Under Terrazas family rule, the state passed a municipal land law in 1905. Land usurpation had been common in frontier Chihuahua for years, but now the state government, controlled by the region's predominant landed family, legally denied the right of ranchero communities to hold lands. The following years brought mass adjudications of former municipal lands—alienations that peaked in 1907 and 1908. This borderlands version of the Lerdo Law came late to Chihuahua, but the results were similar. Rancheros saw their autonomy threatened by legalized actions of a government with obvious class interests. Their protests mounted and became more violent. And while the Terrazas-controlled state led the assault on ranchero community lands, drought and frost caused successive crop failures in 1907, 1908, and 1909—scarcities perhaps worsened by the conversion of estate lands from maize production to raising livestock for export. Again, scarcity pushed social grievances to a peak. Many agrarian rebels who would first take up arms to support Francisco Madero in 1910, and then back Pancho Villa so passionately after 1913, were recruited among the rancheros who faced losses of land, of autonomy, in the boom estate development driven by the export economy of Porfirian Chihuahua.[30]

Other Chihuahua insurgents—those who lived as estate dependents—rebelled after facing the other side of estate development there. Livestock was Chihuahua's primary export. Those who developed estates might evict established tenants who had raised maize to make lands fully available for grazing.[31] That left most estates to employ only the reduced numbers of cowboys needed to tend cattle year round. But the livestock export market was volatile, and the cowboys faced great insecurities. Livestock exports had peaked in the mid-1890s, and then hit a four-year depression from 1904 to 1908. They were just beginning to revive when revolutionary turmoil struck Chihuahua.[32] Many Chihuahua cowboys, armed and mounted—ultimately mo-

---

[30] This discussion of Chihuahua reflects Wasserman, *Capitalists*, pp. 104-116; "Chihuahua"; and "Social Origins"; as well as Katz, *Secret War*, pp. 8-9.

[31] Wasserman, *Capitalists*, p. 112.

[32] *Estadísticas económicas . . . comercio exterior*, p. 350.

bile—having faced the insecurity of estate dependent employment in a volatile export economy, joined Madero and then Villa.[33]

The grievances based on the insecurity confronting families living as estate dependents in the rapidly developing commercial economy of northern Mexico became most acute in the Laguna region of Coahuila and Durango. Before the Díaz years, the region was dominated by large grazing properties. Limited cultivation had been undertaken by tenant families who planted in the aftermath of the annual floodwater irrigation along the banks of the Nazas and Aguanaval rivers. A few estates, or their tenants, introduced cotton on a small scale in the middle of the nineteenth century. But the early development of agriculture in the Laguna was inhibited by the irregularity of the annual floodwaters and the high costs of transportation to distant markets.[34]

Then in March of 1884, the completion of the Mexican Central Railroad linked the Laguna with both El Paso and Mexico City. Four years later, the region was also connected by rail to the Texas border at Piedras Negras. With quick and cheap access to both national and international markets, Laguna cotton production boomed. Estate operators, often beginning as tenants of old grazing estates facing bankruptcy, began to build extensive irrigation systems to control and allocate the annual floodwaters. They shifted from Mexican bush cotton, a perennial, to a North American annual variety. The latter brought large increases in labor demands and costs—but even larger gains in yields and fiber quality. Many of the tenants who led the shift to cotton, and the merchants who financed them, emerged as owners of Laguna estates carved out of the larger but less productive grazing properties.[35]

[33] Katz, *Secret War*, pp. 12-14.

[34] Vargas-Lobsinger, *La hacienda*, pp. 15-18.

[35] Meyers, "La Comarca Lagunera," pp. 247-248; Vargas-Lobsinger, *La hacienda*, pp. 34-35, 37.

The success of the Laguna's cotton entrepreneurs did not bode well for the agrarian poor of the region. The rapid development of irrigated estates by politically powerful elites led to disputes over land and especially over water with the villagers and rancheros already in the district. There were mounting protests, and sporadic violence, in the late 1870s and early 1880s, but these were quieted by the consolidation of Díaz' state power and the boom of the Laguna economy after 1884. The grievances, however, were not resolved, and protests would escalate again after 1905.[36]

The vast majority of the rural poor of the Laguna, however, lived as estate dependents. The boom of cotton development greatly increased that population. The 20,000 rural inhabitants of the Laguna in 1880 grew to about 200,000 by 1910—mostly immigrants from central Mexico drawn into the region by news of expanding production and high wages. When cotton plantings began to expand in the 1880s, most Laguna estates were populated by small numbers of tenants, primarily poor sharecroppers. They lived by taking on the risks of raising food crops in the flood plains whose waters were so variable. But as annual cotton plantings spread and irrigation brought better water control, the original sharecroppers were displaced. They were not generally moved off the estates. But the flood-plain lands they had occupied became the estates' prime cotton fields. Sharecropping survived in the Laguna, but the sharecroppers were moved to the fringes of the estates—at or beyond the margins of the irrigation systems. There they tried to raise food crops, and perhaps a little cotton when especially high waters reached their lands. Facing such uncertain prospects of cultivation, they became a large reservoir of workers to plant, cultivate, and pick cotton on the estates' irrigated fields.

Given the annual variations of floodwaters and the

[36] Meyers, "La Comarca Lagunera," pp. 251-254; Vargas-Lobsinger, La hacienda, p. 56.

changing areas of cotton planted, combined with the vola-
tility of the national and international markets for cotton,
Laguna elites preferred to employ wage laborers. They
sought a work force that could be employed when needed,
and ignored otherwise. The 10,000 to 50,000 seasonal migrants who came to the Laguna annually to pick cotton provided elites with just such labor flexibility—and obviously
imposed extreme insecurities on those poorest of workers.
More permanent estate workers combined tenancies with
seasonal wage labor. At one Laguna estate, La Concha, 63
percent of the permanent dependents who maintained accounts at the estate store were sharecroppers. They were allowed to maintain modest debts. The remaining 37 percent
were laborers, allowed less than 10 pesos' credit each by the
estate. But the sharing of family names among those listed
as sharecroppers and laborers indicates that many belonged to extended families that combined sharecropping
and estate labor to survive in the Laguna.[37]

Mexican peasants traditionally have preferred to maintain some base of autonomy—some independent maize
production. When faced with the highly variable earnings
of seasonal labor in the Laguna cotton fields, estate dependent families clung to their tenancies. But they lost access to
the most productive, irrigated lands and faced the insecurities of growing maize on the marginal estate fields. They
remained estate dependents—and faced deepening insecurities. During the years of transition to cotton cultivation
from 1880 to 1900, the recurrent protests and acts of ban-
ditry by estate dependents expressed their mounting discontent.[38]

After 1900, the economic boom and the social insecurity
in the Laguna reached extremes that led to insurrection.
From 1902 to 1907, a rare combination of favorable mar-

[37] Ibid., pp. 52-58, 110-115; Meyers, "La Comarca Lagunera," pp. 249-
250, 255-258.
[38] Ibid., pp. 255-256.

kets and heavy water flows brought boom expansion to Laguna cotton. Work was plentiful and workers' demands focused on improving their living conditions. Then the
financial panic of 1907 was followed by years of little water
in the Laguna's rivers. Cotton plantings were cut back
sharply, offering little labor to a regional population recently enlarged during years of rapid growth. Meanwhile,
drought struck sharecroppers' maize crops, and estates began to sell that staple for prices increased by 50 percent and
more. Laguna estate dependents faced the liabilities of their
insecurity. When both markets and water levels fell
abruptly after 1907, agrarian grievances became acute.[39]
The parallel with agrarian conditions in the Bajío in 1810
on the eve of the Hidalgo revolt is striking.

When Francisco Madero began his revolt to challenge the
Díaz regime in northern Mexico in the fall of 1910, he
quickly found mass support in the Laguna. His kin owned
cotton estates there and were reputed to be employers who
provided unusually favorable conditions to their workers.
Both dispossessed villagers and small holders, whose protests against estate dominance had escalated since 1905, as
well as larger numbers of estate dependents joined the rebel
movement. By the summer of 1911, as Madero triumphed
nationally, the rebellious villagers and estate workers of the
Laguna controlled their region. Local Maderista leaders attempted to demobilize the Laguna masses and return to cotton production. But once mobilized, the rural poor of the
Laguna would turn to more radical leaders. In September
of 1913, Pancho Villa arrived with his forces from Chihuahua, leading the second and more radical wave of the
Mexican revolution. He found thousands of insurgents
from the Laguna ready to give his movement a vehement
agrarian base.[40]

[39] Ibid., pp. 258-261; Vargas-Lobsinger, *La hacienda*, pp. 81, 86-87, 92,
104, 122; Katz, *Secret War*, p. 15.
[40] Meyers, "La Comarca Lagunera," pp. 254, 266-269; Vargas-Lobsinger, *La hacienda*, p. 130.

Villa's revolutionary forces included dispossessed rancheros from Chihuahua as well as Laguna villagers who had
lost lands and access to water to the cotton estates there. His
Division of the North also included estate dependents from
Chihuahua, and especially the Laguna, who were outraged
by their lives of dependence laced with insecurity. Villa's
agrarian base was thus massive. It was also divided. Those
who took up arms seeking restored land rights did not always share interests and goals with estate dependents demanding better conditions of estate life—often on lands ex-
propriated from villagers and rancheros. The lack of unity
in Villa's agrarian base perhaps helps explain his repeated
general statements in favor of agrarian reform—but his
failure to propose and defend a concrete program to effect
such reform. And the division of Villista agrarian interests,
along with the lack of a formal agrarian program, contributed to the larger lack of unity that early on helped Villa recruit the largest armies of the revolution—but eventually
left him defeated in the pivotal revolutionary confrontations of 1914 and 1915.[41]

## THE NORTH CENTRAL PLATEAU: ESTATE RESIDENTS, DEPENDENT INSECURITY, AND REVOLUTION

The regions ranging from the Bajío and central Jalisco
through the mining and grazing areas around San Luis Potosí and Zacatecas formed the northern half of the Mexican
core during the colonial era. It was there that the great conflicts of the independence era were fought—the Bajío and
Jalisco experiencing massive insurrections, while the estate
residents of San Luis Potosí fought for the preservation of
the colonial order. By the late nineteenth century, however,
as the railroads allowed the rapid settlement and economic
development of the far northern borderlands, the old colonial north became a north central region. It was still "north-

[41] Katz, *Secret War*, pp. 136-145, 279-282.

ern" in the predominance of large estates and the paucity of peasant communities. Yet these regions became increasingly "central" in their greater density of settlement and their economic orientation toward internal markets.

After independence, the landed elites of north central Mexico faced persistent financial difficulties. They curtailed direct estate production and allowed growing numbers of tenants to settle on their properties. Subsistence cultivation expanded while commercial estate cultivation stagnated and perhaps declined. Populations of permanent estate employees remained at many properties, but they were increasingly outnumbered by tenant cultivators. North central Mexico thus acquired a rapidly expanding peasant population during the years after 1821. Given the continued predominance of large estate landholding, it was a most dependent peasantry. Yet as long as elite financial difficulties continued, as long as the era of agrarian decompression endured, the autonomy of that dependent peasantry was apparently enough to compensate for its dependence and potential insecurity.

With the expansion of the tenant population at estates in more arid regions such as Aguascalientes and San Luis Potosí, along with the continued growth of tenant production in the fertile Bajío, during the years after independence the two primary subregions of north central Mexico developed increasingly similar agrarian structures. The striking regional differences that generated mass insurrection in the Bajío and loyalty in San Luis Potosí in 1810 diminished after 1821. By the middle of the nineteenth century, tenant production on estate lands characterized rural life across much of the north central plateau. But the trend toward regional homogeneity did not persist through the Díaz era. After 1880, the accelerating commercialization of agriculture brought new transformations. Agrarian social relations in the fertile Bajío again became different from those in the drier areas just to the north. After 1910, it was San Luis Potosí that generated mass agrarian insurrection, while the rural poor of the Bajío were only secondary participants in the era of revolutionary upheavals.

In the arid states of San Luis Potosí and Zacatecas, the coming of the railroads in the 1880s allowed only limited export cultivation. Estates there got access to a larger national market, but they also had to face competition within that market from producers with better land and water resources. Landed elites could only struggle to compete—and to impose deteriorating conditions on their estate dependents. Tenancies continued to proliferate and cash tenants were often forced to become sharecroppers. Elites demanded increasing shares of crops. And some tried to make their tenants raise wheat rather than maize. Wheat would bring greater profits to estate operators, but tenants would face the insecurities of raising a commercial crop in a region of scarce and variable moisture. Most tenants, however, preferred to raise maize—to retain the minimal autonomy allowed by growing that critical part of their families' subsistence. To press tenants toward wheat cultivation, elites might offer a more favorable division of the harvest. But tenants clung to maize production. They insisted on avoiding the addition of the insecurities of the market to the insecurities of tenancies while raising grain in an arid region.

As these deteriorating conditions struck the estate dependents of San Luis Potosí, population growth slowed dramatically there and in nearby Zacatecas.[42] From 1821 to 1877, the expansion of tenant production while elites struggled and markets were weak had brought many migrants into these regions, resulting in a long era of rapid population growth. But under Díaz, as north central elites faced new opportunities and new competition, agrarian conditions deteriorated and migrants looked for more favorable conditions in the borderlands to the north.

But the population growth of the years before 1880 had increased the numbers of workers and tenants in San Luis

[42] See Appendix C, Table c.4.

Potosí enough to allow elites to begin to impose declining conditions on their dependents during the subsequent years of renewed social compression. Estates began to offer only wages to their employees, and would employ them only seasonally. The year-round work and maize rations that had long guaranteed the security of estate employees began to disappear. Estates in San Luis Potosí began to buy maize from the United States in years of scarcity. But rather than giving that maize to their regular employees, they began to sell the staple to estate dependents at whatever price the market would bear. The expanded population of sharecroppers facing deep insecurities of subsistence gave estates access to growing numbers of workers who had no choice but to accept poorly paid seasonal labor. That, in turn, allowed the estates to maintain fewer permanent employees, and to offer little security to those who remained.[43]

During the Díaz era, the estate residents of San Luis Potosí and other dry areas of the north central plateau faced an accelerating loss of security, and a rapid shift to structural insecurity based on combinations of sharecropping and seasonal wage labor. The agrarian structure of secure dependence that had held the loyalty of the estate residents of San Luis Potosí in 1810 disappeared. And the deteriorating conditions of the late nineteenth century were forced onto estate dependents by landed elites trying to profit in new, more competitive market conditions. After 1880, agrarian social relations in San Luis Potosí increasingly paralleled those of the Bajío a century earlier—conditions conducive to insurrection.

Not surprisingly, then, amidst the political revolt of Francisco Madero in 1910, agrarian insurrection became widespread and persistent in San Luis Potosí. Rebel leaders easily recruited irate small holders and outraged sharecrop-

[43] This analysis relies heavily on materials in Bazant, *Cinco haciendas*, pp. 123-124, 131-132, 163-175 for San Luis Potosí; for parallel developments in Aguascalientes, see Rojas, *La destrucción*, pp. 33-44.

pers in the countryside around Ciudad del Maíz and the Huasteca of eastern San Luis Potosí—regions that had already generated rebellion in the late 1870s. Estate dependents at the large grazing properties in the drier regions of northern San Luis Potosí also rose in arms beginning in 1910.[44] Later in the revolutionary era, agrarian insurrection in San Luis Potosí coalesced around Saturnino Cedillo, a ranchero from near Ciudad del Maíz who championed the region's sharecroppers. Cedillo and his agrarian insurgents became a major force in revolutionary conflicts. They allied first with Villa, the most vocal proponent of agrarian justice among northern leaders. Following Villa's eclipse, Cedillo backed Alvaro Obregón, helping to push the Sonoran general toward greater emphasis of agrarian issues in his conflicts with the more conservative Venustiano Carranza.[45] Cedillo's power in the revolution rested on his ability to mobilize the outraged estate dependents of the countryside around San Luis Potosí—dependents recently forced to endure painful insecurities of subsistence as sharecroppers and seasonal wage laborers.

In the Bajío, the southerly, more fertile segment of the north central plateau country, the Díaz era also brought the proliferation of sharecropping and seasonal labor. But there, estates also underwent a continuing process of fragmentation. The more productive rural properties of the Bajío had never been as large as those in more arid regions to the north. During the era of elite difficulties that followed independence, the fragmentation of estates had begun. The agrarian economy of the Bajío resumed rapid growth after 1880, yet the subdivision of properties continued. At Valle de Santiago, for example, estate fragmentation persisted while agricultural output tripled between

---

[44] Falcón, "Los orígenes populares," documents the agrarian base of the Maderista revolt of 1910 in San Luis Potosí, while emphasizing that the leadership opposed agrarian interests.

[45] Ankerson, "Saturnino Cedillo," pp. 141-145.

1896 and 1906, and land values increased five times from 1890 to 1910.[46]

The exceptionally fertile and well-watered lands of the Bajío enjoyed a favored position in the expanding national market integrated by the railroads—many of which converged in that pivotal region. Bajío staples not only supplied central Mexico, but also regions as distant as Coahuila and Durango.[47] That exceptional position in the market stimulated the rapid increases in production and the rise of land values. Suddenly, Bajío grains and other crops were traded in a larger and more complex national market. Traditionally, Mexican estate operators had marketed their own produce—primarily in nearby cities and towns. The new expansion and complexity of marketing during the Díaz era brought a new class of produce dealers to prominence in the Bajío.

The rise of an increasingly powerful group of grain traders was part of a larger transformation of the agrarian structure in the Bajío. After independence, the expansion of tenant cultivation had reduced the landed elites' direct control of production in the region. Under Díaz, the emergence of the grain dealers diminished their control of marketing. The power of Bajío landed elites was thus declining just as the demand for their produce was expanding. The market brought incentives to increase production, while the loss of profits to the grain traders made it difficult to finance expanded cultivation. The subdivision of estates was a common solution. The income from selling part of an estate could finance the intensification of production on the property retained.[48] And to obtain minimally paid labor for expanding harvests, Bajío estate operators continued to allot marginal, nonirrigated lands to sharecroppers. That ex-

[46] For León, see Brading, *Haciendas and Ranchos*, p. 203; for Valle de Santiago, see Díaz Polanco, *Formación*, pp. 43-47.

[47] Miller, "The Mexican Hacienda," pp. 325-327.

[48] This interpretation is based on materials in Díaz Polanco, *Formación*, pp. 44-45.

panding population of tenants produced much of the region's maize (keeping a portion for their families), while providing seasonal labor to estates.[49]

The agrarian majority in the Bajío thus continued to live as insecure dependents during the Díaz era. But they were part of a regional agrarian society that appeared to become less polarized. Families of sharecroppers and seasonal laborers in the Bajío depended less on great landlords represented by locally powerful managers and more on resident farmers who often directly supervised the work on their smaller but intensively productive estates. And those commercial farmers often complained that they were subject to exploitation by powerful grain dealers—whose operations sharecroppers and laborers could barely perceive.

The agrarian transformation of the Bajío during this period made it difficult to place the blame for poverty and insecurity on a single elite group. And agrarian relations of dependent insecurity were not recent developments in the Bajío. Such conditions had emerged during the late eighteenth century and intensified by 1810 to fuel the Hidalgo revolt. After 1821, the difficulties of the commercial economy relieved some of the pressures on Bajío tenants—but dependent and insecure tenancies combined with seasonal wage labor continued to structure the lives of the rural poor of the Bajío throughout the nineteenth century. Thus by 1910, social relations of dependent insecurity had prevailed in the Bajío for over a century. These difficult means of survival still generated discontent, but many among the agrarian majority had apparently begun to adapt to them.

As a result, the Bajío played a secondary role in the agrarian insurrections that developed across Mexico after 1910. Although discontent was sufficient to sustain several local bands of rural insurgents, the region did not become a major focus of insurrection.[50] Apparently, longer experience

[49] Miller, "The Mexican Hacienda," pp. 325-327.
[50] Díaz Polanco, *Formación*, pp. 49-84.

with dependent insecurity moderated grievances in the Bajío, while a less polarized class structure deprived the poor
of a clear target for their discontent. The favored agricultural basin that was the heartland of agrarian insurrection
in 1810 was but a secondary participant in the agrarian revolution that consumed so much of Mexico after 1910.

## The Central Highlands: Peasant Villagers, Dependent Insecurity, and Revolution

Despite more rapid growth elsewhere, the central highlands remained to the end of the nineteenth century the
most densely settled agrarian core of Mexico. The majority
of rural Mexicans still lived in the villages that were concentrated there.[51] In 1810, social relations of symbiotic exploitation kept most central highland villagers quietly loyal to
the colonial regime. During the next few years, agrarian
guerrillas sustained movements in the arid pulque regions
to the northeast of Mexico City. But those uprisings never
became mass mobilizations. The central highlands remained most notable for their agrarian stability during the
conflicts of the independence era.

That stability began to break down after independence.
Elites facing economic difficulties tried to use the unstable
and financially weak powers of state to assault villagers' land
rights. The result was escalating agrarian conflict that generated waves of uprisings in the central highlands from the
late 1840s to the late 1870s. By the beginning of the Díaz
era, then, the once pivotal agrarian stability of the central
highlands had broken down. Violence was increasingly
common and becoming politicized.

Before 1880, the political assaults on peasant community
landholding came during the long era of agrarian decompression in which economic developments often favored peasants and rural laborers. Population growth was

[51] Tannenbaum, *The Mexican Agrarian Revolution*, pp. 27-34.

minimal in the central highlands from 1800 to 1877, and estates facing financial difficulties turned over much of production to tenants. The rural poor thus found years of respite from economic pressures, while assaults on community land rights escalated tensions more often than they succeeded in taking village properties.

After 1880, the improvement of the commercial economy combined with renewed population growth to shift agrarian social relations back in favor of the elites. The stabilization of the Díaz state allowed implementation of the Lerdo Law, ending community landholding in many villages—with the expected reduction of local cohesion and peasant family autonomy. And the new regime was increasingly successful in preventing or containing rebellious protests.

The period of agrarian compression after 1880 thus accelerated the central highland villagers' loss of autonomy. Growing numbers of agrarian families remained village residents but depended for sustenance on sharecropping estate lands while continuing to labor seasonally in estate fields. The shift to sharecropping in central Mexico, begun in the middle of the nineteenth century, was all but completed after 1880. Estate operators faced competition from maize grown in more fertile regions of Mexico, as well as in the United States—thanks to the railroads. Only estates with good soils, regular moisture, and easy access to major markets could profitably raise maize as a commercial crop. Most central highland estates instead allocated their maize lands to sharecroppers—keeping their best, irrigated lands for other crops. Villagers, no longer able to raise enough maize on village or family lands to sustain themselves, would accept sharecropping as a means of maintaining a remnant of autonomy. Estates found that sharecropping shifted the risks of climatic and market difficulties onto the tenants, whose families would provide labor at no cost to the estate. Handbooks for estate administration written around

1900 emphasized the advantages to most estates of shifting maize cultivation to sharecroppers.[52]

Most central highland villagers thus remained peasants. By combining their remaining community and family resources with lands sharecropped at nearby estates, most villages still produced the largest part of their families' subsistence. But a rapidly expanding part of that subsistence production depended on access to estate lands. The attempt to maintain a semblance of peasant life in the face of expanding village populations and shrinking resources forced many villagers into lives of insecure dependence. They faced a fundamental contradiction: although they remained villagers producing most of their basic subsistence needs, they became dependent on elites for access to the resources essential to that production. The potential for conflict between central highland villagers and landed elites rose markedly.

The alternative to peasant production for most villagers was estate employment. But permanent work had never been available on a large scale in the central highlands because of the availability of villagers for seasonal labor. And under Díaz, the minorities of permanent estate employees began to find their lives changing. They, too, faced new insecurities. At the Tochatlaco estate in the pulque zone northeast of Mexico City, a core of permanent workers had obtained wages, maize rations, and access to credit through the middle of the nineteenth century. But as the estate attempted to increase production in the expanded, but more competitive, pulque market created by the railroads, those benefits were denied all but the few most favored employees. In 1897, maize scarcities drove up the estate's cost of providing rations. The owner responded by eliminating those rations, as well as all credit to workers, and offering instead only small wage increases. The higher wages did not

[52] See Katz, *La servidumbre*, pp. 41-55, 162-169; Miller, "The Mexican Hacienda," pp. 320-324, 329-331.

begin to compensate for the loss of maize rations. And the workers were employed less permanently, and more seasonally. As permanent employment of estate dependents was eliminated at this pulque estate, workers were recruited increasingly from among nearby villagers—many of whom were sharecropping on the estate's least productive lands.[53] A parallel deterioration of estate employment practices had occurred at the San Antonio Xala estate in the same pulque region by 1902.[54]

At the grain-producing and stock-grazing property called Hueyapan, northeast of Pachuca in the state of Hidalgo, the transformation of labor relations during the Díaz era followed a different course to a similar outcome. At Hueyapan, the owner looked to take advantage of expanding markets by investing in expensive new irrigation works and new agriculture machinery. The estate thus increased crop production while introducing "labor-saving" machinery. Total estate labor demand remained stable. But the nature of the work available changed. With much of the processing of crops mechanized, Hueyapan employed fewer permanent workers and began to rely on growing numbers of seasonal hands for planting and harvesting. Once again, permanent, secure estate employment diminished while insecure seasonal labor became increasingly common.

Simultaneously, the estate altered its relations with its many tenants. Cash rents gave way to sharecropping. The estate attempted to dictate what sharecroppers planted. To gain and retain tenancies, poor families had to sign contracts promising half their crops to the estate and accepting an obligation to provide additional labor at estate fields. At Hueyapan, as at so many other Mexican estates during the late nineteenth century, the most insecure combination of sharecropping with seasonal wage labor became the only

[53] Bellingeri, Las haciendas, pp. 43-81.
[54] Leal and Huacujo Rountree, "San Antonio Xala," pp. 88-90, 108.

means of survival open to families struggling to cope with rapid agrarian changes.[55]

Parallel developments occurred in the more westerly regions of the central highlands. At the community of Naranja in Michoacán, the coming of the railroad gave elite investors the incentive to claim a marsh that the villagers had long used for fishing, hunting waterfowl, and gathering reeds for basket weaving. No one held title to the wetlands so important to the villagers' subsistence and thus they could be claimed under Díaz' program of land distribution. The new owners drained the marsh to create an exceptionally fertile estate for grain cultivation. They employed only a few permanent workers, mostly mestizos from outside the region. A minority of villagers, about twenty families, were allowed to sharecrop the least fertile of the new estate's lands. The majority retained only the small plots they received when the community lands were alienated in the 1880s—plots continually subdivided as population grew. Families became ever more dependent on seasonal labor at the fields of the estate that had once been their marsh. Yet the work available at the estate did not sustain many villagers. Naranja began to send a stream of migrants to other regions of Mexico—and toward the United States.[56]

Still farther west, at Amacueca in southern Jalisco, villagers had long enjoyed ample lands and maintained a tradition of intensive cultivation. There, too, the accelerating population growth of the late nineteenth century brought the fragmentation of family holdings. Many in the younger generations had been left land inadequate for subsistence, and they began sharecropping on the lands of rancheros who dominated the nearby valley bottom. After 1900, a new generation found lands even more scarce. Many tried to

[55] Couturier, "Hacienda of Hueyapan," pp. 136, 139, 156-160, 178, 218, 221-226.

[56] Friedrich, *Agrarian Revolt*, pp. 12-25, 22-27, 43-45; Coatsworth, *El impacto*, II, 72-74.

survive by sharecropping in the most marginal uplands. Local cultivation, even when combined with the limited seasonal labor available at the rancheros' farms, progressively failed to sustain the growing population of Amacueca. There, too, migrants left, seeking new means to sustain growing families.[57]

Across the central Mexican highlands, population growth, the privatization of community resources, and the expansion and mechanization of estate production combined during the Díaz era to create an increasingly common structure of rural social relations. More and more peasants could not live by cultivating community or family resources, even when supplemented with seasonal labor. They could continue raising essential subsistence maize only by sharecropping estate lands, while still working seasonally in estate fields. Many villagers approached the final loss of subsistence autonomy.

In large part, that loss was caused by population growth. But a state intent on mobilizing community properties, along with elites quick to expand their landholdings, contributed directly to many villagers' declining autonomy. And they gave villagers clear targets for deepening outrage. Their anger over lost autonomy was bound to heighten as they found that the only means of subsistence left was to sharecrop on marginal estate lands, while working sporadically to plant or harvest estate crops. Rapid social changes, often in a single generation, deprived many central highland villagers of cherished autonomy, while forcing them to face dependent insecurity. The resulting grievances fueled the agrarian insurrections of the revolutionary period from 1910 to 1930.

Beginning with the postindependence financial difficulties of landed elites, the growing conflicts over labor, the mounting political assaults on community lands, and the resulting waves of armed conflicts, the symbiotic exploitation

[57] De la Peña, "Regional Change."

linking central highland elites and villagers began to break down during the long era of decompression from 1821 to 1880. The remnants of that stabilizing agrarian structure collapsed during the Díaz era. The rapid privatization of community lands combined with population growth to leave few villagers with real subsistence autonomy. And without autonomy, symbiotic exploitation was impossible. Villagers increasingly depended on landed elites for access to subsistence lands as well as seasonal labor. Villagers forced to seek such dependent and insecure means of survival could no longer bargain with estates. Their relations lost any semblance of exchange—of symbiosis.

Villagers increasingly lived as mere dependents of landed elites. And from that dependence, they gained only the right to sharecrop marginal lands and to work seasonally for minimal wages. The complex developments of the century from 1810 to 1910 had transformed the lives of most central highland villagers. Relatively autonomous peasants linked symbiotically with estates at the end of the colonial era became starkly dependent peasants, subject to elites, and facing poverty and insecurity by 1910. Grievances became intense, and focused on landed elites and the state that appeared to serve elite interests. The potential for agrarian insurrection in the central highlands escalated after 1900.

Rural developments during the Díaz era in the Puebla-Tlaxcala basin, the eastern section of the central highlands, make clear the tendency of villagers forced to live with dependence and insecurity to risk insurrection and for those agrarian families still favored with secure estate employment to remain passive. In the countryside around Huexozingo, San Martín Texmelucan, and the city of Tlaxcala, most families lived as villagers. Most found subsistence lands scarce by the end of the nineteenth century and had to turn to sharecropping and seasonal labor. These villagers, like so many others, faced the loss of autonomy and a rapid shift to lives of dependent insecurity. They had begun to protest in localized uprisings of the late 1870s. After 1910, they sustained a radical agrarian insurrection led by Domingo Arenas.[58]

In contrast, in the more northerly and easterly zones of the Puebla-Tlaxcala basin, villagers were few and most rural families lived as estate dependents into the twentieth century. Here was a more "northern" agrarian structure in the central highlands. Under Díaz, the railroad linking Mexico City with its port of Veracruz passed through, suddenly opening new markets to the estates of northern Tlaxcala and northeastern Puebla. But to take advantage of the new opportunities, estate operators needed workers—who remained scarce in these arid zones. As a result, estates continued to offer year-round employment, maize rations, and access to credit. They allowed continued security. Typically, workers' earnings far surpassed their wage levels, leaving them indebted to the estates.

State laws allowed estates to force such indebted workers to remain until their obligations were fulfilled. But Herbert Nickel has emphasized that debts in the Puebla-Tlaxcala region far exceeded the levels needed to legally retain workers. He also found that most attempts to enforce labor or debt collection failed. In this dry, highland region where elites were not favored with export earnings, they could not establish a police system capable of sustaining effective coercion on the pretext of debts. Thus, the debts owed by workers to estates around Puebla and Tlaxcala were primarily signs of inflated earnings in regions where labor was scarce. Rural families who obtained such earnings—and the security of maize rations—generally did not risk insurrection. In Puebla and Tlaxcala, estate dependents rarely joined the revolution that developed all around them after 1910. Only in the late 1920s, when the petitions of villagers seeking lands threatened to undermine estate operations,

[58] Buve, "Movilización campesina," pp. 533-538; and Nickel, "Agricultural Laborers," pp. 19-20.

and thus the workers' earnings and security, did groups of estate residents begin to petition through legal channels for lands.[59] Such petitions were perhaps revolutionary, but they were far from insurrectionary. In 1810 as in 1910, estate dependents favored with security generally refrained from insurrection. But by the early twentieth century, security was only a memory for most estate residents across Mexico.[60] As population expanded and independent subsistence production became less and less possible, labor scarcities disappeared across most of central and north central Mexico. Elites found workers ever more plentiful—and thus more malleable. Many villagers and estate residents became doubly dependent on estates as sharecroppers and seasonal laborers. Estate operations became more efficient, that is more profitable, while the grievances generated by widening social relations of dependent insecurity peaked.

Among villagers, the majority of rural Mexicans in 1810 and still in 1910, the retention of subsistence autonomy sharply limited insurrection. Villagers in most of central and southern Mexico in 1810 had such autonomy and ultimately it limited the Hidalgo revolt. By 1910, few regions of villagers retained this autonomy. But where peasants did still hold substantial resources, insurrection again proved minimal. The central valleys of Oaxaca had remained bastions of peasant villagers throughout the colonial era. Surrounded by rugged highlands and situated far from coasts, mines, and major urban markets, central Oaxaca experienced little estate development. Nineteenth-century population growth, slow but steady, left peasant resources less ample than in colonial times. But even the coming of the railroad under Díaz did not break the economic isolation of the region. There was no rapid expansion of demand for estate products, and thus little pressure from elites seeking

---

[59] Ibid., pp. 20-24; and *Peonaje e inmovilidad*, pp. 20-23, 26, 29, 36-37, 44, 51, 54.

[60] Katz, *La servidumbre*, pp. 47-52; Bellingeri, "Del peonaje," pp. 122, 131.

peasant lands. Subsistence production predominated in central Oaxaca until 1910. And the villagers there remained generally passive during the revolutionary years that followed.[61] But across most of central highland Mexico, peasant autonomy was under assault and disappearing rapidly during the Díaz era. Central Mexican villagers, whose forebears had remained passive in 1810, would increasingly join and support the agrarian revolution that engulfed much of Mexico after 1910.

## MORELOS: CRUCIBLE OF AGRARIAN REVOLUTION

The villagers of Morelos, led by Emiliano Zapata, were the most adamant of agrarian revolutionaries in Mexico between 1910 and 1920. Their exceptional dedication to insurrection against those who would rule them resulted from a particularly intense local variant of agrarian difficulties afflicting villagers across central Mexico. The Morelos villagers were strategically placed to lead an agrarian revolution.

Lying just south of Mexico City, the state of Morelos is formed by a warmer, wetter, semitropical basin in the heart of the central highlands. First settled by peasant cultivators, the region became increasingly devoted to sugar cultivation during the colonial era. As was typical of colonial developments in central Mexico, sugar estates shared the fertile Morelos basin with peasant communities. In the surrounding highlands, villagers retained most of the land. To obtain the core of permanent workers for sugar production, Morelos estates first used slavery. Captured Mexican Indians served colonial elites as slaves to about 1550, when Africans were forced to take over that role. Seasonal field workers were recruited from villages near the estates, and especially in the adjacent highlands. By the late eighteenth century, free employees had generally replaced slaves as permanent estate workers, while the Morelos villagers continued to

[61] Waterbury, "Non-revolutionary peasants," pp. 411, 417, 438.

provide the seasonal labor for planting and harvesting cane.

By 1810, there was much local conflict between estates and villagers in Morelos—perhaps more than in the grain-producing regions of the central highlands. But those conflicts of the late colonial era did not generate outrage sufficient to stimulate mass insurrection, even when José María Morelos occupied Cuautla with insurgent forces early in 1812. It was after independence that agrarian conflict escalated in the region. Elites facing economic difficulties attempted to use state powers to claim additional lands and water. Still-entrenched villagers reacted vehemently. By the late 1840s, violent agrarian conflict had become endemic to the sugar region, and Morelos villagers began to gain experience as insurgents.

Then, during the Díaz era, pressures on the peasants of Morelos increased radically.[62] The coming of the railroad early in the 1880s made access to Mexico City easier, while opening a much larger national market to Morelos sugar makers. Estates increased production by expanding their irrigation systems and mechanizing much of sugar refining. Sugar production in Morelos increased four times over between 1880 and 1910.

Such economic success for elite estate operators forced mounting difficulties onto Morelos villagers. New irrigation systems often claimed or drained water previously used by villagers. Railroad transportation eliminated the work that had sustained many local muleteers. And the mechanization of refining allowed massive increases in estate production without comparable increases in permanent employment. Only the demand for seasonal field labor expanded along with sugar production. Meanwhile, the population of

---

[62] This analysis of Morelos is based on Womack, *Zapata*, pp. 43-50; Melville, *Crecimiento y rebelión*; De la Peña, *Herederos de promesas*, pp. 57, 65, 85-90, 97-99; and Warman, *. . . Y venimos a contradecir*, pp. 53-95. Warman's study is especially useful for its detailed analysis of villagers' sharecropping relations with Morelos estates.

Morelos continued to expand between 1877 and 1910, though at a rate slower than that of the rest of central Mexico.[63] By the late nineteenth century, most Morelos villagers controlled only minimal subsistence resources.

Given their estates' growing demand for seasonal workers, Morelos elites had an interest in the minimal survival of the region's peasant population. They responded by allotting increasing areas of nonirrigated estate lands to villagers in complex sharecropping arrangements. Prominent villagers in good standing with the estate management were allotted lands on shares. They were obliged to provide the estates with a stipulated number of days labor each year. Those primary tenants, in turn, generally sublet maize plots on shares to less fortunate villagers, often their kin, who actually cultivated the lands and provided the labor owed to the estate. Growing numbers of Morelos villagers thus obtained access to subsistence lands during the late nineteenth century. And sugar estates held in the region an impoverished peasantry to labor seasonally in their fields.

Once again, agrarian changes of the late nineteenth century allowed peasants to continue their cherished subsistence production, but made that production dependent on access to estate lands. In Morelos, that structural dependence was made painfully obvious by the common practice of reallocating subsistence lands annually. Estates thus avoided claims of ownership from tenants who could point to long use as a basis for proprietorship. Villagers thus had no incentive to improve the lands they cultivated. And any sign of insubordination toward the estate administration could result in elimination from the distribution of lands the next year. Such pressures became especially acute after 1900, when the lands available for sharecropping no longer sufficed to meet the needs of a growing population of villagers. A new generation in Morelos faced the prospect of living primarily by laboring seasonally for wages. And as lo-

[63] See Appendix C, Table c.4

cal labor supplies outstripped estate demands, managers used their power to offer even seasonal work only to those ready to serve most regularly and most loyally. The local organization of sharecropping and labor recruitment added blatant reminders of the dependence and insecurity that plagued Morelos villagers around 1900.

The agrarian social relations based on combinations of sharecropping and seasonal labor that predominated in Morelos, and across much of central, north central, and northern Mexico, around 1900 paralleled the relations of dependent insecurity that had plagued the rural poor of the Bajío around 1800. Such social relations generated the outrage, the sense of deep injustice, underlying the regional Hidalgo revolt of 1810, and the national agrarian revolution after 1910. The changes of the nineteenth century had made social relations of dependent insecurity ever more widespread. The loss of security accompanied by impoverishment that had hurt only Bajío residents in the late eighteenth century had struck estate dependents across the north by the late nineteenth century. And in the central highlands, and especially Morelos, the transition to lives of dependent insecurity was especially radical and painful. There, the agrarian changes of the nineteenth century stripped many villagers of subsistence autonomy and forced them to accept dependence on estates through sharecropping. Although Villa recruited some rebels who had been stripped of autonomy and others facing dependence insecurity, many Morelos villagers suffered both simultaneously—fusing their grievances into an intense outrage that drove the movement led by Emiliano Zapata.

When they began to rebel in 1910 to express that outrage, the villagers of Morelos and other central highland regions were favored by their long traditions of community organization.[64] Community cohesion was an established ideal. Lo-

---

[64] On the importance of village organization, see Womack, *Zapata*; Friedrich, *Agrarian Revolt*; and Knight, "Peasant and Caudillo," pp. 25-27.

cal leaders were steeped in peasant concerns. Thus the rebel movement that looked to Zapata for leadership remained staunchly agrarian in outlook. The importance of such community-based agrarian leadership is evident when the Zapatistas are compared with the agrarian rebels from the Bajío who followed Hidalgo in 1810, or with the many Mexican insurgents from the north who fought under Villa after 1913. Such agrarian insurgents with little tradition of community organization rebelled under leaders less rooted in the agrarian population, and less devoted to agrarian issues. Both Hidalgo and Villa raised massive numbers of insurgents driven to rebellion by agrarian grievances. But their movements proved little able to effect agrarian change. The villagers of central Mexico, spearheaded by the Zapatistas of Morelos, however, used established structures of community power to organize an insurrection that fervently and persistently pressed basic agrarian demands for lands and community autonomy. Their insurrection was eventually defeated—but they led Mexicans to a revolutionary transformation.

# CHAPTER NINE

# Elite Conflicts, State Breakdown, and Agrarian Revolution, 1900–1940

BY THE EARLY twentieth century, agrarian grievances were deepening across wide areas of central and northern Mexico. Simultaneously, escalating conflicts among elites were dividing the dominant class, and the Díaz state was facing new difficulties maintaining its political base. The critical conjunction of agrarian grievances, elite divisions, and state breakdown developed in 1910 and led to three decades of revolutionary conflicts and reconstruction. That complex era of revolution cannot be examined in detail here.[1] But a brief discussion may highlight the central role of agrarian insurgents in the conflicts that created modern Mexico.

## REVOLUTIONARY OPPORTUNITY: ELITE CONFLICTS AND REGIME CRISIS, 1900–1910

The extreme grievances fundamental to the massive and widespread outbreak of agrarian insurrections in Mexico beginning in 1910 resulted from the social transformations of the previous century. That revolutionary potential, however, could not become an enduring revolutionary conflict without the development of an opportunity for sustained insurrection. After 1900, a combination of economic and political crises provided that essential opportunity—a deep

[1] For varying interpretations of the Mexican revolution, see Córdoba, *La ideología*; Gilly, *La revolución interrumpida*; Katz, *Secret War*; Ruíz, *Great Rebellion*; and Womack, *Zapata*; on revolutionary reconstruction, see Hamilton, *Limits of State Autonomy*.

division among Mexican elites accompanied by the breakdown of state power.

In 1810, the apparent opportunity for insurrection created by Napoleon's capture of the Spanish state proved a deadly illusion. That crisis of colonial rule raised unprecedented questions of political legitimacy in Mexico, stimulating often sharp debate among elites. But the colonial elites of 1810 were not deeply divided in economic interests. Nor were they divided in their common expectations of ruling the agrarian masses. Once Hidalgo's revolt began and Mexican elites faced mass rural insurrection for the first time, they quickly united to crush the uprising.

The political crisis that opened the era of revolution in 1910 may appear even less substantial than the imperial crisis of 1810. Porfirio Díaz had ruled Mexico for nearly 35 years and was approaching eighty years of age. A problem of succession faced Mexican elites. Political succession is crucial to the stability of any regime, and frequently it has become a problem for regimes based on personal leadership. But such succession difficulties have often been resolved—or not resolved—without revolutionary consequences. The political crisis of 1910 led to a breakdown of state power not merely because of the difficulty of finding a successor to Díaz, but because of underlying divisions among Mexican elites. It was warfare among elite factions divided by conflicting interests that destroyed the coherence of the Mexican state and allowed revolutionary insurrections to begin in 1910 and endure for nearly two decades.

Díaz had consolidated state power in the 1880s by trading political power for economic benefits with elites in diverse Mexican regions. Those elites generally shared interests in commerce, perhaps mining, and landed estates. All could support Díaz' project of rapid railroad construction and the accelerating commercialization of the economy. It was a fragile structure of political stability, based on a large number of often personal links between regional elites and the national regime. In some states, notably Coahuila, Díaz never built a stable political base. But even there, elites acquiesced in his rule in the 1880s—and looked to profit from the economic developments of the era.[2]

By the 1890s, however, the very success of those developments began to create new and widening divisions among Mexican elites. Some gained substantial wealth and power under Díaz, while others faced stagnation and even decline. Meanwhile, new elite groups emerged, including many of foreign origin, whose power derived from control of new, externally linked economic activities. By 1900, the Mexican elite class had neither coherent economic interests nor unified policy goals. The failure to resolve, or to accommodate, those conflicts during the next decade turned a succession crisis into a regime breakdown—clearing the way for agrarian revolution.

Landed elites with estates in the central highlands and on the north central plateau often found their wealth and power threatened during the Díaz era. Their properties primarily served internal markets, and the importation of maize from the United States during years of Mexican scarcities undermined the one economic advantage that had long profited central Mexican elites. The integration of national markets by the railroads also forced many to face new and often damaging competition. In such conditions, some elite families in central and north central Mexico made gains; many others struggled.

In contrast, landed elites raising livestock for export and cotton for the expanding internal and external markets along the northern border regions made great gains under Díaz. So, too, did those producing tropical products for export along the southern coasts. Mexican landed elites thus began to divide into two segments: one was internally oriented, composed primarily of Mexicans, and faced stagnation and even decline; the other was export oriented, in-

[2] Langston, "Coahuila," pp. 58-63.

cluded Mexicans as well as Spaniards, Germans, and North Americans, and reaped expanding benefits.

And while landed elites diversified and divided, Mexico experienced for the first time the power of foreign capitalists. Outsiders with interests based in the United States and Western Europe began to control pivotal sectors of the Mexican economy. The railroads were built and long controlled by British and United States capitalists, who also controlled public utilities. And they monopolized the petroleum industry that developed after 1900. In all these enterprises, foreigners developed new businesses. They had not taken over enterprises once controlled by Mexican elites.

The role of foreign capitalists in mining, however, was different. The copper mines of the borderlands were new developments often undertaken by foreigners. But silver was among the oldest of Mexican industries—long the engine of the commercial economy. Mexican elites had controlled that industry since the colonial era, except for the brief and largely unsuccessful penetration of British interests after independence. But under Díaz, North Americans, led by the Guggenheim family, used their massive capital resources and advanced technologies of production and refining to oust Mexicans from silver mining. Such direct economic conflicts aggravated emerging resentments of foreign capitalists among many Mexican elites.[3]

Meanwhile, the widening space between Mexican and foreign elites was being occupied by a rising group of immigrant capitalists. Immigrant entrepreneurs have been prominent in Mexico since the sixteenth century. During the colonial era, immigrants from Spain all but monopolized large-scale commerce and participated prominently in silver mining. As immigrants, they established their primary interests in Mexico, eventually investing in Mexican estates and joining the local elite. After independence, im-

[3] On foreign capitalists, see Ceceña, *México en la órbita imperial*; Pletcher, *Rails, Mines, and Progress*; and Cockroft, *Intellectual Precursors*.

migrants from England, France, the United States, and elsewhere joined a reduced number of Spaniards, as newcomers who continued to dominate international commerce. The immigrants from North Atlantic regions, however, were less likely to invest in Mexican estates and join landed elites during the postindependence years of troubles in the agrarian economy.

Under Díaz, immigrants continued to come to Mexico with entrepreneurial ambitions and useful overseas connections. They began to entrench themselves in important new sectors of the economy. As an integrated national economy developed, a banking system became necessary. A group of immigrant Frenchmen used their favored access to the capital and expertise of the bankers of Paris to all but monopolize Mexican banking by the end of the Díaz era. Another group of immigrants, primarily from France and Spain, but including Thomas Braniff from the United States, increasingly controlled the textile industry that also developed rapidly late in the nineteenth century.

Textile production had pre-Hispanic roots in Mexico. During the colonial era, a combination of large obraje workshops and artisan families supplied most of the Mexican market, until the arrival of massive imports beginning late in the eighteenth century. After independence, a group of Mexican elites, mostly political conservatives, attempted to use state subsidies to begin mechanized textile production and to counter the continuing flood of imports.[4] They achieved limited success. Then under Díaz, the integration of the national market, the maintenance of tariffs on imports, and the continuing decline of the value of the silver peso in relation to the gold currency used by the industrialized nations all combined to create a large, protected market for a Mexican textile industry. It was primarily immi-

[4] See Potash, *Banco de Avío.*

grant capitalists with favored access to foreign financing
and imported machinery that dominated the industry.[5]

The new complexity of the Mexican elite, along with the
deepening conflicts among elite factions, made the maintenance of a stable oligarchic regime increasingly difficult. At
the same time, as the Mexican economy became more and
more closely tied to the industrial nations of the North Atlantic, the country became increasingly subject to economic
shocks of external origin. From the 1890s, Díaz faced the
need to realign the elite base of his regime, while grappling
with unprecedented decisions of economic policy. He failed
to reestablish a stable base for his government—a failure
that became obvious during the succession crisis of 1910.

As the power of internally oriented landed elites waned
in relation to rising export producers and industrialists,
Díaz had to juggle his base of support. He would not turn to
foreign capitalists; for while he sought their investments, he
feared their power. Instead, beginning in the 1890s, he
looked to the rising group of immigrant capitalists with interests focused on banking and the new textile industry.
The importance of that faction in the Díaz regime was epitomized by the rise of José Yves Limantour to power as Finance Minister.[6]

At the same time, Díaz brought powerful elites from the
agricultural export sector into his regime. He forged alliances with Luis Terrazas and Enrique Creel from Chihuahua and with Olegario Molina from Yucatán. The Terrazas-
Creel family raised livestock on vast estates along the border
and exported large numbers to the United States, maintaining close ties with financial interests across the border. After
1900, Terrazas and Creel both ruled as Governors of Chihuahua, while Creel also served as Díaz' ambassador to the

[5] On immigrant entrepreneurs, see Leal, *La burguesía*; and Keremitsis,
*La industria textil*.

[6] Cardoso et al., *México en el siglo XIX*, pp. 310-311.

United States.[7] Molina had helped build and operate the Yucatán railroads, developed henequen estates, and finally gained near monopolistic control of henequen exports beginning in 1902 through an alliance with International Harvester. A year later, he was Governor of Yucatán, and would soon become Minister of Development in the Díaz cabinet.[8]

Through such alliances with immigrant bankers and industrialists, and export-oriented landed elites, Díaz shifted the base of his regime toward powerholders primarily based in Mexico—men who controlled the new and more dynamic sectors of the economy and had close relations with foreign financial interests. The goal was a realignment of political power with the most dynamic economic elites based in Mexico. But that realignment also began to break the bargains that had consolidated Díaz' power in the 1880s. Instead of elites generally relinquishing political positions in exchange for economic gains, beginning in the 1890s selected elites were given positions of political power which clearly favored their economic interests. Powerful families such as the Maderos of Coahuila, excluded from political power since 1884, must have resented the favor shown the Terrazas of neighboring Chihuahua. Díaz began his rule by seeking to establish a state with at least limited autonomy from elite class interests. But the realignments that began in the 1890s appeared to make his state the agent of favored factions of that class. Elite unity and support for the regime waned.

While Díaz grappled with such difficult political issues, he also had to face the problems of Mexico's new incorporation into an international economy. His fear of direct control by foreigners of pivotal sectors of the economy led him to take control of major railroads. He could not consider direct expropriation. Such a break with foreign capital was not

[7] Wasserman, "Social Origins," pp. 16-17.
[8] Wells, "Family Elites," pp. 232-242.

within his vision. Thus he had to buy the railroads. But that required capital his regime could not begin to raise within Mexico. So, beginning in 1903, Díaz sold bonds to foreign investors to raise the funds to buy Mexican railroads from other (or perhaps the same) foreigners. Although foreign capitalists thus lost control of major rail operations in Mexico, they did gain new leverage over the Díaz regime, for they held a suddenly enlarged national debt.[9] Ultimately, the Mexicanization of the railroads under Díaz placed his state in the position of mediating between foreign capitalists and the Mexican economy—a position parallel to that of the immigrant capitalists and export dealers who were increasingly important to the support of his regime.

For a state and elites in such positions, Mexico's continuing reliance on silver currency became a growing liability. As the value of silver money declined and the gold-backed currency of the United States became more valuable, enterprises that earned their incomes in Mexico in silver but owed debts abroad in gold faced constant losses. Government railroads bought with foreign loans, banks financed with foreign capital, textile factories financed abroad and buying machinery there, and export production and processing financed in the United States, Germany, or elsewhere all lost heavily to the currency differential. In contrast, export producers who paid for labor and other expenses in inflated Mexican silver, while earning incomes from sales abroad in gold, profited from the differential.

Given its own growing foreign debt, and the foreign financial links of its primary supporters, the Díaz regime moved after 1900 to place Mexico on the gold standard. In 1903, Finance Minister Limantour appointed a national commission to study Mexico's monetary difficulties. He selected the members carefully, guaranteeing a majority tied to the government, the railroads, the banks, and others with large foreign obligations. Limantour thus assured that the

[9] Coatsworth, *El impacto*, I, 59-61; II, 32-38.

final recommendation would be a shift to the gold standard. The change was implemented in 1905.[10]

The shift to gold-backed currency proved both politically divisive and economically disruptive. The regime appeared to serve itself and one powerful elite faction to the detriment of others. Immigrant capitalists, state-owned railroads, and others with large debts to foreign financiers stood to gain substantially. But many producers in the export sector who had profited by paying Mexican workers in cheap silver while selling their produce for gold would face losses. Landed elites who produced primarily for Mexican markets in theory might expect little impact from the monetary change. But the transition from silver to gold proved slow and difficult, creating a severe shortage of capital throughout the economy. Estate financing was difficult. And most damaged were Mexican silver producers. Already facing the stiff competition of the Guggenheims, Mexican mine operators now faced an accelerated decline of the value of silver as it ceased to serve as Mexican money. The shift to the gold standard in 1905 deepened the polarization of the Mexican elites, making Díaz' alliance with one favored faction plain to all.

Díaz and Limantour surely expected that the problems caused by the transition to the gold standard would be short lived. They hoped that by basing the Mexican economy on the same gold-backed currency used in the industrial countries, more foreign capital would come to Mexico, financing a new period of rapid development. They envisioned a period of renewed growth that would be internally planned and controlled, but externally financed. With such expansion, internally oriented landed elites might have found expanded markets for estate produce. Export growers might have found a new equilibrium, allowing profits without the advantages of the old monetary differential. After all, they would still pay low wages to produce goods that sold for rel-

[10] María y Campos, "Los científicos," pp. 167-183.

atively high prices in foreign markets. Had these developments followed the shift to the gold standard, Díaz might
have reestablished a broad base of elite support for his regime, and the succession crisis of 1910 might have been resolved with relative ease.

Such hopes were not realized. The transition of one of
the world's great silver mining nations to the gold standard
proved exceptionally difficult. Silver no longer served as
money, but gold remained scarce. Money and credit were in
short supply after 1905. The hoped-for new infusions of
foreign capital never came, due to the financial panic that
began in 1907 in the United States. With silver demonetized
and foreign capital scarce, the dependent capitalist economy of Mexico was suddenly decapitalized. Mexican banks
cut back on lending, generally by refusing credit to internally oriented landed elites—their weakest customers. The
landowners appealed to Díaz for help, and he attempted to
mediate the dispute between his old landed supporters and
his new banking allies. But compromise failed—and Díaz
ultimately backed the bankers. Meanwhile, export earnings
declined as the financial crisis undermined markets for
many Mexican products in the United States. The successive experiences of the shift to gold currency in 1905 and
the financial crisis of 1907 made Mexican elites confront the
liabilities inherent in the dependent model of development
they had followed under Díaz rule.[11]

Mexican elites were both economically weak and deeply
divided when they began to face the question of who would
succeed Díaz. Opposition to Díaz and his allies in 1910 eventually coalesced around Francisco Madero, the maverick
son of one of the wealthiest families of the northern borderlands. Kept out of political power since 1884, the Madero family had more recently suffered losses in livestock
exporting, silver mining, and regional banking. All could be

[11] Cardoso et al., *México en el siglo XIX*, pp. 427-435; María y Campos,
"Los científicos," pp. 182-183; Leal, "El estado," pp. 719-721.

blamed on Díaz policies. The depth of elite class divisions is perhaps most evident in Madero's willingness to court agrarian support through at least vague proclamations, and more concretely by allying with Zapata and other agrarian rebels, in his fight against Díaz.

## REVOLUTION, 1910–1940

The year 1910 was a one of escalating political and agrarian agitation. Madero attracted growing crowds as he toured Mexico promising political democracy and an undefined agrarian justice. At the same time, widespread crop failures made food scarce and expensive among the poor. In 1910 as in 1810, maize scarcities drove agrarian grievances to peak intensity.[12] In 1910, the importation of maize from the United States helped to alleviate shortages.[13] But the recent elimination of maize rations at many estates forced most of the rural (and urban) poor to pay the high prices demanded by those who imported maize for profit. Amidst heated political debates, agrarian outrage escalated.

The inability of deeply divided elites to find compromise solutions for their political (and ultimately economic) differences, combined with the readiness of Madero and other elite dissidents to court agrarian support, opened the way for the revolution that followed. In the autumn of 1910, Díaz jailed Madero and engineered his own reelection once again. Madero escaped into exile in San Antonio, Texas, and called for rebellion. He found support not only among disaffected elites, but many in the middle classes, frustrated by their long exclusion from politics. Madero's movement also began to tap the rebellious potential among the irate agrarian populations of Chihuahua, the Laguna, San Luis Potosí, Morelos, Puebla, and elsewhere. Few rushed to Díaz'

[12] On the drought, see Bazant, *Cinco haciendas*, p. 178; Díaz Polanco, *Formación*, pp. 49-50; Bellingeri, *Las haciendas*, p. 62.
[13] See Table 8.1.

defense. Following Maderista victories in a few skirmishes in Chihuahua, the aging patriarch left for exile. Perhaps he knew the fragility of his regime better than any other Mexican.

With Díaz gone, Madero had to face the gulf separating his goal of moderate political democratization from Zapata's and others' demands for rapid agrarian justice—the return of lands to dispossessed villagers and rancheros. As Maderistas took control of state governments in 1911, they attempted to restrain and if possible to demobilize the many agrarian rebels who had rallied to the fight against Díaz.[14] But Zapata and the agrarian rebels of Morelos refused to lay down their arms until they obtained lands. Madero refused such precipitous reform, leaving Zapata in rebellion against the regime he had just helped to install. Madero then sent Díaz' army to subdue the Morelos villagers. But the troops' brutality only escalated the conflict. Military aggression stiffened the villagers' resistance, and increasing numbers joined Zapata. The peasants of Morelos would remain in arms, demanding lands and local autonomy, until their leader's assassination in 1919. Their persistence, in turn, facilitated agrarian insurrections in other Mexican regions.

The balance of armies in revolutionary Mexico guaranteed that Zapata and other agrarian insurgents could not "win" that prolonged conflict. They could not defeat factions such as Venustiano Carranza's Constitutionalists who were elite led and internationally supported. Agrarian insurgents could not claim and keep control of the national state. But while agrarian insurgents could not win, many would not lose. Pancho Villa raised massive armies that contended for national power from 1913 to 1915. He recruited mass agrarian support in Chihuahua and the Laguna and other northern regions. But as those who had joined Hidalgo a century earlier had learned, massed agrarian ar-

---

[14] LaFrance, "Puebla," pp. 82-99; Falcón, "Los orígenes."

mies could be decisively defeated and eliminated from subsequent power struggles. In contrast, Zapata and many other agrarian rebels relied on guerrilla tactics—by 1910 a century-old tradition among central Mexican insurgents. Such guerrillas could rarely defeat opposing armies. But armies had trouble even finding Zapata. It was the persistence of the Zapatistas and numerous other agrarian guerrillas that eventually forced all the contenders in the revolutionary conflicts to make agrarian reform the primary social question of the era.

The critical role of agrarian insurgents in the revolutionary struggles is evident in the pivotal conflicts of 1914 and 1915. Backed by the most massive and widespread agrarian mobilizations in Mexican history, Villa and Zapata controlled most of Mexico, occupied Mexico City, and dominated the government known as the Convention during late 1914. Carranza and his Constitutionalists were limited to the coastal fringes. But Villa and Zapata failed to issue a unified program of agrarian reforms that might have consolidated their power across Mexico.

Peasant-based movements are not inherently incapable of exercising state power.[15] The Chinese and Vietnamese revolutions should make that clear. It was disunity, not peasant incapacity, that led to the failure of Villa and Zapata to generate a coherent program of revolutionary reforms, and to maintain their national power. While Zapata's rebels were overwhelmingly villagers who demanded that estate lands be returned to them, Villa had mobilized dispossessed northern rancheros as well as estate dependents seeking relief from the insecurities of sharecropping and seasonal labor. And Villa, too, included within his movement a number of elites who were reluctant to consider any agrarian reform.[16]

[15] For a contrary perspective, see Gilly, *La revolución interrumpida*, pp. 139-175.
[16] Katz, *Secret War*, pp. 258-282.

Just at the time Villa and Zapata failed to coordinate their diverse agrarian constituencies, Carranza began to realize the importance of agrarian issues and insurgents in the revolutionary struggles he seemed so close to losing. Through late 1914 and culminating in January of 1915, his government issued a series of decrees that finally recognized the rights of Mexican peasants to subsistence lands and community organization. For Carranza, perhaps the most elitist of Mexican revolutionaries—devoted to a staunch nationalism, but also identified with landed elites—the acceptance of agrarian reform was a political decision made with deep reluctance. It was only dire necessity that led him to recognize that without substantial agrarian support, he could not triumph. He finally recognized the grassroots power of Mexico's agrarian insurgents.

Carranza's strategy worked. Villa and Zapata failed to compromise their movements' fundamental differences—ultimately the differences of north and center that still divided agrarian societies in Mexico. They became more distant allies early in 1915. The core of Zapata's village supporters in Morelos and adjacent states, and Villa's agrarian rebels from Chihuahua and the Laguna remained loyal to their leaders. But Carranza was able to recruit other agrarian leaders, such as Domingo Arenas of Tlaxcala, attracted by his new agrarian platform as well as the mounting evidence that his Consititutionalists had the elite, labor, and international backing to win. Control of the revenues from Yucatán's henequen exports also aided Carranza from 1915. As in 1810, control of regions that did not generate insurrections was critical to elite victories in social conflicts.

The decisive battles of the revolution were fought in the summer of 1915 in the Bajío. Villa's Division of the North faced the growing Constitutionalist armes led by Alvaro Obregón. Obregón emerged victorious, in large part because Zapata remained in his Morelos homeland. Agrarian disunity allowed elite factions their political victory. Carranza, Obregón and the Constitutionalists would build the new state in revolutionary Mexico.

Once Villa was defeated and forced to retreat to his far northern base in Chihuahua, and while Zapata continued to fight a defensive guerrilla war from Morelos, Carranza turned to agrarian policies closer to his landed elite interests and allies. Despite his promises of January 1915, in 1916 he pursued a quiet but effective policy of returning estates taken by revolutionary forces to their former owners. Left to pursue his own policies, Carranza would have returned Mexico to its agrarian structure of 1910.[17]

But Carranza found that military victory and the office of president did not allow him to follow his wishes in such matters. While estates were being returned to their former owners, a constitutional convention met at Querétaro late in 1916. Carranza would have preferred a modest revision of the liberal charter of 1857, with new safeguards against extended personalist rule. But the majority of the delegates to the convention, led by Obregón, understood the depths of the agrarian grievances that had fueled the years of violence—and that had helped bring them to power. Over Carranza's objections, they incorporated into the Constitution of 1917, via Article 27, the right of peasant communities to hold the lands essential to their survival. Returning lands to elite estate owners while constitutionally guaranteeing the right of peasant villagers to many of the same lands—that was the ultimate contradiction of the Constitutionalist victory in the first phase of the Mexican revolution.

For nearly two decades, the revolutionary state and the rural poor would grapple with that contradiction. After Obregón overthrew Carranza in 1920 with the help of agrarian insurgents, many of the most vehement rural rebels obtained lands. Morelos villagers who had fought with Zapata and the followers of Cedillo in San Luis Potosí were

[17] Ibid., pp. 253-255, 287-297; Vargas-Lobsinger, *La hacienda*, pp. 132-133.

thus rewarded for supporting Obregón's ascent to the presidency. But the new leader was not a confirmed *agrarista*. He would redistribute lands when it served his political interests. He would also back landed elites when that seemed advantageous. Perhaps most important, the revolutionary state led by Carranza, then Obregón, and finally Calles from 1916 to 1934 was entrenched in Mexico City—but it was far from established as the sole legitimate power in the provinces.

Romana Falcón has provided a unique view of the conflicts of this era in San Luis Potosí. There were three predominant factions: one led by Juan Barragán, unabashedly representing landlord interests, and linked to Carranza; one led by Aurelio Manrique and Antonio Díaz Soto y Gama, middle-class reformers calling for state-directed agrarian and labor reforms, and predominant while Obregón ruled nationally; and one directed by Saturnino Cedillo, representing the rural insurgents of eastern San Luis Potosí, linked nationally to Calles, and ready to deal with almost any faction that would accept Cedillo's predominance in his home region.

With such competing factions, the 1920s were a decade of continuing, often violent, conflict in San Luis Potosí. As Falcón emphasizes, many of the state's leaders were ultimately seeking power in an era of conflict and reconstruction. Yet her work also shows that the "agrarian question" was the fundamental issue in these disputes. One of the three contending factions served landlord interests; the other two offered differing visions of agrarian reform. Zapata may have died in 1919, but the issues he fought for remained central to revolutionary conflicts for years after his assassination. Revolutionary leaders might have wished otherwise, but agrarian insurgents remained ready to fight for their vision of a new Mexico through the 1920s—and aspirants to political power could not ignore them.[18]

[18] Falcón, *Revolución y caciquismo.*

The persistence of agrarian violence into the 1920s also reflected the ambiguous positions of Mexican rancheros in the revolutionary period. Rancheros were perhaps the segment of Mexican rural society that had expanded most during the nineteenth century. Neither destitute peasants nor wealthy elites, rancheros shared the subsistence autonomy of peasants and the commercial interests of elites. They occupied the social space between landed elites and the rural poor. They might link those groups, or separate them. They might ally with one, the other, or neither.

Rancheros chose widely varying roles in the conflicts that began in 1910. Some became leaders of the agrarian poor. Emiliano Zapata and Saturnino Cedillo are obvious examples. Others, like the Figueroas of Guerrero, entered the conflicts primarily in search of a political role, seeking to end the exclusion they suffered during the Díaz period. Those who became revolutionary activists among the rancheros of Pisaflores, Hidalgo, were also primarily seeking political advantage. But they also saw gains in the agrarian reforms. Their lands were too small to be targets for expropriation, and they might gain economically from the breakup of larger haciendas. Not surprisingly, such rancheros worked toward agrarian change under the Constitutionalist banner.[19] In contrast, the rancheros of Jalisco and Michoacán generally avoided the conflicts of 1910 to 1920 and were strong opponents of agrarian reform as proposed by insurgents such as Villa and Zapata.

The largest concentration of rancheros in Mexico was in these west central regions of Jalisco, Michoacán, and neighboring states.[20] Only there were ranchero communities the dominant agrarian formation over extended areas. During the decade from 1910 to 1920, many revolutionary bands passed through west central Mexico, but there was little

[19] Jacobs, "Rancheros of Guerrero," pp. 81-83; Schryer, "Ranchero Economy," pp. 441-442; "Sierra de Jacala," pp. 164-166.
[20] See Appendix D, Table D.2.

mobilization there. Then in 1926, massive insurrection erupted among the rancheros of Jalisco and Michoacán—insurrection against the victors in the conflicts of the previous decade. To the regime in power, the revolt of the rancheros was a counterrevolutionary uprising. In a wider perspective, it was one of the last and most vehement of the major agrarian insurrections of the Mexican revolution.

The rancheros of west central Mexico were not rich. Often they were not even comfortable. They occupied less fertile lands, generally in isolated uplands, struggling to sustain their families and produce small surplusses for sale. They were modest peasant farmers. But they were distinguished from the peasants of central and southern Mexico by their more Hispanic origins and culture, and by their reliance on private property. And the rancheros were deeply religious, devoted to their priests and churches. For the rancheros of west central Mexico, social life revolved around the Church, the family, and private property—a clear contrast with the community focus of social organization and landholding among the more indigenous peasants of central and southern Mexico.

Never owning much good land, the rancheros of Jalisco and Michoacán had seen their numbers increase and their lands repeatedly subdivided during the late nineteenth and early twentieth centuries. Most ranchero families held less and less land. And there emerged in many ranchero communities a landless class that lived by sharecropping and providing seasonal labor on rancheros' lands. By the 1920s, the majority of families in ranchero settlements lived as insecure dependents of the smaller numbers of still-propertied rancheros.

But most rancheros were not wealthy and distant landlords. They lived in small towns or on their lands, often working alongside their dependents. Ranchero landowners and sharecroppers often were kin, and generally shared personal relationships. And the landless of ranchero communities clung to the goal, the ideal, of family landownership. The poor of ranchero communities tended to view landed rancheros as patrons to be emulated, not as oppressive elites. The growing landlessness in ranchero communities was the immediate result of population growth and partible inheritances, more than any direct expropriation. Thus, the sharecroppers and laborers of ranchero regions might face dependent insecurity, but their discontent did not generally focus on the landed rancheros. This helps explain the absence of insurrection in west central Mexico during the decade of intense agrarian conflict after 1910.

Developments in the 1920s, however, gave the poor of ranchero communities clear targets for their mounting grievances. Under the constitution of 1917, private property was no longer a presumed right of Mexicans. Yet for Alvaro Obregón and Plutarco Elías Calles who succeeded him as president, land reform was not a primary goal. It was a political tool to be used when necessary to pacify a rural region or to punish a political opponent. Such limited and politicized land redistribution left uncertainties and divisions among the rural poor. In west central Mexico, rancheros might become objects of expropriation. Few were staunch supporters of the revolutionary regime. By taking rancheros' lands, reluctant revolutionary leaders might be able to implement at least limited land redistribution without attacking the holdings of powerful elites. And even when ranchero lands were not targeted, the program of land redistribution was a blunt assault on the rancheros' ideal of private property.

Simultaneously, the revolutionary regimes of the 1920s pressed an attack against the Catholic Church. Ecclesiastical institutions had been stripped of their economic power by the liberal reformers of the mid-nineteenth century. President Calles took office in 1924 and pushed programs aimed at denying the Church its role in education and the spiritual life of the nation. Conflict escalated between the bishops and the government. In 1926, the bishops pressed their point by closing all churches and suspending religious services across Mexico. That was the last straw for the ranchero communities of west central Mexico. They were deeply religious people, closely attached to their priests and churches. The priest was often the pivotal, most respected, and most powerful member of ranchero communities. The closing of the churches and the suspension of religious ceremonies, coming along with the government's assaults on property rights, seemed intended to destroy the religious and landed bases of ranchero community life.

The conflict between the state and the Church both precipitated the rancheros' insurrection, and provided the opportunity for its development. The rebels grievances were rooted in the growing economic difficulties of small landowners, sharecroppers, and seasonal laborers—often members of the same struggling families. Amidst those mounting insecurities, the revolutionary regime's threats to property and the Church brought those grievances to the peak of outrage. For the rancheros and sharecroppers of west central Mexico, a regime claiming to be revolutionary was threatening the landed and religious foundations of already difficult lives.

They spearheaded the massive insurrection known as the Cristero revolt. While Church leaders helped precipitate that conflict, they rarely became involved in the violence. Many elite landlords were pleased that the Cristeros were ready to fight vehemently for private property rights—but great landowners, too, stayed aloof from the deadly combat. The Cristero revolt was led by neither landed elites nor high churchmen. It was a movement of rancheros and their dependent sharecroppers and laborers, joined by many others who were part of their ranchero communities.

The Cristeros' demands were bluntly agrarian. They fought to be left alone in the possession of their lands and the exercise of their religion. Their insurrection was massive and vehement enough to fight to a stalemate from 1926 to 1929 both the federal army and thousands of armed beneficiaries of the government's land reform—at a time when the government faced no other armed challengers. It is estimated that 30,000 Cristeros died in defense of their religion and their way of life. They were never defeated by the government. In June 1929, Church leaders negotiated an agreement with the government that allowed religion to resume its public role and the Cristero rebels to return to peaceful pursuits. Exhausted by months of stalemated warfare, most of the insurgents eventually accepted amnesties and the uprising slowly collapsed.[21]

The extent, endurance, and intensity of the Cristero revolt forced the rulers of revolutionary Mexico to understand that partial and politicized land redistribution would not pacify the countryside and allow the consolidation of state power. Calles, no longer president but still Jefe Máximo, proposed the end of land distribution in 1929—a reflection more of his willingness to compromise with landed elites and his preference for commercial farming than any concession to the Cristeros he had fought so hard. And the move to slow the agrarian reform, enacted in legislation during 1930, surely also reflected the political goals of land redistribution during the 1920s—goals which Calles shared.[22] The Cristero revolt made plain the failure of partial agrarian reform as a pacification program.

Others among the revolutionary leadership reacted differently to the failure of partial and politicized land reform, and to the persistence of agrarian violence. They argued that rather than halting redistribution, it should be accelerated. Their cause was assisted by the great depression that struck Mexico in 1930. Surviving landed elites, plagued by two decades of insurrections and revolutionary uncertainties of politics and land rights, now faced the collapse of the commerical economy. Export producers saw markets for their goods all but disappear. The Cristero revolt left Mex-

---

[21] On rancheros and the Cristero Revolt, see González y González, *Pueblo en vilo*; De la Peña, "Regional Change"; Meyer, *La cristiada*; and Díaz and Rodríguez, *El movimiento cristero*.

[22] Simpson, *The Ejido*, pp. 109-118.

ican leaders to choose between halting or completing the agrarian reform. The depression opened up the possibility of completing it.

In December of 1933, at the convention that met in Querétaro to nominate Lázaro Cárdenas as the next President of Mexico, those who pressed for the acceleration of the agrarian reform won a clear victory over Calles and those who would slow the process. The victors produced a six-year plan that provided for the reconstruction of rural Mexico.[23]

Cárdenas assumed the presidency in 1934 and implemented a program of mass land expropriation and redistribution that finally destroyed the landed base of Mexican elites. Most recipients were organized into ejido communities that received lands from the state and allotted them among member families. This twentieth-century revival of Mexican peasant communities at first appears a return to colonial practices. Lands were allotted to communities, which in turn guaranteed their use by peasant families. But the colonial state had also provided lands to support relatively independent local governments, and had expected peasant families to engage in subsistence production— while providing seasonal labor to commercial estates. The new ejido communities did not obtain resources to sustain local governments, which remained dependent on the favor and resources of the revolutionary regime. And the Cárdenas government and those that followed used their powers in the ejido communities to demand political allegiance as well as commercial production. The reconstituted peasant communities of revolutionary Mexico received more land than autonomy.

Cárdenas worked to resolve the contradictions of agrarian policies that since 1915 had attempted to offer land reform to agrarian rebels while maintaining the power of

[23] Ibid., pp. 123-127, 439-463; Hamilton, *Limits of State Autonomy*, pp. 104-124.

landed elites. He sacrificed landed elites to the search for postrevolutionary stability, an unprecedented victory for Mexico's agrarian insurgents. But Cárdenas' reform was a compromise reform. He would undermine landed elites, but he would not weaken the power of the emerging Mexican state. Nor would he relinquish the goal of accelerating commercial development. The victory of the rural poor under Cárdenas was but a partial triumph. Hundreds of thousands of rural families received lands. Despite government pressures, early on most recipients used their holdings for subsistence production. They found it easy to support the government that finally gave them lands. Pressures toward commercialization could be ignored during the depression—and perhaps dealt with later. The era of agrarian violence that began in 1810 finally ended with the land reform of the 1930s.[24]

Conflict did not disappear from rural Mexico, however. Nor were the problems of rural families resolved. After receiving lands, peasant numbers escalated. In another generation, the lands distributed in the 1930s would no longer suffice to support growing families. And as resources became scarce, the government could press more effectively toward commercial production. Some would prosper. But most rural families by the 1960s retained only miniscule plots and were ever more dependent on seasonal wage labor. The goals of autonomy and security, for which so many fought, have become more distant in recent years.

But the assaults on agrarian ideals now derive from the conjunction of population growth and "impersonal" economic developments. Landed elites are gone. Ejido villagers face a state that gave them land, and presses them toward commercial production. They also face a new class of commercial farmers and produce dealers who profit from increasingly mechanized production, while employing many among the rural poor as seasonal workers. The

---

[24] On the Cárdenas era, see especially ibid.

search for seasonal work sends many across the border into the United States. Meanwhile, commercial farmers have continued to turn away from maize and other staples of the Mexican poor, seeking profits in crops for the wealthier residents of Mexico's cities and for consumers in the United States. There are gross inequalities and persistent conflicts within this new agrarian structure. But since Cárdenas' reforms of the 1930s, Mexico has not experienced the waves of multiple insurrections that characterized the era of agrarian violence. The agrarian reconstruction that finally closed the long era of insurrections is the indelible mark left on Mexico by thousands of "defeated" agrarian insurgents.[25]

[25] On the agrarian reform and subsequent rural developments, see Simpson, *The Ejido*; Hewitt de Alcántara, *La modernización*; Stavenhagen, "Social Aspects"; Barkin and Suárez, *Fin de la autosuficiencia*. For regional case studies, both focused on districts of Morelos, see De la Peña, *Herederos de promesas*; and Warman, . . . *Y venimos a contradecir*.

# CONCLUSION

# CHAPTER TEN

# Social Bases of Insurrection and Revolution

THIS STUDY HAS SOUGHT explanations for the agrarian violence that began in Mexico with the Hidalgo revolt of 1810, expanded and became endemic from the 1840s to the 1880s, and then exploded into revolutionary conflict after 1910. In turn, that analysis may contribute to more general and comparative discussions of the origins of agrarian uprisings, and of social revolutions fueled by such uprisings, during recent centuries. This conclusion summarizes my principal findings about Mexican insurrections and explores briefly their relationship to the analysis of rural uprisings and revolutions elsewhere.

## FROM INSURRECTION TO REVOLUTION IN MEXICO

In 1810, Father Miguel Hidalgo led a massive insurrection of agrarian rebels in the Bajío, Jalisco, and neighboring areas. The uprising occurred during the imperial political crisis caused by Napoleon's capture of the Spanish throne. Yet the Hidalgo revolt was crushed in only four months. Several guerrilla movements continued the insurrection during subsequent years, but they, too, were defeated before Mexican elites imposed their own, more conservative independence in 1821. The years from 1810 to 1821 produced unprecedented social violence and fundamental political change. But powerful elites kept social conflicts separate from political developments. There would be no revolution in the era of Mexican independence.

A century later, a political succession crisis touched off

two decades of political wars and agrarian conflicts that became fully entangled and generated a revolutionary transformation. Why had social violence and political conflicts remained separate and thus nonrevolutionary in 1810? And what had changed by 1910 to generate the revolution that then swept Mexico?

The absence of revolution in early nineteenth-century Mexico resulted from the intersection of two developments: agrarian grievances, and thus insurrections, however intense, remained restricted to small areas of north central Mexico. And Mexican elites, however divided over political issues of empire, remained strongly unified in their opposition to those agrarian insurrections.

In striking contrast, by 1910 agrarian grievances were peaking across Mexico from the central highlands to the far northern borderlands just as political divisions became acute among elites divided over economic interests and policies. By the early twentieth century, grievances were widespread, concentrated in the strategic central highlands, and coming to a head just as elite divisions led to the breakdown of state power beginning in 1910. A social revolution followed that did not lead to a peasant utopia—but did produce a structural transformation of rural Mexico that took account of agrarian rebel demands.

The pivotal questions, then, are these: why were acute agrarian grievances regionally limited in 1810, but widespread by 1910? And why were Mexican elites able to maintain class unity amidst the imperial political crisis of 1808 to 1821, but by 1910 had become so factionalized that they would persist in their political wars in the face of unprecedented agrarian insurrections?

Agrarian grievances were regionally confined during the independence era because the social conditions provoking them were equally limited. In the highlands of central and southern Mexico—where most Mexicans then lived—the Spanish state had sustained a structure of peasant community autonomy that allowed villagers to control local governments and to cultivate community lands—and thus to maintain relations of symbiotic exploitation with estates where they worked as seasonal laborers. They were poor and exploited, but not ready to take the risks of rebellion in 1810. Across the plateau country of arid northern Mexico, most rural families lived as estate dependents at the beginning of the nineteenth century. And thanks to the intersection of commercial expansion with population scarcities, most northern estate dependents retained secure employment that held their loyalty. Many fought in the militias that crushed the insurrections that did develop in 1810.

Only in limited regions had the conditions of peasant autonomy and estate resident security come under thorough assault by 1810. In the Bajío, uniquely fertile, well watered, and situated to supply the major mining centers of Mexico, the combination of economic expansion with population growth ended labor shortages and allowed elites to impose deepening poverty and new insecurities on estate residents. Those deteriorating conditions became deadly in the famine years of 1785 and 1786, and again in 1809 and 1810. And it was the rural poor of the Bajío who made the Hidalgo revolt a major social movement.

But the villagers of the central highlands would not join the uprising, and the estate residents of San Luis Potosí fought against it. It was only among the villagers of central Jalisco, the Sierra Gorda, and a few other regions that the uprising begun in the Bajío found large numbers of new adherents. These were villagers incorporated only recently as subordinates into an expanding commercial economy, and whose landed autonomy was threatened in the process. There were, then, two patterns of agrarian social change, two distinct patterns of grievances, underlying the insurrections that began in 1810. And those grievances remained restricted to important but limited areas primarily in north central Mexico.

Complex social transformations during the century after 1810 made similar grievances more widespread and more

intense by 1910. In the years following independence in
1821, the collapse of the commercial economy across much
of highland Mexico favored the rural poor. Villagers faced
less pressure to labor at estates, as lands were increasingly
let to poor tenants, who thus expanded subsistence production. But Mexican elites, frustrated by their persistent financial difficulties, began to use their new tool, the state,
backed by liberal principles, to try to deny land rights to
peasant communities. The state in postindependence Mexico, however, was always poor and unstable. It was a weak
instrument of domination. Thus, the attempts to use state
powers to attack peasant rights primarily succeeded in set-
ting off waves of regional insurrections from the late 1840s
to the early 1880s. The long era of agrarian decompression
from 1810 to 1880 took some economic pressures off the
rural poor. But two developments simultaneously heightened the potential for insurrections: first; the growing
numbers of tenancies made more rural families direct dependents of landed elites. And second, the decision to make
the destruction of peasant community autonomy a political
priority made villagers acutely aware of the need to defend
their interests.

The period from 1880 to 1910 brought political stability,
commercial expansion, and renewed agrarian social
compression. The laws denying peasant community land
rights were finally implemented in many regions. Combined with population growth, the privatization of village
lands accelerated the loss of autonomy of Mexican peasants.
And to maintain a remnant of autonomy, rural families
across central, north central, and northern Mexico often
found that they could survive only by sharecropping the
most marginal of estate lands, while working seasonally in
estate fields. The Díaz era thus brought together the rapid
loss of autonomy and the forced shift to dependent insecurity across much of Mexico. The two patterns of agrarian
grievances began to fuse, with explosive insurrectionary
consequences.

There were still regions, like the highlands of Oaxaca and Chiapas, where peasant villagers retained important if diminished autonomy in 1910. And there were areas like Yucatán, Soconusco, and parts of Puebla and Tlaxcala where estate residents retained critical security. Those regions produced few insurgents after 1910. Their passivity helped the Constitutionalists to their political victory. But the regions without acute agrarian grievances had shrunk drastically from 1810 to 1910. Agrarian insurgents rose in sufficient numbers in regions widespread and strategic enough to eventually force political leaders to implement a radical agrarian reconstruction in the 1930s.

The regional extension of the social conditions that generated acute grievances was thus the fundamental factor limiting agrarian insurrections in 1810 and making them widespread after 1910. But while such social developments were the ultimate and most necessary causes of insurrections, they were not sufficient causes. The sudden loss of autonomy by peasants and the rapid encounter with insecurity by estate dependents did not alone lead to mass insurrections in Mexico.

For uprisings to develop, the deteriorating conditions afflicting the rural poor had to be perceived by the poor as caused by social actors—by human powerholders. Losses of autonomy apparently caused by population growth alone rarely led to insurrection; losses caused by elite land grabbing and state edicts provoked uprisings. Similarly, insecurity resulting most immediately from climatic difficulties rarely generated rebellion; insecurity produced by landlords forcing estate dependents to sharecrop on marginal lands often led to insurrections. The issue was not perception versus social reality, but rather the perception of social realities. When real losses of autonomy and worsening insecurities could be clearly seen as caused by elites, then grievances became acute. They generated the deep sense of injustice that might be alleviated by social action, by insurrection.

Yet even acute grievances with evident social origins did not lead directly to insurrection. The risks of challenging the powerful generally led people with acute grievances to wait for an opportunity to rebel. They awaited situations in which divided elites and a weakened state would allow their insurrection to begin and endure without immediate repression. The perception of such an opportunity (and here perception more easily differs from reality, for the rural poor are trying to perceive relations among elites) was the final condition necessary for the development of mass agrarian insurrections in Mexico.

The endurance and eventual consequences of those insurrections have also depended on several factors. The depth and distribution of the underlying grievances are critical to the course of insurrections. Also important is the nature of the opportunities that allowed uprisings to begin. Divisions among Mexican elites in 1810 proved minimal. They debated political legitimacy within the empire, but they shared economic goals and the expectation of ruling the rural poor. They united in defense of privilege and profit to crush the insurrections of the independence era— and to prevent a movement toward social reconstruction.

By 1910, the divisions among Mexican elites were deep and enduring. The rapid and complex economic developments of the Díaz era had generated fundamental conflicts among elite factions. The resulting political divisions were so extreme that many were willing to court agrarian insurgents as allies against elite opponents. What followed was a political civil war that persisted in the face of mass and widespread agrarian insurrections—allowing those mass movements to endure and to place their agrarian demands in the center of the political arena.

No agrarian movement has claimed enduring control of the Mexican state. In that ultimate sense, no rural insurrection has been successful. But rural Mexicans took up arms against their rulers repeatedly from 1810 to 1930, knowing that they would probably face defeat. Surely few expected to claim the state and rebuild Mexico as a peasant society.

What did Mexican insurgents seek? That, too, changed over time. The poor who lashed out with Hidalgo in 1810, and most other insurgents of the independence era, apparently rose to take vengeance against those they believed responsible for the intolerable conditions they faced. Vengeance remained a goal during the waves of uprisings that occurred during the era of decompression. But during the middle of the nineteenth century, other objectives entered. Especially in more marginal regions such as Yucatán, the Sierra Gorda, and Sonora, mass insurrections could simultaneously claim vengeance and assert rights to greater autonomy against still weak and divided elites. And in the central regions, villagers' revolts often successfully blocked assaults on community land rights. They, too, rebelled to preserve autonomy. The delays of commercial development and of land privatization achieved by the mid-nineteenth-century insurgents were important if limited successes. They won the chance to live as relatively autonomous peasants for a few more decades.

Mexican rural insurrections long remained local or regional in outlook, protective, even defensive in aims. But after the Liberals took power and made the destruction of community landholding a national policy in 1856, agrarian rebels slowly began to accept alliances with radical political actors and ideologues—who led rural insurgents toward more active participation in national politics. Politicized agrarian insurrections, demanding a reconstruction of Mexico in the interests of the rural poor, began in the late 1860s, recurred in the late 1870s, and became the dominant mode of insurrection after 1910—though the Cristeros of the late 1920s brought a revival of more defensive insurrection. That politicization of goals, and a willingness to deal with other political actors with similar, but rarely identical, aims helped the massive insurrections of the early twentieth

century to endure and bring about revolutionary consequences.

But the politicization of agrarian insurrections also
brought new difficulties. The political necessities of working in a national context might lead agrarian insurgents to
ally with groups and leaders less devoted to agrarian
goals—forces that might eventually sacrifice agrarian interests in efforts to consolidate national power.

In coping with that dilemma, movements based on community organization achieved the greatest gains. Estate dependents, outraged at their lives of dependent insecurity,
rose by the tens of thousands with Hidalgo in 1810, and
with Villa after 1910. But Hidalgo had little understanding,
apparently, of his followers' agrarian grievances. And while
Villa was more sensitive to agrarian demands, he repeatedly
worked to link them to other political goals. The estate dependents of the Bajío in 1810, and of Chihuahua and the
Laguna after 1910, lacked the means to generate leaders
more staunchly tied to agrarian interests. Without established community organizations and leaders, estate residents were forced to rebel under leaders they could rarely
control. Hidalgo's rebels still inflicted vengeful damage
upon Bajío estates, and Villa's insurgents were a major
force pressing agrarian demands within the Mexican revolution. But neither uprising could operate as a fully agrarian movement. And both ultimately faced military disaster—limiting their ability to achieve agrarian goals.

In contrast, the agrarian insurgents whose movements
were based on established community organizations were
more successful in forcing changes onto Mexican society.
Community-based insurgents had two major advantages:
first, they could utilize guerrilla tactics when times did not
favor mass mobilization, using their communities as sanc-
tuaries and bases of support. And second, community-
based leaders generally remained loyal to agrarian goals,
dealing with other leaders only when it did not threaten
agrarian interests. Such community bases were pivotal to

the successes of the rebels of the caste war in Yucatán. They were also essential to the strength and successes of the insurgent villagers of Morelos led by Emiliano Zapata.[1] And it was the adamance of Zapata's insurgents that forced Mexicans toward a revolutionary reconstruction.

The changes that led Mexico from insurrection in 1810 to revolution after 1910 were complex. Most important, agrarian conditions that generated extreme grievances and outrage expanded and took on national rather than regional dimensions. Those deteriorating conditions were perceived by the rural poor as directly caused by offending elites. And elites divided so deeply that they could not reunite in the face of mass insurrections. Given such developments, massive rural uprisings began and endured during the political wars of 1910 to 1930. Agrarian insurgents were ready to insert their demands for justice and rural reconstruction into those political conflicts. And the movement led by Zapata, with solid community foundations, refused to waver for a decade in its demands for land redistribution. All of this was necessary to generate the revolutionary conflicts after 1910, and to lead to the limited but real agrarian gains under Cárdenas in the 1930s.

One can imagine a more radical outcome, a more complete agrarian triumph. If only in late 1914 Villa had left behind his elite and international allies and looked first to his agrarian base. Could he and Zapata have compromised their differences, proclaimed a national agrarian program, and consolidated national power? After all, Carranza with his elite allies, oil and henequen revenues, and international backers was on the verge of being eliminated. And Europe was heading into a world war that limited its and the United States' abilities to intervene in Mexico. Perhaps a complete agrarian victory was possible.

But the regional differences of agrarian societies that had long structured Mexican history remained strong. There

---

[1] See Womack, *Zapata*.

would be no national agrarian front—thus no ultimate agrarian victory. Regional agrarian diversity favored the rule of elites whose visions and powers were national, and whose backing was often international. They could play multiple agrarian movements against each other and assure their own triumph. Although these elites still held the powers of state in Mexico when insurrections subsided, they had learned that they could not ignore the agrarian majority. Revolutionary leaders had to sacrifice the landed elites and redistribute lands to hundreds of thousands of rural families to gain social and political stability in the 1930s. That was the victory of the rural poor.

## Social Bases of Agrarian Revolution: A Perspective from Mexico

Examination of the origins of agrarian insurrections in Mexico from the Hidalgo revolt of 1810 to the revolution that began in 1910 makes clear the importance of analyzing both the grievances that created the outrage essential to mass insurrections and the opportunities that allowed such insurrections to begin and endure. Analysis that treats only the development of agrarian grievances or only the emergence of opportunities for insurrection remains but partial analysis. Agrarian families, however poor and exploited, are not perpetually ready to rebel. Rather, they become increasingly willing to take the risks of insurrection as they suffer particularly detrimental social changes. And the outrage generated by grievances of social injustice does not alone produce insurrection. The agrarian poor know well the futility and deadly danger of taking up arms against powerful elites and entrenched states. Thus, once social deterioration has generated the outrage fundamental to insurrection, the aggrieved poor usually await an opportune moment to rebel. Deep divisions among elites, a breakdown of state power, or both together, provide the essential opportunities for mass insurrection. Such opportunities are often announced to the rural poor by the appearance of agitators, renegade elites or frustrated aspirants to elite power, willing to rally mass agrarian support against those in power. A critical conjunction of grievances and opportunities is essential to the emergence and survival of mass agrarian insurrections.

Such insurrections, as the Hidalgo revolt made clear, do not always lead to revolution. For insurrections to have revolutionary consequences, the grievances provoking them must be deeply felt among large and widespread segments of the agrarian population. And the opportunity for insurrection must be substantial. That is, elites must be so divided that they will continue to fight among themselves, maintaining the division or weakness of state power, even when facing mass insurrections. In such an environment, agrarian insurgents can sustain their uprisings long enough to force elites to take account of agrarian grievances in their attempts to reestablish stability. Since the poor rarely dominate the outcome of revolutionary conflicts, the endurance of mass insurrection long enough to force elites to make major concessions to popular demands seems an accurate description of revolutions.

In explaining the grievances fundamental to agrarian insurrections and revolutions, many analysts have emphasized the disruptive consequences of incursions of capitalism into peasant societies.[2] Mexican developments since 1750 suggest that those explanations are not wrong, but insufficient. The insurrections of the independence era cannot be attributed to sudden impositions of capitalism. From the late sixteenth century on, the Bajío had developed as a commercial society. Late colonial social changes there clearly resulted in large measure from commercial pressures—but these were not radically new forces in the Bajío, despite their radically negative social consequences. In contrast, the grievances that led to uprisings in central Jalisco,

[2] See especially Moore, *Social Origins*; and Wolf, *Peasant Wars*.

the coastal hot country, and especially the Sierra Gorda in 1810 are attributable to recent incursions of commercialism that rapidly undermined the autonomy of peasant peoples.

The era of decompression from 1810 to 1880 might be characterized as a long period of the recession of capitalism. And it was largely elite frustration with that recession that led to political assaults on peasant resources—and ultimately to waves of agrarian insurrections.

The developments of the Díaz era do appear to qualify as an incursion of capitalism. The coming of the railroads and the rapid incorporation of wide areas of Mexico into national and international markets made Mexico suddenly more capitalist—and more a part of the Atlantic capitalist economy. But even these were not totally new developments in Mexico. International trade and silver mining had tied Mexico into an Atlantic commercial economy in the sixteenth century. A commercial agricultural economy, built upon large estate production, had developed by the early seventeenth century. But a large peasant subsistence sector had survived alongside that early colonial commercial economy—linked to it by villagers' provision of seasonal labor.

Mexico's commercial and peasant economies endured together through the colonial centuries, linked by symbiotic exploitation. They both also survived the half-century after independence. But after 1821, their symbiosis began to breakdown and conflict escalated. It was not until the rapid extension of commercial production, combined with population growth, during the Díaz era, however, that there was a general assault on the peasant economy across wide areas of Mexico.

Yet that late nineteenth-century incursion of capitalism did not simply provoke agrarian outrage and insurrection. To cite only three regional examples: in the southern coastal lowlands, long isolated from commercial developments and suddenly turned into export plantations, labor scarcities led elites to provide security to workers—and there was little insurrection after 1910. Along the northern borderlands, an equally sudden development of export production had to draw migrants across long distances to gain a work force. They remained mobile, yet dependent and insecure. When the export economy collapsed after 1907, peaking their insecurities, they rose by the tens of thousands. And finally, the villagers of Morelos, the most adamant agrarian rebels after 1910, had faced losses of water and some land to sugar estates that suddenly expanded production in the national market brought by the railroads in the 1880s. But these were only intensifications of developments in relations between sugar estates and Morelos villagers that had begun in the colonial era. And the shift to endemic, often violent, conflict in estate-village relations came in the middle of the nineteenth century. The Porfirian incursion of capitalism was but the last of the long and complex historical developments that led the Zapatistas to their revolutionary insurrection.

Clearly, rapid incursions of capitalism can generate the agrarian social changes that create acute grievances and eventually lead to insurrections. But they do not always bring such developments. Equally clearly, acute grievances and, eventually, insurrections can develop without capitalist incursions. The comparative examination of agrarian changes and uprisings in recent Mexican history suggests a need to emphasize more concrete social processes in analyzing the origins of agrarian insurrections.

Substantially autonomous peasant cultivators, however poor, insecure, and immobile, have rarely joined extended insurrections. Estate dependents allowed basic security, however poor and immobile, have rarely rebelled. In contrast, sudden and rapid losses of autonomy or security, especially when combined with worsening poverty, have repeatedly generated grievances among the rural poor. Such grievances have become acute when the loss of a customary and accepted way of life is not compensated by the emergence of another that is less customary, but at least minimally acceptable. For example, autonomous peasants generally resent any loss of autonomy. If such a loss, however, is compensated by access to new means of survival which, while making them more dependent on elites, offers increased security, grievances generally remain muffled. But if peasants lose autonomy and become dependent on elites while forced to cope with persistent insecurities of survival, they quickly become outraged. Similarly, agrarian dependents long favored with security, but suddenly deprived of that basic guarantee of subsistence, will become outraged unless they find compensating increases in autonomy or mobility. And deepening agrarian grievances produce acute social outrage when the changes provoking them have clear origins among elites.

Such social changes may result directly from an incursion of capitalism, or be accelerated by capitalist developments. They may also result from different causes. Capitalism is too general and multifaceted an historical process to provide a comprehensive explanation for agrarian insurrections. The Mexican evidence suggests that such uprisings are better explained by analyzing changing ways of agrarian life and the complex historical forces that cause those changes—including the workings of capitalism, as well as related factors from demographics to politics.

The acute social outrage that ultimately causes agrarian insurrections rarely finds an outlet in sustained rebellion unless an opportunity develops to challenge the rule of established powerholders. Only if elites appear divided and the state appears weakened will irate agrarian people take the risks of insurrection. And only if dominant powerholders *are* deeply divided and the state *is* critically weakened can agrarian insurrections endure long enough to lead to revolutionary changes. The appearance of an opportunity is thus an essential, though secondary, cause of insurrections. And the reality of an opportunity to sustain insurrection is an essential, yet still secondary, cause of agrarian revolution. Such opportunities are essential, for without them insurrection will rarely develop. Yet they remain secondary causes, for opportunities become important only after social changes have generated the acute grievances that spread outrage among the agrarian populace.

In her analysis of opportunities for revolutionary insurrections, Theda Skocpol argues that the collapse of state powers caused by failures in international war opened the way for mass agrarian insurrections in the French, Russian, and Chinese revolutions.[3] Her focus on international conflicts that cripple state powers and allow the development of revolutions is an essential correction of analyses that have attempted to explain those revolutions solely in terms of class relations and conflicts. The state, with both its internal and international linkages, is clearly a pivotal actor in the origins and outcomes of revolutionary conflicts.

The evidence from Mexico, however, suggests that Skocpol has overemphasized the importance of state breakdowns and paid too little attention to related social developments. The opportunity that allowed the outbreak of the Hidalgo revolt in 1810 was the breakdown of imperial power caused by Napoleon's capture of the center of the Spanish empire. Yet the massive agrarian insurrection that exploded in the aftermath of the state breakdown did not lead to revolution—thanks to the unity of Mexican elites.[4] A century later, an apparently minor crisis of political succession became a political civil war that allowed the development, expansion, and endurance of revolutionary insurrections precisely because the dominant class in Mexico had become too deeply divided to unite against the poor majority. A more comprehensive analysis of the French, Russian, and Chinese revolutions might suggest that there, too, failures in war led to breakdowns of state powers because elites were also deeply divided.

It also appears that failures in international wars are im-

<hr>

[3] *States and Social Revolutions.*

[4] Revolution also failed to develop amidst the conjunction of state collapse and agrarian uprisings in Spain after 1808. For a regional analysis of these issues, see Ardit Lucas, *Revolución liberal.*

portant causes of state breakdowns primarily in nations that compete actively for world power, or regional predominance. The majority of nations are more dependent actors in world power politics, and are less likely to mobilize their populations in prolonged international conflicts. In such nations, and Mexico is an obvious example, failures derived from international relations—defined broadly—remain central to breakdowns of state powers and the origins of mass insurrections and revolutions. But those international failures in dependent nations are likely to result not from wars, but from external economic pressures. And their first manifestations may be as deepening conflicts among elites—only later leading to state collapse. The shift to the gold standard in 1905 and the financial crisis of 1907, both resulting from the dependent development of Mexico, created the deep elite divisions that turned the succession crisis of 1910 into a civil war. In a parallel development, Skocpol has argued that it was the boom and bust impact of petroleum exports in Iran that created widening conflicts among elites there, and ultimately led to the collapse of the Shah's state and the development of the revolution.[5]

A combination of elite divisions and state breakdown appears essential to creating the opportunity for enduring mass insurrection and agrarian revolution. Crises resulting from the foreign linkages of elites and states are primary causes of such opportunities. In nations that compete for world or regional predominance, failure in war is a common precipitant of state collapse—where elites are already deeply divided. In the majority of more dependent and thus less bellicose nations, externally caused economic crises have often led to deepening elite divisions that result in the breakdown of state powers in times of political conflict.

Ultimately, for mass agrarian insurrection to begin and

[5] Skocpol, "Rentier State," pp. 269-270; see also Keddie, *Roots of Revolution*.

endure long enough to become revolutionary, acute agrarian grievances must become widespread just as an opportunity for sustained rebellion develops. The necessity of that conjunction of agrarian social changes, elite divisions, and state breakdown helps explain why revolutions have remained relatively rare in a world laden with injustice. The simultaneous development of agrarian grievances and state collapse may be fortuitous. Certainly the regional agrarian changes that generated the grievances underlying the Hidalgo revolt in the Bajío and Jalisco were but minimally linked to the European wars that led to the collapse of the Spanish imperial state in 1808.[6]

In other instances, the grievances and opportunities essential to revolution may result from more integrated causes. The agrarian grievances underlying the Mexican revolution of 1910 developed in complex social processes that began in the eighteenth century. They were accelerated and brought to an extreme level in many regions by the dependent capitalist development of the late nineteenth century. The same economic developments of the Díaz era directly caused the elite divisions that led to the collapse of the Mexican state in 1910. Thus, the same process of dependent capitalist development brought the culmination of agrarian grievances and the breakdown of state power in 1910. To that extent, this analysis supports the conclusions of Barrington Moore, Jr., and Eric Wolf that nations undergoing rapid transitions to capitalist development are especially prone to revolution. Societies whose leaders have defined them as "backward" and that have been pressed through forced development programs seem especially susceptible to revolutionary conflicts.

[6] I do not believe that the coincidental nature of these developments was responsible for the failure of the Hidalgo revolt to reach revolutionary intensity. Had agrarian grievances been more widespread and Mexican elites more divided, the fortuitous conjunction of agrarian insurrection in Mexico and the breakdown of the imperial state in Spain could well have led to a social revolution in early nineteenth-century Mexico.

Capitalism is not uniquely capable of generating severe agrarian grievances. Nor is it alone able to generate deep divisions among elites. But accelerated, forced, capitalist development, pressed forward by leaders driven to "close the gap," to catch up in world power competition or in regional economic development, seems uniquely capable of generating acute agrarian grievances and deep elite divisions at the same time. And such forced capitalist development also makes nations increasingly susceptible to the external shocks of war or economy that have led to state breakdowns—precipitating revolutionary conflicts. Analysis of Mexico thus suggests that while incursions of capitalism are not the only causes of massive agrarian insurrections and potentially revolutionary confrontations, such incursions have been common causes of such developments during the last two centuries.

Analysis of agrarian insurrections and revolutions requires examination of the powers, actions, and adaptations of elites, states, and the agrarian masses. This analysis should underscore the importance of including subordinate majorities in historical social studies. Only by analyzing different rural social structures and their varying changes could both the origins and the failures of the Hidalgo revolt be explained. Only by examining the proliferation of agrarian grievances—that were often different in different regions—can the intensity and limitations of the agrarian revolution after 1910 be understood. Certainly the actions of elites and states faced with mounting agrarian grievances cannot be ignored. But the fact that powerful elites and state officials find themselves reacting to grievances and uprisings of the agrarian majority makes it clear that when studying insurrections and revolutions, the majority of society's members cannot be excluded. Agrarian insurgents make that statement more directly.

In Mexico, such statements began on a regional basis in 1810, continued through the nineteenth century, and culminated in the national revolution after 1910. The struc-

ture of modern Mexico, consolidated in the Cárdenas reforms of the 1930s, would be very different without that
century of agrarian violence. Agrarian insurgents did not
make modern Mexican history alone; but they made certain
that elites would not make it without them. Facing social
changes that denied them autonomy and forced them into
deepening poverty, dependence, and insecurity, agrarian
Mexicans became outraged at the injustice of their lives.
They used every opportunity available to mount insurrections, never winning, but insuring that no elites would endure as rulers without addressing agrarian grievances.
That persistence in the face of repeated failure led ultimately to limited victory—the destruction of the landed
elite and the massive redistribution of lands in ejido communities. Surely agrarian rebels could have imagined a
more complete victory. Without their struggle, however,
rural Mexicans would have gotten much less.

# APPENDICES

# Bajío Estates: Production, Population, and Ownership, 1600–1810

THE ANALYSIS of agrarian social change in the Bajío during the colonial era must focus upon the evolving production of the region's estates, and the changing social relations linked to that production. Ideally, such study would utilize quantitative descriptions of estate production, ownership, and labor relations at several times during the seventeenth and eighteenth centuries. Unfortunately, the sources presently available do not allow such a precise reconstruction. However, this appendix presents several tables that include limited quantitative descriptions of various factors at different times. They do not allow a comprehensive analysis of economic and social changes, but they do provide important quantitative evidence for a general analysis that must remain more qualitative.

Around 1630, the exact year is unknown, the Bishop of Michoacán commissioned a survey of estate production in his vast diocese that included the Bajío. His concerns for his tithe income led to the detailed materials presented in Table A.1. Completed at the end of the formative years of Bajío estate building, the survey shows the more rapid agricultural development of the eastern basin over the western reaches and the adjacent uplands. It also establishes the predominance of maize production over wheat during the early period. The bishop was clearly more concerned with tithes than with parishioners, but his survey also provides less complete, but still important, information on the numbers of Indian households then living at Bajío estates. Table A.2 indicates the small size of the rural labor force in the re-

Agricultural and Livestock Production at Bajío Estates, c. 1630

| Product and Range of Production | Number of Estates | | | | Bajío Total[e] |
|---|---|---|---|---|---|
| | Eastern Bajío[a] | Northeast Uplands[b] | Western Bajío[c] | Southwest Uplands[d] | |
| Maize[f] | | | | | |
| 1–100 | 2 | 7 | — | 4 | 13 |
| 101–250 | 4 | 17 | 1 | 2 | 24 |
| 251–500 | 13 | 15 | 10 | 3 | 41 |
| 501–1,000 | 17 | 6 | 16 | 2 | 41 |
| 1,001–2,500 | 26 | 4 | 19 | — | 49 |
| 2,501–5,000 | 11 | 1 | 7 | — | 19 |
| 5,001–10,000 | — | 1 | 1 | — | 2 |
| Wheat[f] | | | | | |
| 1–100 | — | 5 | — | — | 5 |
| 101–250 | 3 | 1 | — | 1 | 5 |
| 251–500 | 13 | 1 | 1 | 2 | 17 |
| 501–1,000 | 23 | — | 6 | 2 | 31 |
| 1,001–2,500 | 20 | — | — | — | 20 |
| 2,501–5,000 | — | — | — | — | — |
| 5,001–10,000 | 1 | — | — | — | 1 |
| Ganado Mayor[g] | | | | | |
| 1–100 | 13 | 9 | 15 | 2 | 39 |
| 101–250 | 3 | 2 | 10 | 4 | 19 |
| 251–500 | — | 7 | 4 | 3 | 14 |
| 501–1,000 | 2 | 3 | 2 | — | 6 |
| 1,001–2,500 | 1 | 2 | 2 | 1 | 6 |
| Ganado Menor[h] | | | | | |
| 101–250 | 1 | 1 | — | — | 2 |
| 251–500 | 1 | — | 2 | — | 3 |
| 501–1,000 | 1 | — | 4 | — | 5 |
| 1,001–2,500 | 1 | — | 1 | — | 2 |
| 2,501–5,000 | — | 1 | — | — | 1 |
| 5,001–10,000 | — | 2 | — | 2 | 4 |
| 10,001–25,000 | 1 | 6 | — | — | 7 |
| 25,001–50,000 | — | 1 | — | 1 | 2 |

SOURCE: My calculations from López Lara, ed., *Obispado de Michoacán*.
[a]137 estates in Apaseo, Celaya, Chamacuero, Salamanca, and Salvatierra.
[b]78 estates in San Miguel and San Felipe.
[c]70 estates in Irapuato, León, and Silao.    [d]24 estates in Pénjamo and Rincón.
[e]309 total estates in the Bajío.    [f]Annual harvest in fanegas.
[g]Annual increase in head of large livestock: horses, cattle, etc.
[h]Total head of small livestock: sheep, goats, etc.

TABLE A.2
Indian Households at Bajío Estates, c. 1630

| Regions and Jurisdictions | No. of Estates | No. of Indian Households | Indian Households per Estate |
|---|---|---|---|
| Eastern Bajío | | | |
| Apaseo | 7 | 400 | 57 |
| Celaya | 54 | 2,390 | 44 |
| Chamacuero | 21 | 600 | 29 |
| Salvatierra | 20 | 400 | 20 |
| Northeast Uplands | | | |
| San Felipe | 31 | 188 | 6 |
| Western Bajío | | | |
| Irapuato | 24 | 300 | 12 |
| León | 27 | 128 | 5 |
| Silao | 19 | 260 | 14 |
| Southwest Uplands | | | |
| Rincón | 11 | 150 | 14 |

SOURCE: My calculations from López Lara, ed., *Obispado de Michoacán*.

gion early in the seventeenth century, as Indians migrated into the Bajío only slowly.

By the late eighteenth century, Bajío estate production had changed substantially. Surveys of recent plantings completed by colonial officials in response to the great famine of 1785 and 1786 reveal the shift away from maize production toward the predominance of wheat, especially on the larger estates of the eastern basin. (See Table A.3.) The unique detail available from the same surveys for the Salamanca jurisdiction, part of the eastern Bajío, shows both the shift of large growers to wheat, and their relegation of maize production to tenants. (See Table A.4.)

What was the impact of these and other changes in estate production on the fortunes of Bajío elites? Apparently they were very positive. Table A.5 indicates that among the most prominent families at Querétaro, estate ownership re-

TABLE A.3
Maize and Wheat Planted at Estates in Several Bajío Jurisdictions,
1785

| Jurisdiction | No. of Estates | Maize Planted[a] | Wheat Planted[a] |
|---|---|---|---|
| Eastern Bajío |  |  |  |
| Acámbaro | 13 | 424 | 560 |
| Salamanca | 29 | 917 | 882 |
| Salvatierra | 19 | 339 | 3,102 |
| Valle de Santiago | 27 | 1,175 | 3,574 |
| Total | 88 | 2,855 | 8,118 |
| Western Bajío and Uplands |  |  |  |
| León | 31 | 911 | 404 |
| San Pedro | 17 | 379 | 730 |
| Pénjamo | 6 | 1,387 | 522 |
| Total | 54 | 2,677 | 1,656 |

SOURCE: FCA, Tables 256, 257, 258, 259, 260; my calculations.
[a]In fanegas of about 1.5 bushels each. I have transposed the amounts of wheat from the cargas listed in the original documents to fanegas.

mained the essential base of power, often complemented
with local officeholding, through the years prior to 1810.
Table A.6 lists the numbers and known values of Bajío estates offered for sale in Mexico City periodicals between
1790 and 1809. Such offerings generally indicated that an
elite family faced financial difficulties and was unable to sell
its properties in the local Bajío region—a double indicator
of elite difficulties. The table suggests that there was general stability in both the numbers and the values of Bajío estates offered to Mexico City buyers after 1790. The years
1806 and 1807 did bring a slight increase in estate adver-
tisements, but the general indication of the table is that
there was no rapid increase in the instability of estate ownership in the Bajío during the two decades prior to 1810.
The provincial elite was not facing a crisis threatening its
landed foundations.

TABLE A.4

Maize and Wheat Planted at Estates in the Salamanca Jurisdiction, 1785

| Estate Operator | Estate Name | Maize[a] Estates | Maize[a] Tenants | Estate Wheat[a] |
|---|---|---|---|---|
| LARGE GROWERS | | | | |
| D Juan de Santa Anna | Mancera | — | 50 | 120 |
| same | Sardinas | 50 | — | 40 |
| D Joaquín de Ríos | Cerro Gordo | 30 | — | 140 |
| same | not given | 13 | — | 46 |
| same | Las Cruces | 20 | — | — |
| D Julian Gamiño | Buenavista | 10 | 163 | — |
| same | Marañon | 42 | — | — |
| D Felipe García | San José del Cerrito | 18 | — | 300 |
| not given | Baltierra | 36 | 100 | — |
| D Tomás Machuca | Sn Bernardo de las Mojadas | 25 | — | 152 |
| Dña Guad. Martínez Conejo | Marigones | 9 | 55 | — |
| Large Growers Total | | 253 | 368 | 798 |
| SMALL GROWERS | | | | |
| Br. D Gregorio Conejo | Balderrama | 6 | 15 | — |
| same | Guadalupe | 5[b] | 5 | — |
| same | Loma Granada | 7[b] | 8 | — |
| D Juan Conejo | Ancon | 6 | 8 | — |
| D Manuel Villseñor | Puerto del Valle | 16 | 40 | — |
| D Vicente de la Concha | Mendoza | 32 | — | — |
| D Juan González | San Cayetano | 9 | — | 18 |
| not given | Temascatía | 8 | — | 18 |
| Convento San Agustín | Molino | 22 | — | — |
| D Juan Moreno | San Antonio | 18 | — | — |
| Los Gallardo | Rancho Gallardo | 15 | — | — |
| D Antonio Alvarado (rents) | La Rosa | 15 | — | — |
| D Luis Almanza | not given | 6[b] | 7 | — |
| Juan Valle (rents) | Santo Domingo | 10 | — | — |
| D José Francisco Aragón | San Juan | 8 | — | — |
| D Antonio Tóvar | Aguilas | 8 | — | — |
| D Pedro Fonseca | Loma Pelada | 7 | — | — |
| Small Growers Total | | 194 | 104 | 84 |
| Salamanca Total | | 447 | 472 | 882 |

SOURCE: FCA, Doc. 260.

[a]In fanegas.　　　　　[b]Divided between estates and tenants.

TABLE A.5
Property Ownership and Officeholding among 46 Members of the
Querétaro Elite, 1780–1810

| Group | No. of People | No. of Estates | No. of Obrajes | No. of Offices |
|---|---|---|---|---|
| Estate Owners | 28 | 49 | — | 19 |
| Estate and Obraje Owners | 9 | 13 | 10 | 9 |
| Obraje Owners | 9 | — | 9 | — |
| All Owners Total | 46 | 62 | 19 | 28 |

SOURCE: Biographical file data compiled from *Gazeta de México*, 1784–1810; the José
Sánchez Espinosa Papers (JSE); and various documents in the Archivo General de la
Nación, Mexico City.

TABLE A.6
Number and Value of Bajío Estates Advertised for Sale in Mexico City,
1790–1809

| Year | No. of Estates Advertised | Estates of Known Inventory Value | |
|---|---|---|---|
| | | No. | Total Value (pesos) |
| 1790 | 1 | 1 | 106,000 |
| 1791 | 2 | 2 | 271,700 |
| 1792 | 1 | — | |
| 1793 | 1 | 1 | 136,000 |
| 1794 | 2 | 2 | 194,100 |
| 1795 | 3 | 2 | 469,913 |
| 1796 | 3 | 2 | 97,271 |
| 1797 | — | — | |
| 1798 | 1 | 1 | 190,000 |
| 1799 | 2 | 2 | 230,400 |
| Total 1790–1799 | 16 | 13 | Mean 130,414 |
| 1800 | — | — | |
| 1801 | — | — | |
| 1802 | 2 | 2 | 236,200 |
| 1803 | 1 | 1 | 128,000 |
| 1804 | — | — | |
| 1805 | 2 | 1 | 235,159 |
| 1806 | 4 | 4 | 672,801 |
| 1807 | 4 | 3 | 367,022 |
| 1808 | 1 | 1 | 106,224 |
| 1809 | 1 | 1 | 44,500 |
| Total 1800–1809 | 15 | 13 | Mean 137,685 |

SOURCE: All Bajío estates advertised for sale in *Gazeta de México*, 1790–1809, and *Diario de México*, 1805–1809.

# Life and Labor at Charco de Araujo, 1796–1800

THE SURVIVING ACCOUNTS of the operations of the estate called Charco de Araujo provide an extremely detailed glimpse of the lives of a group of 74 estate dependents living just north of Dolores, where insurrection would begin only a decade later. These accounts are especially revealing because they detail the years that the estate shifted from stock grazing to increased crop production on marginal lands. The accounts thus provide a view in microcosm of the larger agrarian transformation of the eighteenth-century Bajío.

The accounts not only recorded estate activities, but also the work records of individual employees and sharecroppers. Such accounts have often been analyzed, usually by calculating total numbers of workers, their total remuneration, their total debts, etc. Such calculations are most revealing of the effects of labor on estate operations. My goal is to approximate an understanding of the effects of estate dependence on the lives of the rural poor. Thus, I have used the estate accounts to calculate the work, earnings, and debts of individual employees as well as the plantings and harvests of sharecroppers. I have used those individual work records to seek patterns of life and labor at the estate, for both individuals and the extended family groups to which they belonged. (Thanks to many specific references in the accounts, plus the presumption that shared surnames indicate kinship, the accounts allow an analysis of extended family composition, work efforts, and earnings.)

Table B.1 summarizes the numbers of individual men

TABLE B.1
Employees and Sharecroppers at Charco de Araujo, 1796–1800

|  | Individual Men | | Extended Families | |
|---|---|---|---|---|
|  | No. | % | No. | % |
| Employees Only | 52 | 70.3 | 24 | 60.0 |
| Sharecroppers Only | 10 | 13.5 | 4 | 10.0 |
| Employees and Sharecroppers | 12 | 16.2 | 12 | 30.0 |
| Total | 74 | 100.0 | 40 | 100.0 |

SOURCE: Charco de Araujo accounts: in Microfilm Collection of the Library of the Instituto Nacional de Antropología e Historia, Mexico City; Serie Guanajuato, Roll 11; my calculations.

(women are never listed) and extended family groups engaged in employment, sharecropping, and combinations of both at Charco de Araujo. Table B.2 shows the varying periods that dependents remained at the estate during the four years of the accounts. It should be noted that because the accounts cover years when the estate was taking on

TABLE B.2
Length of Individual and Family Dependence at Charco de Araujo, 1796–1800

| Months at Estate | Individual Men | | Extended Families | |
|---|---|---|---|---|
|  | No. | % | No. | % |
| 0–3 | 10 | 17.8 | 4 | 10.0 |
| 4–12 | 13 | 23.2 | 8 | 20.0 |
| 13–24 | 14 | 25.0 | 9 | 22.5 |
| 25–36 | 8 | 14.3 | 8 | 20.0 |
| 37–48 | 11 | 19.6 | 11 | 27.5 |
| Total | 56[a] | 99.9 | 40 | 100.0 |

SOURCE: Charco de Araujo accounts, my calculations.
[a]Information available for 56 of 72 known estate dependents.

many new employees and tenants, those noted as staying two years or more were generally permanent dependents. Most of those listed as remaining from two to four years were first hired during the period of the accounts, and continued to 1800 when they end. Most presumably remained longer.

By calculating the ratio of actual periods of paid employment to total time affiliated with the estate, Table B.3 reveals the extent that dependents at Charco de Araujo found permanent employment. Table B.4 calculates the ratios between the value of the goods and cash actually received by employees and the incomes that would have resulted from their work for wages. Ratios from .81 to 1.20, indicating receipts from 20 percent below to 20 percent above wage levels, indicate accounts nearly balanced—probably as close to balanced as possible, given the prevailing system of remuneration. Ratios above 1.21 indicate substantial overpayments resulting from workers obtaining goods and cash well in excess of their wage earnings.

Table B.5 summarizes the crop yields on estate fields and those of sharecroppers in terms of the ratios of grains har-

TABLE B.3

Ratios of Employment to Length of Dependence at Charco de Araujo, 1796–1800

| Ratios of Employment to Period of Dependence | Employees' Length of Dependence in Months | | | | | Total | % |
|---|---|---|---|---|---|---|---|
| | 0–3 | 4–12 | 13–24 | 24–36 | 36–48 | | |
| 0–0.50 | — | 1 | 1 | 1 | 1 | 4 | 8.7 |
| 0.51–0.70 | — | 1 | — | 4 | — | 5 | 10.9 |
| 0.71–0.90 | 1 | 5 | 5 | 1 | 7 | 19 | 41.3 |
| 0.91–1.00 | 9 | 3 | 3 | 1 | 2 | 18 | 39.1 |
| Total | 10 | 10 | 9 | 7 | 10 | 46[a] | 100.0 |

SOURCE: Charco de Araujo accounts, my calculations.
[a]Information available for 46 of 64 employees.

TABLE B.4
Ratios of Received Earnings to Wages Accounted for Employees of Charco de Araujo, 1796–1800

| Ratios of Received Earnings to Wages Accounted | Length of Employment in Months | | | | | | |
|---|---|---|---|---|---|---|---|
| | 0–3 | 4–12 | 13–24 | 25–36 | 37–48 | Total | % |
| .81–1.20 | 8 | 8 | 6 | 1 | 3 | 26 | 44.8 |
| 1.21–1.60 | — | 1 | 5 | 6 | 8 | 20 | 34.5 |
| 1.61–2.00 | — | 3 | — | 1 | 1 | 5 | 8.6 |
| Over 2.00 | 3 | 2 | 2 | — | — | 7 | 12.1 |
| Total | 11 | 14 | 13 | 8 | 12 | 58[a] | 100.0 |

SOURCE: Charco de Araujo accounts, my calculations.
[a]Information available for 58 of 64 employees.

TABLE B.5
Maize and Frijol Produced by the Estate and Sharecroppers at Charco de Araujo, 1796–1799

| Year | Estate Crops | | | Sharecroppers | | |
|---|---|---|---|---|---|---|
| | Plant[a] | Harvest | Ratio[b] | Plant | Harvest | Ratio |
| Maize | | | | | | |
| 1796 | 13f00 | 912f09 | 70 | 7f11 | 585f00 | 74 |
| 1797 | 12f06 | 597f09 | 49 | 7f07 | 419f06 | 55 |
| 1798 | 10f00 | 504f00 | 50 | 21f03 | 891f08 | 42 |
| 1799 | 11f03 | 508f06 | 45 | 20f10 | 685f06 | 33 |
| Frijol | | | | | | |
| 1796 | 15f00 | 212f11 | 14 | 6f08 | 97f10 | 15 |
| 1797 | 9f07 | 81f00 | 8 | 8f10 | 178f02 | 20 |
| 1798 | 10f00 | 153f06 | 15 | 21f03 | 474f06 | 22 |
| 1799 | 10f04 | 110f00 | 11 | 20f11 | 289f06 | 14 |

SOURCE: Charco de Araujo accounts, my calculations.
[a]Crop amounts in fanegas (f) and almudes (12 almudes per fanega).
[b]Ratios of grain harvested to planted.

vested to seed planted. Those ratios show declining maize yields, especially among sharecroppers. The tenants, however, produced frijol crops consistently better than those on estate fields. That surely reflected the importance of close attention in frijol production. The benefits of small-scale, intensive production were so substantial that frijol was rarely grown in colonial Mexico as a large estate crop.

The many references in the accounts to members of families working together at the estate indicate that the calculation of total family earnings is essential to evaluate the general material conditions of the agrarian poor at the estate. I have combined the value of wage earnings plus overpayments, the value of maize received as rations, and the value of crops retained by sharecroppers to estimate total receipts of extended families. Table b.6 shows the distribution of the total earnings of the 34 families for which this calculation was possible. Clearly, the families that remained longest at the estate obtained the highest total earnings. Table b.7 presents the distribution of total family earnings when divided by the number of family members who worked as employees and/or sharecroppers to produce them. It makes apparent that the higher incomes of families who remained longer at the estate were created largely by putting more members to work.

Table b.8 presents the mean total incomes per worker of dependent families at Charco de Araujo. It reveals that whether family ties to the estate were quite brief or more lengthy, the addition of family members to the work force resulted in declining earnings per workers. That is, increased family work efforts did not produce nearly commensurate increases in family incomes. The dependent poor at Charco de Araujo were increasing their work efforts substantially—but gaining only modest improvements in total earnings. Such great efforts for minimal remuneration were essential to the survival of the agrarian poor in the Bajío on the eve of the Hidalgo revolt.

TABLE B.6

Annual Cash-Equivalent Incomes of 34 Families at Charco de Araujo,
1796–1800

| Annual Incomes in Pesos | Number of Families | | | | | |
|---|---|---|---|---|---|---|
| | Number of Months Dependence at the Estate | | | | | |
| | 0–3 | 4–12 | 13–24 | 25–36 | 37–48 | Total |
| 11–20 | | 2 | | | | 2 |
| 21–30 | 1 | 2 | 1 | | | 4 |
| 31–40 | 2 | | | | | 2 |
| 41–50 | 1 | 1 | 2 | 1 | | 5 |
| 51–60 | | 2 | 1 | 1 | 2 | 6 |
| 61–70 | | 1 | | 1 | 2 | 4 |
| 71–80 | | | 2 | 1 | 1 | 4 |
| 81–90 | | | | 1 | | 1 |
| 91–100 | | | | | | |
| 101–110 | | | | | | |
| 111–120 | | | | | 1 | 1 |
| 121–130 | | | | | 2 | 2 |
| 131–140 | | | | | | |
| 141–150 | | | | | 1 | 1 |
| 151–160 | | | | | | |
| 161–170 | | | | | 1 | 1 |
| 171–180 | | | | | | |
| 181–190 | | | | | 1 | 1 |
| Total | 4 | 8 | 6 | 5 | 11 | 34 |

SOURCE: Charco de Araujo accounts, my calculations.

TABLE B.7

Annual Cash-Equivalent Income per Economically Accounted
Member[a] among 34 Families at Charco de Araujo, 1796–1800

| Annual Incomes in Pesos | Number of Families | | | | | |
|---|---|---|---|---|---|---|
| | Number of Months Dependence at the Estate | | | | | |
| | 0–3 | 4–12 | 13–24 | 25–36 | 37–48 | Total |
| 11–20 | 1 | 2 | 1 | | 1 | 5 |
| 21–30 | 1 | 4 | 2 | 1 | 1 | 9 |
| 31–40 | 1 | | 1 | | 4 | 6 |
| 41–50 | 1 | | 2 | 1 | 1 | 5 |
| 51–60 | | 1 | | 1 | 1 | 3 |
| 61–70 | | 1 | | 1 | | 2 |
| 71–80 | | | | 1 | 2 | 3 |
| 81–90 | | | | | | |
| 91–100 | | | | | | |
| 101–110 | | | | | | |
| 111–120 | | | | | | |
| 121–130 | | | | | 1 | 1 |
| Total | 4 | 8 | 6 | 5 | 11 | 34 |

SOURCE: Charco de Araujo accounts, my calculations.

[a]Family cash-equivalent incomes presented in Table B.6 are here divided by the number of persons who were accounted as employees and sharecroppers in producing those incomes.

TABLE B.8

Relation of Per-Worker Cash-Equivalent Incomes to Number of Family
Members Employed or Sharecropping at Charco de Araujo, 1796–1800

| Months at Estate | Number of Employees and Sharecroppers per Family | | | | | | | | | |
|---|---|---|---|---|---|---|---|---|---|---|
| | One | | Two | | Three | | Four | | Five | |
| | No.[a] | M[b] | No. | M | No. | M | No. | M | No. | M |
| 0–3 | 3 | 34 | 1 | 19 | | | | | | |
| 4–12 | 6 | 33 | 2 | 23 | | | | | | |
| 13–24 | 2 | 34 | 4 | 31 | | | | | | |
| 25–36 | 6 | 60 | | | | | 4 | 21 | | |
| 37–48 | 3 | 84 | 3 | 46 | 1 | 20 | 3 | 37 | 2 | 30 |

SOURCE: Charco de Araujo accounts, my calculations.
[a]Number of families with given number of employees and/or sharecroppers.
[b]Mean per-worker cash-equivalent incomes of those families.

# Regional Structures of Mexican Population, 1790–1910

AGRARIAN SOCIAL HISTORY studies the evolving relations between human populations and the resources that sustain them. That relation is structured by social organization and mediated by technologies of production. But the size and distribution of population is a fundamental factor in all agrarian social developments.

The tables in this appendix present demographic information basic to the social analysis in the text. Table C.1 presents the available figures for populations of Bajío jurisdictions in the late eighteenth century. It reveals the proportions of the population there that were classed as Spaniards, Castas (that is mestizos and mulattoes), and Indians. Such complete demographic information was not available for every Bajío jurisdiction. Even less has survived for other Mexican regions. To compare regional population structures, only total populations of Intendancies are generally available, plus tributary counts that included only persons classed as Indians or free blacks and mulattoes. Most importantly, tribute counts distinguish between Indians residing in corporate communities, and those elsewhere—in cities or at estates. Table C.2 thus provides figures for total regional populations, plus breakdowns of those classed as tributaries, and the subdivisions of the tributary population. For many of the rural jurisdictions surrounding Mexico City, I have been able to calculate population figures comparable to those for the Bajío. Table C.3 presents these, comparing zones emphasizing grain cultivation with the drier regions engaged in pulque production and stock grazing.

TABLE C.I
Bajío Population Structure, c. 1792

| Regions and Jurisdictions | Total Population | Spaniards | | Castas[a] | | Indians | |
|---|---|---|---|---|---|---|---|
| | | No. | % | No. | % | No. | % |
| Eastern Bajío | | | | | | | |
| Querétaro | 80,497 | 14,821 | 18 | 18,246 | 23 | 47,430 | 59 |
| Celaya | 67,801 | 15,176 | 22 | 18,119 | 27 | 34,506 | 51 |
| Salvatierra | 24,995 | 6,032 | 24 | 6,420 | 26 | 12,543 | 50 |
| Salamanca | 17,771 | 3,541 | 20 | 6,959 | 39 | 7,221 | 41 |
| Acámbaro | 10,074 | 1,997 | 20 | 3,121 | 31 | 4,956 | 49 |
| Northeast Uplands | | | | | | | |
| San Miguel | 22,587 | 3,410 | 15 | 5,247 | 23 | 13,930 | 62 |
| Dolores | 15,661 | 3,131 | 20 | 3,606 | 23 | 8,924 | 57 |
| Sierra Gorda | | | | | | | |
| San Luis de la Paz | 30,745 | 4,315 | 14 | 6,899 | 22 | 19,531 | 64 |
| Western Bajío | | | | | | | |
| Silao | 28,631 | 6,043 | 21 | 8,044 | 28 | 14,544 | 51 |
| Irapuato | 30,701 | 6,293 | 20 | 11,237 | 37 | 13,171 | 43 |
| Pénjamo | 20,952 | 2,670 | 13 | 8,548 | 41 | 9,734 | 46 |
| Mining Center | | | | | | | |
| Guanajuato | 55,412 | 24,160 | 44 | 19,438 | 35 | 11,814 | 21 |

SOURCE: Cook and Borah, *Essays*, II, Table 2.4, pp. 217-219.
[a]Mestizos and mulattoes.

Demographic analysis of nineteenth-century Mexico has just begun. Major problems remain. There were no national population counts before 1877, another consequence of the era of disintegration. In addition, the provinces used in late colonial counts often had boundaries very different from those of the states in the national period. In Table c.4 I have attempted to gauge regional differences in population growth after independence. I begin with the provincial counts of the late colonial era. I have then grouped together the states that once comprised those provinces to present the census figures from 1877. Because boundaries were not identical, the general figures for the four larger regions are

TABLE C.2
Regional Distribution of Tributary Population in Mexico, c. 1800

| Region and Provinces | Total Population | Tributary Population | % Tribs. | Community Indians | | Non-Comm. Inds | | Blacks | |
|---|---|---|---|---|---|---|---|---|---|
| | | | | No. | % | No. | % | No. | % |
| **Central Highlands** | | | | | | | | | |
| Mexico | 1,495,140 | 1,019,865 | 68 | 958,869 | 64 | 14,183 | 1 | 46,813 | 3 |
| Puebla | 821,277 | 469,607 | 57 | 455,135 | 55 | 3,268 | 0 | 11,304 | 1 |
| Valladolid | 371,975 | 171,160 | 46 | 99,771 | 27 | 22,621 | 6 | 48,768 | 13 |
| Regional Total | 2,688,392 | 1,660,632 | 62 | 1,513,675 | 56 | 40,072 | 2 | 106,855 | 4 |
| **North Central Plateau** | | | | | | | | | |
| Guadalajara[a] | 623,572 | 191,846 | 31 | 119,160 | 19 | 1,570 | 0 | 70,734 | 11 |
| Guanajuato | 511,616 | 278,541 | 54 | 75,364 | 15 | 160,309 | 31 | 42,868 | 8 |
| San Luis Potosí | 186,503 | 138,547 | 74 | 57,845 | 31 | 31,569 | 17 | 49,140 | 26 |
| Zacatecas | 151,749 | 90,332 | 60 | 24,862 | 16 | 14,878 | 10 | 50,592 | 33 |
| Regional Total | 1,473,440 | 699,266 | 47 | 277,231 | 19 | 208,326 | 14 | 213,334 | 14 |
| **South** | | | | | | | | | |
| Oaxaca | 528,860 | 416,383 | 79 | 396,545 | 75 | 3,071 | 1 | 16,767 | 3 |
| Mérida | 460,620 | 330,351 | 72 | 299,027 | 65 | 2,288 | 1 | 29,036 | 6 |
| Veracruz | 154,280 | 141,038 | 91 | 130,031 | 84 | 5,158 | 3 | 5,849 | 4 |
| Regional Total | 1,143,760 | 887,771 | 78 | 825,603 | 72 | 10,517 | 1 | 51,652 | 5 |

SOURCES: Population totals from Humboldt; "Tablas geográficas políticas del reino de Nueva España," in FHEM, I, 146; tributary populations calculated from "Estado general de tributos y tributarios," B-AGN, Tercera Serie, 1:3 (Oct.-Dec. 1977), pp. 6-25.
[a] I have taken the tributary figures for the Aguascalientes jurisdiction out of Zacatecas province and added them into Guadalajara, so that provincial totals would correlate to tributary totals.

TABLE C.3

Population Structures in Grain and Pulque Zones of the Central Highlands, c. 1792

| Jurisdictions | Total Population | Spaniards | | Castas[a] | | Indians | |
|---|---|---|---|---|---|---|---|
| | | No. | % | No. | % | No. | % |
| GRAIN ZONE | | | | | | | |
| Chalco | 51,457 | 300 | 1 | 1,172 | 2 | 49,985 | 97 |
| Coyoacán | 19,426 | 2,198 | 11 | 1,733 | 9 | 15,495 | 80 |
| Cuautitlán | 22,213 | 1,014 | 5 | 2,492 | 11 | 18,707 | 84 |
| Tacuba | 39,116 | 1,826 | 5 | 3,861 | 10 | 33,429 | 85 |
| Teotihuacán | 12,016 | 895 | 7 | 654 | 5 | 10,467 | 87 |
| Texcoco | 38,067 | 3,499 | 9 | 1,972 | 5 | 22,596 | 86 |
| Xochimilco | 20,482 | 1,145 | 6 | 793 | 4 | 18,544 | 90 |
| Zumpango | 8,639 | 500 | 6 | 1,669 | 19 | 6,470 | 75 |
| Zone Total | 211,416 | 11,377 | 5 | 14,346 | 7 | 185,693 | 88 |
| PULQUE ZONE | | | | | | | |
| Actopan | 26,429 | 1,474 | 6 | 3,877 | 15 | 21,078 | 80 |
| Apan | 8,086 | 1,295 | 16 | 1,710 | 21 | 5,081 | 63 |
| Ixmiquilpan | 26,427 | 1,471 | 6 | 2,478 | 9 | 22,478 | 85 |
| Otumba | 8,895 | 1,118 | 13 | 1,140 | 13 | 6,637 | 75 |
| Tetepango | 26,104 | 1,762 | 7 | 3,378 | 13 | 20,964 | 80 |
| Tula | 14,834 | 2,003 | 14 | 2,094 | 14 | 10,737 | 72 |
| Zempoala | 6,246 | 315 | 5 | 1,387 | 22 | 4,544 | 73 |
| Zone Total | 117,021 | 9,438 | 8 | 16,064 | 14 | 91,519 | 78 |

SOURCES: Spaniards from Cook and Borah, *Essays*, II, Table 2.4, pp. 217-219; Indians from "Estado general de tributos," pp. 6-9; Castas from both sources. (Where totals for Castas differed, I have selected the higher figures, presuming that undercounting was the more common error.)

[a]Mestizos and mulattoes.

probably more reliable than the provincial calculations. Then, I have also included the census figures by state from 1910, allowing a relatively accurate calculation of population changes during the Díaz era.

Because the accuracy of the counts of c. 1800, 1877, and 1910 varied, the absolute figures and rates of growth should be viewed with healthy skepticism. But the broad regional differences in rates of growth are likely more accurate, and may be used with cautious confidence.

TABLE C.4
Population Distribution and Growth in Mexico, 1800–1910

| Provinces | Population c. 1800 | States | Population 1877 | %[a] | Population 1910 | %[a] |
|---|---|---|---|---|---|---|
| **NORTHERN BORDERLANDS** | | | | | | |
| Durango | 157,970 | Durango | 190,846 | | 483,175 | 4.64 |
| | | Chihuahua | 180,758 | | 405,707 | 3.75 |
| | | Combined | 371,604 | 1.75 | 888,882 | 4.21 |
| Sonora | 120,080 | Sonora | 110,809 | | 265,383 | 4.24 |
| | | Sinaloa | 189,348 | | 323,642 | 2.15 |
| | | Combined | 300,157 | 1.94 | 589,025 | 2.91 |
| Coahuila | 40,000 | Coahuila | 104,131 | 2.08 | 362,092 | 7.52 |
| Nuevo Santander | 38,000 | Tamaulipas | 140,000 | 3.48 | 249,641 | 2.36 |
| Nuevo León | 26,000 | Nuevo León | 189,722 | 8.18 | 365,150 | 2.79 |
| Antigua California | 9,000 | Baja Cal. | 23,195 | 2.05 | 52,272 | 3.79 |
| Borderlands Total | 391,050 | | 1,128,809 | 2.45 | 2,507,062 | 3.70 |
| **NORTH CENTRAL PLATEAU** | | | | | | |
| Guadalajara | 623,572 | Jalisco | 953,274 | | 1,208,855 | .82 |
| | | Aguascalientes | 89,715 | | 120,511 | 1.03 |
| | | Tepic | 92,455 | | 171,163 | 2.58 |
| | | Colima | 65,827 | | 77,704 | .55 |
| | | Combined | 1,201,271 | 1.21 | 1,578,263 | .94 |
| Guanajuato | 511,616 | Guanajuato | 768,208 | .65 | 1,081,651 | 1.24 |
| San Luis Potosí | 186,503 | San Luis Potosí | 525,110 | 2.35 | 627,800 | .48 |
| Zacatecas | 151,749 | Zacatecas | 413,603 | 2.25 | 477,556 | .45 |
| North Central Total | 1,473,440 | | 2,908,192 | 1.26 | 3,765,270 | .88 |

## Region and State — Haciendas and Ranchos, 1877–1910

| Region and State | 1877 Haciendas | 1877 Ranchos | 1910 Haciendas | 1910 Ranchos |
|---|---|---|---|---|
| **NORTH** | | | | |
| California | 17 | 35 | 11 | 1,093 |
| Coahuila | 86 | 168 | 290 | 819 |
| Chihuahua | 123 | 596 | 222 | 2,408 |
| Durango | 143 | 382 | 226 | 2,474 |
| Nuevo León | 247 | 952 | 507 | 1,799 |
| Sinaloa | 98 | 192 | 37 | 3,178 |
| Sonora | 112 | 393 | 314 | 1,290 |
| North Total | 933 | 3,040 | 1,793 | 15,940 |
| **NORTH CENTER** | | | | |
| Aguascalientes | 48 | 464 | 38 | 468 |
| Colima | 29 | 225 | 40 | 292 |
| Guanajuato | 421 | 889 | 511 | 3,788 |
| Jalisco | 385 | 2,646 | 471 | 7,465 |
| Nayarit | | | 43 | 1,658 |
| Querétaro | 121 | 292 | 146 | 495 |
| San Luis Potosí | 159 | 156 | 211 | 1,540 |
| Zacatecas | 121 | 1,084 | 159 | 1,437 |
| North Central Total | 1,284 | 5,756 | 1,619 | 17,143 |
| **CENTER** | | | | |
| Guerrero | 116 | 753 | 92 | 1,620 |
| Hidalgo | 157 | 538 | 208 | 1,461 |
| México | 389 | 259 | 398 | 489 |
| Michoacán | 496 | 1,527 | 397 | 4,436 |
| Morelos | 48 | 53 | 40 | 102 |
| Puebla | 480 | 587 | 377 | 901 |
| Tlaxcala | 136 | 143 | 117 | 110 |
| Center Total | 1,822 | 3,860 | 1,629 | 9,119 |
| **SOUTH** | | | | |
| Campeche | 130 | 158 | 147 | 161 |
| Chiapas | 98 | 501 | 1,076 | 1,842 |
| Oaxaca | 116 | 753 | 191 | 769 |
| Quintana Roo | | | 3 | 24 |
| Tabasco | 67 | 118 | 634 | 1,174 |
| Veracruz | 237 | 652 | 159 | 1,807 |
| Yucatán | 1,145 | 363 | 1,170 | 611 |
| South Total | 1,793 | 2,545 | 3,380 | 6,388 |
| **Grand Total** | 5,832 | 15,201 | 8,421 | 48,590 |

sociales, Table 47, p. 41.

## Population Table

| | 1800 | | %[a] | 1877 | 1910 | %[a] |
|---|---|---|---|---|---|---|
| **CENTRAL HIGHLANDS** | | | | | | |
| Mexico | 1,495,140 | Mexico | | 683,323 | 989,510 | 1.36 |
| | | Federal Dist. | | 327,512 | 720,753 | 3.64 |
| | | Hidalgo | | 427,340 | 646,551 | 1.55 |
| | | Morelos | | 154,519 | 179,594 | .48 |
| | | Guerrero | | 301,252 | 594,278 | 2.94 |
| | | Querétaro | | 173,576 | 244,663 | 1.24 |
| | | Combined | .49 | 2,067,522 | 3,375,349 | 1.91 |
| Puebla | 821,277 | Puebla | | 697,788 | 1,101,600 | 1.76 |
| | | Tlaxcala | | 133,498 | 184,171 | 1.15 |
| | | Combined | .01 | 831,286 | 1,285,771 | 1.67 |
| Valladolid | 371,975 | Michoacán | 1.01 | 661,947 | 991,880 | 1.52 |
| Highlands Total | 2,688,392 | | .42 | 3,560,755 | 5,653,000 | 1.79 |
| **SOUTH** | | | | | | |
| Oaxaca | 528,860 | Oaxaca | .47 | 718,194 | 1,040,398 | 1.36 |
| Mérida | 460,620 | Yucatán | | 282,934 | 348,740[b] | .70 |
| | | Campeche | | 86,170 | 86,661 | .00 |
| | | Combined | -.26 | 369,104 | 435,401 | .61 |
| Veracruz | 154,280 | Veracruz | | 504,950 | 1,132,859 | 3.77 |
| | | Tabasco | | 83,707 | 187,574 | 3.75 |
| | | Combined | 1.77 | 588,657 | 1,320,433 | 3.76 |
| Chiapas | 88,084[c] | Chiapas | 3.65 | 208,215 | 438,843 | 3.36 |
| South Total | 1,231,844 | | .69 | 1,884,170 | 3,235,075 | 2.18 |
| National Total | 5,784,726 | | .83 | 9,481,926 | 15,160,407 | 1.81 |

SOURCES: Provincial figures for 1800 from Humboldt, "Tablas," p. 146; state figures for 1877 and 1910 from *Estadísticas sociales*, pp. 7–8.

[a] Percent population growth per year.

[b] Includes 9,109 for new territory of Quintana Roo.

[c] Chiapas was not part of New Spain in the colonial era. I have estimated its population for 1800 by projecting figures of 40,289 for 1742 and 63,654 for 1777 forward to 1800. Those figures are in Aguirre Beltrán, *La población negra*, pp. 222, 224.

# APPENDIX D

## Land Distribution and Estate Development in the Díaz Era, 1877–1910

ANALYSTS OF THE Mexican revolution repeatedly assert that under the Díaz regime large areas of lands were distributed among favored elites and estate building accelerated rapidly. Such developments did occur in late nineteenth-century Mexico, but they were not equally intense in all Mexican regions.

This appendix presents tables showing the distribution of *baldíos*, previously unclaimed lands, between 1877 and 1910, and the changing numbers of haciendas and ranchos in 1877 and 1910. By presenting the data by state, and by grouping states into larger regional units, important patterns appear. The distribution of lands and the development of new estates were most concentrated in the newly settled, export-oriented regions of the northern borderlands and southern coastal lowlands. In the longer settled and more densely populated zones of central and north central Mexico, few lands were distributed, and while the numbers of ranchos expanded rapidly, large estate development was minimal.

TABLE D.1
Baldío Lands Alienated in M[exico]

| Region and State | | |
|---|---|---|
| NORTH | 82 | |
| Baja California | 583 | |
| Coahuila | 62 | |
| Chihuahua | 848 | |
| Durango | 10,733 | |
| Nuevo León | | |
| Sinaloa | 14,773 | |
| Sonora | | 16, |
| Regional Total | 3 | 11,61 |
| | 1 | 102,286 |
| NORTH CENTER | 9 | 608,450 |
| Aguascalientes | 31 | 47,207 |
| Colima | 37 | 172,263 |
| Guanajuato | 6 | 159,537 |
| Jalisco | 285 | |
| Nayarit | 279 | 1,118,472 |
| Querétaro | | |
| San Luis Potosí | 651 | 17,948 |
| Zacatecas | | 61,474 |
| | 1 | 20,100 |
| Regional Total | 44 | 29,274 |
| | 17 | 9,760 |
| CENTER | 27 | 9,160 |
| Guerrero | 457 | 7,581 |
| Hidalgo | 143 | |
| Mexico | | 147,719 |
| Michoacán | | |
| Morelos | 689 | |
| Puebla | | 826,663 |
| Tlaxcala | 978 | 3,062,413 |
| | 1,255 | 331,663 |
| Regional Total | 17 | 40,180 |
| | 4 | 1,133,738 |
| SOUTH | | 466,618 |
| Campeche | 7,025 | 823,892 |
| Chiapas | 274 | |
| Oaxaca | 12,403 | 6,685,16? |
| Quintana Roo | | |
| Tabasco | 21,956 | 20,824,70? |
| Veracruz | | |
| Yucatán | 38,069 | |
| Regional Total | | |
| National Totals | | |

SOURCE: *Estadísticas sociales*, Table 48, p. 42.
[a] All values in pesos.

Abbreviations

Periodicals:
B-AGN    *Boletín del Archivo General de la Nación*, México
HAHR    *Hispanic American Historical Review*
HM        *Historia mexicana*
RMCPS  *Revista mexicana de ciencias políticas y sociales*

Publishers:
CM       El Colegio de Mexico
CUP      Cambridge University Press
FCE      Fondo de Cultura Económica
INAH    Instituto Nacional de Antropología e Historia
SEP      Secretaría de Educación Pública
UCP      University of California Press

Adams, Richard N. *Energy and Structure: A Theory of Social Power*. Austin: The University of Texas Press, 1975.
Aguirre Beltrán, Gonzalo. *La población negra de México*. 2nd ed. Mexico City: FCE, 1972.
Alamán, Lucas. *Historia de Méjico*. 5 Vols. Mexico: Editorial Jus, 1968-1969.
Altman, Ida. "A Family and Region in the Northern Fringe Lands: The Marqueses de Aguayo of Nuevo León and Coahuila." In Altman and Lockhart, eds., *Provinces of Early Mexico*, pp. 253-272.
Altman, Ida and James Lockhart, eds. *Provinces of Early Mexico*. Los Angeles: UCLA Latin American Center, 1976.
Anderson, Rodney. *Outcasts in Their Own Land: Mexican In-*

*dustrial Workers, 1906-1911*. DeKalb: Northern Illinois University Press, 1976.

Ankerson, Dudley. "Saturnino Cedillo: A Traditional Caudillo in San Luis Potosí, 1890-1938." In Brading, ed., *Caudillo and Peasant*, pp. 140-168.

Anna, Timothy. *The Fall of Royal Government in Mexico City*. Lincoln: University of Nebraska Press, 1978.

Archer, Christon. *The Army in Bourbon Mexico, 1760-1810*. Albuquerque: University of New Mexico Press, 1977.

Ardit Lucas, Manuel. *Revolución liberal y revuelta campesina*. Barcelona: Editorial Ariel, 1977.

Bakewell, P. J. "Zacatecas: An Economic and Social Outline of a Silver Mining District, 1547-1700." In Altman and Lockhart, eds., *Provinces of Early Mexico*, pp. 199-229.

Barkin, David and Blanca Súarez. *El fin de la autosuficiencia alimentaria*. Mexico City: Nueva Imagen, 1982.

Barragán, José Florencio. "La provincia de San Luis Potosí en el Reino de Nueva España." In Florescano and Gil, eds., *Fuentes*, pp. 319-353.

Barrett, Elinore. *La cuenca de Tepalcatepec*. 2 Vols. Mexico City: SEP, 1975.

Barrett, Ward. "Morelos and Its Sugar Industry in the Late Eighteenth Century." In Altman and Lockhart, eds., *Provinces of Early Mexico*, pp. 155-175.

Basalenque, Diego. *Historia de la Provincia de San Nicolás de Tolentino de Michoacán del Orden de N. P. S. Agustín*. José Bravo Ugarte, ed. Mexico City: Editorial Jus, 1963.

Bauer, Arnold. "The Church in the Economy of Spanish America." HAHR, 63:4 (November 1983), pp. 707-733.

Bazant, Jan. *The Alienation of Church Wealth in Mexico*. Cambridge: CUP, 1971.

————. *Cinco haciendas mexicanas: tres siglos de vida rural en San Luis Potosí*. Mexico City: CM, 1975.

————. "La división de las grandes propiedades rurales mexicanas en el siglo XIX." In Moreno García, ed., *Después de los latifundios*, pp. 33-41.

————. "La hacienda azucarera de Atlacomulco, México,

entre 1817-1913." *Jahrbuch für Geschichte von Staat, Wirtschaft und Gesellschaft Lateinamerikas,* 14 (1977), pp. 245-268.

Beato, Guillermo. "La casa Martínez del Río: del comercio colonial al la industria fabril, 1829-1864." In Cardoso, ed., *Formación y desarrollo,* pp. 57-107.

Bellingeri, Marco. "Del peonaje al salario: el caso de San Antonio Tochatlaco de 1880 a 1920." RMCPS, 91 (1978), pp. 121-136.

———. *Las haciendas en México: El caso de San Antonio Tochatlaco.* Mexico City: INAH, 1980.

Benjamin, Thomas and William McNellie, eds. *Other Mexicos: Essays on Regional Mexican History, 1876-1911.* Albuquerque: University of New Mexico Press, 1984.

Benson, Nettie Lee. *La diputación provincial y el federalismo mexicano.* Mexico City: CM, 1955.

Berry, Charles. *The Reform in Oaxaca, 1856-76.* Lincoln: University of Nebraska Press, 1981.

Bloch, Marc. *Feudal Society.* 2 Vols. Trans. by L. A. Manyon. Chicago: University of Chicago Press, 1961.

Borah, Woodrow. *Justice by Insurance.* Berkeley: UCP, 1983.

———. *New Spain's Century of Depression. Ibero-Americana* 35. Berkeley: UCP, 1951.

Brading, D. A. *Haciendas and Ranchos in the Mexican Bajío: León, 1680-1860.* Cambridge: CUP, 1978.

———. *Miners and Merchants in Bourbon Mexico, 1763-1810.* Cambridge: CUP, 1971.

———. "Noticias sobre la economía de Querétaro y de su Corregidor don Miguel Domínguez, 1802-1811." B-AGN, 11:3-6 (1970), pp. 275-318.

———. "La situación económica de don Manuel y don Miguel Hidalgo y Costilla, 1807." B-AGN, 11:1-2 (1970), pp. 15-82.

———. *Caudillo and Peasant in the Mexican Revolution.* Cambridge: CUP, 1980.

Burke, Michael. "Peasant Responses to the Hidalgo Revolt

in Central Mexico, 1810-1813." Unpublished essay, 1980.

Burkholder, Mark and D. S. Chandler. *From Impotence to Authority: The Spanish Crown and the American Audiencias, 1687-1808.* Columbia: University of Missouri Press, 1977.

Buve, Raymond. "Movilización campesina y reforma agraria en las valles de Nativitas, Tlaxcala (1917-1925)." In Frost et al., eds., *El trabajo*, pp. 533-564.

————. "State Governors and Peasant Mobilization in Tlaxcala." In Brading, ed., *Caudillo and Peasant*, pp. 222-244.

Calderón de la Barca, Frances. *Life in Mexico.* Howard T. Fisher and Marion Hall Fisher, eds. Garden City, N. Y.: Doubleday, 1966.

Cardoso, Ciro. *Formación y desarrollo de la burguesía en México: siglo XIX.* Mexico City: Siglo XXI, 1978.

Cardoso, Ciro et al. *México en el siglo XIX (1821-1910).* Mexico City: Siglo XXI, 1980.

Ceceña, José Luis. *México en la órbita imperial.* Mexico City: El Caballito, 1973.

Cerutti, Mario. "Poder estatal, actividad económica, y burguesía regional en el noreste de México (1855-1910)." Presented to 45th International Congress of Americanists, Bogotá, 1985.

Chavez Orozco, Luis and Enrique Florescano. *Agricultura e industria textil de Veracruz.* Xalapa: Universidad Veracruzana, 1965.

Chevalier, François. *La formación de los grandes latifundios en México.* Trans. by Antonio Alatorre. Mexico City: Problemas Agrícolas e Industriales de México, 1956.

Coatsworth, John. "Anotaciones sobre la producción de alimentos durante el porfiriato." HM, 26:2 (October-December 1976), pp. 167-187.

————. *El impacto económico de los ferrocarriles en el porfiriato.* 2 Vols. Mexico City: SEP, 1976.

————. "Obstacles to Economic Growth in Nineteenth-Century Mexico." *American Historical Review*, 83:1 (February 1978), pp. 80-100.

———. "Los orígenes del autoritarismo moderno en México." *Foro Internacional*, 16:2 (1975), pp. 205-232.

Cockroft, James. *Intellectual Precursors of the Mexican Revolution, 1900-1913*. Austin: The University of Texas Press, 1968.

Cook, Sherburne F. and Woodrow Borah. *Essays in Population History: Mexican and the Caribbean*. Vol. 2. Berkeley: UCP, 1974.

Córdoba, Arnaldo. *La ideología de la revolución mexicana*. Mexico City: Ediciones Era, 1973.

Cosío Villegas, Daniel, ed. *Historia moderna de México*. Vol. 8. *El porfiriato: La vida económica*. Mexico City: Editorial Hermes, 1965.

Cossío Silva, Luis. "La agricultura." In Cosío Villegas, ed., *Historia moderna*, Vol. 8, pp. 1-133.

———. "La ganadería." In Cosío Villegas, ed., *Historia moderna*, Vol. 8, pp. 135-178.

Costeloe, Michael. *Church Wealth in Mexico*. Cambridge: CUP, 1967.

———. *La primera República Federal de México, 1824-1835*. Mexico City: FCE, 1975.

Courturier, E. B. "Hacienda of Hueyapan: The History of a Mexican Social and Economic Institution, 1550-1940." Unpublished Ph. D. dissertation, Columbia University, 1965.

Cross, Harry. "Living Standards in Rural Nineteenth-Century Mexico: Zacatecas, 1820-1880." *Journal of Latin American Studies*, 10:1 (May 1978), pp. 1-19.

De la Peña, Guillermo. *Herederos de promesas: agricultura, política, y ritual en los Altos de Morelos*. Mexico City: La Casa Chata, 1980.

———. "Regional Change, Kinship Ideology, and Family Strategies in Southern Jalisco." *Kinship Ideology and Practice in Latin America*. Raymond Smith, ed. Chapel Hill: University of North Carolina Press, 1984.

Del Río, Ignacio. "Sobre la aparición y desarrollo del trabajo libre asalariado en el norte de Nueva España (siglos XVI-XVII)." In Frost et al., eds., *El trabajo*, pp. 92-111.

*Diario de México*, 1805-1810.

Díaz, José and Román Rodríguez. *El movimiento cristero: sociedad y conflicto en los Altos de Jalisco.* Mexico City: Nueva Imagen, 1979.

Díaz Díaz, Fernando. *Caudillos y caciques.* Mexico City: CM, 1972.

Díaz-Polanco, Hector. *Formación regional y burguesía agraria en México.* Mexico City: Ediciones Era, 1982.

Diehl, Richard. "Pre-Hispanic Relationships between the Basin of Mexico and North and West Mexico." In *The Valley of Mexico*, Eric Wolf, ed. Albuquerque: University of New Mexico Press, 1976.

Di Tella, Torcuato. "The Dangerous Classes in Early Nineteenth-Century Mexico." *Journal of Latin American Studies*, 5:1 (1973), pp. 79-105.

Domínguez, Jorge. *Insurrection or Loyalty: The Breakdown of the Spanish American Empire.* Cambridge, Mass.: Harvard University Press, 1980.

Duby, Georges. *The Early Growth of the European Economy.* Trans. by Howard Clarke. Ithaca: Cornell University Press, 1974.

*Estadísticas económicas del porfiriato: comercio exterior de México, 1877-1911.* Mexico City: CM, 1960.

*Estadísticas económicas del porfiriato: fuerza de trabajo y actividad económica por sectores.* Mexico City: CM, n.d.

*Estadísticas sociales del porfiriato, 1877-1910.* Mexico City: Dirección General de Estadística, 1965.

Falcón, Romana. "¿Los orígenes populares de la revolución de 1910? El caso de San Luis Potosí." HM, 39:2 (October-December 1979), pp. 197-240.

―――. *Revolución y caciquismo: San Luis Potosí, 1910-1938.* Mexico City: CM, 1984.

Farriss, Nancy. *Crown and Clergy in Colonial Mexico, 1759-*

*1821*. London: The Athlone Press, University of London, 1968.

————. *Maya Society Under Colonial Rule*. Princeton: Princeton University Press, 1984.

Favre, Henri. *Cambio y continuidad entre los mayas de México*. Trans. by Elsa Cecilia Frost. Mexico City: Siglo XXI, 1975.

Fernández de Recas, Guillermo. *Aspirantes americanos a cargos del Santo Oficio*. Mexico City: Librería de Manuel Porrúa, 1956.

Flores, Caballero, Romeo. *La contrarrevolución en la independencia*. Mexico City: CM, 1969.

Florescano, Enrique. *Estructuras y problemas agrarios de México, 1500-1821*. Mexico City: SEP, 1971.

————. *Precios del maíz y crisis agrícolas en México, 1708-1810*. Mexico City: CM, 1969.

————, ed. *Analisis histórico de las sequías en México*. Mexico City: Secretaría de Agricultura y Recursos Hidráulicos, 1980.

————, ed. *Fuentes para la historia de la crisis agrícola de 1785-1786*. 2 Vols. Mexico City: Archivo General de la Nación, 1981.

Florescano, Enrique and Isabel Gil, eds. *Fuentes para la historia económica de México*. 3 Vols. Mexico City: INAH, 1973-1976.

Fontana, Josep. *La quebra de la monarquía absoluta, 1814-1820*. Barcelona: Ediciones Ariel, 1971.

Forman, Shepard. *The Brazilian Peasantry*. New York: Columbia University Press, 1975.

Fraser, Donald. "La política de desamortización en las comunidades indígenas, 1856-1872." HM, 21:4 (1972), pp. 615-652.

Friedrich, Paul. *Agrarian Revolt in a Mexican Village*. Englewood Cliffs, N. J.: Prentice Hall, 1970.

Frost, Elsa Cecilia, Michael Meyer, and Josefina Vázquez, eds. *El trabajo y los trabajadores en la historia de México*.

Mexico City: CM, and Tuscon: University of Arizona Press, 1979.

Fuentes Mares, José. . . . *Y México se refugió en el desierto*. Mexico City: Editorial Jus, 1954.

Galaviz de Capdeveille, María Elena. "Descripción y pacificación de la Sierra Gorda." *Estudios de Historia Novohispana*, 4 (1971), pp. 113-149.

Galicia, Silvia. *Precios y producción en San Miguel el Grande, 1661-1803*. Mexico City: INAH, 1975.

García, Pedro. *Con el cura Hidalgo en la guerra de independencia*. Mexico City: FCE, 1982.

García Cantú, Gastón. *El socialismo en México: Siglo XIX*. Mexico City: Ediciones Era, 1969.

Garner, Richard. "Price Trends in Eighteenth-Century Mexico: HAHR, 65:2 (May 1985), pp. 279-325.

*Gazeta de México*. 1784-1810.

Gibson, Charles. *The Aztecs Under Spanish Rule*. Stanford: Stanford University Press, 1964.

Gilly, Adolfo. *La revolucíon interrumpida*. Mexico City: El Caballito, 1971.

Goldfrank, Walter. "Theories of Revolution and Revolution Without Theory: The Case of Mexico." *Theory and Society*, 7:1 (January-March 1979), pp. 135-165.

Gómez Cañedo, Lino. *Sierra Gorda: Un típico enclave misional en el centro de México (siglos XVII-XVIII)*. Pachuca: Centro Hidalgo de Investigaciones Históricas, 1976.

González y González, Luis. *Pueblo en vilo*. Mexico City: CM, 1968.

González Navarro, Moisés. *Anatomía del poder en México, 1848-1853*. Mexico City: CM, 1977.

———. *Raza y tierra*. Mexico City: CM, 1970.

Goubert. Pierre. *The Ancien Régime: French Society, 1600-1750*. Trans. by Steve Cox. New York: Harper and Row, 1973.

Greenwood, Davydd. "Political Economy and Adaptive Processes: A Framework for the Study of Peasant

States." *Peasant Studies Newsletter*, 3:3 (July 1974), pp. 6-8.

Hadley, Phillip. *Minería y sociedad en el centro minero de Santa Eulalia, Chihuahua, 1709-1750*. Trans. by Roberto Gómez Ciriza. Mexico City: FCE, 1979.

Hale, Charles. *Mexican Liberalism in the Age of Mora, 1821-1853*. New Haven: Yale University Press, 1968.

Hamill, Hugh. *The Hidalgo Revolt*. Gainesville: University of Florida Press, 1966.

Hamilton, Nora. *The Limits of State Autonomy: Post-Revolutionary Mexico*. Princeton: Princeton University Press, 1982.

Hamnett, Brian. "The Economic and Social Dimension of the Revolution for Independence in Mexico, 1800-1824." Working Paper, Center for Latin American Research, University of Bielefeld, 1979.

————. *Revolución y contrarrevolución en México y el Perú*. Mexico City: FCE, 1978.

————. "Royalist Counterinsurgency and the Continuity of Rebellion: Guanajuato and Michoacán, 1813-1820," HAHR, 62:1 (February 1982), pp. 19-48.

Harris, Charles. *A Mexican Family Empire: The Latifundio of the Sánchez Navarro Family, 1765-1867*. Austin: The University of Texas Press, 1975.

Hart, John. *Anarchism and the Mexican Working Class, 1860-1931*. Austin: The University of Texas Press, 1978.

————. "The 1840s Southwestern Mexican Peasants' War: Conflict in a Transitional Society." Presented to a workshop on rural uprisings in Mexico, Social Science Research Council, New York, 1982.

Herrera Canales, Inés. *El comercio exterior de México, 1821-1875*. Mexico City: CM, 1977.

————. *Estadística del comercio exterior de México, 1821-1875*. Mexico City: INAH, 1980.

Hewitt de Alcántara, Cynthia. *La modernización de la agricultura mexicana, 1940-1970*. Mexico City: Siglo XXI, 1978.

Hu-Dehart, Evelyn. "Sonora: Indians and Immigrants on a Developing Frontier." In Benjamin and McNellie, eds., *Other Mexicos*, pp. 177-211.

―――. *Yaqui Resistance and Survival: The Struggle for Land and Autonomy, 1821-1910*. Madison: University of Wisconsin Press, 1984.

Huerta, María Teresa. "Isidoro de la Torre: el caso de un empresario azucarero, 1844-1881." In Cardoso, ed., *Formación y desarrollo*, pp. 164-187.

Humboldt, Alejandro de. *Ensayo político sobre el reino de la Nueva España*. Mexico City: Editorial Porrúa, 1966.

―――. "Tablas geográficas políticas del Reino de Nueva España." In Florescano and Gil, eds., *Fuentes*, I, 128-171.

Hurtado López, Flor. *Dolores Hidalgo: Estudio económico, 1740-1790*. Mexico City: INAH, 1974.

Jacobs, Ian. "Rancheros of Guerrero: The Figueroa Brothers and the Revolution." In Brading, ed., *Caudillo and Peasant*, pp. 76-91.

Joseph, G. M. *Revolution from Without: Yucatán, Mexico, and the United States, 1880-1924*. Cambridge: CUP, 1982.

Katz, Friedrich. *The Secret War in Mexico: Europe, the United States, and the Mexican Revolution*. Chicago: University of Chicago Press, 1981.

―――. *La servidumbre agraria en México en la época porfiriana*. Mexico City: SEP, 1976.

Keddie, Nikki. *Roots of Revolution: An Interpretive History of Modern Iran*. New Haven: Yale University Press, 1981.

Keremitsis, Dawn. *La industria textil mexicana en el siglo XIX*. Mexico City: SEP, 1973.

Knight, Alan. "Peasant and Caudillo in Revolutionary Mexico, 1910-1917." In Brading, ed., *Caudillo and Peasant*, pp. 17-58.

Ladd, Doris. *The Mexican Nobility at Independence, 1780-1826*. Austin: Institute of Latin American Studies, University of Texas at Austin, 1976.

LaFrance, David. "Puebla: Breakdown of the Old Order."

In Benjamin and McNellie, eds., *Other Mexicos*, pp. 77-100.

Langston, William. "Coahuila: Centralization against State Autonomy." In Benjamin and McNellie, eds., *Other Mexicos*, pp. 55-76.

Lapointe, Marie. *Los mayas rebeldes de Yucatán*. Zamora: El Colegio de Michoacán, 1983.

Lavrin, Asunción. "El convento de Santa Clara de Querétaro: La administración de sus propiedades en el siglo XVII." HM, 25:1 (1975), pp. 76-117.

————. "The Execution of the Law of *Consolidación* in New Spain: Economic Aims and Results." HAHR, 53:1 (February 1973), pp. 27-49.

————. "Problems and Policies in the Administration of Nunneries in Mexico, 1800-1835." *The Americas*, 28:1 (1971), pp. 55-77.

Leal, Juan Felipe. *La burguesía y el estado mexicano*. Mexico City: El Caballito, 1983.

————. "El estado y el bloque en el poder en México, 1867-1914." HM, 23:4 (1974), pp. 700-721.

Leal, Juan Felipe and Mario Huacujo Roundtree. "San Antonio Xala: Contrapunteo del funcionamiento económico de una hacienda pulquera en la segunda mitad del siglo XVIII y en el último tercio del siglo XIX." RMCPS, 91 (January-March 1978), pp. 59-119.

————. "San Antonio Xala: La vida en una hacienda pulquera en los primeros días de la revolución. *Estudios Políticos*, 5:18-19 (April-September 1979), pp. 245-310.

Lerdo de Tejada, Miguel. *Comercio exterior de México desde la conquista hasta hoy*. 1853. Reprinted; Mexico City: Banco Nacional de Comercio Exterior, 1967.

————. *Memoria de la Secretaría de Hacienda . . . México, 1857*.

Lira, Andrés. *Comunidades indígenas frente a la ciudad de México*. Zamora: El Colegio de Michoacán, 1983.

López Lara, Ramón, ed., *El Obispado de Michoacán en el siglo XVII*. Morelia: Fimax Publicistas, 1973.

410     Bibliography

López-Portillo y Rojas. *Elevación y caída de Porfirio Díaz.* 1921. Reprinted; Mexico City: Editorial Porrúa, 1975.

María y Campos, Alfonso de. "Los científicos y la reforma monetaria de 1905." *Estudios Políticos,* 5:18-19 (April-September 1979), pp. 157-187.

Márquez, Enrique and Horacio Sánchez. "Fraccionamiento de las tierras de Felipe Barragán en el oriente de San Luis Potosí, 1797-1905." In Moreno García, ed., *Después de los latifundios,* pp. 49-61.

Martin, Cheryl English. "Haciendas and Villages in Late Colonial Morelos." HAHR, 62:3 (August 1982), pp. 407-427.

Maya, Carlos. "Estructura y funcionamiento de una hacienda jesuíta: San José Acolman, 1740-1840." *Ibero-Americanisches Archiv,* 8:4 (1982), pp. 329-359.

Mejía Fernández, Miguel. *Política agraria en México en el siglo XIX.* Mexico City: Siglo XXI, 1979.

Melville, Roberto. *Crecimiento y rebelión: el desarrollo económico de las haciendas azucareras en Morelos, 1880-1910.* Mexico City: Nueva Imagen, 1979.

Menegus Bornemann, Margarita. "Ocoyoacac: Una comunidad agraria en el siglo XIX." *Estudios Políticos,* 5:18-19 (April-September 1979), pp. 81-112.

Meyer, Jean. *La cristiada.* 3 Vols. Mexico City: Siglo XXI, 1973-1974.

————. *Esperando a Lozada.* Zamora: El Colegio de Michoacán, 1984.

————. *Problemas campesinos y revueltas agrarias en México, 1821-1910.* Mexico City: SEP, 1973.

Meyers, William. "La Comarca Lagunera: Work, Protest, and Popular Mobilization in North Central Mexico." In Benjamin and McNellie, eds., *Other Mexicos,* pp. 243-274.

Migdal, Joel. *Peasants, Politics, and Revolution: Pressures toward Political and Social Change in the Third World.* Princeton: Princeton University Press, 1974.

Mill, John Stuart. *Principles of Political Economy. Collected*

*Works,* Vol. II. Toronto: University of Toronto Press, 1965.

Miller, Simon. "The Mexican Hacienda between the Insurgency and the Revolution: Maize Production and Commercial Triumph on the *Temporal.*" *Journal of Latin American Studies,* 16:2 (November 1984), pp. 309-336.

Miranda, José. "La población indígena de México en el siglo XVII." HM, 12:2 (1963), pp. 182-189.

Molina Enríquez, Andrés. *Los grandes problemas nacionales.* Arnaldo Córdova, ed. Mexico City: Ediciones Era, 1978.

Moore, Barrington, Jr. *Injustice: The Social Bases of Obedience and Revolt.* White Plains, N. Y.: M. E. Sharpe, 1978.

————. *Social Origins of Dictatorship and Democracy: Lord and Peasant in the Making of the Modern World.* Boston: Beacon Press, 1966.

*Morelos: Documentos inéditos y poco conocidos.* Vol I. Mexico City: SEP, 1927.

Moreno García, Heriberto, ed. *Después de los latifundios.* Zamora: El Colegio de Michoacán, 1982.

Moreno Toscano, Alejandra. "Economía regional y urbanización: tres ejemplos de la relación entre ciudades y regiones en Nueva España a finales del siglo XVIII." *Ensayos sobre el desarrollo urbano de México.* Woodrow Borah et al. Mexico City: SEP, 1974, pp. 95-130.

Morin, Claude. *Michoacán en la Nueva España del siglo XVIII.* Mexico City: FCE, 1979.

Nickel, Herbert. "Agricultural Laborers in the Mexican Revolution, 1910-1940." Presented to a workshop on rural uprisings in Mexico, Social Science Research Council, New York, 1982.

————. *Peonaje e inmovilidad de los trabajadores agrícolas en México.* Trans. by Catalina Valdiesco de Acuña. Bayreuth: Universität Bayreuth, 1980

Ocampo, Javier. *Las ideas de un día: el pueblo mexicano ante la consumación de su independencia.* Mexico City: CM, 1969.

Orozco, Wistano Luis. *Los ejidos de los pueblos.* 1914. Reprinted; Mexico City: El Caballito, 1975.

Osorno, Fernando. *El insurgente Albino García.* 1938. Reprinted; Mexico City: FCE, 1982.

Paige, Jeffrey. *Agrarian Revolution: Social Movements and Export Agriculture in the Underdeveloped World.* New York: Free Press, 1975.

Patch, Robert. "Agrarian Change in Eighteenth-Century Yucatán." HAHR, 65:1 (February 1985), pp. 21-49.

Pletcher, David. *Rails, Mines, and Progress: Seven American Promoters in Mexico, 1867-1911.* Ithaca: Cornell University Press, 1958.

Potash, Robert. *El Banco de Avío de México: el fomento de la industria, 1821-1846.* Mexico City: FCE, 1959.

Powell, Philip Wayne. *Soldiers, Indians, and Silver.* Berkeley: UCP, 1952.

Powell, T. G. *El liberalismo y el campesinado en el centro de México, 1850-1876.* Mexico City: SEP, 1974.

Randall, Robert. *Real del Monte: A British Mining Venture in Mexico.* Austin: The University of Texas Press, 1972.

Reed, Nelson. *The Caste War of Yucatán.* Stanford: Stanford University Press, 1964.

Reina, Leticia. "La rebelión campesina de Sierra Gorda, 1847-1850." Presented to a workshop on rural uprisings in Mexico, Social Science Research Council, New York, 1982.

――――. *Las rebeliones campesinas en México, 1819-1906.* Mexico City: Siglo XXI, 1980.

Rojas, Beatriz. *La destrucción de la hacienda en Aguascalientes, 1910-1931.* Zamora: El Colegio de Michoacán, 1981.

Ruíz, Ramón Eduardo. *The Great Rebellion: Mexico, 1905-1924.* New York: Norton, 1980.

Rus, Jan. "Whose Caste War? Indians, Ladinos, and the Chiapas 'Caste War' of 1869." *Spaniards and Indians in Southeastern Mesoamerica.* Murdo MacLeod and Robert Wasserstrom, eds. Lincoln: University of Nebraska Press, 1983.

Sánchez Díaz, Gerardo. "La transformación de un régimen de propiedad en un pueblo: conflictos agrarios en Churumuco, 1869-1900." In Moreno García, ed., *Después de los latifundios*, pp. 63-78.

Sanders, William and Barbara Price. *Mesoamerica: The Evolution of a Civilization.* New York: Random House, 1968.

Schryer, Frans. "A Ranchero Economy in Northwestern Hidalgo, 1880-1920." HAHR, 59:3 (August 1979), pp. 418-443.

———. *The Rancheros of Pisaflores: The History of a Peasant Bourgeoisie in Twentieth-Century Mexico.* Toronto: University of Toronto Press, 1980.

———. "La Sierra de Jacala: Ranchos and Rancheros in Northern Hidalgo." In Benjamin and McNellie, eds., *Other Mexicos*, pp. 145-172.

Scott, James. "Hegemony and the Peasantry." *Politics and Society,* 7:3 (1977), pp. 267-297.

———. *The Moral Economy of the Peasant: Rebellion and Subsistence in Southeast Asia.* New Haven: Yale University Press, 1976.

Septién y Septién, Manuel, ed. *Precursores de la independencia en Querétaro.* Querétaro: Gobierno del Estado, 1970.

Simpson, Eyler. *The Ejido: Mexico's Way Out.* Chapel Hill: University of North Carolina Press, 1937.

Simpson, Lesley Byrd. *The Encomienda in New Spain.* Revised edition. Berkeley: UCP, 1966.

Sinkin, Richard. *The Mexican Reform, 1855-1876: A Study in Liberal Nation-Building.* Austin: Institute of Latin American Studies, University of Texas at Austin, 1979.

Skocpol, Theda. "Rentier State and Shi'a Islam in the Iranian Revolution." *Theory and Society,* 11:3 (May 1982), pp. 265-283.

———. *States and Social Revolutions.* Cambridge: CUP, 1979.

———. "What Makes Peasants Revolutionary?" *Comparative Politics,* 14:3 (April 1982), pp. 351-375.

Spenser, Daniela. "Soconusco: The Formation of a Coffee

Economy in Chiapas." In Benjamin and McNellie, eds., *Other Mexicos*, pp. 123-143.

Stavenhagen, Rodolfo. "Social Aspects of Agrarian Structure in Mexico." *Agrarian Problems and Peasant Movements in Latin America.* Rodolfo Stavenhagen, ed. Garden City, N.Y.: Doubleday, 1970, pp. 225-270.

Stevens, Donald Fithian. "Agrarian Policy and Instability in Profirian Mexico." *The Americas*, 39:2 (October 1982), pp. 153-166.

Steward, Julian. *Theory of Culture Change.* Urbana: University of Illinois Press, 1955.

Super, John. "The Agricultural Near North: Querétaro in the Seventeenth Century." In Altman and Lockhart, eds., *Provinces of Early Mexico*, pp. 231-251.

————. "Querétaro Obrajes: Industry and Society in Provincial Mexico, 1600-1800." HAHR, 56:2 (May 1976), pp. 197-216.

————. *La vida en Querétaro durante la colonia, 1531-1810.* Mexico City: FCE, 1983.

Tannenbaum, Frank. *The Mexican Agrarian Revolution.* Washington: The Brookings Institution, 1929.

Taylor, William. *Drinking, Homicide, and Rebellion in Colonial Mexican Villages.* Stanford: Stanford University Press, 1979.

————. "Landed Society in New Spain: A View from the South." HAHR, 54:3 (August 1974), pp. 387-413.

————. *Landlord and Peasant in Colonial Oaxaca.* Stanford: Stanford University Press, 1972.

————. "Rural Unrest in Central Jalisco, 1790-1816." Presented to a workshop on rural uprisings in Mexico, Social Science Research Council, New York, 1982.

————. "Town and Country in the Valley of Oaxaca, 1750-1812." In Altman and Lockhart, eds., *Provinces of Early Mexico*, pp. 63-95.

Timmons, Wilbert. *Morelos: Priest, Soldier, Statesman of Mexico.* El Paso: Texas Western Press, 1970.

Turner, John Kenneth. *Barbarous Mexico*. Chicago: S. H. Kern, 1911.

Tutino, John. "Agrarian Social Change and Peasant Rebellion in Nineteenth-Century Mexico: Chalco, 1840-1870." Presented to a workshop on rural uprisings in Mexico, Social Science Research Council, New York, 1982.

———. "Creole Mexico. "Spanish Elites, Haciendas, and Indian Towns, 1750-1810." Unpublished Ph. D. dissertation, University of Texas at Austin, 1976.

———. "Family Economies in Agrarian Mexico, 1750-1910." *Journal of Family History*, 10:3 (Fall 1985), pp. 258-271.

———. "Hacienda Social Relations in Mexico: The Chalco Region in the Era of Independence." HAHR, 55:3 (August 1975), pp. 496-528.

———. "Life and Labor on North Mexican Haciendas: The Querétaro-San Luis Potosí Region, 1775-1810." In Frost et al., eds., *El trabajo*, pp. 339-378.

———. "Power, Class, and Family: Men and Women in the Mexican Elite, 1750-1810." *The Americas*, 39:3 (January 1983), pp. 359-381.

———. "Rebelión indígena en Tehuantepec." *Cuadernos Políticos*, 24 (1980), pp. 89-101.

———. "War, Colonial Trade, and Mexican Textiles: The Bajío, 1785-1810." Presented to 45th International Congress of Americanists, Bogotá, 1985.

Urrutía de Stebelski, María Cristina, and Guadelupe Nava Oteo. "La minería, 1821-1880." In Cardoso, ed., *México en el siglo XIX*, pp. 119-145.

Vanderwood, Paul. *Disorder and Progress: Bandits, Police, and Mexican Development*. Lincoln: University of Nebraska Press, 1981.

Van Young, Eric. *Hacienda and Market in Eighteenth-Century Mexico*. Berkeley: UCP, 1981.

Vargas-Lobsinger, María. *La hacienda de "La Concha": una*

*empresa algodonera de la Laguna, 1883-1917.* Mexico: Universidad Nacional Autónoma de México, 1984.

Velázquez, María del Carmen. *Cuentas de sirvientes de tres haciendas y sus anexas del Fondo Piadoso de las Misiones de las Californias.* Mexico: CM, 1983.

Villoro, Luis. *El proceso ideológico de la revolución de independencia,* 4th ed. Mexico: Universidad Nacional Autónoma de Mexico, 1983.

Vizcaya Canales, Isidro. *En los albores de la independencia.* Monterrey: Instituto Tecnológico y de Estudios Superiores de Monterrey, 1976.

Voss, Stuart. *On the Periphery of Nineteenth-Century Mexico: Sonora and Sinaloa, 1810-1877.* Tucson: University of Arizona Press, 1982.

Warman, Arturo. . . . *Y venimos a contradecir: Los campesinos de Morelos y el estado nacional.* Mexico: La Casa Chata, 1976.

Wasserman, Mark. *Capitalists, Caciques, and Revolutions: The Native Elite and Foreign Enterprise in Chihuahua, Mexico, 1854-1911.* Chapel Hill: University of North Carolina Press, 1984.

——. "Chihuahua: Family Power, Foreign Enterprise, and National Control." In Benjamin and McNellie, eds., *Other Mexicos,* pp. 33-54.

——. "The Social Origins of the 1910 Revolution in Chihuahua." *Latin American Research Review,* 15:1 (1980), pp. 15-38.

Waterbury, Ronald. "Non-revolutionary Peasants: Oaxaca Compared to Morelos in the Mexican Revolution." *Comparative Studies in Society and History,* 17:4 (October 1975), pp. 410-442.

Weimers, Eugene. "Agriculture and Credit in Nineteenth-Century Mexico: Orizaba and Córdoba, 1822-1871." HAHR, 65:3 (August 1985), pp. 519-546.

Wells, Allen. "Family Elites in a Boom-and-Bust Economy: The Molinas and Peons of Porfirian Yucatán." HAHR, 62:2 (May 1982), pp. 224-253.

————. "Yucatán: Violence and Social Control on Hene-quen Plantations." In Benjamin and McNellie, eds., *Other Mexicos*, pp. 213-241.

West, Robert. *The Mining Community in Northern New Spain: The Parral Mining District. Ibero-Americana* 30. Berkeley: UCP, 1949.

Wolf, Eric. "The Mexican Bajío in the Eighteenth Century." *Synoptic Studies of Mexican Culture*. New Orleans: Tulane University, Middle American Research Institute, 1957, pp. 178-199.

————. *Peasants*. Englewood Cliffs, N. J.: Prentice-Hall, 1966.

————. *Peasant Wars of the Twentieth Century*. New York: Harper and Row, 1969.

Womack, John, Jr., *Zapata and the Mexican Revolution*. New York: Knopf, 1969.

LIBRARY OF CONGRESS CATALOGING-IN-PUBLICATION DATA

TUTINO, JOHN, 1947-
   FROM INSURRECTION TO REVOLUTION IN MEXICO.

   BIBLIOGRAPHY: p.
   INCLUDES INDEX.
   1. PEASANT UPRISINGS—MEXICO—HISTORY.   2. MEXICO—RURAL
CONDITIONS.   3. REVOLUTIONS—MEXICO—HISTORY.   4. ELITE
(SOCIAL SCIENCES)—MEXICO—HISTORY.   I. TITLE.
HN113.T88   1986      303.6'4'0972      86-12301
ISBN 0-691-07721-5 (ALK. PAPER)

# Land Distribution and Estate Development in the Díaz Era, 1877–1910

ANALYSTS OF THE Mexican revolution repeatedly assert that under the Díaz regime large areas of lands were distributed among favored elites and estate building accelerated rapidly. Such developments did occur in late nineteenth-century Mexico, but they were not equally intense in all Mexican regions.

This appendix presents tables showing the distribution of *baldíos*, previously unclaimed lands, between 1877 and 1910, and the changing numbers of haciendas and ranchos in 1877 and 1910. By presenting the data by state, and by grouping states into larger regional units, important patterns appear. The distribution of lands and the development of new estates were most concentrated in the newly settled, export-oriented regions of the northern borderlands and southern coastal lowlands. In the longer settled and more densely populated zones of central and north central Mexico, few lands were distributed, and while the numbers of ranchos expanded rapidly, large estate development was minimal.

### CENTRAL HIGHLANDS

|  | 1800 |  | 1877 | [a] | 1910 | [a] |
|---|---|---|---|---|---|---|
| Mexico | 1,495,140 | Mexico | 683,323 |  | 989,510 | 1.36 |
|  |  | Federal Dist. | 327,512 |  | 720,753 | 3.64 |
|  |  | Hidalgo | 427,340 |  | 646,551 | 1.55 |
|  |  | Morelos | 154,519 |  | 179,594 | .48 |
|  |  | Guerrero | 301,252 |  | 594,278 | 2.94 |
|  |  | Querétaro | 173,576 |  | 244,663 | 1.24 |
|  |  | Combined | 2,067,522 | .49 | 3,375,349 | 1.91 |
| Puebla | 821,277 | Puebla | 697,788 |  | 1,101,600 | 1.76 |
|  |  | Tlaxcala | 133,498 |  | 184,171 | 1.15 |
|  |  | Combined | 831,286 | .01 | 1,285,771 | 1.67 |
| Valladolid | 371,975 | Michoacán | 661,947 | 1.01 | 991,880 | 1.52 |
| Highlands Total | 2,688,392 | Combined | 3,560,755 | .42 | 5,653,000 | 1.79 |
| **SOUTH** |  |  |  |  |  |  |
| Oaxaca | 528,860 | Oaxaca | 718,194 | .47 | 1,040,398 | 1.36 |
| Mérida | 460,620 | Yucatán | 282,934 |  | 348,740[b] | .70 |
|  |  | Campeche | 86,170 |  | 86,661 | .00 |
|  |  | Combined | 369,104 | -.26 | 435,401 | .61 |
| Veracruz | 154,280 | Veracruz | 504,950 |  | 1,132,859 | 3.77 |
|  |  | Tabasco | 83,707 |  | 187,574 | 3.75 |
|  |  | Combined | 588,657 | 3.65 | 1,320,433 | 3.76 |
| Chiapas | 88,084[c] | Chiapas | 208,215 | 1.77 | 438,843 | 3.36 |
| South Total | 1,231,844 | Combined | 1,884,170 | .69 | 3,235,075 | 2.18 |
| National Total | 5,784,726 |  | 9,481,926 | .83 | 15,160,407 | 1.81 |

SOURCES: Provincial figures for 1800 from Humboldt, "Tablas," p. 146; state figures for 1877 and 1910 from *Estadísticas sociales*, pp. 7–8.

[a] Percent population growth per year.

[b] Includes 9,109 for new territory of Quintana Roo.

[c] Chiapas was not part of New Spain in the colonial era. I have estimated its population for 1800 by projecting figures of 40,289 for 1742 and 63,654 for 1777 forward to 1800. Those figures are in Aguirre Beltrán, *La población negra*, pp. 222, 224.

TABLE D.2

Rural Properties in Mexico, 1877–1910

| Region and State | 1877 | | 1910 | |
|---|---|---|---|---|
| | Haciendas | Ranchos | Haciendas | Ranchos |
| **NORTH** | | | | |
| Baja California | 17 | 35 | 11 | 1,093 |
| Coahuila | 86 | 168 | 290 | 819 |
| Chihuahua | 123 | 596 | 222 | 2,408 |
| Durango | 143 | 382 | 226 | 2,474 |
| Nuevo León | 247 | 952 | 507 | 1,799 |
| Sinaloa | 98 | 192 | 37 | 3,178 |
| Sonora | 112 | 393 | 314 | 1,290 |
| North Total | 933 | 3,040 | 1,793 | 15,940 |
| **NORTH CENTER** | | | | |
| Aguascalientes | 48 | 464 | 38 | 468 |
| Colima | 29 | 225 | 40 | 292 |
| Guanajuato | 421 | 889 | 511 | 3,788 |
| Jalisco | 385 | 2,646 | 471 | 7,465 |
| Nayarit | — | — | 43 | 1,658 |
| Querétaro | 121 | 292 | 146 | 495 |
| San Luis Potosí | 159 | 156 | 211 | 1,540 |
| Zacatecas | 121 | 1,084 | 159 | 1,437 |
| North Central Total | 1,248 | 5,756 | 1,619 | 17,143 |
| **CENTER** | | | | |
| Guerrero | 116 | 753 | 92 | 1,620 |
| Hidalgo | 157 | 538 | 208 | 1,461 |
| Mexico | 389 | 259 | 398 | 489 |
| Michoacán | 496 | 1,527 | 397 | 4,436 |
| Morelos | 48 | 53 | 40 | 102 |
| Puebla | 480 | 587 | 377 | 901 |
| Tlaxcala | 136 | 143 | 117 | 110 |
| Center Total | 1,822 | 3,860 | 1,629 | 9,119 |
| **SOUTH** | | | | |
| Campeche | 130 | 158 | 147 | 161 |
| Chiapas | 98 | 501 | 1,076 | 1,842 |
| Oaxaca | 116 | 753 | 191 | 769 |
| Quintana Roo | — | — | 3 | 24 |
| Tabasco | 67 | 118 | 634 | 1,174 |
| Veracruz | 237 | 652 | 159 | 1,807 |
| Yucatán | 1,145 | 363 | 1,170 | 611 |
| South Total | 1,793 | 2,545 | 3,380 | 6,388 |
| Mexico Totals | 5,832 | 15,201 | 8,421 | 48,590 |

SOURCE: *Estadísticas sociales*, Table 47, p. 41.

Baldío Lands Alienated in Mexico, 1877-1910

| Region and State | No. of Titles | Hectares Alienated | Total Value[a] |
|---|---|---|---|
| **NORTH** | | | |
| Baja California | 692 | 1,152,548 | 140,275 |
| Coahuila | 765 | 1,378,585 | 276,273 |
| Chihuahua | 821 | 3,103,009 | 1,326,355 |
| Durango | 583 | 1,354,227 | 783,111 |
| Nuevo León | 62 | 120,863 | 38,031 |
| Sinaloa | 848 | 1,912,646 | 419,697 |
| Sonora | 10,733 | 3,510,500 | 1,300,477 |
| Regional Total | 14,773 | 12,873,342 | 4,449,447 |
| **NORTH CENTER** | | | |
| Aguascalientes | 3 | 438 | 627 |
| Colima | 1 | 16,674 | 1,010 |
| Guanajuato | 9 | 11,617 | 2,784 |
| Jalisco | 31 | 102,286 | 49,990 |
| Nayarit | 37 | 608,450 | 69,178 |
| Querétaro | 6 | 47,207 | 1,527 |
| San Luis Potosí | 285 | 172,263 | 67,391 |
| Zacatecas | 279 | 159,537 | 22,903 |
| Regional Total | 651 | 1,118,472 | 215,410 |
| **CENTER** | | | |
| Guerrero | 1 | 17,948 | 4,039 |
| Hidalgo | 44 | 61,474 | 3,090 |
| Mexico | 17 | 20,100 | 17,468 |
| Michoacán | 27 | 29,274 | 2,937 |
| Morelos | 457 | 9,760 | 31,309 |
| Puebla | 143 | 9,160 | 10,973 |
| Tlaxcala | — | 7,581 | — |
| Regional Total | 689 | 147,719 | 69,816 |
| **SOUTH** | | | |
| Campeche | 978 | 826,663 | 489,300 |
| Chiapas | 1,255 | 3,062,413 | 1,346,110 |
| Oaxaca | 17 | 331,663 | 129,663 |
| Quintana Roo | 4 | 40,180 | 30,135 |
| Tabasco | 7,025 | 1,133,738 | 885,416 |
| Veracruz | 274 | 466,618 | 106,750 |
| Yucatán | 12,403 | 823,892 | 470,909 |
| Regional Total | 21,956 | 6,685,167 | 3,458,283 |
| National Totals | 38,069 | 20,824,700 | 8,192,956 |

SOURCE: *Estadísticas sociales*, Table 48, p. 42.

[a] All values in pesos.